00668

THINKING AND DOING

PHILOSOPHICAL STUDIES SERIES IN PHILOSOPHY

VOLUME 7

HECTOR-NERI CASTAÑEDA

The Mahlon Powell Professor of Philosophy, Indiana University

Editor of *Noûs*

THINKING AND DOING

The Philosophical Foundations of Institutions

D. REIDEL PUBLISHING COMPANY

DORDRECHT-HOLLAND / BOSTON-U.S.A.

Library of Congress Cataloging in Publication Data

Castañeda Calderón, Héctor Neri.
 Thinking and doing.

 (Philosophical studies series in philosophy ; v. 7)
 Includes bibliographical references and indexes.
 1. Thought and thinking. 2. Act (Philosophy)
3. Deontic logic. I. Title.
BF455.C34   120   75-16169
ISBN 90-277-0610-7

Published by D. Reidel Publishing Company,
P.O. Box 17, Dordrecht, Holland

Sold and distributed in the U.S.A., Canada, and Mexico
by D. Reidel Publishing Company, Inc.
306 Dartmouth Street, Boston,
Mass. 02116, U.S.A.

Printed in The Netherlands by D. Reidel, Dordrecht

To
Sara, Miriam, Xmucane, Kicab,
Hector-Neri, Omar, and Quetzil

TABLE OF CONTENTS

ACKNOWLEDGEMENTS

This book expounds a system of theories on several different aspects of practical thinking and action, the bulk of which were conceived between 1951 and 1955. The ensuing years I have spent, among other things, developing those theories, working out their harmony and unity, gathering the relevant large collection of supporting evidence, and attempting to acquire a modest mastery of the English language so as to give those theories a minimally communicable expression. The results are far from perfect. But I am confident that a reader will both forgive my style, lexicon, and grammar, and build better views upon my errors, if he can appreciate the comprehensiveness and the unity of my theories and the richness of the supporting data.

Naturally, the preparation of a treatise during twenty-four years owes much to many people. The philosophical debts on specific points that I remember are recorded in the appropriate notes. But to the many critics of early statements of my views in private discussions and to the many students in my ethics classes, whose questions and challenges undoubtedly contributed to my developing a better formulation of many a thesis and argument, I can only express, apologetically, my collective and anonymous gratitude.

My main philosophical debt still is to Wilfrid Sellars, who, besides instilling deeply in me an interest in Kant's great philosophical system, taught me both the theoretical nature of the philosophical enterprise and the importance of applying different methods and techniques to philosophical problems. Richard Hare was kind enough to discuss with me both my 1954 doctoral dissertation and his 1952 *The Language of Morals* on Wednesday afternoons during the three Oxford academic terms in 1955–56. He helped me appreciate the significance of imperative inference and led me to the realization of the historical significance of his observations on p. 25 of his book. In 1956–57 I benefited from discussions on the logic of imperatives and norms with Charles Baylis and Romane Clark. During the late 1950's I was privileged to receive critical letters on my views from Robert Binkley.

Perhaps the greatest influence, after Sellars', both on my philosophical methodology and on what I take philosophy to be about is that of my colleagues at Wayne State University during 1957–64, especially Richard Cartwright, David Falk, Edmund Gettier, Keith Lehrer, George Nakhnikian, Alvin Plantinga, and Robert Sleigh. Nakhnikian criticized many of my earlier papers and generously corrected my style and grammar. Keither Leher read in 1972 a draft, written in 1968–71, which included both this book and a history of the philosophical theory of obligation in the Twentieth Century (this history furnishing additional evidence for my theories), and presented me with eight pages of valuable comments.

I owe special gratitude to Juan José Arévalo, the 1945–51 President of Guatemala and his Minister of Education, the late Ricardo Castañeda Paganini, for having made it possible for me to study philosophy under Sellars' guidance. Thanks to the British Council and the Guatemalan University of San Carlos I was able to work on action theory at Oxford University during 1955–56. Wayne State University and the Guggenheim Foundation supported my 1967–68 sabbatical leave during which I planned this book, began its writing, and did some of the final research for it. Since 1969 Indiana University has encouraged my research providing me with valuable peace of mind and stimulating colleagues.

My associate William Rapaport has helped me with some criticisms and with the useful figures in Chapters 1 and 12. Anita Baugh and Elizabeth Meyers wrestled valiantly with my obscure handwriting in order to produce the 1968–71 typescript. Kim Liford, chiefly, and Margaret Dennig have courageously fought their way through the corrections of that typescript and have delivered the final copy. To all of them I am very grateful for their precious aid and their forbearance.

To those this treatise is dedicated I owe the greatest debt for their patient sacrifices that made it feasible for me to write several versions of it.

H-N.C.

Bloomington, Indiana,
January 27, 1975

to project from the rich data a theory, i.e., a system of hypotheses, about the total pattern. I have here attempted to theorize on the basis of abundant data. No data can *prove* any theory, mine or somebody else's. But everybody can test another's theories, and if these theories are fruitful, he can build better and more comprehensive ones on them. This fruitfulness I have striven to achieve. Given the totalitarian or holistic nature of philosophy, *no* philosophical theory, regardless of how comprehensive it may be, is anything but tentative.

This treatise puts forward a very comprehensive theory of action, i.e., of the structure of human action, delving into the normative and practical structures of practical thinking, and the most basic structure of practical reasoning. Yet it does not deal with values. Naturally, in terms of what in Ch. 1 we call the Representational Image of practical thinking, our theory of action has to be complemented with the theory of the implicational relationships between values and intentions and norms. But since values are nothing more than representations to consciousness of facts about needs, desires, wants, and intentions of agents, the theory of the validity of practical thought contents and the truth of normative judgments can connect directly with those facts about needs, wants, and intentions, as we show in Chs. 5, 6, 10, and 11, thus bypassing the value judgments and the theory of values. In general, the peculiarity of values as contents of consciousness makes them more indispensable, not for action, but for esthetic contemplation and the theory of art.

It would be appropriate to end this preface with a list of both the most important theses and the new views I am defending in this treatise. I mean the specific theses over and above the important general claims made above that: (i) the views on the specific topics of practical thinking and action theory must belong to one unified comprehensive theory; (ii) this comprehensive theory must be integrated within a 'larger' theory of the mind and reality; and (iii) the structural simplicity of a theory, which is a crucial desideratum, must yield pride of precedence to the capacity of a theory to conform to the largest possible collection of data. In consonance with these general theses, the system of theories here developed is based on a large amount of data, and its structural cumulative simplicity consists of its threading together a large number of theses on a wealth of topics. It would be too tedious and lengthy to summarize the several theories and their unity here bereft of their evidence. The reader can frame an idea of

the richness of the crucial and novel theses by glancing at the topical
index, in particular, by reading the content of the entry Principles and
other entries like Deontic, Imperative, Ought, Thinking, Mandate, Intention, Action, and Language.

CHAPTER 1

INTRODUCTION: TASKS AND PROBLEMS

In this chapter we both demarcate the subject-matter and formulate the aims of the ensuing investigations. We explain in what sense this is an investigation into the philosophical foundations of institutions and normative systems. We distinguish six sets of philosophical problems which will be dealt with in this book. Our aim is to develop a family of interconnected theories that provide a unitary systematic account of our problems. We will take some pains to collect, describe and organize a large amount of data, so that our theorization can be both comprehensive and well supported.

1. THE FOUNDATIONS OF NORMATIVE SYSTEMS AND INSTITUTIONS

One of our main topics is the philosophical foundations of normative systems. Since a norm is a principle of action, the foundations of normative systems lie ultimately in the nature of action and in the nature of practical thinking, i.e., the thinking, intimately bound up with action, concerning what is right, or wrong, to do in certain circumstances. The study of the philosophical foundations of normative systems is simply the study of the structure of practical thinking, the structure of what is thought in practical thinking, the connection between both of them and action, and the role and status in the world of what is thought in practical thinking. Because of the characteristic involvement of thinking with language, the investigation will have to delve into the functions and structure of the language of action.

Many philosophers have been concerned with the foundations of morality, and many others with the foundations of law. In this book we sharpen and generalize the problem so as to include the general foundations of all normative systems. Roughly speaking, a normative system is a certain set of rules, or norms, or judgments, or statements, that formulate permissions, licenses, rights, obligations, requirements, duties, injunctions, prohibitions, interdictions, or some type of correctness or incorrectness of some course of action – or, alternatively, a certain set of *do*'s or *don't*s and *shall*'s or *shan't*s.

The moral codes of all the different communities and the legal systems of the nations of the world are, of course, among the most important normative systems. But each institution of any society is either a normative system or, more likely, a complex of normative systems which assign roles and duties to the officers of the corresponding institutional hierarchy. Each particular law or ordinance, each by-law of an association, each set of rules of a game, and each agreement, contract or promise is, or determines, a normative system.

One of the tasks of the present investigation is to clarify the very concept of normative system. Such a task includes that of explaining the relationships between any two of the different items mentioned above as composing a normative system. We will, for instance, explain how in general licenses or rights relate to requirements or oughts, and how these relate to *do*'s and *don't*s, and how all of the preceding relate to *shall*'s and *shan't*s. For the time being let us say for convenience that normative systems are (at least in part) systems of *norms* or *deontic judgments*.

A normative system is (in part) a system of norms determined by a special characteristic set of considerations, through which it partitions all actions into three classes: (i) those actions that are *required* by those characteristic considerations; (ii) those (different) actions that are *un-required*, i.e., whose no-performance is required by those same considerations, and (iii) all other actions, which are thus the actions the normative system leaves open, or free, for every agent to perform or not to perform as he pleases. (We may allow as a limiting case that normative system that has actions neither of type (i) nor of type (ii).) Thus, each normative system determines a type or kind of *requiredness*. And each norm either assigns to some action the normative character of being required, or assigns to it the normative character of being non-required, by the considerations characteristic of the normative system to which the norm belongs. Thus, the elucidation of the nature of a normative system consists (at least in part) in the elucidation of the nature of its characteristic requiredness. This is tantamount to the elucidation of the nature of the norms characteristic of the system. Now, the characteristic norms of a normative system N are of the following canonical form:

(F)   X is required *by N* [or ought *Nly*] to do A,

where the adverbial phrase *'by N'* [or *'Nly'*] signals the type of required-ness determined by system N. Consider for instance:

(1)   One is required *by the local traffic regulations* to stop before a red light;

(2)   X ought *morally* to forgive Y;

(3)   Jones ought, *in accordance with his promise to his wife of June 15,* to buy himself a new suit.

In these examples the italicized adverbial phrases clearly indicate the types of requiredness involved, and they also indicate in the proper contexts of utterance to what normative systems the norms they would express belong to.

The full theory of a given institution *i* is at bottom, then, the total theory of the norms characterizing, or, better, constituting, the normative system N(*i*) that determines institution *i*. This is the theory that accounts for the logical form of such norms, their implication relationships, and their truth conditions. For example, the total theory or philosophy of morality is the theory of the norms of the form 'X ought *morally* to do action A' as well as of the complex statements composed of such norms. Likewise, the theory or philosophy of law is the theory of the norms involving the form 'X must (ought, should) *legally* do A'. Similarly for the other institutions. In short, the *total theory of an institution i* is composed of two parts:

(a) the *general* theory of norms, i.e., the general theory of the sense and truth constraints built into the matrix:

(F.1)   X ought [is required, is obligated]_____ to do A, and

(b) the *special* theory of the particular institution *i*, that is, the theory of the contributions to the truth conditions of the norms composing the corresponding normative system N(*i*) by the special considerations characteristic of N(*i*); in brief, the special theory of institution *i* is the theory of what the adverbial phrase entering in the blank in form (F.1) above expresses.

Thus, the special theory of morality is the theory of the adverb 'morally', rather than the theory of *ought*, as is often said. The special theory that constitutes the distinctive part of the philosophy of law is simply the theory of the adverb 'legally'. But neither the philosophy of morals (or morality) nor the philosophy of law has anything to say about general requiredness.[1]

In this book we develop a series of theories that deal with the general normative matrix (F.1). We place it in a still larger context, relating it to other types of statements and to the general mechanisms of action. These theories are the foundation for the special theories (b) of particular institutions. The specific theories of type (b) are, so to speak, adverbial theories that modify the theory of requiredness in general, when superimposed upon it. Naturally, the adverbial character of the special theories of given institutions does not prevent such theories from being more complex and more difficult to formulate than the general theory of their foundational matrix (F.1). Furthermore, the complexity of a special theory may depend on the fact that the institution the theory deals with is a complex of sub-institutions. This is indeed the case both with morality and with the law. Morality is, as I have explained elsewhere[2], a complex of three interacting normative subsystems. That is, the adverb 'morally' has a threefold ambiguity; or, if you prefer, it is an adverb that needs specification by one of three subsidiary adverbs that modify it. A system of law, especially in contemporary societies, is a most complex normative system: it is a huge system of systems, some of which are also systems of systems of norms.

To sum up, the preceding explains briefly a sense in which our study of norms and requiredness in general provides foundations for the studies of institutions, especially morality and the law. It also indicates how the study of normative systems can be concentrated at least in part on the study of the structure of norms, their interrelationships, and their relationships to other things, especially circumstances, thinking, and action.

The involvement of a normative system with the production of action is precisely its *raison d'être*. However useful it is to consider a normative system as an abstract system of norms, the crucial thing is that a normative system is adopted by a special domain of agents. Even when there is a process of enactment carried out by a representative set of norm-makers or legislators, the normative system is meant to be adopted by the agents of the domain, so that they can guide their actions by it. The life of a normative system lies, so to speak, in the internalization of the norms composing it into the action mechanisms of the agents for whom the system formulates its own special brand of requiredness. That internalization of a normative system makes the agents possessing it rational producers of action in two ways. On the one hand, an agent is rational, superficially speaking, both by contemplating different courses of action as within his power and by being aware of the actions he performs. On the other hand, an agent is a rational producer of action, in a profound sense, when he chooses courses of action for performance from the very conception of the requiredness of the action he believes to be required by the sum total of his circumstances, or by the balance of the special considerations of the diverse requiredness impinging on him in his current circumstances. More generally, to think endorsingly at a certain time that an action is somehow required through some existing circumstance by virtue of one's having adopted a certain normative system, is to nudge oneself to some degree to perform the action in question. Normative thinking is a thinking with an internal causality, i.e., a causality involving what is thought and what one is inclined to do.

The connection between the performance of an action and the thought of a norm formulating a special requiredness, is one of the main topics on which this investigation is to shed some light. But in order to increase the flood of light we must, once again, generalize the problem. This time we generalize beyond the practical dimension of normative systems, and consider the general problem of how practical thinking, whether normative or not, connects with action.

2. PRACTICAL THINKING

We exercise our thinking powers in learning what things are and how they relate to, and affect, one another. We postulate hypotheses and invent theories about what things are and how they affect one another. These are all instances of thinking in which one contemplates the world, its contents, and its laws. They are variously referred to as descriptive, or theoretical, or contemplative, or pure uses of reason. Here we shall call them instances of *contemplative* or *propositional thinking*.

But we also exercise our thinking powers in finding out or deciding what to so, as well as in helping others to decide or learn what to do. Knowing what to do is an intimate and subtle blending of contemplation and causation. Thinking what to do oneself, or what another person is to do, consists partly in the contemplation of several fragments of future possible worlds, all beginning at the terminal point of a past history shared by those worlds. Thinking what to do is much more than comparing alternative fragments of the future of the world. It is also to be at least dimly aware of oneself as housing causal powers that can alter, even if slightly, the future of the world. To come to know what to do is to have a thought which itself consists of an awareness of its bringing about an action, or of its bringing about at least a re-arrangement of the causal powers in oneself, so as to create a state of readiness for action in the appropriate circumstances. To advise or, in general, to tell another agent what to do is to guide him to, or even to force him into, a contemplation of the alternative fragments of the future of the world that impinge on his manifold of causal powers; moreover, it is to lead him to contemplation on the presupposition that those powers will be activated, or at least re-arranged into a state of readiness, by the agent's very contemplation of those alternative possible futures of the world.

Thinking what to do oneself, or what another is to do, intending or deciding to do something (whatever it may be), advising or telling others what to do, are just some of the practical uses of reason; they are forms of *practical thinking*. They and their cognates are the locus of the investigations carried out in this book. We will explore here the 'nature' of practical thinking.

The causational dimension is the most profound mystery in the nature of practical thinking. That dimension is the coalescence of contemplation and causation, we said; but it is more: it is the coalescence of contemplation and the causation of that contemplation, and the contemplation of that causation. Practical thinking is a most intricate intermeshing of awareness and action, and of action and *what* one is aware of. Thus, however it is that a man's thinking reorganizes his tendencies to act and even eventuates in action, practical thinking consists of a massive and obscure awareness of one's, or other's, causational powers through some characteristic concepts and some characteristic thought contents. We shall call them *practical concepts* and *practical thought contents*. Among the practical concepts are the concepts of *ought, right,* and *wrong,* the concept expressed by the imperative mood, and the concept expressed by the future tense in declarations of resolution or intent.

In the case of purely contemplative thinking, the units of thought content are variously called *propositions, statements,* and *judgments.* They are characterized by being true or false, and by other aspects discussed in Chapters 2 and 3. In order to avoid begging any questions we shall use the Greek work *noema* (plural *noemata*), meaning *what is thought* or *conceived, planned* or *purposed,* to refer both to propositions and to the similar counterpart units of content of practical thinking.

Among the fundamental noemata that appear to consciousness in practical thinking are:

(1)   *what* one thinks when one intends to do something (hereafter called an *intention*); *what* one thinks when one makes up his mind to do something (hereafter called a *decision*);

(2)   *what* one thinks when one considers, even without issuing it a command, an order, a piece of advice, a request, or an entreaty;

(3)   *what* one thinks when one conjectures or comes to believe that a man has an obligation, or a duty, to do something, or that he ought to, or is required to, do this or that;

(4)   *what* one thinks one supposes that it is wrong, or unlawful, or forbidden, for a certain agent to perform a given act;

(5)   *what* one thinks when one considers or thinks that it is right, or permissible, for a man to do some action A.

Of course, some contents of practical thinking are propositions. This is the case when one considers a proposition as a condition, or a circumstance, or a qualification, of a decision, obligation, order, or prohibition. Propositions also enter practical thinking in the identification of agents thought of as possessors of obligations, permissions, or rights, as well as in the identification of objects as persons affected by obligatory or forbidden actions. (These crucial distinctions will be elucidated in Chapters 4–9.)

We shall *theorize* that decisions are intentions that appear at the tail end of deliberations. For convenience we shall call:

(1) *intentions,* all noemata of type (1);
(2) *mandates* or *imperatives,* all members of type (2);
(3) *ought-judgments,* the noemata of type (3);
(4) *wrong-judgments,* those of type (4), and
(5) *right-judgments,* those of type (5).

We shall refer to ought-, wrong-, and right-judgments as *deontic noemata*. In Chapter 7, we shall argue that *deontic noemata* are propositions. Non-commitally, i.e., without implying that they are genuine properties, we shall call oughtness (obligatoriness, dutihood), wrongness (unlawfulness, forbiddenness), and rightness (permissibility, allowedness) *deontic properties*. The categories of noemata are further explained in Chapter 2, and in the ensuing chapters they receive full clarification.

Undeniably, there is practical thinking. Undeniably, its contents are more variegated than those of purely contemplative thinking, as the preceding list shows. Yet there is an obvious sense in which purely contemplative thinking and its contents have an ontological primacy over practical thinking and its contents. This is the sense in which there is no inconsistency in the supposition that there might be a purely contemplative creature, endowed with the capacity to think and the power to cognize the world, but deprived of the power to act deliberately on the world: that is, deprived of the power to conceive intentions or mandates and unable to consider deontic noemata. On the other hand, if a creature is an agent endowed with practical reason, he is, a fortiori, endowed with contemplative thinking.

This is why propositions are also contents of practical thinking. Our intentions and our duties to act depend on our circumstances. This is as it must be: we want to change the *same* world we find ourselves in, i.e., the world our perceptions and beliefs are about. The comprehensiveness of practical thinking that includes and requires contemplative thinking is characteristic of a mind that has the adequate mechanism, with great survival value, for keeping fast to the needed *unity* of the world of contemplation and the world of action. While contemplative thinking is, as explained, ontologically prior, and could in principle appear pure in an angelic creature, practical thinking becomes psychologically dominant and logically encompassing. The ultimate unity of reason *is* the unity of practical reason.

There is still a series of more profound ontological problems about reality surrounding practical thinking. In ordinary contemplative thinking we consider propositions, which are true or false, and if a proposition is true, there is then in the world a fact corresponding to (or, in some theories, identical with) that proposition. This naturally raises the question whether anything similarly corresponds to the practical noemata or not. Perhaps, deontic judgments correspond to some facts. After all, we do say that it is true that one ought morally to do such and such, and that it is false that one is required in accordance with this or that institution to do a certain action. Perhaps, the words 'true' and 'false' do not mean exactly the same thing in these cases as they do in the case of brute facts, e.g., in 'it is false that the earth is flat' or 'it is true that cats are afraid of dogs'. These are questions we shall decide later on. (See both Chapter 7, §1, and Chapter 8) But there is another problem. To the extent that norms or deontic judgments are true or false, we seem to be committed to there being in the world such properties as requiredness or rightness or wrongness. Perhaps there are such properties, but certainly they are most peculiar; e.g., non-existent entities, like unperformed actions, seem to have them. A full understanding of the nature of practical thinking, and of normative systems, demands that such properties, if so they are, be placed in their proper position in the structure of reality. (See Chapter 13) Furthermore, intentions and mandates do not seem to correspond to facts in any way analogous to that in which true ordinary propositions of observation and of scientific research correspond to their facts. In what sense, then, are intentions and mandates real, if at all, over and above the sense in which the mental states of intending and endorsing mandates are real? In what sense are they real over and above the sense in which intentions appear in declarations of intention, and mandates appear in acts of issuing orders, requests, etc.?

These last questions bring in the most profound issues of philosophy: the nature of the mind, and the connections between thinking and language, on one hand, and the connections between thinking and reality, on the other. These are, of course, part and parcel of the ultimate framework within which we must find the foundations of normative systems. But we will not deal with such large issues here, except to the extent that some of them take on a special aspect in the context of practical thinking. Our design is to deal with the *local* problems, so to speak, within the field of problems pertaining to practical thinking. We hope to provide solutions to those problems bringing the investigation up to the point where the problems have to be dealt with within the larger setting of general philosophy.

The preceding discussion demarcates our area of investigation and gives an idea of the main problems that will occupy us in our journey.

But before we set off we must complete some preparations. We need a better chart of the area to be traveled and we also need some indispensable equipment.

3. OUR SIX TYPES OF PHILOSOPHICAL PROBLEMS

To the initial reflection on deliberate action by an agent, the agent's mind appears as a mechanism that is both representational of the world and causal. Thus, what appears to initial reflection is partitioned into three systems: (i) the agent, his internal mechanisms of action and thinking, and his internal episodes of thinking; (ii) the representational system of noemata; (iii) the rest of the world. They appear to be embedded in a large network of relationships connecting the elements of one to those of another. Each of those relationships must be elucidated.

The representational system we call the *phenomenological image*. It raises two internal types of problems: (i) the *ontological problems* pertaining to the constitution of noemata: their elements and structure; and (ii) the *logical problems* pertaining to the implication relationships between noemata. The problems pertaining to the relationships between the representational image and the Rest of the World we call *metaphysical*. The problems about the connections between the representational image and the internal mechanisms of the agent we call *meta-psychological,* and the problems about the organization of the internal representational mechanisms of the agent belong in *rational psychology.*

In short, we distinguish the following six types of philosophical problem in which we are interested in this investigation:

(A) *The phenomenologico-ontological problems,* which we will for brevity call *ontological problems,* of practical thinking in general (and of normative thinking in particular) are the differentiation from one another of the practical noemata, and the formulation of the structural relationships between practical noemata. Specifically, here belong questions like these:

(1)   What are the differences and structural relationships between mandates and propositions? For instance, is the command *Jones, go home* reducible to the corresponding proposition *Jones is going or will go home*? I.e., is the command the result

of some operation on the proposition or is it a complex having the proposition as a component?

(2)   What are the structural relationships between intentions and mandates?

(3)   Is what is intended a proposition?

(4)   Is the structure of a deontic judgment of the form *X ought Nly to go home* that of the adverbial qualification *Nly* modifying the deontic matrix *X ought _____ to go home*? Is this matrix the result of the operation of ought on the simpler matrix *X ... _____ to go home*? Is this latter matrix a proposition, namely the proposition *X is going (will go) home*?

(5)   What sorts of structural relationships are there between intentions and deontic noemata?

(B) *The logical problems* of practical thinking are those of formulating the networks of implication relationships between and among the noemata thought in practical thinking. Since propositions are also thought of in practical thinking, included here are the implications from contemplative propositions to practical noemata, and vice versa. It should be stressed that simple principles like so-called Hume's guillotine and Poincaré's principle are lame attempts at solving the logical problem of practical thinking in one fell swoop. Poincaré's 'principle' claims that no imperative (i.e., mandate) follows from any set of propositions; and Hume's guillotine asserts that no ought judgment follows from non-deontic propositions. *Fortunately,* the logical problem of practical thinking is more complex, and cannot be solved by such wholly segregating principles. We say 'fortunately' because our brief remarks above about the unity of reason and the proposition-encompassing character of practical thinking strongly suggest that, rather than logical principles segregating the different types of content of practical thinking, what we must have are *bridging* principles of implication. Such bridging principles are the ones that hold together, so to speak, the unity of the world as both a world of contemplation and a world of action.[3] Our task is to produce not only the principles of implication internal to practical noemata, but also some of the most important principles bridging the difference between propositions and deontic noemata.

Evidently, the solutions to the logical problems are to be built upon

answers to the questions of type (A). They are both very closely related
that sometimes we will speak of the logico-ontological structure of a
noema to refer both to its internal structure and to the network of
implication relations at whose intersection it lies.

(C) *The semantical, or proto-metaphysical problems* of practical thinking
are those concerning the analysis (not necessarily reduction) of the values
of practical noemata involved in practical reasoning. If deontic judgments
or norms are true or false, then in this rank we are to reveal the structure
of deontic truth. Since the word 'truth' suggests some correspondence
with facts or something in the world, we are dealing here with the reality
content of deontic judgments. That is why I prefer to call this the proto-
metaphysical rank. The word 'semantical' suggests in one of its uses
something linguistic, and in another something having to do with set-
theoretical models. While both connotations relate to something important as we shall see, we will also be dealing here with something more
fundamental and concrete. The same considerations apply to intentions
and mandates and their inferential values.

The problems of this rank presuppose solutions to some of the problems
of ranks (A) and (B).

(D) *The meta-psychological problems* of practical thinking are those
pertaining either (i) to the involving of practical noemata with mental
states or states of consciousness, or (ii) to the special way in which
practical thinking is involved with action. The problems of type (i) can
be grouped under the heading of problems in the *rational* (or*philosophical*)
psychology of practice (or action). In the case of contemplative thinking
philosophers often speak of propositional attitudes (referring to believing,
supposing, and the like), and to propositional states of consciousness
(like perceiving, thinking or imagining that something or other is the
case). We shall speak of *practical* (and later on, of *practitional*) *attitudes,*
and of *practical* (and *practitional*) *states of consciousness.* Here one of the
main problems is the relationship between the practical and propositional
attitudes and states. This is an ontological problem, pertaining to the
structural relationships between the operations of the mind and the
practical noemata. The other problems of type (i) pertain to the formulation of the differences between any two of the practical attitudes or states
of consciousness. These are for the most part logical problems in that the
different practical attitudes characteristically differ from one another

in their implications. Clearly, these problems presuppose at least partial solutions to the problems of types (A) and (B), and some of them presuppose solutions to the problems of type (C).

The meta-psychological problems of type (ii) are those pertaining to the practicality of practical thinking in all its manifestations. Included here are the special discussions of the structure of the way in which each type of practical noema is involved with action. This investigation here is theoretical and connects both with profound metaphysical issues and with most difficult problems in empirical science. Among the former are the issues about universal causality and the indeterminism of the will, as well as the issue of the self's intervention in the physical world. The empirical problem of describing the neuro-physiological mechanism of intended and deliberate action is the one that at this juncture plugs in with our philosophical discussion.

(E) *The metaphysical problems* of practical thinking pertain to the degrees and type of reality of practical noemata. We shall examine what sort of entities actions are. But, more importantly, the investigation must reveal the sense in which the world is, as most of us think it is after a brief reflection, primarily composed of non-normative and non-practical facts. This includes an account of the status of deontic properties as not being really part of the ultimate furniture of the world. This investigation clearly presupposes solutions to problems of all the preceding ranks. In general, metaphysical claims about what is real, or not, in the deep sense of something being in no way a by-product of the mind, or of the use of language, are supervenient claims. They have to be grounded on pervasive phenomenal features of the relevant categories of entities, or concepts. Only after we have gone through the development of the answers to the basic questions of ranks (A)–(D) can we consider some features of those answers as metaphysical clues – i.e., as clues that, if at all possible, take us, after careful tooling, from the several accounts of what appears to consciousness in practical thinking, to reality in itself.

(F) *The philosophico-linguistic problems* of practical thinking are of three main types: (i) problems having to do with the deep structure underlying the sentences expressing noemata thought in practical thinking; (ii) problems pertaining to the different speech acts performed by the utterance of given sentences, and (iii) special problems pertaining to the theory of communication. Clearly, solutions to problems of type (i) are presupposed by the solutions to the other types, and solutions to problems of type (ii) are presupposed by solutions to problems of type (iii). Communication is a transference of noemata from person to person through the performance of some speech acts. An act of communication can be successful, even if a noema thought by the speaker when he makes an utterance U expressing it is not the same as the noema thought by the hearer when he apprehends U. But in such cases the noemata thought by the speaker and the hearer must be related in certain ways that include some sharing of structures. Problems of type (i) are, evidently, the crucial ones in this rank.

The deep structures underlying the sentences of a given language are structures of the noemata the sentences express. The grammatical categories correspond to some logico-ontological structures of noemata, so that the apprehension of the former by a hearer or reader allows him to apprehend the latter. Thus, the study of the problems of type (i) of this rank goes hand in hand with the study of the problems of rank (A). But the former must reach beyond (A) to ranks (B)–(D). The reason is that often we cannot separate two akin ontological structures except by their implications. To illustrate, there are many concepts of necessity, and their differences do not consist of perceptually different properties, but of different implication principles. Some concepts of necessity are, for instance, such that if a proposition is not necessarily true (in the relevant sense), then it is necessarily (in the same sense) not necessarily true; on the other hand, other concepts of necessity do not abide by this law.

The distinctions among the main types of practical noemata we made in §2 above is of fundamental importance for the theory of speech acts. But this theory includes more specific problems, like distinguishing commands from requests, and within each of these their several species.

The preceding hierarchy of problems is the framework of our investigation. We shall deal fully and in great detail with the basic problems in ranks (A) and (B). (See Chapters 3, 4, 6, 7, and 9.) The problems in rank (C) will receive full treatment (in Chapters 5, 6, and 8). But we will be able to touch on some of the problems of type (i) in rank (D), while discussing the main problems in the other ranks. (See especially, Chapter 4 §1, and Chapter 10 §1). The full treatment of the rational psychology of action is a massive enterprise that would require a very fat volume just for itself. Here is, then, thanks to the theories dealing with ranks (A),

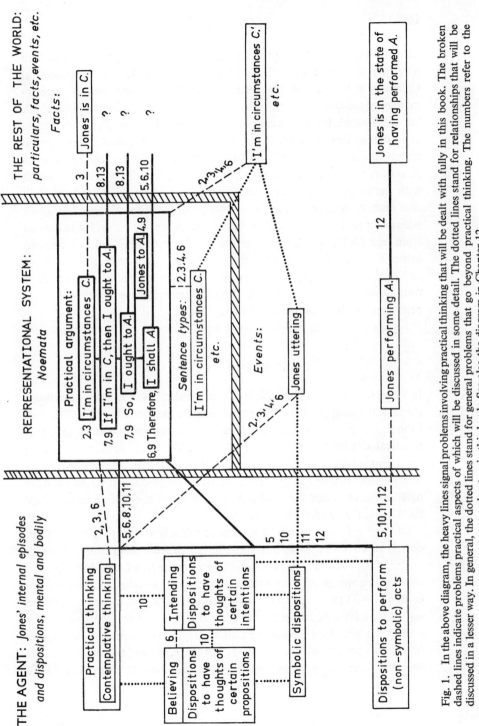

Fig. 1. In the above diagram, the heavy lines signal problems involving practical thinking that will be dealt with fully in this book. The broken dashed lines indicate problems practical aspects of which will be discussed in some detail. The dotted lines stand for relationships that will be discussed in a lesser way. In general, the dotted lines stand for general problems that go beyond practical thinking. The numbers refer to the chapters in this book. See also the diagram in Chapter 12.

(B), and (C), a foundation for the rational psychology of action. The narrow philosophical problem of type (ii) in rank (D) will be treated in Chapters 9, 10–12. But the general metaphysical problems of indeterminism of the will and of the role of the self in action will not be broached. We shall attack the problems in rank (E), both the one about what sorts of entities actions are and the one about the metaphysical status of deontic noemata. (See Chapters 12 and 13, respectively.) Finally, the main problems of type (i) and (ii) in rank (F) will be treated in the process of dealing with the other problems, especially those in ranks (A) and (B). We will also discuss some features of the contents of less general speech acts like promising and formulations of intention. However, we will not deviate from our route, which traverses the problems of practical thinking, to attempt to articulate a detailed theory of speech acts or deep structure of practical language. We limit ourselves to providing the specific required foundations for such a theory. (Specific references to these and other problems can be found in the Index.)

Figure 1 indicates the framework and the scope of our investigation.

4. PRACTICAL LANGUAGE

In §1 we formulated the problem of the foundations of normative systems through the contrast between some linguistic matrices. In §2 and §3 we formulated the main and the large bulk of our problems in terms of practical thinking and practical noemata. We have already mentioned the intimacy between thinking and the production of symbols. Some philosophers equate thinking with the use of language. But we do not have to endorse or reject this view. At the pre-theoretical level in any case thinking is the crucial phenomenon.

Of course, it may very well be that to think is always to use language, overtly or covertly, or to have something like sentences running through one's brain or body. In such a case the proper theory of thinking will have to have an appropriate account for the fact that episodes of thinking have contents. And the theory may very well establish that those contents do not really have a status in the world. Yet nothing of this is precluded by posing our problems about the nature of practical thinking directly, as problems about thinking, not about language. Posing the problems that way has several absolutely important virtues. Among them are: (a) we have not begged *any* questions concerning the nature of the relationship between thinking and language; (b) we side neither with the physicalists, who claim to reduce the mental to the physical, nor with the dualists, nor with the neutral monists; (c) we side with no position on the possibility of a private language, i.e., a language that is a means of thinking without being a means of communication.[4] Furthermore, (d) our attentive study of the structures that appear to consciousness in practical thinking has the enormous value of providing data that any theory about the nature of the mind has to take into account.

It is often said that a rational being who lives all by himself, outside all social intercourse, needs not conception of *ought* or *right*. Thus, it might be thought that practical thinking by its very nature requires a minimal social organization and, hence, a language that as a means of communication ties the social organization together. It might be thought that even if the logical and ontological problems of purely contemplative thinking could be treated without reference to language, the logical and ontological problems of practical thinking must perforce be formulated as problems about the structure of communicative language. But the fundamental assumption about the presupposed sociality of practical thinking seems to be false. *A being who acts and changes the world can have the power to make decisions and adopt goals, whether he has always been entirely alone in the world or not.* Likewise, certain courses of action will be right for him to perform, others will be required, and others will be wrong, even if this is so only in relation to his own purposes or goals. Hence, such a being still has to think, and perhaps equally hard, to determine what are his long-range goals and what he ought to do in order to attain them. Therefore, the crucial philosophical problems of understanding the structure of *what* that being thinks remain unaltered. That general structure is the same as that of the practical thinking of a social creature. He, of course, needs no moral thinking. But this is another matter.

Now, *we* live in communities and engage and indulge in social intercourse. We learn from each other, and we are interested in presenting our views to others in order to help them, or be helped by their criticism. In short, our practical thinking is certainly richer by thinking and expressing it through language. But a person living all alone and with only personal practical thinking will most likely have a language – private if you wish.

But its structure must be the general one. To the extent that a language is fit for the exercise of practical thinking, that language has syntactico-semantical categories that reflect the structures of practical noemata. Since we are anxious to understand the very structures and categories of what appears to us in our actual practical thinking, we must study those structures and categories as they are present in the language we use to face the world, both in pure contemplation and in action. Hence, an examination of the syntactico-semantical categories of ordinary language is the proper method to follow in our investigation in its early stages. Ordinary language contains all the concepts we need in our ordinary experience and thinking of the world; thus it contains all the philosophical clues. But these clues do not come labeled, or naked, or isolated. They come mixed with empirical beliefs and even superstitions. They must be mined, and sometimes subjected to elaborate processes of refinement and distillation. For instance, the fact that we in daily life do not say certain things, or do not use certain syntactical constructions, can be due to all kinds of reasons: because it is impolite, because it is cruel, because it is cumbersome, because it is in fact obviously false, because it is necessarily false, because nobody has thought of it, because.... Only some of those reasons can have philosophical significance. Sometimes we do not use a given string of words because there is no proposition or other noema they could express. But that this is the reason for our not using certain words does *not* follow from the mere fact that we do not use the words in question[5].

At any rate, especially when one is philosophizing for, or before, or with others it is unavoidable that one engages in examinations of ordinary language. We shall do so here in order to apprehend structural and implicational (-like) aspects of practical noemata. But we shall feel free to modify ordinary English sentence structure and vocabulary in order to gain more perspicuous representations of the (deeper) structures of the practical noemata we are studying. Naturally, we shall not be proposing that ordinary language be changed. We shall sometimes introduce notations that make certain structures more perspicuously similar to their cognate structures, yet our notations should not be construed as implying adverse criticisms of ordinary grammar.

For a further discussion of philosophical methodology and theorization in a detailed context see Chapter 6 §2.

5. CONVENTIONS ON QUOTATION MARKS

We are, therefore, in part to engage in an examination of ordinary language. And we shall often need to talk about a sentence or phrase as well as about the noemata or 'parts' of noemata it expresses, given the ordinary syntactical and semantical conventions of ordinary language. For the sake of brevity we adopt the following conventions:

C1   Single quotes around a sentence, clause, locution or word form a name of the sentence, clause, locution or word in question.

Thus, 'Jones' is a family name widely used in English, and "Jones" is a name of that family name. Similarly, the sentence 'Mary went with Jones' has as its name "Mary went with Jones", and the sentence, *not* the name, is made up of the words 'Mary', 'went', 'with', and 'Jones' in that order.

C2   Single asterisks, i.e., '*'s, around a sentence, clause, locution or word produce a name of *what* is expressed by the sentence, clause, locution, or word *in a given context of discussion.*

Convention C2 must be used with care. As is well known, sentences and words are ambiguous and may express different contents or parts of contents of thought. That is why we must assume a certain context given, so that the name can refer uniquely to a certain item of thought. Thus, during a limited discussion we may refer to the proposition a man formulates when he says "I am happy" as the proposition *I am happy*. In such a case it should be understood that the word 'I' refers to the speaker in question at the time of his assertion. In general, of course, there is *no* single proposition *I am happy*. But this is exactly the same as with ordinary proper names. The name 'Jones' is used to refer to given persons (or other entities) when the context of conversation or previous agreement fixes the reference. There is no single man named 'Jones'; yet we do manage pretty well quite often when we use it intending to make unique references.

In short, in a given context we can refer to a certain proposition by using the name '*Karl will go home*', and to the corresponding order by means of the name '*Karl, go home*'. Hence, in discussing examples of noemata, whether practical or purely contemplative, we shall assume that there is a method for determining (often with success) which noema a given sentence expresses. But we shall not discuss here the problem of the general method or methods for ascertaining which noemata are, or would be, expressed by which sentences in this or that type of circumstances. Indeed, we shall not discuss how noemata are paired with sentences, unless some remarks to that effect are crucial for the development of an argument or a distinction.

Given convention C2 a certain noema can easily, in a given context, receive several names. For instance, if a man named Gaskon asserts that he himself is a millionaire, he has in fact said "I am a millionaire". Thus we can refer to Gaskon's first-person proposition at that time as *I am a millionaire*. Clearly, that proposition is the one we have just expressed in the clause 'he himself is a millionaire'; hence, in the present context Gaskon's proposition *I am a millionaire* is the same as our proposition *he himself is a millionaire*. Of course, we can agree to call that proposition G, so that 'G' is another name of it.

C3   Numerals or letters, sometimes within parentheses or brackets, preceding indented sentences, phrases or other locutions will be used either as names of the noemata or 'parts' of noemata the sentences, phrases, or locutions express, or as names of the sentences or expressions themselves. The context should make clear which one is intended.

For example, the expression 'C3' can, in accordance with convention C3, be either the name of the two sentence paragraph it precedes, or a name of the convention this paragraph formulates.

Convention C4 is introduced at the end of §4 of Chapter 2.

NOTES TO CHAPTER 1

[1] The thesis that general requiredness characterizes morality is, in different forms, part of a persistent error in the history of moral philosophy. It often appears as the claim that a moral ought is overriding or vice versa. See H-N. Castañeda, *The Structure of Morality* (Springfield, Illinois: Charles Thomas Publisher, 1974), Ch. 7 for a critical examination of those and other theses, which are versions of the identification of moral thinking with practical thinking. This is a pervasive thesis. It is propounded by Kant, e.g., in the *Grundlegung* when he discusses the third proposition of moral value (A.K.K. ed., pp. 400–402). (See Chapter 1 §5 below.) Prichard follows Kant on this matter and even chastizes him for calling hypothetical imperatives imperatives, where 'imperatives'

refers to ought-judgments. See his 'Moral Obligation' (1937) in *Moral Obligation* (Oxford: The Clarendon Press, 1950). Leonard Nelson holds the same view in his *System of Ethics*, transl. from the German original of 1932 by N. Guterman (New Haven: Yale University Press; London: Oxford University Press, 1956). Hare's uneasy equating of oughts with moral oughts comes from both his characterization of ought-judgments as implying imperatives and his view that 'ought' if used evaluatively is universalizable. See his *The Language of Morals* (Oxford: The Clarendon Press, 1950), especially pp. 164–178, and his *Freedom and Reason* (Oxford: The Clarendon Press, 1963), especially 7–50 and 86–224. Hare's view on 'ought' is examined in H-N. Castañeda, 'Imperatives, Decisions, and Oughts', in H.-N. Castañeda and G. Nakhnikian, eds., *Morality and the Language of Conduct* (Detroit, Michigan: Wayne State University Press, 1963).

² See H-N. Castañeda, *The Structure of Morality*, Chapter 8.

³ For a detailed reformulation and rebuttal of Hume's guillotine see H-N. Castañeda, 'On the Conceptual Autonomy of Morality', *Nous* 7 (1973), where there is an argument for bridging implications connecting *Ought* and *Is*. Some philosophers have argued that Hume himself did not spouse Hume's guillotine. I believe that he did spouse it when he formulated it, but perhaps he did not spouse it at other times. On this issue see the papers by A. C. MacIntyre, A. Flew, R. F. Atkinson, G. Hunter, and W. D. Hudson in W. D. Hudson, ed., *The Is-Ought Question* (London: Macmillan and Company Ltd., and St. Martin's Press, 1969). See below Chapter 11 §4–§5 and Chapter 13 §1.

⁴ I have expressed my views on the possibility of a private language in detail. See H-N. Castañeda, 'The Private Language Argument', with replies to comments by V. Chappell and J. F. Thomson, in R. O. Jones, ed., *The Private Language Argument* (London, England: Macmillan and Company Ltd., 1971), and 'The Private Language Problem', in Paul Edwards, ed., *The Encyclopedia of Philosophy* (New York: Macmillan and Free Press, 1967).

⁵ To mention only a famous example, from the fact that we do not in daily life say "I know that I am in pain" it does *not* follow that there are no such facts as one being in pain or as one knowing that one is in pain. Another famous example: from the (alleged) fact that we do not say truly 'I am now dreaming' it does not follow that dreams are not states of consciousness. See Norman Malcolm, *Dreaming* (London: Routledge & Kegan Paul; New York: The Humanities Press, 1959), and H-N. Castañeda, 'Criteria, Analogy, and Other Minds', *The Journal of Philosophy* 69 (1962): 533–546.

PART I

THE LOGICO-ONTOLOGICAL STRUCTURE OF THE REPRESENTATIONAL IMAGE OF PRACTICAL THINKING

PRACTICAL THINKING: DRAMATIS PERSONAE

In this chapter we begin our study of the formal structure of *what* we think when we are engaged in thinking practically. We start unfolding our story about the contents of practical thinking by developing its main characters. Our concern in this chapter is with role delineation. Each of the units of practical thinking is sketched out in basic outline, sufficient to bear the character development of the rather intricate plot to be unveiled in the following chapters.

We are intensely committed to providing a true story. Our *dramatis personae* are, must be, real creatures to be met in daily life. Thus, the characterizations to be given in the sequel are meant to be sufficient for anybody acquainted with practical thinking to recognize and identify the creatures of his world our story is about. Yet these characterizations are not meant to constitute a precise and fully detailed picture in pana-vision, so to speak, of each of the units of practical thinking. Indeed, there is no such picture of each unit by itself. Full color and precise details we can have only in a family portrait, and such a portrait belongs *within* the theory of the structure of what is thought in practical thinking. In short, the ensuing characterizations, even definitions, of the units of practical thinking are at most semi-technical: they provide entrance into the story that ends up in a theory in which technical characterizations that are the former's philosophical successors can be given. The preliminary characterizations are mechanisms for collecting data, while the ultimate theoretical characterizations constitute philosophical elucidation of the preliminary ones.

1. DELIBERATION

Our story is about *what* we think when we are exercising our powers of practical thinking. Inevitably, there are isolated episodes or occurrences of practical thinking, as, for instance, when one merely issues an order or makes a request. But the most fascinating general feature of thinking is that the contents of thought have systemic relationships. What appears to consciousness in unitary episodes are nodes that belong into a systematic network most of which remains beyond the horizon of consciousness. Thus, the most natural unit of study is not an isolated thought, but a train of thoughts that make up a reasoning. In the case of practical thinking such reasonings are called *deliberations*. Primarily, we deliberate in order to find out what to do ourselves in given circumstances. Secondarily, we deliberate before others in order to advise them what to do in the circumstances under consideration. Whatever its ultimate purpose, a deliberation is a sufficiently large piece of practical thinking that can show the units of practical thinking in a natural habitat.

As it befits the seriousness of philosophical problems, let us consider a most grave case of practical thinking. We are all familiar with the plight of the title heroine in Sophocles' *Antigone*. As you recall, in the immediate background of the tragedy lie the deaths of her two brothers, Eteocles and Polyneices. But while the former dies defending their motherland, Thebes, the latter dies in the process of invading it. King Creon, maternal uncle of the three, has both executed a hero's funeral for Eteocles and ordered the posthumous punishment of Polyneices. He has decreed that whoever buries Polyneices' corps will be sentenced to death. Knowing all this Antigone is suffering not only the demise of both of her brothers but also the harshness of Creon's decree. This decree cuts profoundly into the fiber of a most basic duty of Greek religion, namely, the deeply-felt sacred duty to honor one's closest kin by means of a proper funeral. Undoubtedly, as a politically involved Greek citizen, Antigone also feels a deeply-ingrained respect for the law of the land. She opts for both transgression of the law and forfeiture of her life in the fulfillment of her sacred duty. The play begins just soon after that. She takes her sister Ismene out of the royal palace. There Antigone tries to persuade Ismene to join her in providing a proper burial for Polyneices:

What, hath not Creon destined our brothers, the one to honored burial, the other to unburied shame? Eteocles, they say, *with due observance of right and custom* [my italics], he hath laid in the earth, for his honor among the dead below. But the hapless corpse of Polyneices – as rumour saith, it hath been published to the town that none shall entomb him or mourn, but leave unwept, unsepulchred, a welcome store for the birds, as they espy him, to feast on at will.

Such, 'tis said, is the edict that the good Creon hath set forth for thee and me – yes, for *me* – and is coming hither to proclaim it clearly for those who know it not: nor counts the matter light, but who disobeys in aught, his doom is death by stonning before all the folk. Thou knowest it now; and thou wilt soon show whether thou are nobly bred, or the base daughter of a noble line. [Verses 21–38, from the translation by Richard C. Jebb, *Sophocles: The Plays and Fragments* (Amsterdam: Servio, Publishers, 1962), Vol. III, pp. 13–17.]

This is a grave speech. Antigone is laboring under the tremendous weight of her decision. She is anxious to obtain Ismene's cooperation, but apprises her that in this case compliance with the sacred traditional duty demanded by the gods can be fatal. Yet for her everything is clear: there is after deliberation just one duty that rules her will. Naturally, she acknowledges that the King's edicts have a claim to obedience. She evinces this acknowledgement by her unqualified recognition that the burial honors bestowed upon Eteocles do conform to what justly [*dykes*] is demanded both by the divine law and by the law of the land (through Creon's decree). That is why she is experiencing a conflict of duties.

A reasoning very much like the following must have flashed through Antigone's mind when she reached the tragic decision to bury Polyneices:

A. 1.   Polyneices is dead.
    2.   One ought (legally) to do what one's own King decrees.
    3.   My King Creon has decreed that nobody bury Polyneices (under penalty of death)

Hence,

    4.   I ought (legally) not to bury Polyneices.

On the other hand,

    5.   One ought (as a religious person) do what the gods have decreed.
    6.   The gods have decreed that a dead man be buried by his closest kin.
    7.   I and Ismene are Polyneices' closest kin.

Hence,

    8.   I ought (as a religious person) to bury Polyneices.
      What shall I do?

Now,

    9.   The decrees of the gods always override the decrees of the kings; i.e., if one cannot obey both a divine decree and a

kingly one, one ought ultimately (everything being considered) to do what the gods have decreed.

Hence,

10. I ought ultimately (everything being considered) to bury
Polyneices (even if I must die for disobeying Creon).

Therefore,

11. I *shall* bury Polyneices.

We dismiss here the question whether the word 'ought' is the most
adequate at every place it appears in *A*, or whether other words like
'must' or 'should' would be more appropriate at some places. 'Ought' is
well enough. We are not concerned with the words, but with what these
words express; we are interested in the common and peculiar idea they
would all express in sentences expressing deliberation. Thus, for convenience we call that common and peculiar aspect *ought*, without
implying that it is a real property or a thing.

It would obviously be unfounded, and irrelevant, to conjecture that
Antigone went through the eleven steps of deliberation *A*, pondering each
one of them equally, or that eleven sentences of Ancient Greek trans-
lating the above eleven English sentences ran through her mind, or that
events in her brain corresponded to our eleven sentences. Most likely,
without verbalizing each of the steps, Antigone 'saw' the fundamental
premises and immediately reached her conclusion. Given her religious
upbringing and her intense love for her brothers, it was not necessary for
her to dwell upon premise 9 (that divine law overrides kingly law). Most
certainly, steps 9 and 5 (that one has the religious duty to obey the divine
law) and 6 (that a divine decree demands burial by closest kin) were built
in, by training, into her mechanisms of practical thinking. Thus, her
learning of Polyneices' death, and the ever present knowledge that
Polyneices was her brother, prompted in her, automatically, the thought
of steps 10 (that she ought ultimately to bury Polyneices) and 11 (to bury
him). Be this as it may, here we are not interested in the study of Antigone's psychological processes of cognition or of reasoning.

We are interested in the eleven steps of deliberation *qua* possible contents of occurrences of thought, i.e., in the terminology of Chapter 1,
qua noemata. Now, regardless of the actual details and ordering of what

she thought, whatever the noemata on which her consciousness focussed may have been, and regardless of the clarity of her focussing consciousness, Antigone was certainly aware of all the eleven noemata making up deliberation A. Furthermore, she conceived of them as being related in the ways signaled by our connecting English words 'hence', 'on the other hand', and 'therefore'.

Suppose, however, that Antigone was not able to make up her mind, and that she and Ismene consulted with, say, Socrates of Thebes. Suppose that Socrates shared Antigone's *Weltanschauung,* particularly in that he put religious considerations above the law of the land and believed that a man ought to sacrifice his life for his religious duties. Clearly, Socrates of Thebes would not have been able to go precisely through deliberation A in response to Antigone's request for advice. He could have gone through a reasoning very much like A, but differing from it in having second-person noemata instead of the first-person ones that Antigone thought in deliberation A. It is obvious how Socrates' deliberation for advice could have run:

B. 1.   Polyneices is dead.
    2.   One ought (legally) to do what one's own King decrees.
Your King Creon has decreed that nobody bury Polyneices.

Hence:

    4.   You ought (legally) not to bury Polyneices.

On the other hand,

    5.   You ought (*qua* religious person) to do what the gods have decreed.
    6.   The gods have decreed that a man be buried by his closest kin.
    7.   You, Antigone and Ismene, are Polyneices' closest kin.

Hence,

    8.   You both ought (*qua* religious persons) to bury Polyneices. *What* are you to do my children?

Well, now,

    9.   The decrees of the gods do override the decrees of the kings, etc.

Hence,

    10.   You ought ultimately (everything being considered) to bury
            Polyneices

Therefore,

    11.   Ismene and Antigone, *do* bury Polyneices.

Hence,

    12.   Antigone, *do* you bury Polyneices.

A quick glance at deliberations *A* and *B* prompts some general remarks. *First,* the connective words 'hence' and 'therefore' are interchangeable. This suggests that the same sort of implicational relationships connect all kinds of noemata. Nevertheless, at this juncture this is merely a *problem* to be dealt with in detail later on. But it is also a *datum* to be reckoned with by any theory about the contents of practical thinking. *Second,* the multiplicity of ought- or deontic judgments (regardless of which word is used to express them) is impressive. It must be fully understood; no theory of the contents of practical thinking can be adequate unless it provides a satisfactory account of the multiplicity of *ought*s. *Third,* the conflict-solving ought-judgments need not be *effectively* practical in that they may fail to lead to action or to a readiness for action. This is palpably shown by deliberation *B*. On hearing Socrates deliberate for her and Antigone, Ismene *thinks* step *B*10, that she and Antigone ought ultimately to bury Polyneices; yet Ismene may very well be having an ineffective thought of a conflict-solving ought-conclusion. This shows, *fourth,* that there is an important difference between first-person practical noemata, on the one hand, and second- and third-person practical noemata, on the other hand. We shall say something about this later on, especially in Chapter 10.

    The noemata making up deliberations *A* and *B* naturally group into several categories:

    I.   *Propositions* about the facts of the case:
        (A) *Propositions of brute fact:*
            Polyneices is dead (*A*1, *B*1)
            Ismene and Antigone are Polyneices' closest kin (A7, B7)
        (B) *Propositions about special facts:*

King Creon has decreed that nobody bury Polyneices
(*A*3, *B*3)
*The gods have decreed that a man be buried by his closest
kin* (*A*6, *B*6)

II. *Deontic noemata:*
  (A) *Conflicting ought-judgments:*
    (a) Legal deontic noemata:
      (1) General legal principle:
        *One ought (legally) to do what one's own
        King decrees* (*A*2, *B*2)
      (2) Legal conclusion:
        *Antigone and Ismene ought (legally) to refrain from
        burying Polyneices* (*A*4, *B*4)
    (b) Religious deontic neomata:
      (1) General Principle:
        *One ought (*qua* religious person) to do what the
        gods decree* (*A*5, *B*5)
      (2) Religious deontic conclusion:
        *Ismene and Antigone ought (*qua* religious persons)
        to bury Polyneices* (*A*8, *B*8)
  (B) *Overriding and conflict-solving ought-judgments:*
      (1) General principle:
        Divine decrees override kingly decrees (*A*9, *B*9)
      (2) Overriding ought-conclusion:
        *Ismene and Antigone ought ultimately to bury
        Polyneices* (*A*10, *B*10)

III. *Intentions:*
Antigone's intention *I *shall* bury Polyneices* (*A*11)

IV. *Mandates:*
*Ismene and Antigone, *do* bury Polyneices* (*B*11)
*Antigone, *do* bury Polyneices* (*B*12).

In this investigation we are devoting our efforts to an elucidation of the general structure undergirding the differences and relationships among the main categories of noemata that are contents of practical thinking. These are the categories whose names we have italicized in the above chart. We proceed now to get better acquainted with each one of them.

2. PROPOSITIONS

Our main topic is practical thinking. Propositions are, but not exclusively, contents of practical thinking. Thus, it would be a long preliminary detour to engage here in a full study of propositions. We shall make only a brief introduction solely to lay down distinctions for later parallels. These furnish valuable premises for later use.

We assume the Strawson-Cartwright[1] distinction among a *statement* (i.e., a *proposition*), the *sentences* formulating it, and the *meanings* of such sentences. We adopt the view, congenial to logicians, that Strawson has called the "more impersonal view of statement ... a picture in which the actual needs, purposes and presumptions of speakers and hearers are of slight significance" for determining the entailments or implications and the truth-value of a statement, all of which remain constant, even if the statement is not made.[2] That is, we distinguish from each other what is entailed by a statement S, what is entailed by statements of the forms *X stated S*, *X stated S with purpose P*, and *X stated S on the assumption (or presumption) that p*, and what is presupposed by the interlocutors in normal or efficient communication.

More precisely and fully, we distinguish each of the following from one another:

   (i) the sentences that express a given proposition.
   (ii) the meanings of such sentences.
   (iii) the proposition in question.
   (iv) the acts of uttering one or other of such sentences.
   (v) the acts of formulating the proposition in question.
   (vi) the acts of asserting the given proposition.
   (vii) the acts of endorsing or coming to believe such a proposition.
   (viii) the acts of communicating such a proposition, i.e., the acts of successfully telling someone that such-and-such is the case.

Here are eight distinct types of items. But there are philosophical theories that attempt to reduce some types to others. For instance, some philosophers have proposed to reduce propositions to sentences, while others have suggested the reduction of propositions to speech acts of either type (iv) or of type (vi) or of type (viii) or some combination. Other philosophers want to reduce the mental acts of type (vii) to speech acts of some type or other. We simply cannot enter into such controversies. We assume no reductionist theories of any sort; nor we assume the denial of any reductionist theses. We simply stay firm on the fact that at the phenomenological level the above eight items are distinct. This is a fact that any reductionist thesis has to take into account and even explain satisfactorily. Let us briefly discuss this phenomenological fact.

A proposition is characterized by being true or false, by being the possible content of a belief or cognition, by being the possible content of acts of assertion, i.e., by being *what* is asserted or stated; propositions are among the messages that pass from person to person in acts of communication. They are clearly different from each of the acts performed on them, with them or by them. For one thing, acts are neither true nor false, whereas propositions are true or false. For another thing, the acts have an agent and belong to him, while propositions (or most of them in any case) belong to no one. What a person communicates to another by saying to the latter "Bonita loves Karl" belongs to no one: anybody can receive the information from anyone and can relay it to any one. The piece of information has no agent.

That propositions or units of information or misinformation are not actions or acts is perfectly clear. What is more tempting is the assimilation of propositions to either sentences or meanings of sentences. We must at all costs resist a naive assimilation, even if in the end we adopt some theory that reduces propositions to sentences *and something else*. Consider again the case of, say, Brown who tells Gaskon that "Bonita loves Karl!" Brown can perform his act of communicating such thing, *the very same thing,* to Gaskon by using different sentences – not to mention the case of communication without words. Naturally, if Brown speaks English he may simply assert the sentence 'Bonita loves Karl' and this is the sentence most naturally thought to be the proposition or information Brown conveys to Gaskon. But Brown can use the Spanish sentence 'Bonita ama a Karl', or, for that matter, any other sentence in another language or in English. He can use the English sentence 'Karl is loved by Bonita'. Indeed, Brown can formulate the very same proposition by means of an expression which is not a sentence. For instance, if Brown says "It is impossible for Bonita to love Karl" the infinitive clause 'Bonita to love Karl' may very well express, within the context of the larger sentence, of course, the very same thing expressed by the sentence 'Bonita ama a

Karl'. Clearly, then a proposition cannot be identical with the linguistic means of expressing it.

It might be thought that a proposition is identical with the class of all sentences that express it and nothing else. This excludes the sentence 'It is impossible for Bonita to love Karl' from the class to be equated with the proposition *Bonita loves Karl*, since that sentence clearly expresses something more by means of the frame 'It is impossible for...'. This suggestion faces at least one further serious problem. The well-known Cantor's theorem about power sets says, roughly, that a given set or class of objects has more subsets than it has members. For example, the triple $\{a, b, c\}$ has three members and eight subsets: the null set, the three sets $\{a\}$, $\{b\}$, and $\{c\}$, the three pairs $\{a, b\}$, $\{a, c\}$, $\{b, c\}$, and, of course itself. Similarly, the infinite set of natural numbers $\{1, 2, ...\}$ yields a class of subsets which is of higher degree of infinity.

For convenience, the word cardinality is used to cover both natural numbers and degrees of infinity. Let us use '$<$' to indicate that the class mentioned on the left has lower cardinality than that mentioned on the right, and '$\leqslant$' to mean '*has the same cardinality as, or lower cardinality than*', then we have:

(a)   class of sentences $<$ class of classes of sentences;

(b)   class of classes of sentences $<$ class of classes of classes of sentences;

(c)   class of classes of classes of sentences $\leqslant$ class of propositions attributing to a certain class of sentences membership in a class of classes of sentences.

Therefore,

(d)   class of sentences $<$ class of propositions.

Propositions come in pairs: for every true one there is its negation, which is false, and vice versa. Furthermore, every class of classes of sentences yields as many true propositions as there are classes of sentences that attribute membership to each of the latter in the former. Nevertheless, we cannot replace in (c) above the sign '$\leqslant$' with '$<$'; for the infinite cases we may still get the same degree of infinite cardinality.

From (d) above it follows that a large number of propositions are not identical with classes of sentences – let alone sentences. Now, the rationale for identifying some propositions with classes of sentences cannot be, it seems, but a rationale for identifying *all* propositions with classes of sentences. Thus, it seems that no proposition is a class of sentences. Exactly the same argument can be given against the identification of a proposition with a class of classes of classes of ... sentences.

In spite of the preceding argument it may still be true that every proposition one can think, one can express – even if one express more propositions than one has sentences. This is an ontological justification of ambiguity. Perhaps propositions can be reduced to classes of sentences *and something else,* e.g., speech acts, behavior, and circumstances, capable of disambiguating sentences.

In this book, however, we cannot pursue the topic of the metaphysics of propositions. We leave it open whether propositions are reducible to physical or psychological entities, or not. We also leave it open whether or not propositions are identical with states of affairs, and whether or not true propositions are identical with facts.[3] We simply insist on maintaining a metaphysically non-committal description of the apparent structure enveloping propositions and the practical noemata. We make distinctions that beg no questions, and our *macro* theories will at least collect and organize data to be accounted for by an adequate nominalistic *micro* theory.

We must also distinguish a proposition from the meaning or meanings of a sentence that expresses it. For instance, we must distinguish *what* Brown asserted when he said to Gaskon "Bonita loves Karl" from the meaning of the sentence 'Bonita loves Karl'. The meaning of the sentence is the same regardless of what different propositions it expresses by virtue of the fact that the names 'Bonita' and 'Karl' refer to different persons. The meaning of the sentence is known by a Spanish speaker still in the process of gaining the basic mastery of English when he knows that 'Bonita loves Karl' means the same as 'Bonita ama a Karl'. And clearly, such a Spanish speaker need *not* know any proposition, any truth (or falsehood), that the English sentence has ever expressed. Indeed, as of this writing the author knows no such proposition, and he has complete understanding of the meaning of such sentence. In fact, it seems that *the meaning of a sentence is better conceived of as the type and range of propositions it can express, given the conventions of the language to which the sentence belongs.* To speak is to choose proposition from such ranges.

Obviously, the suggestion that a proposition is to be identified with a class of synonymous sentences has to face the above problem arising from Cantor's theorem, which applies to all classes of sentences.

Naturally, we have to assume that propositions have constituents or 'parts' in some sense. But we simply cannot go here into a discussion of the nature of such constituents. We shall, however, assume as little as is strictly necessary for the development of our theories and investigations. Since sentences express propositions we shall assume that some sentences reveal in their grammatical structure structural aspects of the propositions they express. Indeed, a good deal of philosophy consists precisely in the search for perspicuous analyses of sentences and notations that reveal transparently and in fine detail the structure of certain propositions.

We must emphasize that propositions are abstract possible *whats* or contents of cognitive operations of the mind; they need not be actual contents of any cognitive operation. For instance, many a scientific discovery involves the thinking by a scientist of a proposition that nobody has ever thought before at all. The same is true of the invention of many novels or pieces of science fiction.

Since many philosophers use the term 'statement' to refer to *what* is asserted and has truth-values, we shall use it to refer to propositions. The term 'statement' has an unwelcome slant, to wit: on propositions being contents of speech acts of asserting or stating. But it must be remembered that what is a statement in our sense is a possible content of an act of stating. Thus, if we do not say that some statements have never been stated, perhaps we should use the word 'statement' to refer to propositions that have actually been stated. Then, statements are like claims, declarations, and reports, namely, propositions which *have* played the role of being contents of some speech act. Likewise, beliefs, conjectures, hypotheses, and prediction among others, are propositions that have been the contents of certain psychological acts or attitudes. However, at the present level of our investigation all such differences of linguistic or psychological roles are of no significance.

3. MANDATES

We also adopt here toward practical thinking the same point of view described above that we adopt toward theoretical or factual or contemplative thinking. More specifically, we generalize the distinctions discussed above to commands, orders, requests, pieces of advice, petitions, and entreaties, all of which will be, generically, called *mandates,* or *imperatives.* They are all: (i) possible straight answers to a question of the form *Shall I do A?* asked in interpersonal discourse, or (ii) combinations of such possible answers with others or with propositions. Again, we adopt the impersonal view of mandates, taking their relations analogous to entailment to remain constant, even when they are not issued or considered. Thus, we distinguish from each other:

    (i) a sentence formulating a given mandate,
    (ii) the meaning of such a sentence,
    (iii) the mandate in question,
    (iv) the act of uttering the sentence,
    (v) the act of formulating the mandate,
    (vi) the act of issuing the mandate,
    (vii) the act of endorsing or adopting the mandate, and
    (viii) the act of communicating the mandate, i.e., the *telling* of someone *to* do something or other.

Since these distinctions are exactly parallel to the ones drawn above for the case of propositions, we can be brief here. The difference between a sentence expressing a mandate and the meaning(s) of such a sentence is obvious. Two entirely different sentences of that sort may have the same meaning; for instance, the English sentence 'Bonita, go home' and the Spanish sentence 'Bonita, vete a case' have the same meaning: they are each other's translation. As in the case of propositions, the difference between a mandate and a sentence expressing it is revealed by the fact that one imperative sentence may express different mandates, and by the fact that the very same mandate can be formulated by two or more different sentences. On the one hand, clearly, the sentence 'Bonita, go home' has expressed different orders or requests on different occasions of its use. On the other hand, the same mandate may be expressed with different sentences. Suppose that Jones issues the order *Bonita, go home*, and that Jones suddenly notices that Bonita tarries, perhaps because she did not hear him, so that he repeats his order by saying "Do go home", or "Bonita, I want you to go home". In this case we have the three different sentences 'Bonita, go home' 'Do go home' and 'Bonita, I want you to go home', which have different meanings, and yet express the very same mandate, in those circumstances.

The meaning of an imperative sentence is, of course, a range of mandates. By considerations similar to those made above in §2 we can see that a mandate (or imperative) is neither a sentence nor the meaning of a sentence. This does not, however, preclude, as some philosophers want to have it, that a mandate be at bottom reducible to a class of sentences, imperative or otherwise, together with something else. Again, we shall not discuss this here. But we must insist that such a reduction, if viable, has to respect the phenomenological differences between a mandate and an imperative sentence, as well as the differences between a mandate and the meaning of a set of synonymous imperative sentences.

That a sentence formulating a given mandate is different from all acts listed as (iv)–(viii) above is obvious: a sentence is an abstract pattern illustrated by physical objects and, not being an act, it has no agents. Similarly, (ii), the meaning of a sentence formulating a mandate, differs from acts (iv)–(vii), since a sentence has always the same meaning or meanings given it by the rules of the language, even if nobody is at a certain time using it. Now, a mandate is not an act, either: it is an abstract entity on which acts can be performed: acts like enacting or issuing it, rejecting or endorsing it, obeying or fulfilling it. But while all acts are brought into existence by some agent at a given time and place, a mandate, i.e., a possible answer to a possible, but perhaps unasked question *Shall I (we) do...?* is not brought into existence by anybody at any place or time. A mandate is not a property of anybody, since it is what unifies the diverse acts, owned by the speakers of a language, when several people issue or consider the same order, command or request. Like a proposition, a mandate does not belong to any given language, since it can be issued or uttered or grasped or understood in any other language.

The difference between (iv), uttering an imperative sentence, and (v), formulating a mandate, is evident from the fact that one can utter a sentence that naturally formulates a mandate without intending to issue a mandate, as in sleep or in practicing the pronounciation of the sentence. That difference is also evident from the fact that when a person issues a mandate by uttering a certain sentence he may re-issue it by uttering another sentence, even if this sentence is a translation of the former.

Similarly, formulating or expressing a mandate differs from (vi), issuing a mandate, in that a person or a sentence can do the former without the use of the sentence doing the latter. For example, if one issues the order *Go home or be quiet* one formulates the order *Go home* without issuing it.

Issuing a given mandate is not the same as endorsing the mandate in question. On the one hand, one may endorse a mandate and be ready and willing to issue it, but fail to issue it because one's tongue suddenly becomes paralyzed, or because one considers at the same time that it would be improper or pointless to issue it. On the other hand, one may issue a mandate that one does not endorse. This may be done, for instance, when one is merely a carrier of other person's issued and endorsed commands. But one may issue a mandate one does not endorse in a case analogous to lying. A man, for example, may ask his child girl to do something, without in the least caring whether she does the thing in question or not – his purpose just being to have her occupied elsewhere so that she does not hear something that is about to be said.

Finally, actually telling a person to do something is different from all the other listed psychological and linguistic acts on mandates. For one thing, the success of the communicating act depends on circumstances surrounding both the speaker and his addressess on which circumstances neither may have complete control. Sometimes the phrase 'telling to' is used to refer to the general act of issuing any mandate, and sometimes to refer to a special type of issuing that is somehow between commanding and requesting. But this does not destroy the difference between communicating and issuing a mandate.

4. PRESCRIPTIONS

We have already spoken of the endorsement of a mandate. But the words 'believe' and 'belief' are not used to refer to attitudes toward mandates. Those words just denote propositional attitudes. The practical term corresponding to 'believe' is 'approve'. But the correspondence is not quite parallel. Yet this lack of paralleligm reveals a very important aspect of practical thinking that we must examine now. Suppose that we are considering what a man, Jones, say, is to do. Let the relevant alternatives of action available to him be getting a job now and registering for a study course. Suppose that we approve that Jones registers for the study course, i.e., we approve of Jone's registering for the study course. The whole content of our attitude of approval is clearly not a proposition; but neither is it a mandate. The whole content of our approval is neither a command nor an order nor a piece of advice nor a petition: it is, however, an abstract content which can be formulated or put forward or communicated in the form of a command, or a piece of advice or a request or a petition. The whole content of our approval is, in fact, the core common to a set of related mandates. We must refer to this common core from now on, it will be called a *prescription*.

Prescriptions are characteristically "unassertable" units by themselves, i.e., they are issuable only under the guise of a mandate of some type or other Thus, it seems that in the case of practical discourse counterparts of propositions as units of content of linguistic acts are, not prescriptions, but mandates. On the other hand, prescriptions seem to be counterparts of propositions as units of thought content and of other attitudes, like approval, as we pointed out. We shall see that prescriptions, not mandates, are, like propositions, possessors of implication relationships.

Consider the sentence 'Mary, go home'. It can be used to express different mandates or imperatives: (i) an order, (ii) a command, (iii) a request, (iv) an entreaty, (v) a suggestion, (vi) a piece of advice. The type of mandate being issued will normally be clear to the addressee and to others, because of the context, or the speaker's tone of voice, or because of classificatory signals like the word 'please' to signal a request, 'This is an order', 'I beg you', 'I advise you', or 'My advice is', which unmistakably reveal the type of mandate in question. Again, our interest does not lie in language, but in what is thought or expressed. The point is that all those mandates are structurally akin; they present a person called "Mary" as an agent of the action of going home and as the subject of the *demand* to perform this action. In other words, all those mandates embody a common thought content: *a structure of agent and action connected in a special way,* which could be called *a demanding way.* Let us call such a structure a prescription. Let the prescription embedded in the previously listed mandates (i)–(vi) be ∗Mary (to) go home∗. This prescription is like the proposition ∗Mary will go home∗ in having the same subject and the same predicate constituents. Are they the same?

At this juncture we must leave this as another question that has to be answered in this investigation.

In any case, prescriptions are the cores of families of mandates, namely, families that demand of exactly the same agents the performance of exactly the same actions in exactly the same circumstances. Obviously, prescriptions must be distinguished from speech acts, from psychological acts or attitudes, from sentences and other locutions, and from meanings of sentences or locutions.

For convenience we shall introduce the following convention to be adjoined to those introduced in Chapter 1 §3:

C4   Pure expressions of prescriptions are obtained as follows: take an imperative sentence that expresses a mandate, delete the imperative commas after the grammatical subjects, and insert right after the imperative subjects the locution 'to'.

5. INTENTIONS

An intention is a possible first-person answer to the question *Shall I do that?* or the question *What shall I do?*, *asked* of oneself, provided the answer does constitute a solution to the problem posed by the question. The proposition *I do not know* does not count as answer, but as an evasion or postponement of the solution to the problem. Intentions are the practical noemata *par excellence*. Intending to do something is to be already in the process of doing it, even if merely by having undergone a re-arrangement of the causal powers within oneself in the direction of the action one intends to do.

The word 'intention' is, like the word 'belief', ambiguous between a certain operation of the mind and the content, or noema, of that operation. Here we use both terms to refer to noemata only. Thus, we contrast the acts or attitudes or operations of intending and their intentions. Intending is obviously, a practical counterpart of believing; likewise, intentions are practical counterparts of propositions. Intentions appear to be different from propositions. For one thing, propositions are either true or false, while intentions are neither. An intention is closely related to a prediction. Both refer to the future, and both are expressed by the future tense. Yet the difference is enormous. The intention *I [Castañeda] shall finish this book* is neither true nor false, and it is one that I have de-

finitely endorsed. Yet the preliction *I [= Castañeda] will finish this book*
is either true or false, but I do not know which one. Furthermore, it is a
prediction that at my age and at my present weight I cannot endorse.
I simply hope that it be true.

Consider a typical expression of a proposition that attributes an intention to a man, say, 'Jones intends to go home'. Such proposition
attributes to Jones both a noema and an operation. But what is the intention, the noema, it attributes to Jones? A faithful attention to the
sentence may suggest that the intention is simply the act of going, i.e.
to go home, which is expressed by the whole of the locution that follows the verb 'intends' in the above sentence. Clearly, *to go home* is
neither true nor false, so that the identification of the action with the
intention does not run afoul the data mentioned in the preceding paragraph. We will argue that intentions are not actions. (See. Chapter 6.)

Here are other problems our investigation must solve. We must provide
an account of both the relationships between intentions and propositions,
and of those between intentions and actions. Particularly, we must answer
the ontological questions: whether or not intentions are reducible to
propositions; whether or not intentions are reducible to actions; whether
or not they are unique practical noemata wholly irreducible to any other
types of noemata. (See Chapter 6.)

Decisions, i.e., the outcomes of deliberation, as Antigone's *I *shall*
bury Polyneices* at the end of deliberation *A* in Section 1, are the same
thought contents as intentions. Deciding to do something is the practical
counterpart of coming to believe that something or other is the case. What
one comes to believe after a difficult search is, of course, the same type of
content, namely, a proposition, as what one believes all of a sudden, with
no effort at all. Likewise, it is the same type of thought content a person
intends, whether his intending comes about all of a sudden, effortlessly, or
whether his intending comes after a long-drawn and painful deliberation.

Intentions are obviously different from mandates. In particular, intentions are *not* self-commands. A self-command is a command addressed
by a person to himself. But a command is never a thought content that
includes a first-person reference. The *self*-feature of a self-command is
external to it, and it accrues to the self-command by virtue of both an
underlying intention and an undergirding first-person proposition. For
instance, feeling a slight wavering of her ability to face death for burying

her brother Polyneices Antigone encourages herself by self-commands that she voices out loud: *Antigone, be steady, be brave, have courage, you die just once and then the gods below will reward your courageous fulfilment of duty*. These self-commands are, internally, mere commands, i.e., possible contents of acts of commanding, just like any other command. What makes them *self*-commands is *external* to them, namely, the related pair of noemata about herself that Antigone has in fact endorsed, namely: the proposition *I am Antigone* and the intention *I [=Antigone] *shall* bury Polyneices*.

To conclude this introduction of intentions, we must distinguish intentions from sentences, phrases, locutions, and words. The reasons for these are exactly parallel to those given for the differentiation of propositions from sentences and phrases, and for the differentation of mandates from imperative sentences and other clauses. Again, intentions are neither the meanings of sentences nor the meanings of phrases or words. Nor are intentions speech acts or psychological operations. Yet, once again, all of these distinctions cannot prejudge the viability of a profound metaphysical reduction of intentions to structures of other entities, physical or orherwise. These are problems we will not be able to tackle this time.

6. PRACTITIONS

For convenience we introduce the term 'practition' to refer generically to both prescriptions and intentions. Since the word does not seem to exist at present in the English language it should fend some misinterpretations of the views expounded in this book. In particular, it should be patent that we are *not* here reducing intentions to prescriptions, much less to mandates or imperatives, and even less to imperative sentences, or psycho-linguistic acts of issuing mandates. In earlier publications[4] I used the term 'prescription' in a more generic sense than the one introduced in Section 4 above. Prescriptions were introduced there as cores of families of mandates *and* intentions. Thus, I said: intentions are first-person prescriptions. That statement invited the reply that intentions are not self-commands. Of course, they are not, regardless of which sense of the word 'prescription' is employed, as has been carefully recorded in the penultimate paragraph of the previous section.

The view I have always advocated is this:[5] intentions and mandates

| | Propositions | Mandates | Practitions | |
			Prescriptions	Intentions
Examples	The executioner killed (is killing, will kill) Jones	Order: Executioner, kill Jones Request: Executioner, please kill Jones	Executioner to kill Jones	*Asserted form:* I[= Executioner] shall kill Jones *Unasserted form:* I[= Executioner] to kill Jones
Complete Linguistics Acts on Them	Expressing Asserting Communicating: telling that	Expressing Issuing Communication: telling to	(Expressable clothed in the guise of some mandate)	Expressing Declaring Communicating
Characteristic Expression	Declarative sentence	Imperative sentence	(Second- and third-person infinitive and subjunctive clauses: also gerundial clauses)	*Asserted form:* first-person future-tense indicative *Unasserted form:* first-person infinite and subjunctive clauses
Complete Psychological Acts	Coming to believe; Considering, thinking (that), Believing, endorsing	(Derived from corresponding acts on the constituting prescriptions)	Coming to endorse Thinking what (x is) to do Approving, endorsing	Coming to endorse = adopt Thinking what (one is) to do Intending, endorsing
Logical Properties	Implications Truth-values	(Derived solely from properties of prescription)	Implications values (to be named)	Implications values (to be named)

are mutually exclusive and complementary. Mandates are second- and third-person practical noemata while intentions are the complementary first-person noemata. But this *non-reductionistic* view has to be defended. We shall do so in Chapter 6.

The word 'practition' denotes a very natural class of noemata, if the view mentioned in the preceding paragraph and yet to be defended turns out to be correct. It has the symbolic property of rhyming with 'proposition'. Since we also argue for the view that deontic noemata are propositions, we will be adhering to the thesis that practical noemata are either propositions or practitions. Thus, the word 'practition' is a nice term to express the fundamental categorial partition of practical noemata. Furthermore, in more than one sense, it will turn out in the theory we are in the process of developing, that both intentions and mandates are the basic units, *qua* practical, of practical thinking. Thus, the word 'practition' carries on its forehead, so to speak, this important thesis of the theory.

For convenience we summarize some of the linguistic and psychological points made about propositions, mandates, prescriptions, and intentions in Figure 1.

7. NORMATIVES OR DEONTIC JUDGMENTS

We have seen in Section 1 of this chapter that there is a rich category of ought-judgments. They are a species of deontic judgments or noemata, sometimes also called *normatives*. In general, the thought contents of speech acts expressing that some persons have duties, obligations, permissions, or prohibitions or interdictions, are all deontic noemata. So are rules that specify what agents of certain kinds are to do in given circumstances. Thus, laws of countries, municipal ordinances, institutional statutes and by-laws, contractual and promisory commitments, are all deontic noemata. Indeed, these are all noemata, but not pure and naked; they are noemata that have been adopted by the communities that constitute the countries, the cities, institutions, contractants, or promise-partners in question. Such deontic noemata are like believed propositions or intended intentions.

Deontic noemata of the kind we are interested in have been referred to by some philosophers as judgments pertaining to the category or realm of the Ought-to-do. There is no harm in introducing this term as a compact way of referring to the problems concerning the general nature of deontic judgments. Such philosophers have often contrasted the Ought-to-be with the Ought-to-do. The former is the one involved in noemata like *The world ought to have been without pain*, *There ought to be life after death*, and even in *Women ought to give birth to children without pain*, where there is no suggestion that there is something that women ought to do, but only that the world would be *better* if they suffered no birth pains. In these investigations we are concerned exclusively with the Ought-to-do. We are concerned only with deontic noemata involving agents and actions. Agentless noemata expressible by sentences like 'Every car ought to be licensed' are within our compass only to the extent that such noemata as those sentences express involve an agent implicitly alluded to when the sentence is uttered. For instance, to say that every car ought to be licensed may be short for saying that everybody who drives (or owns or manages) a car ought to get a license for it.

Philosophers have debated whether the Ought-to-be applies to states of affairs, or facts or propositions. Naturally, we leave this matter undecided here. We also leave undecided whether the Ought-to-be is reducible to the Ought-to-do or vice versa. Note in this connection, however, that the Ought-to-do appears to be much more complex than the Ought-to-be. The role of agency, crucial to the former, is a complex one demanding a special relationship between subjects conceived as agents and the actions they are to perform. (See Chapter 5.)

Hopefully, the preceding examples of deontic judgments suffice to produce some definite idea of what we call here deontic noemata. Perhaps the contrast between the Ought-to-be and the Ought-to-do is helpful to give more substance to our category of deontic noemata. Nevertheless, we must do better than that. Annoyingly enough, many of the crucial words in the preceding discussion, like 'rule', 'right', 'ought', and 'obligation' are often used to formulate propositions that are not deontic noemata in the sense relevant to our study. We must, therefore, try to introduce a sharper characterization of deontic noemata.

The sentences 'I ought to go now, for my class begins in five minutes' and 'He has no right to leave, for his class begins in five minutes' in their normal use do express deontic noemata. But 'He is to the right of Jones' and 'It ought to rain today according to the Weatherman's report' do not normally express deontic noemata. Moreover, an utterance of a sentence containing the word 'ought' may fail to express a deontic judgment because it may be simply the expression of a command or an order. In this case, however, the utterance of the 'ought'-sentence would of course express a practical noema. Clearly, it is not incumbent upon us here to determine whether it is ever the case, or how it is the case when it happens, that an English speaker proffers the sentences 'You must go home' or 'You ought to go home' as a mere emphatic version of the command or order *Go home*. Yet we must furnish some criteria for distinguishing such cases from those in which the man proffers either sentence meaning to put forward a deontic judgment. We proceed to do this by means of a sequence of informal definitions.

DEFINITION 1. A mandate or intention (i.e., a practition) P can *reinforce* a noema N, if and only if there is no absurdity, or there has been no absurdity, of any kind in any of the apparently inferential sequences: *Since N, P*; *Because N, P*; *P, for N*; *N, hence P*, and *N, therefore P*. Furthermore, P does in fact reinforce N in such sequences.

For example, in deliberation *B* in Section 1 above the mandate *Antigone, do bury Polyneices* reinforces the noema *Antigone ought to bury Polyneices.*

DEFINITION 2. Each of the expressions in the following list is a *positive normative term:*
'ought to', 'has a duty to', 'must', 'it is obligatory', 'may', 'it is right', and 'it is permissible'.

DEFINITION 3. Each of the expressions in the following list is a *negative normative term:*
'it is wrong', 'it is forbidden', 'cannot', and 'it is improper'.

DEFINITION 4. A noema expressed by a sentence containing a normative term is called a *prima facie deontic* (or *normative*) *noema.*

Clearly, Definition 4 does not imply that a prima facie deontic noema is really a deontic noema. *It ought to rain by 3 p.m.* is a proposition about the great likelihood of it raining by 3 p.m.; it is prima facie normative, but it is not genuinely so, because there is no agent that is overtly, or covertly demanded to do something.

DEFINITION 5. A verb in the imperative mood in a clause or sentence is *negated* by prefixing to it the negated verb 'don't' or 'don't do the following'. A chain 'don't don't' is replaced either by 'don't fail to' or by 'don't fail to do the following:'.

Example: The main verb in 'Mary, love those who admire you' is negated by producing 'Mary, don't love those who admire you'.

DEFINITION 6. The imperative or mandate *corresponding* to a prima facie deontic noema is the one expressed by the imperative sentence which results from the sentence expressing the latter as prima facie normative by: (i) dropping the normative terms it contains; (ii) putting the remaining part of the clause most immediately affected by (i) in the imperative mood, and (iii) negating each verb affected by (ii) if in the original sentence it is subordinated to a negative normative term.

For example: to *You ought to go home* corresponds *Go home*; to *You, Arthur, may go home* corresponds *Arthur, go home*; to *If Quintus does not go home, it is wrong for Mary to call him up* corresponds *If Quintus does not go home, Mary, don't call him up*.

Let S be a sentence that expresses a noema D as a prima facie deontic noema. Let *n* be the only normative term of S. Let 'Not-S' be the sentence obtained by prefixing the locution 'It is not the case that' to S. Then we can define:

DEFINITION 7. Prima facie deontic noema D is a *deontic noema*, i.e., a genuine deontic noema, if and only if: D can be reinforced by its corresponding mandate, and there is a sentence expressing D such that the sentence 'Not-S' expresses a different noema from the one expressed by putting the appropriate negation expression before the sentence or clause subordinated to the normative term *n* in S.

This definition shows how the sentence 'The tornado ought to be near downtown by midnight' does not, as is *customarily* understood by twentieth century English speakers, express a deontic judgment. *The tornado ought to be near downtown by midnight* is a prima facie noema. Its corresponding mandate is *Tornado, be near downtown by midnight*.

Clearly, the former cannot be reinforced by this mandate; as we custo-marily understood the former we do not regard it as capable of supporting advice to the tornado. Notwithstanding, the sentence 'The tornado ought to be near downtown by midnight' *can* be understood in such a way that it expresses a deontic judgment: an animist, i.e., a man who conceives of winds and other natural forces as composites of physical substances and spirits or souls that animate the physical substances, conceives of the tornado of the example as a genuine agent, like he himself and his friends. But, of course, the animist also conceives of the mandate *Tornado, be near downtown by midnight* as capable of reinforcing his deontic judgment about the tornado. If the tornado ought, really ought, to be near downtown, the animist can consistently urge it to move. The animist's prima facie deontic noema is a genuine deontic noema; the contemporary English speaker's is not. Hence, they are different noemata.

From the general structure of practical thinking it cannot be deter-mined whether the animist or the contemporary sophisticated English speaker has the correct view of tornadoes. Indeed, we must be *unable* to adjudge what the correct view is. Thus, our imperative test for deter-mining genuine deontic noemata is, as it should be, neutral with respect to animism.

Now, suppose that Parko uses the sentence 'Orlo, you ought to (must) shut the door' meaning to issue a command, and nothing but a command. Obviously, Parko's command is a noema reinforceable by itself. Some purists may argue that it makes no sense to proclaim: *Shut the door, therefore, shut the door*. However, it makes even more sense than the propositional counterpart *You will shut the door, therefoıe, you will shut the door*. The reason is transparent: the repetion of the command *Shut the door* has at least the point of psychologically reinforcing the causal "push" that often accompanies the hearing of a command. In any case, Definition 7 provides a criterion for taking our Parko's utterance of the sentence 'Orlo, you ought to (must) shut the door' as not formulating a deontic judgment. The reason is that if Parko merely intends to express a command, then his 'you ought to' or 'must' is simply a signal of his emphasis on his utterance of 'Orlo, shut the door'. Parko cannot dis-tinguish the noema expressed by the sentence 'It is not case that you, Orlo, ought to (must) shut the door' from the one expressed by 'Orlo, you ought not to (must not) shut the door', where both of these two negated sentences are meant to preserve exactly the sense of his own utterance of 'Orlo, you ought to (must) shut the door'. Of course, the fact that there is no difference in the noemata expressed by the two negations as Parko would use them on that occasion does not imply that they both express the same noema. It may very well be the case that the sentence 'It is not the case that you, Orlo, ought to shut the door' expresses, as Parko uses his words, no noema at all.

DEFINITION 8. If a prima facie deontic noema is expressed as such by a sentence containing more than one normative term, then if one subsentence containing a normative term expresses a genuine deontic judgment, then the whole prima facie deontic noema is a genuine deontic noema.

The point of this definition is to extend the character of being a deontic judgment to compound judgments that have at least one component which is a deontic judgment. Thus, the sentence 'You ought to be inside your house before midnight, if the tornado ought to be near downtown by midnight', as normally used, expresses a genuine deontic judgment, regardless of whether one is an animist or not, because 'You ought to be inside your house' expresses one.

The semi-technical definitions of deontic noemata given above apply only to noemata expressed in sentences. Yet, as in the case of the other noemata, we must insist that deontic judgments are not sentences, and that some of them may perhaps never be conceived or formulated by anyone. This is, of course, a limitation. But it is a limitation that should not sadden us. After all, any deontic judgment we can think we can express.

NOTES TO CHAPTER 2

[1] See P. F. Strawson, *Introduction to Logical Theory* (London: Methuen and Company; New York: John Wiley & Sons, 1952); Richard Cartwright, 'Propositions', in R. J. Butler, ed., *Analytic Philosophy* (Oxford: Blackwell Ltd.; New York: Barnes & Noble, 1962): 81–103; Richard Cartwright, 'Propositions Again', *Nous* 2 (1968): 299–246. For further enrichments of my conception of propositions, see my 'Indicators and Quasi-indicators', *American Philosophical Quarterly* 4 (1967): 85–100, especially pp. 90ff, and 'On the Logic of Attributions of Self-Knowledge to Others', *The Journal of Philosophy* 64 (1968): 439–456. These enrichments arise from an examination of demonstrative reference and the attribution to others of demonstrative reference. For yet further enrichments involving an analysis of predication see H-N. Castañeda, 'Thinking and the Structure of the World', *Philosophia* 4 (1974): 3–40.

² See P. F. Strawson, 'Identifying Reference and Truth-values', *Theoria* 30 (1964): 109ff.

³ After careful study of the structure of contemplative thinking and its relations to its contents and the world, I have adopted the simplified view that: so-called states of affairs are just propositions, true propositions are just facts, and that thinking refers to facts without intermediaries. These and other theses are placed in their proper niche in H-N. Castañeda, 'Thinking and the Structure of the World', mentioned in note 1 above.

⁴ Especially in my 'Actions, Imperatives, and Obligations', *Proceedings of the Aristotelian Society* 68 (1967–68): 25–48, and in 'Intentions and Intending', *American Philosophical Quarterly* 9 (1972): 139–149. In the earlier 'Outline of a Theory on the General Logical Structure of the Language of Action', *Theoria* 26 (1960): 151–182, practitions were called *imperative-resolutives*; but this term was also used to refer to expressions of practitions.

⁵ This view is formulated in the papers mentioned in note 4 as well as in my 'Imperatives, Decisions, and Oughts: A Logico-metaphysical Investigation', in Hector-Neri Castañeda and George Nakhnikian, eds., *Morality and the Language of Conduct* (Detroit: Wayne State University Press, 1963; paper-back, 1965): 219–299.

CHAPTER 3

PROPOSITIONAL STRUCTURE AND
PROPOSITIONAL IMPLICATION

In this chapter we deepen our characterization of propositions and study the basic structures of propositional implication. Here is, then, a short, but slightly unconventional (because more philosophical), introduction to standard two-valued logic. We need this introduction, not only for completeness, given that propositions are contents of practical reasoning, but primarily because the implicational structure of propositions is the paradigm of implicational structure. This is part of the ontological primacy of the contents of contemplative thinking. We make use of most of this chapter in the following ones.

We take more pains than usual to separate the ontological from the linguistic aspects, and both from the purely logical ones. For later use we include an analysis of the main roles of ordinary logical words in communication and thinking. All of this helps the extermination of some common confusions vitiating many discussions of the logic of mandates and deontic judgments.

The discussion of the logic of propositions develops crucial premises in the arguments to be erected in Chapters 4 and 6 in defense of the claim that mandates and intentions have implicational relationships, and must have "semantical" values analogous to truth and falsehood, which are elucidated in Chapters 5 and 6. Specifically, we shall make use of Meta-theorems I and II, the completeness theorems of the propositional calculus, formulated in §14.

1. PROPOSITIONAL FORMS

We have introduced propositions and have adopted the '∗' -quotes to equip ourselves with names for propositions. Unofficially we have already on occasion talked about certain forms of propositions. From now on it will be economical and perspicuous to have official names for proposit onal forms. To that effect, we shall abide by the conventions below, to be added to those introduced in Chapter 1 §5 and Chapter 2 §4.

C5   The small letters *'p'*, *'q'*, *'r'*, *'s'*, and *'t'*, with or without subscripts, will be used as blanks to be filled in with sentences, or other locutions that express propositions in whose internal analysis we are not at the moment interested. They will be called *propositional variables* or *schematic letters*.

Thus, any propositional variable whatever represents the most general form of a proposition, regardless of how the proposition is expressed and regardless of what inner structure it may have. Propositional variables are governed by two rules:

C5.1   In a given context of discussion each occurrence of a propositional variable is to be filled in with sentences expressing one and the same proposition; preferably the filler should be the same sentence so as to highlight the sameness of the proposition in question.

C5.2   In a given context of discussion different propositional variables may very well, but need not, represent different propositions.

Neither propositional variables by themselves nor sentence schemata containing occurrences of propositional variables express propositions, i.e., things that are true or false: they express, not propositions, but only *forms of propositions*, i.e., *propositional forms*. We shall say that propositional forms are expressed by sentential forms. For instance, the schema or form 'John believes that *p*' is a sentence matrix. Genuine sentences result from it by "filling" in the slot represented by *'p'* with sentences. The resulting sentences express things that are true or false, but the schema itself does not. Thus, the schema generates the sentences 'John believes that he does not believe anything' and 'John believes that $2+2=5$', which may be used to express propositions.

C6   We shall use asterisks around sentence schemata containing propositional variables to form names of the propositional forms the schemata represent.

Thus, there is the propositional form *John believes that *p**, which underlies every proposition that ascribes belief that something or other is the case to some person named 'John'. Similarly, there are the propositional forms *If p, then q*, and *p, but q*. These names are like ordinary names in referring to different forms, but are less dependent on context than ordinary names. Since the reference of the name 'John' is not fixed, the reference of the name '*John believes that p*' is not fixed. Similarly, inasmuch as the word 'if' may have different meanings or uses, the name '*if p, then q*' may refer to different propositional forms. But once the meanings and uses of 'if', 'and', 'or', and 'neither-nor' are fixed, it is clear what the following propositional forms are: *If p, then q*; *p, and q*; *p or s*; *neither q nor p*; *if p and q, then neither r nor s*. We shall presently discuss these forms in detail.

2. TRUTH

We simply cannot engage here in a detailed analysis of truth. For our present purpose it will suffice to list some of the fundamental assumptions about truth that jointly provide a partial elucidation of truth, thus clarifying even more our concept of proposition, since by our characterization of propositions a truthvalue is both necessary and sufficient for propositionhood. The principles to be enunciated involve references to propositions, belief, fact, etc.; they are, thus like axioms that simultaneously, though partially, characterize all the concepts in question.

In spite of challenges from many quarters, the traditional view of proposition and truth is not only the simplest but the most serviceable. It is essentially made up of principles and principle schemata about truth some of which are listed below, where by *truth-value* is meant truth, falsity, and at this very moment any (if there is any) other value of propositions relevant to belief and implication:

(T.1)   Each proposition has exactly one truth-value.

(T.2)   A proposition is true, if and only if it is not false.

(T.3)   The truth-value of a proposition does not change from time to time.

(T.4)   The truth-value of a proposition does not change from place to place.

(T.5)   The truth-value of a proposition is not altered by the psychological attitudes or acts that have the proposition as their content.

(T.6)   The truth-value of a proposition is not altered by the linguistic
         acts that have the proposition as content.

Principle (T.1) is the *principle of non-contradiction*. Nobody rejects
it. Even those who argue that there are more than two values, still adopt
(T.1). From (T.1) and (T.2) together it follows that no proposition is both
true and false, and this corollary is actually what is often referred to as
the principle of non-contradiction.

Principle (T.2) is often called the *principle of excluded middle,* for it
allows no truth-value between truth and falsity. Some philosophers and
logicians reject it, but so far no overwhelmingly persuasive applications
of more-valued logic have been made.

Several principles connect truth to reality, to belief, and to implication.
Their precise formulation involves certain technical and metaphysical
complexities, but by means of the following principle schemata we can
express some sets of those principles using '*p*' in accordance with convention C5 above:

(T.7)   The proposition that *p* is true, if and only if there is a fact
         corresponding to it, namely the fact that *p*.
(T.8)   That *p* is true, if and only if *p*.
(T.9)   If X believes that *p*, then he takes that *p* as true, i.e., he has
         a propensity to perform acts of assenting to it being the case
         that *p*. (Cf. Chapter 10 §1–§2).
(T.10)   If X knows that *p*, then X believes truly that *p*.
(T.11)   Implication is truth-preserving, i.e., a proposition is true if it
         is implied by a set of true propositions.

Principle schemata (T.7) and (T.8) collect *principles of correspondence*.
It might be thought that either of these two could be used to define truth,
but that is not the case. Since (T.7) and (T.8) are only principle schemata,
they would not in general be wholly satisfactory as definitions. In particular, they are incapable of yielding the principles (T.12)–(T.16) to be
given in §5 below. Furthermore, (T.7) can be a satisfactory definition
only if the concept of *fact* is already properly clarified, or only if we
already know what exactly the relation of correspondence is. But neither
condition can be met without circularity. Indeed, as we said above, all
of the above principles of truth should be regarded as axioms that provide

a simultaneous partial analysis of the concepts *fact, truth, proposition. belief,* and *knowledge.* They all hang together, spanning the whole structure of our confrontation of the world. The circle these concepts constitute closes up with the principle schema

(KF)   If someone knows that *p*, then it is a fact that *p*.

The illumination of this circle of concepts is indeed one of the most fundamental problems of philosophy. Epistemology, metaphysics, the philosophy of mind, the philosophy of language, and logic all converge together to shed their lights on that circle.

Here we also see one of the basic predicaments of philosophy: an unavoidable circularity. As the principles (T.1)–(T.11) evidence, there can be no complete clarification of one of the fundamental concepts of the above circle, if there is no complete clarification of the other members of the circle. Yet we must start doing philosophy somewhere. The only way to proceed is to engage in the task of clarification with as much awareness of assumptions as is possible, so that we can go back and examine them at intermittent intervals. What logic does, in what below we shall call the semantical approach, is to set a floodlamp on the segment *truth* of the circle and to try to floodlight the segment *implication:* at least a penumbra is bound to reach the other segments of the circle.

Principles (T.9) and (T.10) show the extremely important role that truth plays in the purely intellectual operations of the mind These operations are directed toward truth, thus making of truth the *psychologically preferred value* of propositions. We shall not argue here, but we do want to raise the question whether or not it is possible that there exist (non-human) beings with exactly the opposite psychological make-up, so that their acts of endorsement of propositions would be directed, not to truth, but toward falsity. Such beings would, then, have attitudes of *anti-belief* and *anti-supposition* and *anti-conjecture,* as compared with us. Undoubtedly, such beings would have an exceedingly difficult time adjusting to their environment, so that, if they are logically possible, they would probably have to be disembodied angelic natures who contemplate the world, but do not act on it. But perhaps even a purely contemplative mind cannot exist if all it performs are anti-operations on propositions and it has nothing but anti-attitudes toward propositions.

By (T.9) to believe is to take a proposition as true, and this must be carefully understood. (T.9) does not require that when a person believes that p, for some proposition that p, that person ascribes or attributes to this proposition the property truth. According to (T.9) to believe is to have placed, so to speak, the proposition on the side of true propositions, to have the attitude of reacting to it as a member of the class of true propositions; but for this, one need not have an *exact* idea of what the property truth is, hence, one need not engage in the second-order operation of judging that the proposition that p is true. A comparison may be helpful. Thinking that p is analogous to acts of separating, say, apples from peaches. A man can separate apples from peaches and place them in an apple pen without realizing that the things he is handling are apples and peaches. Likewise, a man can think that p, thus placing that proposition that p on his truthpen, without thinking or being aware that the items he is so placing are truths. Of course, a man can separate apples from peaches by means of *classifying* them, i.e., judging that each of the things in question is an apple or a peach. Likewise, a man can rise up from merely believing that p to judging that (the proposition) that p is true.

Principle (T.11) establishes truth as the *logically preferred value.* That is, to speak anthropomorphically, implication prefers truth in the sense that it preserves it. Undoubtedly, there is among propositions a relation of *anti-implication,* which is, like implication, a matter of the form or structure of propositions, but differs from implication in being falsity-preserving. Indeed, by an operation known to logicians as dualization one can pick out the anti-implicational principles from the corresponding implicational ones.

We shall say that *truth is the designated value of propositions* as a summary way of referring both to the preferred role that it plays in implication and to the preferred role it plays in the purely intellectual operations of the mind.

3. REASONING

Principles (T.9) and (T.11) above explain why men not only have beliefs, but also engage in reasoning, or draw inferences. To infer is primarily to proceed from believing certain propositions to believing other propositions because one purportedly sees that the former propositions imply the latter ones. Given that truth is by (T.9) the polar star of belief and supposition, a finite mind cannot but be a reasoning being: reasonings multiply the true propositions of which a mind is aware – provided it gets hold of some true propositions. Again, if a thinking creature who has anti-beliefs is possible, such a creature would be engaged in *anti-reasoning,* pursuing the lines of *anti-implication* whenever possible.

We are reasoning creatures. And we do our reasoning by thinking propositions through a language. Thus, we have a battery of words and phrases that we use, not to formulate compound propositions, but to perform acts of reasoning. These words and phrases, called *inferential terms,* are used simply to express the speaker's *purported* seeing of an implication relationship together with his assertion or non-assertion of the propositions in question. Naturally, the inferential terms must not only indicate that the speaker is making a reasoning, but they must signal which propositions are taken by the speaker to imply, i.e., to be the *premises* of his reasoning, and which ones he takes to be implied, i.e., to be the conclusions of his reasoning. The distinction between premise and conclusion is a logical one. Nevertheless, there is a distinction to be called *thematic,* to be made in the case of a reasoning. The reasoner's primary interest may lie on the propositions he is committed to once he endorses certain propositions; but, alternatively, the reasoner's interest may lie on the reasons for his endorsing a certain proposition. For instance, the reasoner may want to increase his, or somebody else's, inventory of (alleged) truths by concentrating on new conclusions, or he may want to explain or justify a certain belief. In general, a reasoner may have certain purposes, which would make him focus his attention primarily on some premises, or on the conclusion. We shall say that the *theme* of a person's reasoning is the set of premises (or a premise), or the conclusion, depending on which one lies on his main focus of attention or interest. The reasoner's choice of inferential terms often signals what the theme of his reasoning is. This thematic role of inferential terms is crucial for a full understanding of language in general, especially practical language as we shall see in Chapter 4. It will help us avoid some confusions about imperatives and their logic.

The following chart analyzes the most typical inferential expressions of English. It will be useful later on in Chapter 4.

A. *Inferential Expressions*

We use ' + ' to indicate the thematic role of signaling that the proposition expressed by the sentence following the inferential expression in question is in the main focus of attention; '−' indicates subtraction from the main focus, and '=' indicates that the conclusion and the premises share the highlight of attention.

I. *Conclusion signals:* the following expressions herald the conclusion or a reasoning by immediately preceding a sentence, or clause, that expresses the conclusion:
'therefore' (+);   'in consequence' (=);   'thus' (+);
'hence (+);   'consequently' (+);   'so' (+);

II. *Premise signals:* the following expressions herald a premise or set of premises by immediately preceding a sentence, or clause, that expresses a premise:
'since (−);   'for' (−);
'given that (=);   'because' (+);
'as is shown (established, implied) by the fact that' (=);
'as is shown (established, implied) by the following reasons (circumstances)' (=).

4. THREE APPROACHES TO IMPLICATION

The study of propositional implication has proceeded along three different avenues, which are, naturally, very intimately related. In fact, some of the most important results of logical theory in the last fifty years are precisely the proofs of a battery of theorems that establish the virtual equivalence of: the semantical approach, the inferential approach, and the analytic or strictly axiomatic approach.

The *semantical approach* to logic is at once the most recent and the most profound from the philosophical point of view. In its classical form it is the attempt to analyze and illuminate the concept of propositional implication from certain general and rather simple properties of truth, or of truth-values. These properties are mainly (T.1)–(T.6) listed in §2 and others to be given throughout the chapter. That is, it bases the study of the implication among propositions on truth-values; and this is why it is more profound than the other two approaches. An unhappy by-product has been the dogmatic acceptance by philosophers of the incorrect thesis that all implication is propositional; but this is a human failure, and not a failure of the approach or method.

The *inferential approach* assumes, or at any rate need assume, nothing about truth. It assumes, however, a relationship of immediate implication, which is characterized by a set of primitive principles; it provides an analysis of general types of implication in terms of immediate implication. Alternatively, this approach may be viewed as assuming the validity of certain simple reasoning operations of the mind, from which the validity of more complex reasoning operations is accounted for. This is the oldest approach, begun by Aristotle in the fourth century B.C. It is less profound in that it provides a merely internal analysis of implication, but by not assuming anything about truth-values it allows of a broader and more liberal conception of logic. Thus, it is not a mere coincidence that Aristotle himself spoke of practical syllogisms, which he conceived as reasonings whose conclusions are, not propositions, but *actions*. In Chapter 4 we shall take Aristotle' cue and will adopt the inferential approach for the logic of imperatives.

The *analytic approach* is a somewhat indirect study of implication. In its customary form it studies types of necessary truth and has been concerned primarily with explicating the systematic structure of necessary truths by organizing classes of them as consequences of finite sets of necessary truths (axioms) or of finite sets of structures of them (axiom-schemata). Naturally, this approach has to assume some concept of immediate implication as the core of the consequence relation linking a system of necessary truths. But it does provide an analysis of general types of implication in terms both of the assumed type of immediate implication and of certain necessary and, hence, vacuous or eliminable premises. Since this approach has assumed something about necessary truth, it also has fostered the incorrect idea that all implications are relationships between or among propositions. We shall follow this approach in Chapter 9

We proceed now to a brief discussion of each of these three approaches to propositional implication and to the structures of propositions

A. *The Semantical Approach*

5. TRUTH-FUNCTIONAL CONNECTIONS

The simplest forms of proposition composition are those that yield propositions out of propositions. They are called logical connections. The simplest connections are those that always fully determine the truth-value of the resulting compound proposition from the truth-values, whatever they may be, of the component propositions. They are called *truth-functional connections*.

Negation. There are four unary truth-functional connections, i.e., structures that form out of one proposition another proposition with a truth-value fully determined by the structure. But in practical life the most interesting is called negation. This is expressed in English typically by a variety of mechanisms: (i) adverbs, like 'not'; (ii) adjectives, like 'no' (in 'no one'); (iii) propositions, like 'without'; (iv) verbs, like 'fails'; (v) prefixes, like 'un-', 'im-'; (vi) suffixes, like '-less'; (vii) phrases, like *'it is not the case that'* and *'the following is not the case'*. The last two expressions in (vii) are, literally speaking, the most cumbersome, but they are the most apt, logically. They can always be depended on to produce a sentence that expresses the negation of a given proposition, regardless of how complex the latter may be. For example, the proposition *If May and Saul come, but Mary doesn't, then Irving will not call Irwin* has as its negation: *The following is not the case: If May and Saul come, but Mary doesn't, then Irving will not call Irwin*.

Since we are interested in studying the structures of propositions, the diversity of expressions of negation in ordinary language is a *logical* nuisance. We adopt the sign '$\sim$' as a canonical notation that expresses negation, pure and simple, as an abbreviation of 'the following is not the case:'. Thus, using convention C5 of §1 above, we can represent the general form of negation in many different ways, e.g., $(\sim p)$, $(\sim q)$, $(\sim p_1)$, $(\sim q_{17})$. By availing ourselves of conventions C5 and C6 we have different names for the form or structure of propositional negation, e.g., $*(\sim p)*$ and $*(\sim r_{11})*$.

The truth functional character of negation is determined by the principle

TABLE I

(T.12)

p	$(\sim p)$
T	F
F	T

that the negation of a proposition has the opposite value to the proposition it negates. This is shown in Table I.

C7 'T' abbreviates 'truth' or 'true' as is needed.
'F' abbreviates 'falsity' or 'false' as is needed.

Binary connections. A pair of propositions determine four combinations of truth values: (a) both true, (b) both false, (c) one true and the other false, and (d) the reverse of (c). Thus, there are sixteen binary truth-functional types of compound proposition. It is customary to single out four of them for special study, because they are so practically important that in many languages they have distinctive and syntactically simple expressions. They are exhibited in Table II.

TABLE II

p, q	(T.13) Conjunction $(p \& q)$ p and q	(T.14) Disjunction $(p \lor q)$ p or q	(T.15) Conditionalization $(p \supset q)$ if p, q; p, only if q	(T.16) Biconditionalization $(p \equiv q)$ p, just in case q
TT	T	T	T	T
TF	F	T	F	F
FT	F	T	T	F
FF	F	F	T	T

6. ENGLISH SEMANTICAL CONNECTIVES

There really are no words in ordinary English that can translate *exactly* the formal connectives. The English connectives not only express logical connections, but also express other things at the same time. In particular, ordinary English connectives have the *thematic role* of highlighting one or another component as the focus of attention, the formal connectives are, in contrast, entirely devoid of a thematic dimension. The formal binary connectives have exactly the sense given them by Table II. On the other hand, the English connectives are naturally endowed with a multiplicity of senses.

In brief, there are some non-logical rules that govern both the use of connections and the asserting or inferring of propositions. But *such rules cannot decide questions of logic and ontology as, e.g., to whether there are certain propositions or certain implications.* Such rules, among which are the following, govern acts of communication, and may be called:

Dialectical Principles:[1]

Dial. I. The assertion of a proposition should have a point or serve a purpose.

Dial. II. In the course of straight-out communication, which is to convey information, the propositions asserted should be relevant to the interest of some of the interlocutors.

Dial. III. Everything else being equal, one should always assert the stronger proposition. That is, if one has a choice between asserting a proposition P and a proposition Q which is implied by P, but does not imply P, one should assert P, unless there is an important overriding purpose served by asserting Q.

These are vague principles, and since the interests and purposes of human beings are so variegated, it is not easy to improve upon Dial. I–III. In spite of their vagueness and imprecision they do determine a minimal ethics of communication, and since man is unavoidably a social creature they do tend to be obeyed much more than it might seem at first sight. Dial. III, which will be useful in Chapters 4 and 7, explains why in daily life when one knows that p, one normally asserts that p, rather than any other statement of the forms $*(\sim p \supset q)*$ or $*(p \vee q)*$, implied by that p, regardless of whether that q is relevant to that p or not. Inasmuch as the conditional or disjunctive statement is weaker, one is actually withholding information, one is deceiving, unless, of course, there is a special reason for making the weaker claim, e.g., to make a joke.

Aside from the dialectical rules, ordinary connectives serve several roles, so that they also abide by the following:

Formal Principles Governing Ordinary Connectives:

OC. I. An ordinary binary connective has an *ontological dimension* that consists of its signaling a logical connection.

OC. II. An ordinary binary connective has a *thematic dimension* that consists of its signaling focussing of attention on, or withdrawal of attention from, one proposition rather than another.

OC. III. An ordinary binary connective has an *ordering dimension* that consists of its signaling the role or position of the proposition expressed by the sentence immediately following it in the compound proposition whose connection it expresses.

These three principles provide together a profile of *one* of the typical senses of the ordinary connectives, as shown on the following chart, in which: '1' signals that the connective heralds the first component of the logical connective, and '2' that it heralds the second component, the logical order being expressed from left to right on Table II above, '+' signals that the heralded component is the main focus of attention, '−' that it is not, and '=' that both components are of equal interest.

Conjunction:
'and': &, =, 2;   'both ...': &, =, 1;
'but': &, +, 2;   'although': &, −, 1 or 2;
'in spite of': &, −, 2;   'as well as': &, =, 2;
'without': &, =, 2;   [preposition] 'like': &, −, 2;
'who', 'where', 'which', 'that', 'where', used as the prefixes of specifying clauses: &, =, 2;
the same pronouns used as prefixes of amplifying clauses: &, −, 2.

Disjunction:
'or': ∨, =, 2; 'unless': ∨, −, 2; 'one of them': ∨, =, no specific order

Conditionalization:
'if': ⊃, −, 1;
'in case that': ⊃, −, 1;   'only if': ⊃, −, 2;
'on condition that': ⊃, −, 1; 'only in case that': ⊃, −, 2;
'provided that': ⊃, −, 1;   'only on condition that': ⊃, −, 2;
                            'only provided that': ⊃, −, 2;

Bioconditionalization:
'if and only if': ≡, −, 2 oftener; 'just in case that': ≡, −, 1 or 2;
'in case that only in the case that': ≡, −, 1 or 2;
'if ... and conversely': ≡, =, 2;
'exactly if': ≡, −, 1 or 2; 'if ... and vice versa': ≡, =, 2.

In conclusion, certain statements often made, especially in logic text-books, about the relationship between the formal and the ordinary English connectives must be rejected: The truth is as follows:

(1) The formal connectives are *not* abbreviations of the English connectives that express the same logical connections.

(2) The meaning of a formal connective is *not* what is common to the meanings of all the English expressions used to express the logical connection that it expresses. For instance, the meanings or uses of the word 'and' and 'but' do not intersect at logical conjunction.

(3) The meaning of '⊃' is *not* the core common to all the meanings of 'if', for the word 'if' has always a thematic dimension that is not part of the meaning of '⊃'.

(4) The fact that certain sentences with certain words are never used in daily life to make assertions does *not* establish that such sentences do not express propositions or that the propositions they express are not true.

To sum up, the formal logical connectives are a wonderful invention that allows the expression of propositional forms, pure and simple, without concern for dialectical rules, or thematic roles, or stylistic considerations.

7. 'IF', 'ONLY IF', AND '⊃'

The ordinary conditional connectives all have the index '−'. None of them makes the whole conditional proposition the theme of apprehension or assertion. As a fact about English this is somewhat tantalizing, but when one considers that it is also a fact about the ordinary conditional connectives of Spanish, French, German, Greek, and many other languages of different families, it becomes a really exciting thing. It will be of great value in Chapter 4. I do not have a wholly satisfactory explanation, but I do have a:

HYPOTHESIS. The thematic role of ordinary simple conditional connectives is enhanced by always expressing the asymmetry of the theme-nontheme relationship as built on the asymmetry of the antecedent-consequent relationship. In the case of the other connections, when the whole compound is the theme of apprehension, the components are equally and not-orderly non-themes.

My hypothesis is that the characteristic thematic dimension of ordinary simple conditional connectives satisfies a deep principle of economy and efficiency in the determination of themes of apprehension. In Chapter 4 §4 we shall see that there is yet a further surface characteristic of ordinary conditional connectives that is also rooted in that deep principle of economy and efficiency. We have here not a mere surface linguistic phenomenon, but a phenomenon that may be said to belong to *philosophical* anthropology. As pointed out on p. 8, there is a psychological primacy of practical reason over pure reason. Given the logical, theoretical asymmetry of the connection $* \supset *$, we, creatures who do our thinking by means of a language, do not have an ordinary simple connective expressing $* \supset *$ with a thematic ordering $(+, x)$ or $(=, x)$, which contravenes the logical ordering; we have instead two (sets of) simple conditional connectives to express the two thematic orderings that the logical asymmetry allows for: namely, the '*if*'-type and the '*only-if*'-type.

The sentences governed or announced by the ordinary simple conditional connectives do not, again, express what is of primary interest in apprehension or communication: they express propositions that are of derivative interest as mere *conditions* for something else. The members of the group with index '$(-, 1)$' typically represented by 'if', announce sufficient conditions; the members of the group with index '$(-, 2)$', typically represented by 'only if', announce necessary conditions. *Being a condition, whether sufficient or necessary, is not, therefore, a matter of logic, but a matter of the thematic dimension of our apprehension or communication of propositions.* As we have emphasized, '$\supset$' does not have a thematic dimension, so that from the point of view of pure logic, $*$(He comes on Monday) $\supset$ (he will see you on Tuesday)$*$ can be expressed, indifferently, by the sentence 'If he comes on Monday, he will see you on Tuesday' or by the sentence 'He comes (will come) on Monday only if he will see (sees) you on Tuesday'. But the two translations are *not* synonymous: the former clearly indicates that the primary concern is the man seeing the interlocutor, whereas the other presents the man's trip as the main theme. Since we are dealing with actions, an entirely different array of purposes and plans is being pointed to when the 'if' construction is used, from the one being pointed to when the 'only if' construction is used.

We can summarize the main propositional thematic role of 'if' by saying that what it announces is a *sufficient condition for knowing, or for being justified in endorsing,* the consequent. On the other hand, the main propositional thematic role of 'only if' is to announce a *necessary condition for knowing, or endorsing justifiedly,* the antecendent.

The preceding discussion suggests that if a fundamental English expression of connection should have the thematic pattern $(=, x)$, then the fundamental expression of '$\supset$' in English is not, or should not be, a conditioning expression like 'if' and 'only if', but an expression like 'either not ... or _____' or '... unless it is not the case that _____'. Since the English biconditional connectives including conditional terms also have minus patterns $(-, x)$, we should regard as the fundamental expressions of $*\equiv*$ compound connectives like '... or _____, but not both'. Thus, *there is a sense in which the fundamental ordinary simple connectives are '$\sim$', '&' and '$\vee$'.* This provides a deeper sanctioning of our confining ourselves to $*\sim*$, $*\&*$ and $*\vee*$ from now on. This will simplify our argument, by avoiding irrelevant linguistic side issues, for the claim that mandates have implication relationships and abide by a two-valued logic. (See Chapter 4 §4.)

8. Logical form

We have so far studied truth-functional composition of propositions; yet it is obvious that some propositions are made up of components that are not themselves propositions. For instance, the propositions $*5$ is even$*$ and $*4$ is even$*$ are not constituted by proper "parts" that are also propositions, yet they obviously have a nonpropositional common "part" expressed with the sentence fragment 'is even'. Thus $*5$ is even$*$ and $*4$ is even$*$ have overlapping logical forms, and a complete study of logical form or logical composition must reach nonpropositional components. But even before discussing the logical behavior of such components, we can see that the following principles hold for all types of logical form.

(LF.1)   There is no such thing as *the* logical form of a proposition: every proposition has several logical forms.[2]

Evidently, the simplest proposition must have at least two forms: the general form of proposition, say, $*p*$, and at least one form that analyzes the proposition in terms of some nonpropositional components. $*$If he comes, he'll see you or Mary* has many forms: $*p*$, $*(p \supset (q \lor r)*$, and the deeper ones involving nonpropositional components.

Let us say that a logical form ϕ is a *refinement* of a logical form ψ just in case whatever proposition has ϕ also has ψ. That is, more crudely, ϕ is a deeper refinement of ψ if and only if ϕ includes ψ. Now:

(LF.2)   If a proposition X is a connective compound of other propositions, whether truth functionally or not, then the logical forms of X that have X made up of nonpropositional components are refinements of forms that have X as a connective compound.

(LF.2) records the fact that truth-functional form is the shell of the other types of logical form. This is particularly significant given that there is no precise definition or analysis of logical form in general. Of course, sharp demarcations can be made, but they are betrayed by their arbitrariness of confining the study of logic, on the one hand, and the concepts of implication, logical form, tautology, etc., on the other hand, to the realm of propositions. In Chapter 4 we shall study some logical forms of imperatives, which are non-propositions; and in Chapter 7 we shall argue that imperative non-propositional logic is at the base of deontic logic.

The next principles pertain to the hierarchical structure of the logical forms of a proposition.

(LF.3)   If a proposition X has two logical forms ϕ and ψ, then either ϕ is a refinement of ψ, or ψ is a refinement of ϕ, or there is a logical form of X that is a refinement of both ϕ and ψ.

For example, consider a proposition that is: (i) a conditional, (ii) a conditional with conjunctive antecedent, and (iii) a conditional with disjunctive consequent; that is, it has the logical forms exhibited below by the formulas:

(i) $(p \supset q)$
(ii) $((p \mathrel{\&} q) \supset r)$
(iii) $(p \supset (q \lor r))$.

Obviously, forms represented by (ii) and (iii) are both refinements of the form represented by (i): a conditional with this or that special feature is still a conditional. On the other hand, neither the form represented by (ii) includes the form represented by (iii) nor vice versa. The proposition in question must, perforce, be a conditional with both a conjunctive antecedent and a disjunctive consequent; that is, it has also the form represented by

(iv) $((p \,\&\, q) \supset (r \vee s))$.

The form represented by (iv) is a refinement of both the form represented by (ii) and the one represented by (iii), as well as of the form represented by (i).

We can picture the relationship of being a refinement that holds between logical forms by means of a relationship of substitution that holds between formulas representing logical form. *First, we uniform* the representations, or names, of logical forms involved, by representing the same component with the same symbol throughout the set of forms involved. Thus, in the example above, comparing (ii) and (iii) we can see that letter q may represent a different component of the proposition having forms (i)–(iv). We eliminate this ambiguity of 'q' throughout the sets of forms (i)–(iii) by letting the same propositional variable represent the same proposition throughout the whole set of forms under consideration. This uniformation can be done in many different ways, for, as we know, there are infinitely many propositional variables at our disposal. We choose, for example, the following uniformation:

(iia) $((p_1 \,\&\, p_2) \supset q)$
(iiia) $(p \supset (q_1 \vee q_2))$
(iva) $((p_1 \,\&\, p_2) \supset (q_1 \vee q_2))$.
(LF.4)   A form ϕ is a refinement of a form ψ, if a uniform pair of representations of ϕ and ψ, call them, R_ϕ and R_ψ, show that R_ϕ results from R_ψ by the substitution throughout R_ψ for every occurrence of one or more symbols, say s_j, of occurrences of a string S_j of symbols such that S_j represents an analysis of the component of a proposition represented by s_j.

In our example above: (iia) arises from (i) by substituting '$(p_1 \,\&\, p_2)$' for 'p'; (iiia) arises from (i) by substituting '$(q_1 \vee q_2)$' for 'q'; (iva) arises from (iia) by substituting '$(q_1 \vee q_2)$' for 'q'; and (iva) arises from (iiia) by the substitution of '$(p_1 \,\&\, p_2)$' for 'p'.

(LF.5)   If a logical form ϕ has just true [alternatively: false] instances, i.e., is had by only true [false] propositions, then every form which is a refinement of ϕ has also just true [false] instances.

This is a fundamental principle about logical forms. We can see immediately that if a logical form ϕ is a truth-functional form, then (LF.5) holds. Suppose that ϕ is a truth-functional form, and that every single one of its instances is true. That is, suppose that, regardless of whether the component propositions are true or false, a compound proposition having form ϕ is true. Then regardless of how deeply we refine ϕ to find a form ψ, even if the components brought out by ψ are not propositions, all that ψ can do is to determine more ways for the components of the instances of ϕ and ψ to be true or false. But since ϕ makes its instances true, regardless of the truth-values of the latter's components, then ψ only determines more ways for its instances to be true. Patently, the same holds for the case in which ϕ has just false instances. Suppose now that logical form ϕ in no way shows a proposition X to be made up of other propositions, i.e., at every stage of the analysis of X that leads to ϕ we have nonpropositional components. Let ψ a form of X which is a refinement of ϕ. Then ψ contains an analysis of some components of X taken as unanalyzed by ϕ. Clearly, no proposition can be an instance of ψ which is not an instance of ϕ. Since all the instances of ϕ are true, [alternatively: false], so are the instances of ψ.

9. SEMANTICAL IMPLICATION

We are now in a position to provide the semantical characterization of propositional implication in general:

(S.I)   Propositions $X_1, X_2, \ldots X_n$ *imply* a proposition Y, i.e., $X_1, X_2, \ldots, X_n \vDash Y$, if and only if the conjunctive proposition $X_1 \& X_2 \& \ldots \& X_n \& \sim Y$ has a logical form such that every proposition having that form is false.

(S.I*)   A set α of propositions *implies* a proposition Y, i.e., $\alpha \vDash Y$, if and only if for a natural number n some members of α, say, $X_1, X_2, \ldots,$ and X_n imply Y.

We are calling these principles "characterizations", rather than "definitions", because of their intrinsic vagueness. They are vague to the extent that we do not have an exact concept or analysis of the logical form of propositions. The machinery developed in §5 provides us with an analysis of merely the most superficial layer of proposition composition. It gives us a sufficient, but not a necessary condition, for general propositional implication, But we can define:

(S.I.t.)   Propositions $X_1, X_2, ..., X_n$ *tautologically imply,* proposition Y, i.e., $X_1, X_2, ..., X_n \mathrel{\underset{t}{\vdash}} Y$, if and only if the conjunction $X_1 \mathbin{\&} X_2 \mathbin{\&} ... \mathbin{\&} X_n \mathbin{\&} \sim Y$ has a logical form with a truth-table whose last column has only 'F's.

10. SEMANTICAL EQUIVALENCE

An important relationship between propositions occasionally alluded to already is that of equivalence. In the semantical approach we can define it as follows:

(S.E.)   Proposition X is *semantically equivalent* to proposition Y, or semantically co-implies Y, i.e., $X \mathrel{|=|} Y$, if and only if $X \vDash Y$ and $Y \vDash X$.

Inasmuch as our conception of semantical implication is still fragmentary, our conception of semantical equivalence must also remain fragmentary. Our conception of equivalence is clear, so far, only for the most superficial case:

(S.E.t.) Proposition X is *tautologically equivalent* to proposition Y, i.e., $X \mathrel{\underset{t}{|=|}} Y$, if and only if $X \mathrel{\underset{t}{\vDash}} Y$ and $Y \mathrel{\underset{t}{\vDash}} X$.

In general we have:

(S.E.1) $X \mathrel{|=|} Y$, if and only if $X \equiv Y$ has a logical form with only true instances.

11. LOGICAL TRUTHS: TAUTOLOGIES

An important concept is that of logical truth, i.e., the concept of a proposition that is true by virtue of its form alone. Its main characterization is this:

(LT.G) A proposition X is a *logical truth,* if and only if X has a form
ϕ such that every proposition which is an instance of ϕ is true.

Logically, the concept of logical truth has the importance of allowing another characterization of implication as well as of allowing shortcuts in the testing for implication. The fundamental principle is

(LT.I) $X_1, ..., X_n \vDash Z$, if and only if
$X_1 \& ... \& X_n \supset Z$ is a logical truth.

Epistemologically, the concept of logical truth is extremely important in that it determines a class of propositions that can be known to be true by a mere consideration of their logical forms, without any appeal to empirical evidence.

But, as we did in §8 in the case of logical form, we must emphasize here that (LT.G) and (LT.I) are, rather than finished precise analyses, the goals or guides of the study of logic. Since there is no exact general definition of logical form, there is no exact general definition of logical truth. One's concept of logical truth has to gain its elucidation piecemeal in steps that parallel the piecemeal elucidation of one's concept of logical form. At this juncture, we are only in possession of a clear concept of full-propositional form, and this concept can yield a clearly delineated concept of a species of logical truths, to wit:

(LT.t) A proposition X is a *tautology,* if and only if it has a full-propositional form ϕ all instances of which are true.

(LT.t∗) A tautology is a logical truth.

From (LT.t) and the principles of truth governing full-propositional forms we can derive:

(LT.ti) $X_1, ..., X_n \underset{t}{\vDash} Z$, if and only if $X_1 \& ... \& X_n \supset Z$ is a tautology.

B. *The Inferential Approach*

12. THE NATURE OF THE APPROACH

Independently of their having truth-values, propositions can be considered as possessing certain structures or forms of composition. Such

forms can be characterized in terms of fundamentel implicational relationships between, or among, propositions. No doubt, propositional
implication is ultimately to be understood in terms of truth-values. But
one can abstract from truth-values altogether and consider implicational
relationships as ordering relationships that arrange all propositions in a
certain hierarchical system. For instance, if a proposition X implies a
proposition Y, X may be said to be logically prior or basic to Y; if in its
turn Y implies Z, then X also implies Z and X is also prior to Z. We have,
then, the ordering X_____ Y_____ Z, which can be grasped without
reference to truth-values. More specifically, the difference in form between a proposition X & Y & Z and a proposition X ∨ Y ∨ Z consists,
on the one hand, in that X & Y & Z does, while X ∨ Y ∨ Z does not, allow
the partial ordering (a) below, and, on the other hand, in that X ∨ Y ∨ Z
does, while X & Y & Z does not, allow the partial ordering (b):

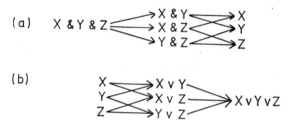

Once we have the concept of semantical implication, developed in the
preceding sections, we are of course in possession of principles that
determine partial orderings of sets of propositions. But we can, alternatively, assume certain principles for partially ordering propositions
without reference to truth-values, and then raise the question whether or
not the partial orderings so obtained are also (semantical) implicational
partial orderings. On the ordering alternative, the form of a proposition
is characterized by the place of propositions having that form in certain
partially ordered sets of propositions: propositions that have the same
form occupy corresponding positions in corresponding partially ordered
sets of propositions. This abstract approach to the ranking of propositions in their "natural" implicational order is not unlike the formal study
of numbers as given in their "natural" order (0, 1, 2, 3, ...), regardless

of whether this order has anything to do with counting or measuring objects, or not.

Evidently, entirely different sets of things can have exactly the same patterns of partial orderings of their elements. Thus, even if in the end it is dependent on truth-values, propositional deducibility is a general relationship that can in principle be exemplified by *other kinds* of things. At any rate, even if 'deducibility' is defined as a certain partial ordering that holds for propositions, these partial orderings are in principle generalizable, and it is only a purely terminological matter whether things other than propositions stand in deducibility – like relationships or not. This is an extremely important point to which we shall return in Chapters 4 and 6.

There is a sense in which the study of deducibility that starts from primitive, unanalyzed principles of relative ranking of propositions lacks *philosophical* depth. Inasmuch as there are many different ways of partially ordering propositions, the choice of our primitive principles must have some justification. Undoubtedly, the justification will in the end bring in semantical implication and truth-values. Furthermore, the philosophical clarification of the fundamental set of concepts: proposition-truth-implication-belief-knowledge-fact, mentioned in §2 above, must culminate in a revelation of all the links among all the members of the set. Hence, truth values are ultimately going to come in anyway. Nevertheless, we can postpone the reference to truth-values and yet provide a foundation for the study of deducibility. The relationship of deducibility we are interested in may be viewed as the relationship that partially orders propositions, or better: sets of propositions, in terms of the *relative reasonableness* of our endorsing or believing the propositions in question. Thus, proposition X is deducible from proposition Z, just in case it is reasonable to endorse or believe X if one endorses or believes Z. We have here the reason for calling the study of deducibility the inferential approach to implication. For if a person believes X, and Y is deducible from X, then that person is justified in inferring Y from X. Thus, the principles of deducibility are, or correspond to, the principles of derived reasonableness of belief. Correspondence is enough. The idea is that principles of reasonableness are principles of criticism of belief, which *reveal* deducibility relations. The "natural" order of deducibility is, then, the order natural for a fully rational mind: the order of reasonableness.

For convenience we adopt the following conventions:

C21   '$X_1, X_2, ..., X_n \vdash Y$' means that Y is deducible from the set $\{X_1, X_2, ..., \text{and } X_n\}$.

C22   '$\alpha \vdash Y$' means that there is a natural number n such that Y is deducible from some n members of α.

C23   '$\alpha, \beta, X_1, ..., X_n \vdash Y$' means that if γ is the set whose members are just $X_1, ..., X_n$, the members of α and those of β, then $\gamma \vdash Y$.

For example, the following are true:

(1)   *Mary loves John*, *Mary loves Peter* ⊢ *Mary loves both John and Peter*.

(2) α, *Mary runs and kicks* ⊢ *Mary runs*.

Deducibility, like implication, depends on the logical form of propositions, so that as long as there is no complete characterization of logical form there is no complete characterization of deducibility. We must therefore, also proceed piecemeal in the analysis of deducibility, providing at each step a cumulative partial characterization of it. Here we shall study the fundamental layer in which propositions are structurally related to other propositions and nothing but propositions. We shall refer to this layer as the layer of connective deducibility, or as the $\left|\overline{}\right._c$ layer, which is the counterpart of the tautological layer, or $\left|\overline{\overline{}}\right._t$-layer, studied above. As in the case of implication, connective deducibility is a special case of general deducibility i.e.:

MT.D.1. For any propositions Y and Z, if $Y \left|\overline{}\right._c Z$, then $Y \vdash Z$.

13. CONNECTIVE DEDUCIBILITY

We now start the study of propositional form anew; but we shall assume the conventions lined up for the use of quotation marks, propositional variables, etc. We consider as fundamental three forms of proposition: (a) the general form of proposition which is equally represented by all propositional variables, (b) the negative form variously represented by '(∼...)' around a propositional variable which occupies the place of

'...', and (c) the conjunctive form represented by '(... & _____)' or expressions obtained by this by putting propositional variables in the blanks. We must keep in mind that as of this moment the expressions '$(\sim p)$' and '$(p \,\&\, q)$' are assumed to represent uniquely certain propositional forms, but it is left in abeyance whether or not these forms are characterizable by the truth principles (T.12)–(T.16) in Section II.1. As of this moment we merely assume that propositions are partially ordered in different sequences and that each proposition has just one proposition which is its negative, and that two propositions uniquely determine a conjunctive one. Since this is not enough to give us a working idea of the negative and conjunctive forms, we characterize these forms by means of certain inferential principles, as follows, where β and α are sets of propositions and X and Y are propositions:

D1.   If X is in β, then $\beta \,\big|_{c}\, X$.

D2.   If $\beta \,\big|_{c}\, X$, then $\beta \,\big|_{c}\, \sim X$.

D3.   If $\beta \,\big|_{c}\, \sim X$, then $\beta \,\big|_{c}\, \sim(X \,\&\, Y)$.

D4.   If $\beta \,\big|_{c}\, \sim Y$, then $\beta \,\big|_{c}\, \sim(X \,\&\, Y)$.

D5.   If $\beta \,\big|_{c}\, X$ and $\beta' \,\big|_{c}\, Y$, then $\beta, \beta' \,\big|_{c}\, X \,\&\, Y$.

D6.   If $\beta, \sim X \,\big|_{c}\, Y$ and $\beta, X \,\big|_{c}\, Y$, then $\beta \,\big|_{c}\, Y$.

D7.   If $\beta \,\big|_{c}\, \sim(X \,\&\, \sim Y)$, then $\beta, X \,\big|_{c}\, Y$.

∗D100.   If in the above formulations of principles D1–D7 we delete the subscript 'c' we formulate valid principles for general deducibility.

For convenience we introduce the following abbreviations:

D8.   '$(X \vee Y)$' for '$(\sim((\sim X) \,\&\, (\sim Y)))$'.
D9.   '$(X \supset Y)$' for '$(\sim(X \,\&\, (\sim Y)))$'.

D10.　'$(X \equiv Y)$' for '$((X \ \& \ Y) \vee ((\sim X) \ \& \ (\sim Y)))$'.

In analogy with semantical co-implication and tautologyhood, we define:

D11.　X is *connectively co-deducible* from Y, i.e., $X \mid \overline{}_c \mid Y$, if and only

if $X \mid \overline{}_c Y$ and $Y \mid \overline{}_c X$.

D12.　$\mid \overline{}_c X$, i.e., X is *connectively null-deducible,* if and only if $\vee \mid \overline{}_c X$

and $\vee$ is the null set of propositions.

Again, if we drop the subscript 'c' we obtain definitions for 'co-deducibility' and 'null-deducibility' in general.

C. *Implication and Deducibility*

14. EQUIVALENCE OF IMPLICATION AND DEDUCIBILITY

An important result of logical theory is the establishment of the formal equivalence between the semantical and the inferential approaches to propositional implication. If we identify the structures $*(\sim p)*$ and $*(p \ \& \ q)*$ discussed in the theory of semantical implication with the identically represented structures discussed in the theory of deducibility, we have the following:

META-THEOREM I:　$\alpha \mid \overline{}_t Y$, if and only if $\alpha \mid \overline{}_c Y$.

META-THEOREM II:　Y is a tautology, if and only if $\mid \overline{}_c Y$.

We shall not prove these meta-theorems here; but proofs for them can be easily adopted from proofs in logic textbooks of similar meta-theorems.

　　Let us remark that one of our main claims in Chapter 4 is defended by an argument that makes essential use of meta-theorem I.

15. INFERENTIAL ENGLISH CONNECTIVES

Strictly speaking we should have used in §13 other connective symbols than '$\sim$' and '&', so as not to prejudge the issue whether the operations studied there are the same as the semantical operations we called negation and conjunction in §5. As we said in §13, the inferential or ordering principles given there characterize a purely inferential sense of '$\sim$' and

'&', which need not have anything to do with negation and conjunction. Meta-theorems I and II amount to the discovery that if we are concerned with conjunction and negation, the purely inferential characterization of negation and conjunction of §13 coincides with the purely semantical characterization of §5. This in its turn shows that the logical meanings of the ordinary English connectives discussed in §6 can be analyzed in at least two alternative ways, each of which yields the same set of implications for each proposition. In particular, we can put it in our philosophical inventory that the fundamental common logical meaning of 'and', 'but', and 'although' consists precisely in linking expressions so that the resulting complex sentences come to express compound propositions that, regardless of their truth-values, satisfy the deducibility principles D1–D2. *These principles are indeed the inferential criterion for deciding whether a given expression of English, or of some other language, expresses the form of conjunctive propositions or not.*

We shall utilize this important result about English connectives in Chapters 4 and 6.

D. *The Analytic Approach*

16. THE NATURE OF THE APPROACH

In §9–11 we saw that there is a very intimate relationship between implication and logical truth, since principles of implication are determined by the logical forms of propositions, and that logical forms of propositions determine classes of logical truths. Now, conversely, a logical form may be adequately characterized in terms of certain classes of logical truths determined by it. Since logical truths are said by philosophers to be the central type of *analytic truths,* we call the study of logical forms as determining classes of logical truths the *analytic approach* to the study of logical form and of implication. On this approach, first we characterize some logical forms in terms of certain minimal sets of logical truths; secondly we provide some rules for the derivation of all the other logical truths determined by the logical forms under study. The initial logical truths are called *(logical) axioms,* and the derived logical truths *(logical) theorems.*

The emphasis of the analytic approach lies both on the derivation of logical truths from other logical truths and on the finiteness of the set of (classes of) axioms. The interest lies on the construction of an axiomatic calculus, conceived with a certain interpretation in mind, but which does not need that interpretation for its development. The emphasis on the derivation of logical truths immediately abstracts from truth; and the principles of derivation thus formulated can in principle be applied to the derivation, or production, of entities out of other entities where the entities in question are related in ways that parallel logical forms, but can be entities of other types and sorts. This makes the analytic approach to implication at once both philosophically illuminating and philosophically precarious. It is illuminating in that it shows that the types of derivational relationships between, and among, logical forms do not depend on propositions having truth values, but on propositions having values, *whatever they may be,* with certain properties of truth-values. But the approach is precarious. It needs a deeper foundation that can support the derivational relationships in question. In the end, naturally, that foundation is constituted by the semantical principles of truth-values (T.1)–(T.16).

There is a partial foundation for the analytic approach in terms of the reasonableness of the endorsement of propositions. We may very well take the logical axioms and theorems, studied by the analytic approach to logical form, to be forms (or types) of proposition such that it is the maximum of irrationality to refuse to endorse or believe propositions of those forms (or types). Thus, *the minimal foundation for the inferential approach provides also a partial foundation for the analytic approach.* This foundation has the advantage of allowing the study of logical form to proceed still in abstraction of truth-values. In fact the analytic approach can be viewed as an alternative, *within the inferential approach,* to the rule treatment represented by the deducibility principles D1–D10 given in §14.

Again, as discussed in §8, there is no general characterization of logical form, so that the analytic approach still has to proceed gradually. On this approach what we find are cumulative layers of axiomatic structures.

In general, and axiomatization of a layer of implicational relationships introduces within the class of propositions an organization of the class whereby some propositions represent the whole class by virtue of selected implications. But, of course, alternative axiomatic organizations are available. Thus, each axiomatization of a layer of logic has its own slant; it has the role of focusing attention or emphasis on certain propositions and certain implications. The axiomatic approach has, then, a *systemic* thematic dimension, which goes beyond the thematic dimension of language discussed in §§6–7.

Given our goals in this book, there is no need to engage in a detailed discussion of axiom systems for logic. We can, of course, develop an axiom system. It would be very convenient to present one that takes negation and conjunction as primitive logical structures, as, for instance, the system formulated by J. Barkley Rosser.[3] Then we would have another characterization of the common logical meanings of the English words 'and', 'but', and 'although'. This would provide us with another route to argue, as we shall argue in Chapters 4 and 6, for the parallelism among the logic of propositions, the logic of mandates, and the logic of intentions. This route has been traveled elsewhere,[4] but we will not run it again.

We will develop in Chapter 9 an axiomatic system for deontic noemata. The present discussion should suffice as a foundation for it.

E. *Axioms, Implication, and Deducibility*

17. THE EQUIVALENCE OF THE THREE APPROACHES

The analytic axiomatic approach to the study of propositional implication leads to several axiomatic systems. Such systems are, of course, equivalent, if they deal with exactly the same subject-matter, have the same logical truths as theorems, or have as theorems logical truths that are representatives of the same classes of logical truths. A similar equivalence has been established between some axiom systems for tautological implication and the semantical system of truth principles (T.1)–(T.16) of §2 and §5. Thus, similar equivalence holds between such axiom systems and the deducibility system put forward in §13. Naturally, we cannot state the meta-theorems involved, without formulating any particular axiom system.

F. *Propositional Quantification*

18. QUANTIFIERS AND PROPOSITIONAL FUNCTIONS

We have explained in sufficient detail general characterizations of *implication, equivalence,* and *logical truth.* We have emphasized that these concepts gain specificity piecemeal, to wit, by the specification of successive layers of analysis of logical form. So far we have specified the layer of tautological form determined by the rules of truth (T.12)–(T.16), given in §5 above. We have also explained the formal relationship of deducibility that turns out to coincide with implication. Again, we only discussed in some detail the layer of connective deducibility that coincides with tautological implication. We proceed now to specify another layer of logical form: the layer of quantification. Again, there are the same three approaches to be distinguished, and, again, their coincidence is the subject-matter of very important theorems in logical theory.

Quantifiers are the structures expressed by expressions like 'all', 'everything', 'anybody', 'everybody', 'most', 'few', 'someone', 'something', and 'there is an object (person) such that'. We shall call these expressions themselves quantifiers, too. The main structural principle in the case of propositions is, roughly, that quantifiers express certain operations on what are called propositional functions where the results of the operations are propositions. *Propositional functions* are sorts of incomplete propositions, i.e., frames of propositions with empty "positions" for missing constituents. Here again we recall the assumption that language is ontological, so that certain syntactical structures of sentences reveal the structure of the propositions they express. Yet, again, our primary concern is with *what* appears to consciousness and is somehow carried by language. Thus, we shall drop the scare quotes around 'position' and 'part'. These words can literally, in a new sense if you wish, name what in a proposition corresponds to parts and positions in a sentence expressing the proposition in question. Now, propositional functions are expressed by incomplete sentences to be called *sentential functions*. For instance '_____ is blue' expresses a propositional function, where the blank '_____' neatly indicates that the function is predicative, being, so to speak, the predicate frame, of a proposition obtained by subtraction of the latter's subject. There are also subjective functions, where the subtracted part of the generating proposition is the predicate; for instance, 'John is _____' expresses the subjective function embedded in the propositions *John is happy* and *John is angry*. We shall consider here only the predicative functions.

The standard logic of propositions studies three types of generation of propositions from propositional functions. The first one is called *instantiation* and consists of the generation of propositions by completion of the propositional function with particular constituents in non-predicative empty positions. For instance *_____ is red* is instantiated into *John is red* and *The box on the table is red*. The other two types of generation are called *generalizations*. In both, the empty positions are not really filled in, but are closed, so to speak, by the application of an operator on the whole propositional function. Roughly, the idea is this: the operator *everything* applies to *_____ is red* yielding by *universal generalization* the proposition *Everything is red*, which is the same as *Everything (_____ is red)*, showing that 'everything' is not a name of an expression that refers to any single person, but an expression with altogether different logical properties. Likewise, the proposition *Someone is red* is the result of an operation of *existential generalization* on the propositional function *_____ is red*, which we may provisionally refer to as *Someone (_____ is red)*. The reason for calling 'someone' an *existential quantifier* is that it is taken to mean the same as 'There is (exists) an object such that.'

Consider now the proposition *Karl is older than Bonita*. Here we have an instantiation of several different propositional functions: *Karl is older than _____*, *_____ is older than Bonita*, and *_____ is older than _____*, not to discuss *Karl is _____ than Bonita* or *Karl _____ Bonita*. Let us concentrate on *_____ is older than _____*. We use two different blanks to indicate that the two empty positions of the function *may* be filled in with different constituents, as in *Karl is older than Bonita*; but they *may* also be filled in with the same constituent as in the false proposition *Karl is older than Karl (himself)*. Thus, this latter proposition is also an instantiation of the propositional frame *_____ is older than _____*. Obviously, we may have to use any number of blanks and types of blanks, depending on how complex the proposition is. An example with five blanks is *_____ gave _____ _____ and _____ borrowed _____ from _____*. For convenience it is preferable to dump the use of blanks and resort instead to letters, especially 'x', 'y', and 'z', with or without subscripts. These letters will be called *individual variables*. Thus, the last mentioned form can be more succinctly referred to as *x gave y to z and x_1 borrowed y from z_1*, where the repetition of 'y' indicates that the same propositional constituent fills the two positions of the propositional function in the propositions which instantiate the latter.

Consider the propositional function *x touches y*. Here there are several ways of generalizing, depending on which quantifier operates on which empty position of the function, i.e., *x* or *y*. We need, therefore, some way of indicating the relationship between a quantifier and the positions it close up. We do this by attaching to each quantifier expression the individual variable that indicates that a certain set of blanks are to be filled in with the same constituent. Thus, we have among the generalizations of *x touches y*:

(1)   Everything x everything y (x touches y):
        Everything touches everything.
(2)   Everything x something y (x touches y):
        Everything touches something (or other).

At this juncture we make our canonical notation more perspicuous by shortening 'everything x' and 'everything y' to '$\forall x$' and '$\forall y$'; we also abbreviate 'something x' and 'something y' as '$\exists x$' and '$\exists y$'. Thus, the propositional function *x touches y* yields the following generalizations:

(1) $\forall x \forall y$ (x touches y):   Everything touches everything
(2) $\forall y \forall x$ (x touches y):   Everything is touched by everything
(3) $\forall x \exists y$ (x touches y):   Everything touches something
(4) $\exists y \forall x$ (x touches y):   Something is touched by everything
(5) $\exists x \forall y$ (x touches y):   Something touches everything
(6) $\forall y \exists x$ (x touches y):   Everything is touched by something
(7) $\exists x \exists y$ (x touches y):   Something touches something
(8) $\exists y \exists x$ (x touches y):   Something is touched by something.

Another example. *Whoever likes someone is liked by somebody* is the same proposition as *Everybody [you choose, call him x] is such that: if he [x] likes someone, then he [x] is liked by somebody*, which is *$\forall x$(x likes someone $\supset x$ is liked by somebody)*. Here we can offer a deeper analysis of the structure of this proposition, since the propositional function *x likes someone* is *there is at least one person [call him y] such that x likes y*, which is in canonical notation *$\exists y$(x likes y)*. Similarly, *x is liked by somebody* is the same as *$\exists y$(y likes x)*. Hence our proposition *Whoever likes someone is liked by somebody* is the proposition *$\forall x$($\exists y$(x likes y)$\supset \exists y$(y likes x))*. Of course, which variables we use is immaterial, so that our proposition is the same as $*\forall z(\exists x(z$ likes $x)\supset\exists y(y$ likes $z))*$.

Now we can see that the truth principles (T.12)–(T.16) introduced in §5 do *not* constitute the full characterization of the propositional structures negation, conjunction, disjunction, etc. Those principles would provide a full characterization only if these structures applied exclusively to propositions. But they also apply to propositional functions; e.g., *Karl hates x but loves $y*$ is a conjunction of *Karl hates $x*$ and *Karl loves $y*$. In short, the logical connections we studied in §§5–17 connect items which are neither true nor false. This is a liberating simple point that will be useful in Chapter 4 §2, as well as in Chapter 6 §4. In any case, here we have the structural principle:

Con. Prop. Fu. If $*f*$ is a propositional function, so is $*(\sim f)*$; and if $*f*$ or $*g*$ is a propositional function, then $*(f \& g)*$, $*(f \vee g)*$, $*(f \supset g)*$, $*(f \equiv g)*$ are also propositional functions.

19. SEMANTICAL APPROACH

The fundamental semantical property of the quantifiers is their presupposing a domain of entities, called the *universe of discourse*. Thus, in its widest range the expressions 'nobody', 'somebody' and 'everybody' express quantifiers that have as their universe of discourse the total class of persons, past, present, and future. But often we say, e.g., "Everybody came to the party", using the word 'everybody' to express a quantifier that ranges over a small domain of persons, namely, those invited, or those expected. Naturally, the sentence 'Everybody came to the party' expresses different propositions depending on the universe of discourse of the quantifier expressed by the word 'everybody'. Thus, the general truth-conditions crudely formulated below characterize the logical meaning of the two sets of quantifier expression we are at present most interested in: *(for table III see next page)*

We are now in a position to characterize a second layer of semantical implication, equivalence, and logical truth. All we need do is to extend the tautological characterizations of implication, equivalence, and logical truth to the quantificational characterizations by including both the rule of truth (T.12)–(T.16) and the rules of truth (T.17)–(T.18). We shall not stop to formulate these extensions.

TABLE III

U is the presupposed non-empty universe of discourse; '$\phi(x)$' is a sentential function having one or more blanks labelled "x", that expresses a propositional function:

> (T.17) or U(T), $*\forall x\phi(x)*$ is true if and only if every member
> of U has the property expressed by '$\phi(x)$'
> (T.18) or E(T). $*\exists x\phi(x)*$ is true, if and only at least one member
> of U has the property expressed by '$\phi(x)$'.

Rules (T.1) and (T.18) explain why inferences like the following are valid:

> A1.   Everybody will take the course, therefore, John will take the course.
> A2.   All students (of a certain kind) took the course.
>   John is a student (of the kind in question) therefore,
>   John took the course.
> B.   John opened the door, therefore, someone opened the door.

20. SET-THEORETICAL MODELS

The standard, rigorous theory of quantificational logical truth and implication treats these concepts in terms of set theory. Since we shall need to refer to this theory in Chapter 4 §1, we shall discuss it briefly. In the standard logical theory it is sentences that are said to be true or false, but we can always construe this as a way of referring to the truth-values of the propositions expressed by the sentences under consideration. Let us, then, consider sentences and sentential functions.

We use the letters 'f' and 'g' to represent sentential functions that have no connectives or sentential functions that we are not interested in analyzing. They are called *predicate variables* and are said to be of *degree* n when they represent sentential functions with n individual blanks or variables. We define:

> *Pred. For. Predicate formulas* are sequences of symbols of the following kinds: (1) $\phi(x_1, ..., x_n)$, where ϕ is a predicate variable of degree n and $x_1, ..., x_n$ are names or individual variables; (2) $(\sim\phi)$, $(\phi \& \psi)$, $(\phi \vee \psi)$, $(\phi \supset \psi)$ and $(\phi \equiv \psi)$, and (3) $(\forall x\phi)$ and $(\exists x\phi)$, where ϕ and ψ are predicate formulas.

Predicate formulas represent forms of propositional functions.

Now, let ϕ be a predicate formula and let x be an individual variable. If x occurs in ϕ in a part of the form '$(\forall x\psi)$' or of the form '$(\exists x\psi)$', x is *bound in* ϕ [and in ψ]. A variable that occurs in ϕ in parts not of those forms is *free in* ϕ. For example, 'x' and 'y' are free in the formula '$(\exists z)f(x, y, z)$' while 'z' is bound in it. If a formula has no free individual variables it represents a predicate propositional form.

Let α be a set of predicate formulas. Consider now a non-empty set D of entities whatever and a set S whose members are sets of ordered n-tuples of members of D, for at least all values of n which are degrees of predicate variables occurring in formulas in α.

DEFINITION 1.   An interpretation i of α on the pair $\langle D, S \rangle$ is both: (1) an assignment of a member of D to each name or free individual variable occurring in at least one formula in α, and (2) an assignment of a member of S of degree n to each predicate variable of degree n occurring in at least one formula in α. Let $i\,(t)$ be the entity i assigns to a term t.

DEFINITION 2.   The triple $\langle D, S, i \rangle$ is a *model* for α, if D and S are as above described and i is an interpretation of α on $\langle D, S \rangle$. For example, the set $\alpha = \{$'$\exists x f(x, y)$', '$\exists x \exists y (\sim f(x, y))$'$\}$ has as model the triple $\langle D, S, i \rangle$, where D $= \{$Napoleon, Caesar, Alexander$\}$, S is a set with two members: a set of singletons, A $= \{\{$Napoleon$\}, \{$Caesar$\}\}$ and a set of ordered pairs, B $= \{\langle$Napoleon, Caesar$\rangle, \langle$Caesar, Napoleon$\rangle, \langle$Alexander, Caesar$\rangle, \langle$Alexander, Alexander$\rangle\}$, and i is the assignment of Napoleon to 'x', Alexander to 'y' and set B to 'f'.

DEFINITION 3.   A valuation v of a set α of predicate formulas on a model M $= \langle D, S, i \rangle$ is an assignment of T (for truth) or F (for falsity) to each member of α by means of the following rules:

(1) v assigns T, or F, to predicate formulas of the forms '$\sim \phi$', '$(\phi \,\&\, \psi)$', '$(\phi \vee \psi)$', '$(\phi \supset \psi)$', and $(\phi \equiv \psi)$' T, or F, in accordance with the truth-tables of §5.

(2) v assigns T to a predicate formula ψ of the form '$\phi(x_1, ..., x_n)$', where ϕ is a predicate variable of degree n, if and only if the ordered n-tuple $\langle i\,(x_1), ..., i\,(x_n) \rangle$ belongs to $i\,(\phi)$. Otherwise v assigns F to ψ.

(3) v assigns T to a predicate formula ψ of the form $\forall x\phi$ if and only if every interpretation like i, except for assigning a different member of D to 'x', yields a valuation of T for ϕ. Otherwise v assigns F to ψ.

(4) v assigns to a predicate formula of the form '$\exists x\phi$' exactly what it assigns to the corresponding formula of the form '$\sim(\forall x(\sim\phi))$'.

DEFINITION 5*.   A predicate formula ψ is *logically valid* if and only if ψ is assigned T by every model for $\{\psi\}$.

DEFINITION 6*.   A set α of predicate formulas *implies* a predicate formula ψ, i.e., $\alpha \vDash \psi$, if and only if every model that assigns T to each formula in α also assigns T to ψ.

Definition 5* and Definition 6* elucidate properties of propositional predicate forms. They provide the basis for a set-theoretical semantical characterization of quantificational implication between propositions and quantificational logical truth. But we shall not do so here, since it is not necessary for our purposes in this book.

21. INFERENTIAL APPROACH TO QUANTIFICATION

We continue the discussion of §12. There we considered a natural partial ordering of propositions and classes of propositions. We extend that natural partial ordering to propositional functions. Thus, the principles governing the quantifiers are principles establishing precedence between propositions and propositional functions. Again, the naturalness of that partial ordering pertains to the reasonableness, or unreasonableness, of a thinking creature's endorsements of the propositions and propositional functions involved. We must explain, however, what it is for a man to endorse a propositional function. Since a propositional function is neither true nor false, a man cannot endorse it by believing it, or by believing that it is true.

A man endorses a propositional function ϕ when he has the propensity to believe the propositions that are instances of ϕ. We leave it open whether it is possible to endorse a propositional function without believing the fully universal instance of it. On the other hand, a man who endorses, i.e., believes the fully universal generalization of a propositional function ϕ does endorse ϕ. This is principle D11 below.

In any case, the inferential approach characterizes the quantifiers by means of the following inference principles. We assume the machinery developed in §13. We introduce the symbol '$\alpha \left|\dfrac{}{q}\right. X$' to mean that X is deducible from (i.e., follows in the natural order after) α by the rules of §13 or by the rules governing quantifiers, which are:

D11. $(\forall x \phi) \left|\dfrac{}{q}\right. \psi$,

         where ψ stands for predicate formula like the one represented by ϕ, except for containing occurrences of a name, or free occurrences of an individual variable, wherever ϕ contains free occurrences of x.

D12.   If $\alpha \left|\dfrac{}{q}\right. \psi$, then $\alpha \left|\dfrac{}{q}\right. (\forall x \phi)$,

         where ϕ and ψ stand for predicate formulas obtainable from each other by replacing just free occurrences of an individual variable y for free occurrences of x, and neither x nor y appear free in any predicate formula in α.

D13.   (a) $(\exists x \phi) \left|\dfrac{}{q}\right. (\sim \forall x (\sim \phi))$

         (b) $(\sim \forall x (\sim \phi)) \left|\dfrac{}{q}\right. (\exists x \phi)$.

22. COINCIDENCE OF THE THREE APPROACHES

Quantifiers can also be treated axiomatically, as an extension of the treatment of the connections discussed briefly in §16. Indeed, we shall treat quantifiers axiomatically in Chapter 9.

The crucial thing is that the three approaches coincide. In particular

META-THEOREM XI. $\alpha \left|\dfrac{}{q}\right. {=} X$, if and only if $\alpha \left|\dfrac{}{q}\right. X$.

We will need refer to this result. But we will not establish it here. It can be found in most intermediate textbooks in logic. Note that Meta-theorem XI includes as a special case Meta-theorem I of §14.

NOTES TO CHAPTER 3

[1] This name is adopted from Wilfrid Sellars, 'Presupposing', *The Philosophical Review*, **63** (1954): 197–215. Keith Lehrer has informed me that these dialectical principles are similar to what Paul Grice has called rules of conversational implicature.

[2] Since there is *no* ultimate form of a proposition or an argument, it follows that *there is no purely formal proof of non-implication, consistency or non-validity.* Since philosophical analyses are strong co-implications, the non-analyzability of a concept cannot be proven formally. This is a most important principle that philosophers often forget. And this is often joined to the idea that unanalyzable concepts cannot be related by implications. This denial of bridging implications leads to false principles like the so-called naturalistic fallacy or Hume's guillotine. (See pp. 21 and 332ff.)

[3] J. Barkley Rosser, *Logic for Mathematicians*, McGraw-Hill, New York. 1953, Chapter IV, pp. 55–76.

[4] In H-N. Castañeda, 'On the Semantics of the Ought-to-Do', *Synthese* **21** (1970): 449–468, reprinted in G. Harman and D. Davidson, eds., *Semantics of Natural Language* (Dordrecht: Reidel Publishing Co., 1972).

CHAPTER 4

IMPERATIVES AND PRESCRIPTIONS

In this chapter we argue, first, that prescriptions are not propositions. We also collect and codify data from which we argue, secondly, that there are logical relationships, in the same formal sense studied in Chapter 3, among imperatives or prescriptions, as well as between imperatives and propositions. We construct a theory of prescriptive implication, which theory will be the basis of the theory of deontic implication to be erected in Chapters 7–9. We widen the customary scope of logic right at its inception, that is, at the point of selection of its subject-matter, in contrast with later deepenings that consist of the introduction of new types of propositions and of principles of implication characterizing such types.

The high point of this chapter is the proof that there is a class of prescriptions and mandates that have an implicational structure that parallels thoroughly the implicational structure of propositions. This proof uses the resources furnished by Chapter 3, especially §12 and §13. Given the equivalence, discussed in Chapter 3, §14, between the semantical and the inferential approaches to implication, the just-mentioned parallelism yields the result that a class of prescriptions and mandates has a two-valued logical structure.

That parallelism establishes that prescriptions and mandates have then two values analogous to truth and falsity. What exactly are they? This question is reserved for Chapter 5. The counterpart case of intentions is treated in Chapter 6.

1. PRESCRIPTIONS AND PROPOSITIONS

As we characterized them in Chapter 2, §3 prescriptions are the cores of families of mandates that demand of the same agents the same actions in the same circumstances. That is, prescriptions are the cores of mandates that differ only in their social modality, e.g., being an order, or a command, or a request, or a piece of advice, or a petition, or an entreaty. We also noted that the approval of a person's doing something is an attitude that has a prescription as its content. Thus, our term 'prescription' does not blur any distinction between psychological and linguistic acts. It merely identifies a structure of subjects and properties and objects which is conceived as related, not by the way in which the elements of a fact or a proposition are related, but in the way in which that structure appears to practical thinking, to wit, as one to be actualized. The word 'prescription' identifies that structure throughout the different mental operations and the different speech acts on it. The typical and distinctive structural feature of a simple prescription is to have, not a mere arrangement of a subject and a property, but an arrangement of an action and a subject from which the action is demanded, i.e., an agent. Thus, the primary difference between *John goes (is going, will go, has gone) home* and *John, go home* seems to be a difference in the way in which the property or action of going home is predicated of John. This difference has nothing to do with whether *John, go home* is a command, an order, a request, an entreaty, or a piece of advice. It is a difference between propositions and prescriptions, and not between propositions and mandates. And it seems to be a difference in the way the action of going is thought to be *tied* to John, i.e., it is a difference belonging to the *copulation* of subject and predicate.

To make this more clearly, consider the following command, or order, or request:

(1)   Karl, please do the following: if it rains, *close the windows,* if and only if the awnings are not up, and if it hails, *turn circulator A on* if and only if circulator B is off.

This is a somewhat complex mandate, whose complexity should help us avoid the traps of oversimplification. It exhibits several very important structural features of mandates and prescriptions. Let us perform an anatomic analysis of it.

First, mandate (1) is a request, as is signaled by the word 'please'. The expression 'Karl, please do the following' expresses here a request operator which transforms (1.C) below into a request:

(1.C)   if it rains, [Karl] *close the windows* if and only if the awnings are not up, and if it hails, [Karl] *turn circulator A on* if and only if circulator B is off.

Clearly, the same syntactical prefix 'Karl, do the following' can be used to express an order or a command or a piece of advice, depending on the context of utterance and on the tone of voice. That is, the locution 'Karl, do the following' *cum* given context and tone of voice, expresses an operator that transforms prescription (1.C) into a command, or an order, or a petition, as the case may be. Interesting prefixes are 'Karl, I beg you [I entreat you, I command you], do the following'. These prefixes express, of course, entreaty and command operators, respectively. But they also express a proposition, namely, the proposition that the corresponding psycho-linguistic act is being performed. Some philosophers, like John L. Austin,[1] have denied the expression of the proposition, but their main reason has been the uncompelling one that those prefixes do express the issuance of a mandate. Of course they do, but why should they not do both? In any case, whether or not these prefixes have the dual role of expressing a mandate and a proposition, they express a mandate, and this is what concerns us here.

Let us pause to pay homage to ordinary language. It possesses a perspicuous mandate operator expression that applies to any clause formulating a prescription namely, '$a_1, ..., a_{n_1}$ *do the following:* C', where each of the 'a's is a name of an agent and 'C' represents a clause expressing a prescription. For example;

(2)   Paul, Mary, and Ted, do the following: if it rains, Paul mow the lawn, and Ted keep the sprinkler off; and if it does not rain, Ted open the windows, and Mary paint the window sills.

Some actions involve several agents. For instance, the opening of the doors of certain bank strongboxes requires that two or three men turn their respective keys. Such actions can be demanded by prescriptions and mandates that can also be expressed in the canonical notation described above. If the list of agents is too long, we can substitute a description of the class they form; to wit, 'α, do the following: C'.

Second, prescription (1.C) is the core of the mandates expressed by sentence (1) and by the sentences differing from (1) by having other imperative prefixes like those mentioned in the preceding paragraph. Prescription (1.C) is a complex of two different types of constituents:

(a)   *Propositions:*
       it rains; *the awnings are not up*;

      it hails; *circulator B is off*.

(b)   *Simpler prescriptions:*
     [Karl] close the windows;
     [Karl] turn circulator A on.

Thus, in this example we must distinguish prescriptions from propositions. Even though the whole complex prescription (1.C) is the core of mandate (1), nevertheless it is the two simpler prescriptions in that core that constitute the substance, so to speak, of the mandate. More formally, the mandate operator *Karl, please do the following* has in its scope the whole of prescription (1.C); the propositions do not, while the simpler prescriptions do, appear essentially in that scope. The operator *Karl, please do the following* would not be effective in transforming a proposition into mandate: it requires a prescription to *hook on* to. For instance, the strings of words 'Karl, do the following: it is raining' and Karl, do the following: Karl is alive' are nonsensical, i.e., they express no noema. This is a purely structural point that must be carefully distinguished from the implicational point depending on it that will loom important later on, namely, the point that the propositions (a) in mandate (1) can be *taken out* of the scope of the request operator *Karl, please do the following*. That is to say, request (1) does imply requests that have the same constituents as (1), and in which some or all propositions (a) are not in the scope of the operator *Karl, please do the following*. For instance, mandate (1) implies

(3)   If it rains, Karl please do the following: *close the windows if and only if the awnings are not up;* and if it hails, Karl please do the following, too: *turn circulator A on if and only if circulator B is off.*

It might be thought that mandate (1) can be analyzed without introducing such a sharp distinction between propositions and prescriptions as we affirmed above. It might be suggested that the reason why the operator *Karl, please do the following* hooks on to certain parts of (1.C) is not because such parts are prescriptions and not propositions. All the parts of (1.C), it might be said, are propositions. Their different behavior with respect to *Karl, please do the following* can be explained by the fact that some parts of (1.C) have Karl as an agent, not just as subject, while the other parts of (1.C) are propositions that do not involve Karl. Undoubtedly, a quick glance at our list of constituents of (1.C) shows that list (a) contains propositions not involving Karl, while list (b) contains constituents each involving Karl.

Can we, then, take prescriptions as a special class of propositions? Can we adopt the thesis that imperative operators of the form ∗X, do the following∗ operate on propositions involving the agent referred to by names represented by 'X'? This would be a nice theory. It would unify the contents of contemplative and practical thinking. Unfortunately, it oversimplifies the structure of prescriptions. It fits mandate (1) very snuggly. Yet it cannot do justice to other examples. Consider, for instance:

(4)   Karl, please do the following: if you come late, not *close the windows* if you raise the awnings, but *raise the awnings* if it is raining.

In mandate (4) we have both the proposition ∗You [Karl] raise the awnings∗ and the prescription ∗*[Karl] raise the awnings*∗. The former occurs inessentially in the scope of the operator ∗Karl, please do the following∗; the latter, however, occurs essentially in that scope. Indeed the derivative inferential point holds, so that (4) implies

(5)   If you come late and you-raise-the-awnings, Karl, please do the following: not close the windows; but if it is raining, Karl, please do the following: raise the awnings.

Thus, the imperative operators of the form ∗Karl, do the following∗ operate on items that involve Karl, to be sure, but such items are not propositions. We can see that this is so in the case of (4) and (5), for palpably the proposition ∗[Karl] you-raise-the-awnings∗ and the prescription ∗*[Karl] raise the awnings*∗ have exactly the same constituents: ∗Karl∗ as agent and ∗raise the awnings∗ as predicate. Thus, either (i) the prescription ∗*[Karl] raise the awnings*∗ is itself the result of an operation on the proposition ∗you [Karl]-raise-the-awnings∗, or (ii) the prescription is a structuring of the same constituents of the proposition in a different way from the one they are structured in the latter. At any rate, even if a prescription results from an operation on a proposition, a prescription is not a proposition.

In the preceding examples we can see that prescriptions that are com-

pounds of both propositions and prescriptions are prescriptions because
of their prescriptional components. This suggests that prescriptions are
not the results of applying a prescriptional operator to any proposition;
if an operator yields a prescription from a proposition, the proposition in
question must be a simple one, in which subjects are structured with
properties. This is further supported by mandates and prescriptions like:

(6)   Everybody, do the following: go home,

and

(7)   The following is an order: Everybody to go home.

In (7) the clause 'Everybody to go home' expresses the same prescription
that enters in mandate (6): it expresses this prescription exactly in the
notation introduced in Chapter 2, §4. The prescription *Everybody to
go home* embedded in the two mandates (6) and (7) seems to be anatomi-
cally analyzable as the universal quantifier *everybody* operating on a
prescriptive basis *to go home*, just as the corresponding proposition
Everybody goes (is going, will go) home is constituted by the universal
quantifier *everybody* operating on a propositional basis *goes (is
going, will go) home*. Such propositional bases as this were called
propositional functions in Chapter 3, §18.

   Thus, it appears that the fundamental contrast between a proposition
and a prescription lies at the very structuring or junction of subjects and
predicates. This contrast can be conceived in two different ways: (a) as
a contrast between two forms or patterns of composition in which the
very same constituents can enter, or (b) as a contrast between a predicate
that enters with subjects in a structure either naked or embellished, as it
were. In view (a) the difference between a pure prescription and its corresponding proposition is one of *copulation* of subjects and predicates.
In case (b) there is a prescriptional operator that operates on predicates,
yielding *prescriptional predicates,* which combine with subjects by means
of the same old copula. In other words, on view (b) the difference between
a pure prescription and its corresponding proposition is the difference
between the categories of predicates involved. Let us call view (a) the
prescriptional copulation view, and (b) the *prescriptional predicate view.*

   Now, which of these two views shall we adopt? The prescriptional predicate view is more complex: it includes six types of items and two of them are probably infinite. It recognizes: two (probably infinite) kinds of properties, the prescriptional operator, the copula, and the two categories of prescriptions and propositions. On the other hand, the prescriptional copulation view is more economical: it recognizes just one kind of property, two kinds of copulation, and the two categories of noemata. It may be thought that ordinary language adopts the economical view by signaling the distinction between propositions and mandates by means of a verbal mood, the verb being the expression of copulation. Since my earlier writings[2] I have adopted the economical copulation view.

There is one consideration that some philosophers would regard as persuasive in favor of the prescriptional predicate view. It will be developed in §9 below. It is this. As noted in Chapter 3, §20, the standard theory of logical truth explains logical truth of quantified propositions in terms of the extensions of properties. To this effect (propositional) copulation is paired with class membership and properties are paired with classes. The generalization of that theory to prescriptions makes it very natural, and very simple, to continue to pair the structuring of subjects and properties with class membership, and then treat the properties involved in prescriptions as special prescriptive properties that have extensions different from those of their corresponding propositional properties. The naturalness of this procedure is persuasive and it *must* be counted in favor of the prescriptional predicate view. But it is not conclusive. A resourceful logician set on defending the prescriptional copulation view can invent other types of set-theoretical models for prescriptions in order to test logical for validity. In any case ontology does not have to follow any purely logical theory of validity. Although it is nice, of course, if we can bring ontology and logic to a unison.

Now, there is an obviously easy correspondence between the two theories. Any claim or thesis involving one view can be translated into a claim or thesis involving the other. Let A be an action that involves n agents and m patients. A proposition to the effect that A has been (or is being or will be performed) is $*A(a_1, ..., a_n, b_1, ..., b_m)*$, where the parentheses express propositional copulation, the 'a's the agents and the 'b's the patients. On the prescriptional copulation view the corresponding prescription is $*A[a_1, ..., a_n, b_1, ..., b_m]*$, where the square brackets represent prescriptional copulation. On the other hand, if we adopt the prescriptional predicate view we can let the mere insertion of names of agents and patients in a predicate expression represent copulation, i.e., the only copulation the view allows. Then we can represent the propositional predicate of the action A by 'A(,..., ...,)', and the corresponding prescriptional predicate by 'A[,..., , , ...,]', both with n slots for names of agents and m slots for names of patients. Then, the proposition involving action A and the same n agents and m patients mentioned above is, once again, $*A(a_1, ..., a_n, b_1, ..., b_m)*$, and the corresponding prescription is, again, $*A[a_1, ..., a_n, b_1, ..., b_m]*$.

Thus, there is *no* logical difference between the two views. The difference is strictly *ontological*. It will not matter for our logical purposes here which view we adopt. Thus, we submit to ontological economy and continue adhering to the prescriptional copulation view. If an extension of our present investigations requires a shift to the prescriptional predicate view we will, certainly, make that shift. (In Chapter 10 we shall study the nature of the practitional copula).

Some philosophers, including myself during some periods of reflection, have proposed to analyze *all* actions as bringings about of some state affair. On one view of such a type, the attribution to John of the action of opening the door made by the action proposition *John opened the door* is really the proposition *John brought it about that the door became open*. This view is, however, glaringly incorrect. Clearly, John can bring it about that the door becomes open, without himself opening it, e.g., by having Marilyn open it. A better view analyzes *John opened the door* as *John brought it about that John *opened* the door*, where the italicized 'opened' expresses a mere physical relation between John and the door, deprived of the actional or performing aspect normally built into the meaning of 'opened'. That physical relationship is exactly like the one existing between a swinging tree branch and a steady kite in contact with it, i.e., the one we would express by saying "the swinging tree branch hit the kite". I have found this view tempting. On it, for each set α of agents, there is a family of action operators of the form *α brings it about at time t at place l that*, which operate on propositions, and *there are no other action propositions than those resulting from the action,* so to speak, *of those operators*. This closing statement is what constitutes the view, for obviously there are such operators and there are the resulting action propositions.

We shall not decide on that view at this juncture. We must note, however, that every action proposition of the form *α brings it about at t at l that $p*$ corresponds to a prescription of the form *α to bring it about at t at l that $p*$. This is so regardless of whether there are other action propositions or not. Patently, the prescriptional operator *α to bring it about at t at l that* must be carefully distinguished from the propositional action operator *α brings it about at t at $l*$. Again, we must view the connection between α and bringing about in either of two ways: (a) as involving one of two ways of copulation, or (b) as involving the same copulation but two types of bringing about: a propositional and a prescriptional one. Again, we need not decide this issue, and for convenience we adopt at least temporarily the economical view (a).

In conclusion, there is an apparently irreducible aspect characteristic of prescriptions and mandates. Because of it *prescriptions are not propositions.*

2. IS THERE A LOGIC OF IMPERATIVES?

A very important difference between propositions and mandates or prescriptions is this: propositions are said to be true or false, but neither mandates nor prescriptions are said to be true or false. Even if there are propositions having no truth-value, as some philosophers have proposed, nevertheless combinations of such propositions with other propositions yield compound propositions which are true or false. Mandates and prescriptions, on the other hand, are wholly devoid of truth values: *none* of them is either true or false.

This difference has led some philosophers[3] to claiming that there are no logical relations between, or among, imperatives: that there is no logic of imperatives. Others[4] have argued that the following two formal analogies between statements and imperatives show that imperatives stand in logical relations

(A) The logical words 'all', 'some', 'not', 'and' ('but', 'although', 'both'), 'neither ... nor', 'without -ing', 'or', 'if' ('only if'), etc. are correctly used in sentences formulating imperatives, without exhibiting a change of meaning. For instance, we have negated orders (like *Don't open the window*), conjunctive commands (like *Stop the tank and get out*), conjunctive negative advice (like *Neither borrow nor lend money*), conjunctive semi-negative directives (like *Prepare yourself to go without telling anyone, even your wife∗), conditional requests (like ∗If he comes, please tell him to wait∗), etc.

(B) The inferential words 'so', 'hence', 'therefore', 'because', 'since', etc. are, without any apparent change in meaning, used to express inferential or inferential-like, relations between imperatives and other imperatives, or among imperatives and statements. For instance, we reason, or seem to reason, as follows: ∗He will be engaged the whole morning, thus, *(hence, therefore, so),* please come back tomorrow∗, or ∗*Since* it is too drafty, close the window∗, or ∗Close the window, for *(since, given that, because)* it is too drafty∗.

To see the strength of (A) and (B) it must be noted that, e.g., no difference in the meaning of 'and' is established by the fact that ∗Napoleon and Caesar were conquerors∗ is true while ∗Paul, close the window, and, you, Peter, close the door∗ is neither true nor false. Two complexes may have different properties, even when they have one identical component, or exactly the same form of composition. There is in principle no mystery in the logical connections yielding both statements, i.e., complexes with truth-values, in one case, and imperatives, i.e., complexes without truth-values, in the other case. The difference is, or can be, fully accounted for by the nature of the elements they connect or relate. Moreover, the words 'and', 'but', and 'or' do not change meaning when they express connections between properties which are neither true nor false, as, e.g., in 'Something is blue and (but, or) round'. (See principle *Con. Prop. Fu.* at the end of Chapter 3, §18).

Furthermore, there are other important parallellisms between statements and mandates:

(C) The inferential or inferential-like relations involving imperatives clearly divide into two groups: (1) those which seem *invalid,* e.g., ∗If he comes, give him this book; therefore, burn the book∗, and (2) those which seem *valid,* e.g., (i) ∗If he comes, give him this book; he is coming, hence, give him this book∗, and (ii) ∗Give this book to him, if and only if he comes; Oh! but he won't come; hence, don't give it to him∗.

(D) Many patterns of relations exhibited by what seem to be valid reasonings involving imperatives are the same patterns of relations between premises and conclusions that make valid a reasoning involving statements only. For instance, in (C) above we have the familiar valid patterns: (i) ∗If p, then q; p; hence q∗ and (ii) ∗$p \equiv q$; not-(q); hence not-(p)∗.

In sum, (A)–(D) do show that imperatives have relationships which both parallel the logical relationships of statements, and *must* be studied whether we call them "logical" or not. (A)–(D) strongly suggest that a generalization of the logical principles governing statement and statemental inference is profitable. For convenience at any rate, we shall use the words 'logical', 'logic', 'inference', 'reasoning', 'valid', 'invalid', etc. in this fruitful generalized way.

It must be acknowledged, of course, that if a philosopher wants to use these words only for the case of statements, he is absolutely correct in saying that there are no imperative inferences, no imperative logic, and no logical relationships between imperatives. The issue, then, whether or not there is a logic of imperatives is in part verbal. What is *not* verbal is, by (A)*(D), that the relationships between, and among, imperatives, are analogous and even, perhaps, parallel to the relationships we studied in Chapter 3 for the case of propositions. Furthermore, it is not a verbal matter that the study of such relationships between imperatives is of great importance for understanding the structure of what we think in practical thinking, which deals with prescriptions as well as with orders, commands, requests, pieces of advice, or other types of mandate. Thus, we may grant the purist philosopher his terminology, and introduce a new set of terms for the study of the principles governing the classification of the sequences of mandates that are analogous to valid reasonings. Because of the parallelism pinned down by (A)–(D) above we may naturally use the old terms, which the purist philosopher applies to propositions, prefixed by the morpheme '*sh-*'. Thus, we would speak of imperative sh-reasonings, which divide into those which are sh-valid and those which are sh-invalid, the latter being those in which the sh-premises sh-imply the sh-conclusions, and so on.

We can now agree to use the old words 'logic', 'implication', 'valid', etc. in the *sense* in which it covers the old meanings of these words as well as the meanings of the new 'sh'-words. And we shall use them in the new extended sense, unless a warning to the contrary is made. Thus, the issue whether there is a logic of imperatives has the trivial answer *No*, *if* 'logic of imperatives' is used in the "old" sense of 'logic'. And it has a trivial answer *Yes*, if 'logic' is used in the "new" sense. But can anybody prove that the "new" meanings of all logical words mentioned in (A)–(D) are not really the meanings of those ordinary words?[5] This is

really all there is to the general question *Is there a logic of imperatives?*
What is important and not verbal is the formulation and systematization
of the principles that govern valid imperative inference, or sh-valid imperative sh-inference, if you wish.

In Chapter 3, §§12–13 we studied implication relationships between
propositions without reference to truth-values. We called them deducibility relationships. Thus, even without terminological disagreement with
purist philosophers we can study the deducibility relationships between
mandates, or between prescriptions. In Chapter 3, §12 we characterized
propositional deducibility as the "natural" partial ordering of proposition
such that a thinking being who endorses (believes) a set α of propositions
is not only justified in endorsing (believing) the propositions that come
after α in that "natural" ordering, but would be acting irrationally were
he to refuse endorsement of the negations of such propositions that follow
α in the "natural" order of propositions. Clearly, mandates or prescriptions
are such that if one endorses some set α of them one would be irrational
were one to refuse endorsement of other mandates or prescriptions. Thus,
mandates and prescriptions also have a "natural" order of their own. For
instance, a commander who endorses the order *Jones, call Smith up and
report your call* is justified in endorsing the simpler order *Jones, call
Smith up*; furthermore, that same commander would be acting irrationally if without rescinding his previous endorsement he also endorses
the command *Jones, do not call Smith*

Evidently, then, mandates and prescriptions cannot help but stand in
relationships of deducibility, as this was characterized in Chapter 3, §12
above. This is precisely what the above facts (A)–(D) in §1 establish conclusively about the connectives and the inferential words of English. It is
only because in the case of propositions we know that the inferential and
the semantical approaches are virtually equivalent, that we find a problem
about the logic of imperatives when we do not find semantical values of
prescriptions really available, waiting for us. But it is only rashness that
leads to a denial of the logic of imperatives (i.e., of prescriptions and
mandates). It would be more appropriate to hold that prescriptions and
mandates show that the inferential and the semantical approaches to
implication are not after all universally isomorphic.

In any case, prescriptions and mandates do have a "natural" order
determined by deducibility relationships, and we must study it if we

are to deepen our understanding of the structure of practical thinking.

As in the case of propositional deducibility, imperative deducibility depends on the logical forms of mandates or, rather, prescriptions. Thus, once again, we must keep in mind, as we learned in Chapter 3, that there is no general complete characterization of logical form in one piece. We must, therefore, study logical form by stages, each stage determining a layer of deducibility relationships. This is exactly as it should be, given what we know from Chapter 3 about propositional deducibility. Taking advantage of our study of propositional deducibility, we can distinguish right away three cumulative layers of deducibility:

(i)   the layer of *connective deducibility relationships,* i.e., relationships that depend solely upon the logical forms exemplified by mandates or prescriptions made up of nothing but components that are either whole prescriptions or mandates or whole propositions;

(ii)   the layer of *quantificational deducibility relationships,* i.e., relationships that depend upon connective forms and quantificational composition;

(iii) the layer of *identity deducibility relationships,* i.e., relationships that depend on principles of type (i) and (ii) as well as on principles governing identity.

We shall for convenience continue to sue the sign '⊢' to mean deducibility, and '$\frac{}{c}$' to mean connective deducibility. That is, '$\beta \frac{}{c} X$' means that X is deducible from the set β of noemata by the deducibility principles governing connections. For short, we may read '$\beta \frac{}{c} X$' as 'β c-implies X'.

3. THE INFERENTIAL APPROACH: PURE PRESCRIPTIVE COMPOUNDS

In Chapter 3, §6 and §12 we saw that ordinary English connectives have thematic and stylistic roles, besides their logical ones. Thus, there is reason to suppose that ordinary English connectives are not used indiscriminately to combine expressions of propositions and to combine expressions of mandates or prescriptions. The thematic or stylistic roles of the connectives may, expectably, prevent them from freely expressing logical form regardless of the type of components. Thus, as always, we must be very careful to distinguish the grammatical form of a sentence or clause from the logical form of what is expressed by that sentence or clause.

In consequence, in studying the deducibility of prescriptions it is a good tactical precept to concentrate our study during its initial stages on the ordinary English connectives that are thematically and stylistically as transparent as possible. This suggests that we should start by considering those English connectives that have the thematic role of putting, not one component, but the whole compound on the focus of attention. That is, we should start by examining the connectives with patterns of the form $(=, x)$, as given in the chart at the end of Chapter 3, §6. Hence, in accordance with Chapter 3, §7, we should not consider in our initial discussion the connectives for conditionality or biconditionality. Furthermore, because of the dialectical principles given in Chapter 3 §6, expressions of disjunction are dialectically restricted. Thus, we may profit by limiting the first round of our discussion of the fundamental deducibility principles governing prescriptions to the principles that determine the forms expressible with ordinary connectives like 'and' and 'not'. These connectives are as transparent as is possible both thematically and stylistically.

In the case of negation we must note that the primary connective 'it is not the case that', which most characteristically expresses propositional negation, does not express prescriptive or mandate negation. The most characteristic way of expressing imperative negation is the imperative prefix 'don't', as in 'Don't run', which is normally used to express the negation of the mandate expressed by 'run'. Thus, one of the primary English connectives for mandate negation is 'don't do the following', which, as the counterpart of 'the following is not the case', contains 'do the following' as the indicator of the largest scope of negation in the mandate in question. For example, consider

(1)   Mary and Paul, don't do (both of) the following: you, Mary, call Peter up when Martha arrives, and you, Paul, not call Aracelly up when Martha arrives.

Other primary English connectives that express mandate negation are 'fail to do the following', 'leave the following undone', and 'make sure that the following is not done'. Thus (1) may also be put as follows:

(1a)   Mary and Paul, make sure that the following is left undone:
that when Martha arrives Mary call Peter up, but Paul do
not call up Aracelly.

Naturally, the negative prefixes just discussed also express the overall
negation of the maximal prescription constituting the mandate whose
negation those prefixes help to formulate. Thus, we may analyze those
prefixes as having one component that is simply the overall negation of a
prescription. Such a component is, in the case of sentence (1), 'Mary and
Paul not do (both of) the following', and, in the case of (1a), it is 'Mary
and Paul make sure that the following is left undone', such components
patently lack the conjugated form of a main verb.

In the light of facts (A)–(D) discussed in §2 above we may frame the
hypothesis that imperative or prescriptional logic is parallel to propositional logic. Now, we have justified our initially limiting ourselves both
to the (=, x)-connectives expressing conjunction and to the connectives
expressing negation. Thus, our first task is simply to examine our ordinary
conception of the different types of mandates in order to determine
whether or not mandates and prescriptions abide by the seven principles of
deducibility D1–D7 given in Chapter 3 §13, which govern negation and
conjunction. Where X and Y are proposition and α and β sets of propositions, those principles are:

D1.   If X is in α, then $\alpha \left|_c - X\right.$:

If X is in α, then α c-implies X.

D2.   If $\alpha \left|_c - X\right.$, then $\alpha \left|_c - \sim\sim X\right.$:

If α c-implies X, then α c-implies
the double negation of X.

D3.   If $\alpha \left|_c - \sim X\right.$, then $\alpha \left|_c - \sim(X \& Y)\right.$.

D4.   If $\alpha \left|_c - \sim X\right.$, then $\alpha \left|_c - \sim(Y \& X)\right.$.

D3 and D4: If α c-implies the negation of X, then α c-implies
the negation of the conjunction of X with any
propositions Y, regardless of order.

D5.   If $\alpha \left|\frac{}{c}X\right.$, and $\beta \left|\frac{}{c}Y\right.$, then $\alpha, \beta \left|\frac{}{c}(X \& Y)\right.$:

If α c-implies X and β c-implies Y, then union
of α and β c-implies the conjunction of X and Y. (See
C21–C23 in Chapter 3, §12.)

D6.   If $\alpha, \sim X \left|\frac{}{c}Y\right.$ and $\alpha, X \left|\frac{}{c}Y\right.$, then $\alpha \left|\frac{}{c}Y\right.$:

If α and $\sim X$ c-imply Y and α and X c-imply Y, then
α alone c-implies Y.

D7.   If $\alpha \left|\frac{}{c}\sim(X \& \sim Y)\right.$, then $\alpha, X \left|\frac{}{c}Y\right.$:

If α c-implies the negation of the conjunction of X
and not-Y, then α and X together c-imply Y.

As explained in Chapter 3, §12 and §21 (which should be recalled), the
deducibility principles are correlated with principles of derived reasonableness of belief, or endorsement of noemata, in more general terms.
Reasonableness is not a psychological phenomenon, but a relational
property of states of endorsement, related to the deducibility connections
between the noemata the (possible) states of endorsement are about. The
idea is that the principles of, or intuitions about, the criticism of (possible)
states of endorsement of certain noemata reveal the deducibility connections between the noemata. Thus, reasonableness is not the same as,
or even the *ratio essendi* of, deducibility, but it is its *ratio cognoscendi*.
Let us apply this idea to mandates. Reader, therefore, mobilize your
intuitions concerning *your* implicit principles about what is warranted
criticism, both condemning and praising, of a person who endorses, even
issues sincerely, some mandates and refuses to endorse, or issue other
mandates, and there is no difference in circumstances, psychological or
physical, that are relevant, the *only* relevant thing being the actions
prescribed by the mandates in question. That is, the mandate endorser
is *just* motivated by the fulfillment of those mandates.

Suppose then that α is a set of mandates by a person to be called *Impera-
tor*. Clearly, if a mandate $*$Do A$*$ is in α, it would be most irrational of
Imperator to refuse to continue endorsing α while refusing to endorse
$*$Do A$*$, or, to continue to endorse α without refusing to endorse $*$Don't

do A∗. Thus, in the "natural" order of the reasonable endorsement of mandates and prescriptions, a set α containing a prescription or mandate X is *"prior" to X,* i.e., α c-implies X. Hence, we have:

D1.i.   If X is in α, then $\alpha \mathrel{\Big|_{c}} X$.

Consider now the unspecified order, where A is any prescription as complex as desired:

(2)   Mary and Paul, do the following: A.

Clearly, whoever endorses or issues (2) would act irrationally if he were to refuse to endorse or issue the corresponding counter-order:

(2a)   Mary and Paul, *don't* leave the following undone: A.

Hence, if endorsing certain prescriptions or mandates commits Imperator to (2), that endorsing commits him to (2a). Thus, letting $'x_1',\ldots,'x_n'$ represent the agents of a prescription represented by 'A', and taking

$'x_1,\ldots,x_n$, do A' as an abbreviation of
$'x_1,\ldots,x_n$, do the following: A',

we have, more generally, that:

D2.i.   If $\alpha \mathrel{\Big|_{c}} *x_1,\ldots,x_n$, do A∗,

then $\alpha \mathrel{\Big|_{c}} *x_1,\ldots,x_n$, don't fail to do A∗.

Suppose now that Imperator endorsingly issues the order ∗Smith, don't go home∗. He then is committed to, in the same sense of it being unreasonable for him to adhere to his previous endorsement and refuse endorsement of, the orders: ∗Smith, don't do the following: go home and talk to Mary∗, ∗Smith, don't do the following: go home and drive my car∗, ∗Smith, don't do the following: go home without driving my car∗, and, in general, any order of the form ∗Smith, don't do the following: go home and ...∗ as well as any order of the form ∗Smith, don't do the following: ..., but go home∗. Thus, we have for a normal sense of 'and' the imperative counterparts to D3 and D4:

D3.i.   If $\alpha \,\Big|_{c}\!\!-\! *x_1, ..., x_n$, don't do A*, then

$\qquad \alpha \,\Big|_{c}\!\!-\! *x_1, ..., x_n$, don't do (A and B)*.

D4.i.   If $\alpha \,\Big|_{c}\!\!-\! *x_1, ..., x_n$, don't do A*, then

$\qquad \alpha \,\Big|_{c}\!\!-\! *x_1, ..., x_n$, don't do (B and A)*.

Suppose that Imperator has issued two sets of orders α and β, that because of having issued α he is committed to order *Smith, clean up the kitchen*, and that because of having issued β he is committed to order *Jones, sweep the hall floor*. Then Imperator is committed to the conjunctive order *Smith, clean up the kitchen, and Jones, sweep the hall floor*. More generally:

D5.i.   If $\alpha \,\Big|_{c}\!\!-\! *x_1, ..., x_n$, do A* and $\beta \,\Big|_{c}\!\!-\! *y_1, ..., y_m$, do B*, then

$\qquad \alpha, \beta \,\Big|_{c}\!\!-\! *x_1, ..., x_n$, do A, and, $y_n, ..., y_m$, do B*.

Now let α be a set of orders issued by Imperator. Suppose that if Imperator were to add the negative order *Smith, don't go home* he would be committed to the order *Jones, read the *Bible**; suppose further that if he were to add to his set α the order *Smith, go home* he would *still* be committed to the order *Jones, read the *Bible**. Then, his order to Jones to read the *Bible* does not depend at all on what Imperator *demands* from Smith: he is committed to it even if he endorses no more orders. Then:

D6.i.   If $\alpha, *x_1, ..., x_n$, don't do A* $\Big|_{c}\!\!-\! *y_1, ..., y_m$, do B*, and

$\qquad \alpha, *x_1, ..., x_n$, do A* $\Big|_{c}\!\!-\! *y_n, ..., y_m$, do B*, then

$\qquad \alpha \,\Big|_{c}\!\!-\! *y_n, ..., y_m$, do B*.

Finally, suppose that Imperator is committed to, or has endorsed and issued, the order:

(3)   Smith, don't do the following: go home and fail to read.

Suppose that then Imperator issues the order *Smith, go home* as an addition to this repertoire of orders to Smith, or to a group of agents that includes Smith. Then, clearly, Imperator is committed to the order *Smith, read*. Since the *only* way for all of his orders to be fulfilled is that Smith reads when he is at home, it would be unreasonable for Imperator to stand pat on his actually issued orders and refuse to endorse, even issue if necessary, the order *Smith, read*. Then, more generally, for perfectly ordinary senses of English negative and conjunctive connectives:

D7.i.   If $\alpha \left|\dfrac{}{c}\right. *x$ and y, fail (x to do A and y not to do B)*, then

α, *x, do A* $\left|\dfrac{}{c}\right. *y$, do B*.

It appears, then, that mandates stand in exactly the same deducibility relations to other mandates of the same type, at least at the level of connective composition. Thus, the imperative ordinary connectives, 'don't (do the following)', 'leave the following undone', 'fail to (do the following)', and the simple 'not', all *qua* expressions of logical structure, have the same inferential properties possessed by their propositional counterparts 'It is not the case that', 'the following is not the case', and 'not'. The difference, then, between the two sets of negative connectives is not really a logical one, but a *thematic* one: they signal the presence of different types of content for psychological and linguistic operations. Hence, we can introduce a formal connective that simply expresses negation, regardless of the type of content to which it applies. For convenience we let the old sign '∼' be used to express the general form of negation, pure and naked.

The words 'but' and 'and' are already used in ordinary English to express a form of composition that has as elements propositions as well as mandates or propositions. Thus, we need not plead convenience or useful generalization in order to justify making '&' the formal connective that expresses mere conjunction, pure and naked, regardless of the types of the conjuncts.

In short, we extend the use of '$\sim$' and '&' in accordance with the following two rules:

R1.   A prescription X, determines uniquely the prescription $(\sim X)$, and vice versa; the latter is called *the negation* of the former.

R2.   A prescription X and a prescription Y uniquely determine the prescription $(X \,\&\, Y)$, and vice versa. The latter is called *the conjunction* of X and Y.

Evidently, then, conjunction and negation are, in their more general sense, characterized as forms of composition not only by the propositional principles of deducibility listed in Chapter 3, §13, but also by the prescriptional counterparts of such principles, D1.i–D7.i.

Before leaving pure prescriptive compounds we must consider disjunctions of prescriptions or mandates. First of all, we have the rule

R3.   A prescription X and a prescription Y uniquely determine the prescription $(X \lor Y)$, and vice versa, which is called *the disjunction* of X and Y.

Now, in the case of propositions, the crucial principle linking disjunction to conjunction is

D8. $(X \lor Y)$ is equivalent to $(\sim((\sim X) \,\&\, (\sim Y)))$.

It is readily seen that mandates and prescriptions conform to their counterpart of D8. The following obviously valid imperative inferences and their converses illustrate that counterpart of D8 as well as its variations in the light of the principle of double negation:

(3)   John, don't both fail to do A and fail to do B.
       Hence, John, do A or do B.
(4)   Mary, neither drink nor smoke.
       Hence, Mary, don't drink or smoke.
(5)   Luke, work hard, but don't quit.
       Hence, Luke, don't do the following: fail to work hard or quit.

It would be unreasonable for anyone to endorse the premise of (3) or (4) or (5) while refusing to endorse the corresponding conclusion, and vice versa. Thus, for prescriptions and mandates we have, then:

D8.i. $(X \vee Y)$ is equivalent to $(\sim((\sim X) \ \& \ (\sim Y)))$.

Because the expressions of conditionality never have the thematic pattern $(=, x)$ of Chapter 3, §6, we cannot proceed immediately to a discussion of the prescriptive counterparts of the conditional and biconditional propositional principles D9 and D10 formulated in Chapter 3, §13.

4. THE INFERENTIAL APPROACH: CONDITIONAL MANDATES

As noted above, we use very much the same words to express inferential logical connections, regardless of whether the connective compound formed with such connections are propositions or mandates. We also noted that a characteristic expression of imperative negation is 'don't (do the following)', since the characteristic expression for propositional negation, 'it is not the case that', cannot, *grammatically,* be employed to form a sentence formulating a negative mandate by prefixing it to a sentence in the imperative mood. The results of such prefixings are not genuine sentences of English, as, for instance 'It is not the case that John, go home'. This fact about imperative sentences is only a special case of a general grammatical fact of great significance[6]:

(M.G)   Ordinary sentences formulating mandates are never what grammarians call subordinate clauses.

As a consequence of (M.G), English connectives ending in 'that' (like the negative connective 'it is not the case that', the conditional connective 'provided that', and the biconditional connective 'in case, and only in case, that') cannot be prefixed to sentences formulating mandates. Likewise, none of the expressions grammarians call subordinating conjunctions or adverbs (like 'that' itself, 'if', and 'only if', 'when', 'where', etc.), or relative pronouns (like 'which', 'who', 'what', etc.) can be prefixed to a sentence formulating an imperative. Again, the results of such prefixings are not genuine sentences of English, as the following examples illustrate: 'If Peter, go home, then it is raining', 'That is the house where Peter, go in', and 'Peter, who, go home, is drunk'. Since the English words that form ordinary conditional sentences, with the exception of 'then', are all subordinating expressions, (M.G) leads to the interesting result that

(M.G1) All conditional mandates formulated by means of a gram-
          matically conditional sentence are mixed compounds: one
          component is a mandate, the other is a statement.

(M.G) and (M.G1) suggest that the logic of imperatives is deficient,
as compared with the logic of propositions, in that not all possible types
of connective composition are present among compound mandates. This
suggestion cannot, however, be conclusively established. The reason for
this lies on the fact that ordinary connectives perform many different roles
at the same time, as we discussed in Chapter 3, §6 and §7. It cannot be
conclusively shown that these other roles are the ones that make them
inapplicable to imperative sentences, or, in general, to prescription-
(or mandate-) formulating sentences or clauses.

At the level of mixed combinations of mandates and propositions there
is a question about the character of such hybrid combinations. In purely
abstract terms one may suppose that there are in the metaphysical realm:

(i)   mixed compounds which as wholes are mandates or pres-
         criptions;
(ii)   mixed compounds which as wholes are propositions and
(iii)   mixed compounds which as wholes are neither prescriptions
         nor propositions.

Certainly ordinary language could in principle have had all kinds of connective expressions performing the two roles (besides others, in all
probability): (a) of indicating the type of connection of given mixed
compounds, and (b) of indicating the type of content of cognition to which
a given mixed compound belongs. However, for some reason which we
cannot go into here, but which is also philosophically (or metaphysically)
important, *human beings in their normal lives are not interested in (ii)
or in (iii)*. Here we have both an interesting metaphysical discovery and
a very important problem for *philosophical anthropology*. The discovery
consists of finding that there are forms of mixed composition of prescriptions and propositions not given to our ordinary and practical consciousness, as this consciousness is organized through our use of ordinary
language. The problem for philosophical anthropology is that of accounting
why ordinary human consciousness deals only with compounds of type (i),
but not of types (ii) or (iii). The answer lies in the logico-psychological
primacy of practical reason over pure reason mentioned on page 8.

At any rate, a full and exciting life can, apparently, be lived by dealing only with mixed proposition-prescription compounds which are prescriptions. Thus, ordinary language has just the mechanisms for formulating compound statements, compound pure mandates, and mixed compounds which are as wholes mandates. This mechanism consists primarily of (M.G), which insures that ordinary sentences formulating mixed compounds formulate mandates, not statements or something else. Thus, (M.G) is the fundamental clue for principle (M.R):

(M.R) A connective compound with a mandate (or prescription) as component is itself a mandate (or prescription).

But clearly (M.R) is the rationale for (M.G), given that our conceptual and linguistic frameworks embody fact (i), and not facts (ii) or (iii).

In particular, as we know from Chapter 3, §7, ordinary conditional words do not merely serve to express logical conditionalization. They also serve, *thematically,* to pinpoint the content in which we are more interested, namely, the content for which we want to formulate necessary or sufficient conditions. This role of flagging the primary object of a person's attention has nothing to do with the mere logical form of the content in question. This explains in part, why, as we discussed in Chapter 3, §7, natural languages have two sets of terms, like 'if' and 'only if', to express conditionalization: sometimes we are primarily interested in the antecedent of a conditional assertion, and express this by flagging the consequent through prefixing 'only if' to it; other times we are primarily interested in the consequent, and to express this we flag the antecedent by prefixing 'if' to it. The point, then, that (M.R) and (M.G) bring home is simply that human beings, who are primarily agents in, and only derivatively contemplators of, the universe, are fundamentally concerned with actions. Thus, prescriptions and mandates are mixed compounds. Mandates, we shall say, are never conditioned, but always *conditioning* components. Yet they can be antecedent (as in *Only if he comes, give him this book*) as well as consequents (as in *If he comes, give him this book*).

In sum, ordinary English conditional words do not allow us to express with their help purely imperative conditionals, simply because they perform a thematic role that has nothing to do with the form conditionalization. From this, nevertheless, it does not follow that there cannot be a *mere* conditional whose antecedent and consequent are both mandates. It only follows that purely imperative conditionals are *inexpressible* by the traditional simple conditional signs available to ordinary language. Now, in Chapter 3, §5 we introduced the sign ' ⊃ ' to represent conditionalization bare and clean; and we characterized conditionalization by the fact that a conditional proposition (say, *If he comes he will see you*) is logically, though not thematically, equivalent to a disjunction (in this case, *(Either he will not come or he will see you)*) and to a negated conjunction (here *It is not the case that he will come but not see you*). These equivalences are for the case of propositions the crucial part of *one* of the logical meanings of 'if' and 'only if' that ' ⊃ ' represents. Similarly, ' ⊃ ' represents the part of the meaning of these words that, for the case of mixed conditionals, is characterized by the logical, though not thematic, equivalence of, say, *If he comes, give him this book* both to *(Either he won't come, or give him this book* and to *Don't do the following: while it is the case that he comes you not give him this book*. Thus, there is no disortion of ordinary language at all if, in *supplementing* it, we allow ourselves to speak of a purely imperative conditional like *(X, go home) ⊃ (Y, go with him)*, equivalent to *X, don't go home, or Y, go with him*. We must, of course, be careful to add that this use of ' ⊃ ', as a *mere* sign of conditionalization, cannot be translated into ordinary English conditioning expressions. Here is the culmination of the thematic neutrality of ' ⊃ ', discussed in Chapter 3, §6 and §7, by virtue of which ' ⊃ ' *is an important addition to ordinary language,* rather than a mere abbreviation of, or regimentation of one meaning of, 'if'. We shall, therefore, consider such purely imperative conditionals on a par with ordinary mixed conditionals and with conditional propositions. We have, then, the important rule:

R4. A prescription X and a prescription Y determine uniquely their *conditional* prescription $(X \supset Y)$, with X as antecedent and Y as consequent.

We conclude, then, that given the thematic and stylistic roles of ordinary conditional connectives, the greater combinatorial freedom of the negative disjunctive and conjunctive connectives does make them the fundamental connectives, as we pointed out at the end of Chapter 3, §7. This is an important point that really jumps into view in the field of imperative logic. Thus, as we have just seen, the imperative counterpart of deducibility principle D9 given in Chapter 3, §13 holds trivially:

D9.i. $(X \supset Y)$ is equivalent to $(\sim((X \;\&\; (\sim Y)))$.

Now, the biconditional connectives 'if and only if', 'in case that and only in case that', 'if ... and vice versa', 'if ... and conversely', etc. convert wholly naturally into a compound of conjunctive and conditional connectives. Thus, it is immediately apparent that rule R5 and the imperative counterpart of D10 hold:

R5.　　A prescription X and a prescription Y uniquely determine the biconditional $(X \equiv Y)$.

D10.i.　$(X \equiv Y)$ is equivalent to $((X \supset Y) \;\&\; (Y \supset X))$.

5. THE INFERENTIAL APPROACH: GENERAL AND MIXED CONNECTIVE MANDATES

In §4 we recognized principle (M.R), according to which a mixed connective compound one component of which is a prescription or a mandate, is itself a prescription or a mandate. This requires that we discuss the deducibility principles governing mixed mandates or prescriptions. Fortunately, a simple examination of examples shows that mixed deducibility is governed by principles exactly analogous to D1–D10, that govern propositions, and D1.i–D10.i that govern pure prescriptions and mandates. To start with, we must take note of principle (M.R), which governs *our* conceptual framework. Since we are considering conjunction as the primitive binary connective, we need only

R6.　　A proposition X and a prescription Y determine uniquely the mixed prescriptions: $(X \;\&\; Y)$ and $(Y \;\&\; X)$; $(X \vee Y)$ and $(Y \vee X)$; $(X \supset Y)$ and $(Y \supset X)$, and $(X \equiv Y)$ and $(Y \equiv X)$. The latter also determine uniquely their components as the proposition X and the prescription Y.

We shall not bother to discuss the metaphysically interesting connectives mentioned in (ii) and (iii) in §4 above, which yield from prescriptions and propositions, either mixed propositions or a new type of noema that is neither proposition nor prescription. Given the fact that our ordinary conceptual framework excludes these two types of mixed connective compounds, we may simply regard these types as of mere marginal importance in our study of the logical structure of practical thinking.

We must, therefore proceed to formulate the deducibility principles that govern our generalized logical connections. We introduce asterisks as superscripts to indicate that we are dealing with either propositions or prescriptions (or mandates), as the case may be.

> Let $\alpha*$ and $\beta*$ be sets (possibly empty) of just propositions, or just mandates, or both. Let $X*$ and $Y*$ each be either a proposition or a mandate. Then the general inferential connections are characterized by the following general deducibility principles:

D*1.   If $X*$ is in $\alpha*$, then $\alpha* \vdash_c X*$.

D*2.   If $\alpha* \vdash_c X*$, then $\alpha* \vdash_c {\sim} X*$.

D*3.   If $\alpha* \vdash_c {\sim} X*$, then $\alpha* \vdash_c {\sim}(X* \,\&\, Y*)$.

D*4.   If $\alpha* \vdash_c Y$, then $\alpha* \vdash_c {\sim}(X* \,\&\, Y*)$.

D*5.   If $\alpha* \vdash_c X*$ and $\beta \vdash_c Y*$,

then $\alpha*,\, \beta* \vdash_c (X \,\&\, Y*)$.

D*6.   If $\alpha*,\, {\sim} X* \vdash_c Y*$, and $\alpha*,\, X* \vdash_c Y*$, then $\alpha* \vdash_c Y*$.

D*7.   If $\alpha* \vdash_c {\sim}(X* \,\&\, {\sim} Y*)$, then $\beta*,\, X* \vdash_c Y*$.

D*8. $(X* \lor Y*)$ is equivalent to $({\sim}(({\sim} X*) \,\&\, ({\sim} Y*)))$.

D*9. $(X* \supset Y*)$ is equivalent to $({\sim}(X* \,\&\, ({\sim} Y*)))$.

D*10. $(X* \equiv Y*)$ is equivalent to $((X* \supset Y*) \,\&\, (Y* \supset X*))$.

We have already encountered examples of these principles for the special cases D1–D10 and D1.i–D10.i. As a matter of fact, we have already confronted some mixed cases. Clearly, D*1 has a mixed application only if α* is a set of mandates. By (M.R) in §4, if α* is just a set of propositions, then no component of those propositions is a mandate.

*D*3 and D*4*:

(i) If mandate *X, don't do A* is deducible from a set α* of mandates and propositions endorsed by Imperator, then obviously, it would be unreasonable for Imperator to continue endorsing α* and to refuse to endorse each of the following mandates:

> X, don't do A while it is the case that it has rained;
> X, don't while it is not raining, do A;
> X, don't do the following: while it is the case that p do A;
> X, leave the following undone: A while it is not the case that p;
> X, don't make it the case that both it is the case that p and you do A.

(ii) Let the proposition *It is not raining* be deducible from a set α* of mandates and propositions endorsed by Imperator. Then it would be unreasonable for Imperator to continue to endorse α* while refusing to endorse each of the following mandates:

> X, don't do the following: A while it is raining;
> X, don't make it the case that both it is raining and you do A;

*D*5*:

Let Imperator endorse a set α* from which the mandate *X, do A* is deducible, and let him endorse also a set β* from which the proposition that p is deducible. Then it would be unreasonable for Imperator to continue endorsing both sets α* and β* while refusing to endorse each of the following:

> X, do A it being the case that p;
> X, do the following: while it is the case that p do A.

*D*6*:

(i) If endorsing both α* and a mandate *X, do A* commits a person to the proposition that p, and so does commit him endorsing both α* and the corresponding mandate *X, don't do A*, then the endorsements of the mandates in question are irrelevant to the person's commitment to the p once he endorses $\alpha*$.

(ii) Let a person be committed to endorsing a mandate Y by endorsing a set $\alpha*$ of amandates and propositions, whether he endorses also a proposition that p or the proposition that not-p. Then simply endorsing $\alpha*$ commits that person to Y.

$D*7$:

(i) Let Imperator be endorsing a set $\alpha*$ of mandates and propositions, which endorsement commits him to endorsing the mandate

X, don't run in the rain.

Clearly, if Imperator also endorses $*X$, run$*$ while continue endorsing $\alpha*$, then he is committed to endorsing, i.e., believing that it is not raining (or that it will not rain). In general endorsing $*X$, don't do the following: A while it is not the case that $p*$ commits one to endorsing that p if one also endorses $*X$, do A$*$.

(ii) Endorsing $*X$, don't do the following: not A while it is the case that $p*$ commits one to endorsing $*X$, do A$*$ if one also endorses $*$It is the case that $p*$.

$D*8$:

Evidently, the imperative $*X$, go unless he comes$*$ or $*$Either he comes, or X, you better go$*$, putting aside thematic, stylistic and dialectic features, demands essentially the same as the mandate $*X$, don't do the following: fail to go while (it is the case that) he does not come$*$.

$D*9$:

$*X$, if he came the week before, signal$*$, again ignoring thematic, stylistic and dialectic features, demands the essentially same mandate as $*X$, don't make it the case that both you don't signal and he came the week before$*$ and as $*X$, don't do the following: that while it is the case that he came the week before you fail to signal$*$.

$D*10$:

Obviously, $*X$, do A if and only if $p*$ demands very much the same as $*X$, do A if p, and do it only if $p*$, when 'p' represents the same proposition throughout and 'X' the same agent(s).

6. The semantics of imperative logic: the values of prescriptions

In Chapter 3, §14 we saw that for the case of propositions the deducibility principles D1–D10 yield a system of implications, equivalences and logical truths that is isomorphic to the semantical system characterized by the two-valued truth-tables discussed in Chapter 3, §5. Hence, *the deducibility principles D*1–D*10 also yield a system that is isomorphic to the two — valued system characterized by the truth-tables of Chapter 3, §5.* Clearly, it makes no difference whether we call the values in question 'T' and 'F', or '1' and '0', or any other names. Thus, if we continue to take D*8–D*10 as primary characterizations of the meanings of our general connectives '~', '&', '∨', '⊃' and '≡', then the primary two-valued tables that correspond to D*1–D*7, where '1' represents the designated values and '0' the undesignated ones, are:

p*	~p*	p*,	q*	(p* & q*)
1	0	1	1	1
0	1	1	0	0
		0	1	0
		0	0	0

The Value-tables corresponding to D*8–D*10 are:

p*,	q*	p* ∨ q*	p* ⊃ q*	p* ≡ q*
1	1	1	1	1
1	0	1	0	0
0	1	1	1	0
0	0	0	1	1

This is an extremely important result. *We can test inferences involving prescriptions or mandates by using the ordinary truth-tables.* We simply use '1' for 'T' and '0' for 'F', and all the definitions and principles developed in Chapter 3 apply to the general logic of prescriptions and propositions. That is, we can save a lot of space and time by merely reinterpreting Chapter 3 in the new generalized way: we supply all the symbols for propositions with an asterisk and read *'T' as the designated value, whatever it may be, and 'F' as the undesignated value, whatever it may be.*

Doubtless, there is a tremendous computational advantage in knowing that the truth-table technique can be applied to ascertaining whether sets of mandates or prescriptions stand in deducibility relationships. But the truth-table technique raises a serious philosophical problem, namely: *What exactly are the meanings of '1' and '0' when these are applied to prescriptions or to mandates?* It is perfectly clear that when they are correlated with a proposition '1' means 'true' and '0' means 'false'; but we simply have no idea at all at this juncture as to what these marks can mean when they are correlated with non-compound prescriptions.

Nevertheless, we must reckon with these most important facts: (1) mandates and prescriptions *do* stand in deducibility relationships; (2) these deducibility relationships are, at the basic layer of connective inference, governed by principles D*1–D*10; (3) these principles determine a two-valued structure for propositions and *for mandates;* (4) this two-valued structure includes as a special case the two-truth-valued structure of propositions; (5) this two-truth-valued structure of propositions is precisely what justifies or accounts for the fact that our propositional inferences are governed by the propositional principles D1–D10, and, *a fortiori,* by the general principles D*1–D*10. Thus, if we are, as we ought, to provide an account of why our imperative inferences are governed by principles D*1–D*10, we must acknowledge that: (6) *prescriptions and mandates have ontological, or "semantical" values that are formally, logically exactly analogous to truth-values.*

On the one hand, inasmuch as, according to facts (A)–(D) of §2, there are valid and invalid inferences that involve mandates and, hence, prescriptions, there is a prescriptional value analogous to truth, i.e., a value of prescriptions that enters in a valid imperative inference in exactly the way in which truth enters in a valid propositional inference. That is:

Presc. 11. Some prescriptions have a preferred value that is preserved by deducibility; that is, if $\alpha \left|\frac{}{c}\right. X$, then if all the propositions in α are true and all the prescriptions in α have that prescriptional preferred value, then X has that value, too.

On the other hand, inasmuch as deducibility principles D∗1–D∗10 yield a two-valued tabular system, we also have:

> *Pres. 12.* Prescriptions are logico-ontologically two-valued: those that lack the preferred value have one and the same non-preferred value.

We know that the full analysis of truth is an extremely complicated matter. There is no reason to suppose that the full analysis of the prescriptional preferred value is any easier. For one thing, prescriptions presuppose propositions. A prescription can be understood only as depending on facts and as pointing to facts, the latter being the ones corresponding to it, namely, the facts that exist if and only if the prescription is fulfilled. Fortunately, for the study, in this chapter, of the logical properties of prescriptional inference we do not need an analysis of prescriptional "semantical" values. However, in order to account for the fact that imperative inferences are governed by principles D∗1–D∗10 we must acknowledge that the preferred value of prescriptions mentioned in *Presc. 11* is also the analogue of truth with respect to mental operations:

> *Presc. 13.* The prescriptional value preserved by deducibility is also psychologically the preferred value: thinking beings are interested in endorsing prescriptions that have that value.

As in the case of truth, as a summary way of referring to the logical and psychological preferred character mentioned in *Pres. 11* and *Presc. 13,* we shall say that the prescriptional truth analogue is the *designated prescriptional semantical value.* Now, for reasons that will become apparent in the next chapter, ordinary language has no words that predicate the semantical values of prescriptions in the characteristic clear way in which 'true' and 'false' predicate the semantical values of propositions. We shall use the words 'Legitimate' and 'Non legitimate', with capital letters, in a new technical sense, to predicate, respectively, the designated and the undesignated prescriptional values. *These capitalized words are not applicable to events or objects or persons, but only to prescriptions and mandates.* Perhaps the words *'orthotic'* and *'anorthotic'* (from the Ancient Greek ὀρθότης = correctness, rightness, upright standing) can prevent confusion, given that they are not ordinary English words with different meanings ready at hand. Indeed, we shall use them, too, for that very reason. Thus, we shall speak of *Legitimacy* or of *orthotes,* and of *Non-legitimacy* or of *anorthotes.*

Given that we handle prescriptions, i.e., that we endorse them and issue mandates, and that our handling of prescriptions is not necessarily empty, it is necessary that sometimes we issue mandates on the expectation or hope that they will be fulfilled, but with no logical guarantee that they will in fact be fulfilled. Thus, however orthotes is to be analyzed, it is immediately clear that:

> *Presc. 14.* The orthotes (or Legitimacy) of a prescription X and of a mandate M fully constituted by X is generally independent of the truth of the proposition $c(X)$ corresponding to X. That is, we do not have
>
> $c(X) \left|_{c} X \right.$ or $X \left|_{c} c(X)\right.$ for every arbitrarily chosen proposition X.

In the next chapter we develop an account of orthotic values that satisfy the above criteria *Presc. 11–Presc. 14.*

7. GENERAL AND CONNECTIVE NOEMATIC IMPLICATION AND TAUTOLOGIES

As we said above, every single principle and definition developed in Chapter 3 allows of a prescriptional–propositional generalization. We shall not carry out this generalization in detail, but limit ourselves to introducing the fundamental definitions of 'connective implication' and 'tautology'. After that we shall regard ourselves justified in applying all the principles of Chapter 3 to propositions as well as to prescriptions and mandates.

(G.1∗) A set $\alpha*$ of noemata *implies* a noema $Y*$, i.e., $\alpha* \vDash Y*$ if and only if for some natural number n there are noemata $X_1*, ..., X_n*$ in $\alpha*$ such that the conjunctive noema $X_1* \& ... \& X_n* \& \sim Y*$ has a logical form every instance of which has an undesignated value.

(G.1∗.t) A set $\alpha*$ of noemata *tautologically implies* a noema $Y*$, i.e., $\alpha* \left|_{t} \right.$, if and only if there are noemata $X_1*, ..., X_n*$ in $\beta*$ such that the conjunctive noema $X_1* \& ... \& X_n* \& \sim Y*$ has a logical form with a value-table whose last column has only undesignated values.

(G.E∗) A noema X∗ is *semantically equivalent to,* or co-implies, a noema Y∗, i.e., X∗|=|Y∗, if and only if X∗ ⊨ Y∗ and Y∗ ⊨ X∗.

(G.E.∗.t) A noema X∗ is *tautologically equivalent* to a noema Y∗,

X∗ $\left|\underset{t}{=}\right.$ Y∗, if and only if X∗ $\left|\underset{t}{=}\right.$ Y∗ and Y∗ $\left|\underset{t}{=}\right.$ X∗.

(LD∗) A noema X∗ is *logically designated* (or *logically valid*), i.e., ⊨ X∗, if and only if it has a logical form ϕ such that every noema of form ϕ has a designated value.

(LD∗.t) A noema X∗ is *tautological,* or a *tautology,* i.e., $\left|\underset{t}{=}\right.$ X∗, if and only if X∗ has a connective form all instances of which have a designated value.

(G.R∗) A reasoning R is *formally valid* if and only if the set of the premises of R implies the conclusion of R.

8. IMPERATIVE QUANTIFICATION

In §1 we have argued for a fundamental difference between propositions and prescriptions (and, hence, mandates). We pointed out the ontological simplicity of the prescriptional copulation view, and we opted for it. According to it a prescription of the form ∗X do A∗ differs from the corresponding proposition ∗X does A∗ in that the predicate ∗doing A∗ relates to the agent X in a different way; i.e., they differ in the copulation of subject and predicate. Thus, besides propositional functions, studied in Chapter 3 §§18–22, there are, then, *prescriptional functions.*

Let us start by appropriating an official canonical notation that reveals the different logical structures of prescriptions and propositions as different copulative mechanisms. We adopt the notation suggested in §1, which tallies with the propositional notation introduced in Chapter 3, §§19–20. We continue to use parentheses to indicate propositional copulation, and we shall use square brackets to signal prescriptional copulation. Consider ∗Karl, kick Paul∗. We represent the prescription at the core of this mandate as ∗Kick [Karl, Paul]∗, we distinguish that prescription from the reverse prescription ∗Paul to kick Karl∗, by the usual convention of putting the agents earlier on in the copulative schemata '[...]' and '(...)'. Since the agents enter as constituents of both the prescription, or prescriptional function, and the corresponding prop-

osition, or propositional function, the role of agency is sufficiently
signaled in both by the order of the copulative *n*-tuple.

Some actions have several agents. Consider, for instance, the door to
the treasury vault of a bank that can be opened only by the simultaneous
turning of several keys by the manager, the assistant manager and the
purser of the bank. In this case the action of opening that door has three
agents and one object. Hence, the prescription issued by the manager
when he gives the orders *Jim [the manager] and Paul [the purser], let
us open the door* is the prescription *Open [I, Jim, Paul; the door]*.

We have then a canonical notation for the copulative prescriptive
functions, which parallels copulative propositional functions. Patently
our discussion of general propositions in Chapter 3, §18 extends rather
trivially to general prescriptions. Given a prescriptive function *x do
write*, which is the same as *Write [x]*, we have instantiational prescriptions like *John to write* and *The man with the red coat to write*. We
also have the existential prescription *Someone to write* and the universal prescription *Everybody to write*. The former is *∃x write [x]*,
while the latter is *∀ x write [x]*.

Recall from Chapter 3, §6 that philosophers have argued that the
connectives 'and', 'but', 'or', etc. have one meaning when they link
sentences expressing propositions and another meaning when they link
imperative sentences. Likewise some philosophers might argue that the
quantifiers do not mean the same in 'Everybody, go home' and 'Everybody went (or will go) home'. We do not think this view is correct, but
even if it were correct the difference in meaning would be amply indicated
by the context.

Actually, the logical, formal meaning of the quantifiers is given by
rules D11–D13 in Chapter 3, §21 above. These are, where again '$\alpha \left|\frac{}{q}\right. x$'
means that x is quantificationally deducible from α:

D11. $(\forall x\phi)\left|\frac{}{q}\right.\psi$,

D12.   If $\alpha\left|\frac{}{q}\right.\psi$, then $\alpha\left|\frac{}{q}\right.(\forall x\phi)$,
        where ψ and ϕ satisfy the conditions for D11 or D12 given
        on p. 89.

D13. $(\exists x\phi)$ is quantifically equivalent to $(\sim\forall x\sim\phi)$.

As explained in Chapter 3, §12 and §21, deducibility is a natural order of propositions with respect to what is reasonable, or what is unreasonable, for a reasoning truth-oriented creature to endorse or not to endorse.

Now, if a man issues a universal order or request *Everybody, do A* it would be most unreasonable for him to refuse to endorse (whether he issues it or not) the order or request *John, do A* if he believes that John is in the universe of discourse of his mandate. Whoever endorses a universal prescription would be most unreasonable if he did not endorse the prescriptional function involved, so that he would be ready to endorse the prescriptions that instantiate that function. Thus, the prescriptional counterpart of D11 holds.

Evidently, the prescriptional counterpart of D12 also holds. Whoever would be unreasonable by refusing to endorse a prescriptional function, because he endorses a set α of prescriptions, would be unreasonable were he to refuse the corresponding universalization as long as he continues endorsing set α.

The prescriptional counterpart of D13 is marvelously illustrated by the equivalence of the following mandate forms:

(1)   Everybody, do A.
(2)   Don't, anybody, do the following: fail to do A.
(3)   Nobody do the following: fail to do A.

In short, just as in §7 we found the generalized inferential principles D*1–D*10 that govern logical connections in their stark formality, we must now set forth the distilled formality of the primary quantifiers by means of the principles D*11–D*13. All we need do is to read D11–D13 in Chapter 3, §21 as having $\phi*$ and $\psi*$ instead of ϕ and ψ. As a consequence of D*11–D*13 the following inference is deductively valid:

A.   John, open the door.
       Hence, someone, open the door.

Some philosophers[7] have objected to A. Indeed, it would be rather silly for a person to issue an order *John, open the door* and then issue the order *Someone, open the door*. His second utterance may suggest a change of mind. It can be safely said that there is a certain impropriety in drawing inference A for the benefit of an audience. But this impropriety is dialectical; it depends exclusively on the purpose of communication. It has nothing to do with the logical correctness of the inference. This is evident from the fact that the corresponding propositional inference agreed to be valid by the greatest majority of people, also suffers from a dialectical impropriety. If a man predicts *John will return* to an audience disputing about John's sudden departure, it would be very silly for the predictor to go on to say *Somebody will return*. Since the issue is about John and John alone, the weak statement *Somebody will return* is too mild to be nearly irrelevant. This is exactly what happens to the general mandate *Someone, open the door*; it is nearly irrelevant once the actual *issuing* of the mandate *John, open the door* has settled the question about the agent of the opening of the door. But both in the case of propositions and in the case of prescriptions the silliness of the utterance or of the making of the inference depends on the previous *act* of asserting the premise. This has nothing to do with the validity or formal correctness of the inference. It is simply a matter of the dialectical rule, enunciated in Chapter 3, §6:

Dial 1.   For more effective communication always make as strong an assertion as you can.

Now, recall the coincidence of deducibility and implication, discussed in Chapter 3, §14 and §22. Recall that in §6 above we have already taken advantage of that coincidence to introduce the values Legitimacy (L) and Non-legitimacy (N), analogous to truth-values, which govern prescriptional implication. Thus, there are the prescriptional counterparts of the truth principles (T.17) and (T.18) presented in Chapter 3, §19. They are these:

Convention: U is the universe of discourse presupposed by the quantifiers; 'A[x]' is a sentential function expressing a prescriptive function and having one or more occurrences of empty positions indicated by 'x'; 'A[a]' expresses the prescription which is an instantiation of A[x] that has in the x-positions the constituent denoted by 'a'.

(QJ.1)   *∀xA[x]* is L, i.e., has the prescriptive designated value, if and only if for every member a of U *A(a)* is L.

(QJ.2) $*\exists xA[x]*$ is L if and only if for some member a of U
$*A[a]*$ is L.

9. SET-THEORETICAL MODELS FOR PRESCRIPTIONAL-PROPOSITIONAL SYSTEMS

It has emerged from the preceding examination of the structure of prescriptional implication that that structure is quite parallel to that of propositional implication. Thus, the discussion of logical validity by means of set-theoretical models outlined in Chapter 3 §20 needs but minor modifications to be applicable to quantificational systems of both propositions and prescriptions. For the sake of brevity we simply list the emendations to Chapter 3 §20.

First, the characterization of predicate formulas in Chapter 3 §20 is the characterization of propositional predicate formulas. We consider two kinds of individuals: objects, and agents; and we also consider two kinds of predicate variables: the *ordinary* ones, which are divided into n-adic degrees, one degree for each number $n = 1, 2, ...$, and *actional* predicates, which are divided into $(r+m)$-adic degrees, one for each pair (r, m), for $r, m = 1, 2, ...$

Second, we characterize basic prescriptional predicate formulas as sequences of symbols of the form $g[x_1, ..., x_r; y_1 ... y_m]$, where g is a predicate variable of degree $r+m$, and $x_1, ... x_n$ are names of agents or are agential variables; and $y_1, ... y_m$ are names or individual variables, whether agential or objectual. Molecular prescriptional predicate formulas are sequences of symbols of the forms $(\sim\phi)$, $(\phi \& \psi)$, $(\phi \vee \psi)$, $(\phi \supset \psi)$, and $(\phi \equiv \psi)$, where either both ϕ and ψ are prescriptional or one is prescriptional and the other a propositional predicate formula. Quantified prescriptional formulas are sequences of symbols of the form $(\forall x\phi)$ and $(\exists x\phi)$, where ϕ is a prescriptional predicate formula.

Third, we characterize predicate formulas, thus: a predicate formula is either a propositional predicate formula or a prescriptional predicate formula.

Fourth, the definitions of bound and free variables remain, as given in Chapter 3, §20.

Fifth, a model for a prescriptional language is an ordered quintuple $\langle D, A, S, R, P \rangle$, where D is a non-empty domain of objects; A, a set of agents, is a subset of D; S is a non-empty set of sets of ordered n-tuples of D, for $n = 1, 2, \ldots$; R and P are not necessarily different non-empty sets of ordered pairs $\langle a, d \rangle$, where a is an r-tuple of members of A and d is an m-tuple of members of D, for $r, m = 1, 2, \ldots$

Sixth, an interpretation i of a set α of predicate formulas on a model $\langle D, A, S, R, P \rangle$ is: (1) an assignment of a member $i(x)$ of D to each name or free individual variable x occurring in at least one member of α; (2) an assignment of an n-adic member $i(f)$ of S to each ordinary n-adic predicate variable f occurring in at least one formula in α; (3) an assignment of a member $i(a)$ of A to each agent name or agent individual variable a occurring in at least one formula in α; (4) an assignment of both an $(r+m)$-adic member $i(g)$ of R and an $(r+m)$-adic member $i[g]$ of P to each $(r+m)$-adic actional predicate variable occurring in at least one member of α.

Seventh, we must take 'T' as meaning *designated value,* and 'F' as meaning *undesignated value.*

Eighth, the definition of valuation needs two new clauses, namely:

2a. v assigns T to an atomic predicate formula ψ of the form $g(x_1, \ldots, x_r; y_1, \ldots, y_m)$, if and only if the ordered $(r+m)$-tuple $\langle \langle i(x_1), \ldots, i(x_r) \rangle, \langle i(y_1), \ldots, i(y_m) \rangle \rangle$ belongs to $i(g)$. Otherwise, v assigns F to ψ.

2b. v assigns T to an atomic predicate formula of the form $g[x_1, \ldots x_r; y_1, \ldots, y_m]$, if and only if $\langle \langle i(x_1), \ldots i(x_r) \rangle, \langle i(y_1), \ldots, i(y_m) \rangle \rangle$ belongs to $i[g]$.

Every other definition or characterization remains the same as it is in Chapter 3, §20.

NOTES TO CHAPTER 4

[1] J. L. Austin, for instance, so claims in 'Performative-Constative' in Charles E. Caton (ed.), *Philosophy and Ordinary Language* (Urbana, Illinois: University of Illinois Press, 1963). On page 23 we read: "to say 'I promise to...' – to issue, as we say, this performative utterance – *just* [my italics] *is* the act of making a promise; not, as we see, at all a mysterious act. And it may seem at once quite obvious that an utterance of this kind can't be true or false – notice that I say it can't *be* true or false, because it may very well *imply* that *some* other propositions are true or false, but that, if I'm not mistaken, is a quite different matter". On page 31 we find: "Let us suppose that I say to you 'I advise you to do it'; and let us allow that all the circumstances are appropriate, the conditions for success are fulfilled. In saying that, I actually do advise you to do it – it is not that I *state*, truly or falsely, *that* I advise you". Note that Austin does not bother to argue,

because he finds it obvious, that an utterance simply cannot perform both the act of stating and the act of promising or the act of giving advice. Obviously, what is obvious for one may cry out for the proof of another.

[2] My earliest statement appears in *An Essay on the Logic of Commands and Norms* an M.A. thesis presented to the University of Minnesota in 1952.

[3] For instance, A. J. Ayer, *Language, Truth, and Logic* (London: Victor Gollancz, 2nd,/ed., 1948), pp. 108–9, and C. L. Stevenson, *Ethics and Language* (New Haven: Yale University Press, 1944), p. 113.

[4] For instance, R. M. Hare, *The Language of Morals* (Oxford: The Clarendon Press, 1952), p. 25, and H-N. Castañeda, 'Imperative Reasonings', *Philosophy and Phenomenological Research* **21** (1960), pp. 23–4.

[5] This question paralyzes Gary Wedeking's attack, in his 'Are there Command Arguments?', *Analysis* **30** (1970): 161–166, against the above argument that facts (A)–(D) establish that there are imperative reasonings. Wedeking's paper is a reply to my paper mentioned in the preceding footnote. An ingenious argument of Wedeking's is this. Inferential words that announce premises, like 'since' and 'for', never precede an imperative sentence; hence, imperatives cannot be premises: at most they can be conclusions. The linguistic *premise* is, of course, true. But Wedeking's conclusion does not follow. In *John, go home and study, therefore, John, go home* we have an imperative premise. Wedeking forgot to note that the inferential words announce a premise, or a conclusion, and thereby they mark the *other* elements of the argument as conclusion, or premise. (See Chapter 3 §3.) My rejoinder to Wedeking appears in 'There are Command Sh-inferences', *Analysis* **31** (1971): 13–19. See end of next footnote.

[6] For a philosophical application of (M.G) see the examination of Hare's analysis of Ought, in H-N. Castañeda, 'Imperatives, Decisions, and Oughts', in H-N. Castañeda and G. Nakhnikian, eds., *Morality and the Language of Conduct* (Detroit: Wayne State University Press, 1963). Principle (M.G) is the one that misled Wedeking in the argument of his discussed in the preceding footnote.

[7] See, for instance, Thomas Storer, 'The Logic of Value Imperatives', *Philosophy of Science* **13** (1946): 25–40. He argues that *Someone, kill the criminal* is not derivable from *Executioner, kill the criminal* (p. 38).

CHAPTER 5

IMPERATIVE DESIGNATED VALUES: ORTHOTES
AND ANARTHOTES

In the preceding chapter we argued that the logic of imperatives (i.e., mandates and prescription) is two-valued. We established that prescriptions have a semantical designated value analogous to truth, which we call Legitimacy or orthotes, in that it is both preserved by implication and preferred by practical attitudes of approval and endorsement. In this chapter we provide an account of that value, satisfying both the basic requirement of two-valuedness and the other criteria of adequacy set forth in Chapter 4, §6, as *Presc.* 11–*Presc.* 14. The account connects the semantical values of prescriptions both with the mechanisms of action and with the reasonableness of action.

This chapter shows how, although prescriptions are *not* ontologically reducible to propositions, their Legitimacy values *are* reducible to the truth-values of propositions. This is a proto-metaphysical result.

1. Orthotes-in-context-c (a, e)

We know from the preceding chapter that mandates and prescriptions have a two-valued implicational structure. We also know that, being finite and limited creatures, we have a deep metaphysical need to reason, to draw inferences. In the case of contemplative thinking we reason in order to specify propositions on which to focus our thinking. In the case of strict practical thinking we reason in order to determine and guide action, ours in the case of intentions, others' in the case of mandates. Thus, since there are imperative inferences, imperatives have values that: (i) are involved in such inferences, (ii) relate to the action and circumstances rather than to the intentions of the speaker, but (iii) do not imply the actual performance of the action. One of these values is the *designated* one, i.e., such that in the case of an inference, it is both assumed to be possessed by the imperative premises, if any, and claimed to be inherited by the imperative conclusion. It is also the value that (it is presupposed in the use of imperative discourse) the listener's recognition that it is

possessed by the conclusion will normally elicit his willingness to perform, insofar as he is a reasonable agent, i.e., one whose behavior is
guided by general and rational principles.

The aim in commanding, advising, recommending, or requesting to do
something when the command, advice, recommendation or request is
given in an inferential or quasi-inferential dress is to appeal to the agent's
reason: the point is to attempt to persuade the agent to perform by con-
vincing him by reasons that the action recommended, ordered, or requested, has certain reasonableness. In ordinary language there is no
standard word to refer to the designated value of imperatives. We allude
to it when we say that the action demanded by an imperative is reasonable
or convenient, or allright, or proper, or correct, or appropriate, or
justifiable, or due, or the right one in given circumstances. All these terms
signal a basic common aspect, but they also signal important differences.
This very multiplicity is a philosophical clue of great significance. We
shall illuminate it, and conform with it, in two different but related ways.
First, we shall introduce in this chapter several imperative values analogous to truth. Second, in Chapters 7 and 8 we shall relate to each of these
imperative values a corresponding type of deontic judgment. Before we
put forward our formal analysis of Legitimacy-values, we shall discuss
the motivating background informally.

Consider, then, a mandate demanding of certain agents actions that are
allright, or proper, of fine, or convenient for those agents to perform,
given certain circumstances. We shall say, as in Chapter 4, §6, that an
imperative in that position is *Legitimate,* or *orthotic,* with respect to the
circumstances in question. We shall speak of the Legitimacy-values, or
of the orthotic values, of imperatives.[1] Our claim is that orthotic values
are the values of prescriptions and mandates involved in inferences. Since
mandates have the same implications of their core prescriptions, we have
the principle:

> *Imp. Value.* A mandate M constituted by prescription P is orthotic
> if and only if P is orthotic. Hence, we can speak indiscriminately of
> mandate or of prescriptional values. We shall also speak of imperative
> values. It must be remembered, however, that by imperatives we do
> not mean sentences, but noemata.

Let us return to the fact that we use so many different words to allude to the Legitimacy of imperatives. This suggests that an imperative can be orthotic in several different ways, and even that it may be orthotic in one respect and not in another, depending on the circumstances. Such is indeed the case. Imagine, for instance, a boy playing chess with his father and wondering whether he should let his father win at least one game. The boy's mother comes in and decides to help her child. She recommends the boy to check with his white bishop, so that in a few moves he can checkmate. Here, in the context of winning the game, the imperative *Check with your white bishop* is legitimate, whereas in the context of letting the father win (without his knowing it, of course) this imperative is not legitimate. The mother acted from the former context in ignorance of the latter. We must elucidate the structure of her speech act.

Another example of different Legitimacy-values in relation to different contexts is provided by the moral principle *A private person ought not to kill except in self-defense.* This principle guarantees that in the moral context the imperative *Smith, kill Jones* is Nonlegitimate. Yet if one is giving advice as to how Smith can become a millionaire, the imperative *Smith, kill Jones* may formulate the correct advice; i.e., the imperative may be orthotic in the context of *the adviser and Smith* both wanting Smith to become a millionaire.

Before going any further, let us emphasize the distinction between the orthotes of an imperative and the justification of a given *employment* of the imperative.[2] To employ an imperative in its basic use is to command, or to give advice, or to request, or to tender an invitation, or to entreat, etc.; thus, to employ an imperative is to *perform* a certain act, a linguistic act. But the speech act of commanding, or entreating, or advising, etc., is *not* the act mentioned in the imperative issued in the speech act that commands, or entreats, or advises. Doubtless, the acts of commanding, advising, requesting, inviting, etc., are intimately related to the acts the hearers are commanded, advised, requested, or invited to perform; so, the former may often be justifiable when, and because, the latter are appropriate, i.e., when, and because, the imperatives formulating the command, advice, request, etc., are orthotic. Yet in general the speech acts of issuing mandates are justifiable by virtue of other considerations. Thus, a mandate of the form *X, tell the truth* may be orthotic even if the corresponding mandate of the form *Y, tell X to tell the truth* is not orthotic. Conversely, in some situations, your requesting from somebody

his doing of some action may be justified or appropriate, even though
your *request* itself may be *Nonlegitimate* or *anorthotic*. Your advice to
Smith to go may be excellent, but you advising him to go may be wrong.
Legitimacy is, in short, not a property of an event or action, but of a
noema.[3]

Every context in which imperatives are issued is constituted by a set of
ends and a related set of procedures, as well as by a set of possible circumstances logically or casually related to those ends and procedures and
those who subscribe to them. In ordinary parlance we do not say that
every case of proposing an end to oneself is a case of making a decision,
nor do we always speak of choosing an end in connection with every
making of a decision. However, taking up an end, making the decision
to perform a given act, and adopting a convention are all cases of choosing
and belong in a natural family, as we shall explain in Chapter 10. The
acceptance of a convention and the adoption of procedural decision are
not often said to be adoptions of ends; nevertheless, the adoption of a
convention or of a procedural decision does modify some ends pursued by
the adopter of the convention or decision. We shall, for convenience,
call all of them *ends*. In general, an end will be said to be a state of affairs
(or proposition) that an agent wants to some degree to be the case (or
true). See Chapter 10 §5 for our account of wants.

The situation we are trying to get at is this. The Legitimacy or orthotes of
a prescription or imperative is, like the truth of a proposition, an objective
matter: it depends on certain relationships between the purposes of a
domain of agents, their powers, and their environment. Of course, just
as some propositions are true, because of certain mental states of some
persons, some prescriptions may be Legitimate primarily because of
certain mental states or acts of certain agents.

One of the fundamental facts about practical thinking is that it hinges
on the agent's *presupposition* that he can choose from several alternative
courses of action open to him. This does not, of course, imply, as Kant
firmly stressed, that the agent is free in the sense that his acts, or his
volitions, are uncaused. Perhaps the presupposition is just a dialectical
illusion (to use Kant's term) of practical thinking. If it is, the universe
is *ugly:* given the biological and psychological primacy of practical over
contemplative thinking, we are, thus, condemned to presuppose a falsehood in order to do what we must think practically. We *must* in any

case include the presupposition of freedom in our analysis of practical thinking, and we must do it *without* committing ourselves here to the metaphysical thesis that the actions of the will are not causally determined by the circumstances of the agent and the laws of nature. On the other hand, we do not endorse the denial of the thesis either. We must, therefore, in order to hold firmly to the presupposition without relying on the metaphysical thesis, adopt the first-person point of view, the agent's point of view, and contemplate the structure that appears to it. We generalize it to the point of view of a domain of agents acting in consort.

Consider a set A of agents who are engaged in carrying out some plan of action E. They are located at a certain timeplace *t*. For them the history of the world falls into two parts: the Past, and the Future, which are connected not only by logical laws but also by the laws of nature. The Past is full and inalterable. The Future is for them only partially full: it divides into two parts: *the Future Framework,* and *the Future Zone of Indeterminacy*. The Framework is the large part of the Future that is, automatically and fully, determined by the circumstances of the present and the laws of nature. The Zone of Indeterminacy may, metaphysically speaking, be not such, if the thesis of metaphysical determinism is true. But for the agents in our set A this is a moot question. The Zone of Indeterminacy is the part of the Future that allows alternatives: one is the realization of plan of action E as well as the realization of all the actions that are means to E; other alternative is the non-realization of any of these, and other alternatives lie in between. In short, the plan of action E determines for the agents in A a set of actions that are relevant to their purposes. Given the purposes and the conception of the world the agents have, there is then a set of *practical actions,* namely, those through whose performance they think (perhaps erroneously) that they can fill in the Future Zone of Indeterminacy with their plan E and its concomittant actions. Thus, being a *practical action* is relative to a time as well as to both a set of agents and their plans; and it consists of being an action earmarked by the agents as the junctures where on their view they can shape the Future.

Clearly, in considering situations of action (and choice) as just described, it makes a great deal of difference who and how many agents are involved.

Furthermore, it makes a great difference whether a certain person is considered as an agent in the relevant sense, i.e., one whose actions are not part of the Future Framework determined by the past and the laws of nature, or as an object, so to speak, whose actions *are* part of the Framework. In terms of noemata, the above distinction grounds the distinction between propositions (or states of affairs) and practitions. In Chapter 7 it will appear as the distinction between actions prescriptively considered and actions considered as circumstances. The distinction is fundamental for understanding the nature of practical thinking and the roles of norms and normative systems and institutions in our lives.[4] Another point to stress is this. The Legitimacy of a practition has to do with what the agents can do to fill in the Future of Indeterminacy. Hence, if under a certain plan of action a certain person is treated as an object, whose properties, including actions, are part of the Future Framework, then they are not agents of actions in the relevant, practical sense under consideration with respect to the given plan of action. Obviously, an agent can be conceived as both doing certain things that fall within the Future Framework and doing other things that are practical, i.e., are junctures through, in accordance with the plan of action, he can shape the Future. Consider, for example, the case of George who plans today to play tennis tomorrow morning and plans to go to the movies tomorrow afternoon. His first plan of action may include as *practical actions* playing with Bo, who is very tough and competitive, as well as playing with David, who is easygoing. George's afternoon plans will be affected by the way he carries out his tennis project. If he plays with Bo, he will be very tired to enjoy the flick at Cinema I, but would then go to see the comedy at Cinema II. In George's afternoon plan the actions of playing with Bo and of playing with David are part of the Future Framework, not only at noon tomorrow, when he has finished (or not) his tennis plan, but *also* today as he sees tomorrow afternoon's plan.

Actions earmarked as practical depend not only on the presupposition of an open future, but also on the presupposition that our will is causally effective in filling in the Future Zone of Indeterminacy with the desired contents. Furthermore, actions are earmarked as practical in relation to some specific project or plan. (See Chapter 12.)

Consider a set A of agents and a set E of ends pursued by those agents at a certain time t. The agents in A are in circumstances that together with the laws of nature would determine the Future Framework at t. Some of the circumstances are specifiable, perhaps not fully by all the agents in A, but by some of them or others. Let us call them S. The laws of nature, ends E and situation S determine a set α of practical actions: those which the agent can perform and would, if performed, bring about E. Clearly, the agents in A need not know exactly what the members of α are. We shall call a *context of* Legitimacy a set C(A, E, S, α, t) whose members are: (i) true propositions formulating the situation S at t of all the agents in A; (ii) true propositions formulating the facts of endorsement of, or subscription to, ends E at t by the members of A; (iii) true propositions formulating the laws of nature (applicable at t). Note that since S is not a total description of the universe at time t, the laws of nature can leave open a Future Zone of Indeterminacy at t. The parenthetical qualification in clause (iii) indicates that the practical use of reason does not presuppose that the laws of nature remain constant throughout time, but it does presuppose that there are laws of nature linking not only the Future Framework to the Present and the Past, but also the free choices of the agents to the realization of their plans. Without the latter practical thinking is absolutely useless. (See Chapter 10, §2–§3 and Chapter 12).

The practical actions determined by a Legitimacy context are the ones that constitute the characteristic subject matter of practical thinking. So far as our discussion will proceed in this chapter, they are unitary actions, but they may be complex. For instance, in the George example above the action of playing tennis with Bo may be *practically* simple in a given context, but it may be very complex in reality. This is a topic we shall take up in Chapter 12.

Our characterization of contexts of Legitimacy allows that some contexts be self-contradictory. We will assume, however, that from now on all contexts referred to are self-consistent. Even more, we shall concentrate our discussion on those that are compatible with the set R of propositions formulating the realization of the ends in E. The union of the sets R and C(A, E, S, α, t) will be called C'(A, E, S, α, t), and the closure under implication of this will be called C$^+$(A, E, S, α, t). (Recall that a set β of noemata is closed under implication if and only if every proposition implied by some members of β is also a member of β. See Chapter 3, §9.) We shall say that C$^+$(A, E, S, α, t) is *the total description of the context of Legitimacy* C(A, E, S, α, t).

We can now elucidate the Legitimacy values of prescriptions and mandates. In this section we provide an account of the preliminary, but very useful concept of relative Legitimacy, i.e., Legitimacy with respect to certain contexts. In Section 3 below we consider what we call absolute contexts, which are the ones involved in the actual use of imperative language. In Chapter 7 we shall relate the special contexts to the qualified norms and *oughts,* and the absolute contexts to the overriding *ought.*

Recall that for every prescription there is a *corresponding performance proposition.* It is one that, roughly put, predicates of the agents referred to in the prescription the performance of the very same actions demanded by the prescription in exactly the same circumstances. Precisely put, it is the proposition that has exactly the same components as the prescription, in exactly the same order, except for having a propositional copula corresponding to a prescriptional copula. Let us represent the performance proposition corresponding to a prescription P by $c(P)$. As explained in Chapter 3, a prescription P and its corresponding proposition $c(P)$ are generally independent, neither one implying the other. Yet the orthotic values of a prescription P can be elucidated in terms of the truth-values and certain implication properties of $c(P)$. This is part of what in Chapter 1 (p. 8) we referred to as the ontological primacy of pure reason over practical reason, which is at bottom the metaphysical primacy of what contemplative thinking thinks over what practical thinking thinks.

For the sake of brevity let us say that each pair of noemata of the corresponding forms $p*$ and $(\sim p*)$, whether propositions or practitions, is the *negative* of the other. If one of them is $q*$, we shall let the other be $n(q*)$. Clearly, if P is a practition (e.g., a prescription), then $n(c(P))$ is the same as $c(n(P))$.

Consider now a context of Legitimacy C(A, E, S, α, t), and a prescription P whose agents are all in A, and whose predicates are all in α. We shall call P a *primary prescription with respect to* C(A, E, S, α, t) just in case all the predicates in P are predicated of their subjects through the prescriptional copula.

(L.1)   A primary prescription P with respect to context C(A, E, S, α, t) is *Legitimate-in-context*-C(A, E, S, α, t), or *orthotic-in-context*-C(A, E, S, α, t), if and only if one of the following conditions obtain:

(i) The total description $C^+(A, E, S, \alpha, t)$ implies $c(P)$; or

(ii) $C^+(A, E, S, \alpha, t)$ implies neither $c(P)$ nor $c(n(P))$, and some agents in A, including those in P, endorse P, and none of the agents in A endorse $n(P)$; or

(iii) $C^+(A, E, S, \alpha, t)$ implies neither $c(P)$ nor $c(n(P))$; and condition (ii) is false, but $c(P)$ is true.

(L.2)   A primary prescription P with respect to $C(A, E, S, \alpha, t)$ is *Non-legitimate-in-context*-$C(A, E, \alpha, t)$, or *anorthotic-in-context*-$C(A, E, S, \alpha, t)$, if and only if $n(P)$ is *Legitimate-in-context*-$C(A, E, S, \alpha, t)$.

The principles for conjunctions, disjunctions, etc., of prescriptions, whether pure or mixed, are included in the generalized value tables given in Chapter 4, §6. These tables should be especially consulted for conditional and biconditional imperatives.

(L.1) and (L.2) exclude third orthotic values. For quantificational truth see Chapter 4, §8. Clauses (i)–(iii) of (L.1) establish the ontological primacy of propositions over prescriptions and mandates. Clause (i) establishes the general independence of Legitimacy and truth. Clearly, the set of propositions $C^+(A, E, S, \alpha, t)$, which makes a prescription X Legitimate-in-C, may very well make X so by virtue of false propositions, e.g., that ends E are attained and that X is fulfilled. Likewise, clause (ii) allows that a prescription X be Legitimate-in-C even if its corresponding performance proposition is false. Finally, (L.1) above and (L*) and (E.P*) in §3 below reveal how orthotes is a psychologically preferred value, in accordance with *Presc.* 13 in Chapter 4 §6.

2. ENDORSEMENT

In the sense intended here, a person does not have to perform a very special act of choice to subscribe to certain ends or procedural conventions. If he does, much the better. In some cases there is, of course, a deliberate and protracted process that ends in the adoption of an end. But often ends are adopted as a matter of acquiring propensities to do certain things, propensities to prefer certain things and courses of actions, and propensities to criticize and appraise actions in certain ways. Thus the citizens of a country, by simply maintaining their citizenship, subscribe to the policies and laws of their country. Undoubtedly, a person fully determined to relinquish his citizenship may perhaps always find some avenue of escape. At any rate, what matters here is not whether one is forced by biological or physical or social circumstances to subscribe to certain ends and conventions, but whether the person has accepted them in the sense that he has in himself the appropriate inclinations and propensities. In this spirit we assume that normally everyone pursues the goals of self-preservation, avoidance of pain and intense cold, and self-enjoyment. We have not chosen to pursue them; but it will require a special act of choice in special circumstances to subscribe to the opposite ends; as, e.g., when one decides to commit suicide or to sacrifice oneself for the welfare of his beloved ones. A large part of our behavior consists in finding ways to avoid death, pain, intense cold, etc. And we go about it in full awareness of what we are doing, even planning many of our acts so as to prevent clashes among our several pursuits. Thus, a person subscribes to those:

(a) ends to which a psychobiological account of his conscious behavior may make reference;

(b) those ends of his community with which he has come to be, at least partially and in practice, identified himself, and

(c) those which he spontaneously proposes for himself.

As we are using the term 'subscribes to' here there is a systemic *unity* or indivisibility in the case of the procedural conventions, such that, whenever no choice is explicitly included as part of the conventions themselves, the acceptance of a part of the procedures involves acceptance of the whole set. This is part and parcel of the minimal rationality inherent in a being by the mere fact that he thinks. Outstanding procedural conventions are the different types of legislation enacted in the country of one's citizenship. In particular, the procedural conventions include the set of constitutional laws of one's own country. One subscribes to the whole of the constitution of one does not give up, or takes up, his citizenship. Likewise, the morality of his culture is subscribed to completely by the person who subscribes to part of it. Similarly for the case of the statutes constituting any other institution one belongs to. (See Chapter 11.)

Consider the case of a father who is taking his small child somewhere. The child is trying to get dressed, but gets all tangled up when it comes to his shoes. He cannot decide which shoe and stocking to put on first. Finally, the father decides on a procedure and tells the child "Put on your left shoe first". In the context in question, constituted by the end of getting the child ready to go out, any procedure is in principle quite open, but the decision to have the child put on his left shoe first makes the imperative Legitimate (orthotic). It satisfies clause (ii) of (L.1). That procedural decision is like the procedural convention of driving on the left-hand side of the road or stopping at a red light – the very enactment of the convention bestows legal Legitimacy (orthotes) on the imperative.

At least part of the elements that may be classified as the ends or conventions forced upon the individual by the society he belongs to *may* be taken by him, as well as by those issuing commands, requests, or entreaties to him, as falling on the side of the causal factors, which together with certain ends justify or not such commands, requests, entreaties, etc. For instance, certain laws that are carefully enforced may be taken by the agent and his advisers, etc., as if they were propositions asserting that if he does certain acts he will be fined, or imprisoned, or hanged, etc. He may object to such laws and refuse to identify himself with them in any manner whatever except insofar as he wants to avoid inconveniences, imprisonment, etc. He may even go so far as to violate them whenever his chances of being caught are very slim. Perhaps, there is an inconsistency in such a way of life. But here we are concerned only with noting that a different parsing, so to speak, of the elements of a context $C(A, E, S, \alpha, t)$ is feasible, so that they belong in a different context $C(A, E', S', \alpha', t)$ with respect to which certain imperatives are said, or supposed, to be Legitimate or not. This is another commentary on the distinction between the Future Framework and the Future Zone of Indeterminacy.

3. UNQUALIFIED ORTHOTES

We are very much interested in elucidating the semantical values of imperatives relevant to imperative inferences. A quick reflection reveals that orthotes with respect to this or that context is not what we want. The ordinary use of imperatives, whatever their variety of prescriptive discourse, often goes without any indication of a context with respect to which the imperatives are Legitimate. We issue, e.g., *Read that book*, *Pay your debt to Jones*, or *Pass the salt please* without even an apparent hint that they would not be Legitimate in other contexts. There is a certain absoluteness or finality to our issuance of mandates.

Yet many of those imperatives are not thought of by the speaker as correct or orthotic (whatever word they may use) in any context whatsoever. They are merely quietly taken to be correct in the context of utterance, given that the ends involved are obvious. It is the obviousness of the ends, too, what often makes it unnecessary to employ such imperatives inferentially. Without any aid, the hearer can "see" the ends involved and the relevant causal connections, and any statement of reasons is superfluous. Consider, for instance, the case of a man sitting at a banquet table who asks his neighbor to pass the salt. The orthotic context is wholly obvious and before the guests' eyes. The relativity to context is there, clearly there. Nevertheless, the claim of Legitimacy, and also the Legitimacy itself of the request *Please pass the salt (here now)* transcends the context of utterance. That request, although relative to some ends and circumstances of the banquet guests, is taken to be Legitimate for *all* times and *all* future circumstances. In short, the Legitimacy context of the banquet bestows overriding Legitimacy on that request. Thus that context includes an *implicit* comparison of all other contexts applicable to the banquet in those circumstances. It is an absolute context of sorts.

The fact that there is a unity in the life of a person indicates that all the ends or goals the person subscribes to allow of comparison and ranking. Whenever a situation is such that an agent believes that in it two ends of his cannot both be attained, a choice is forced upon him. And he chooses, of course, in the light of what he wants most. So, either one end is by itself stronger than another at a given time, or it is strengthened by one which is higher or stronger. In any case, the person's ends form a complex more or less organic and hierarchic. A human being is a complicated hierarchical array of ends and purposes varying in the depth of their endorsement, as well as in the breadth of actions and experiences they cover. This makes it a nearly unfeasible task to know oneself. Surely, we are unclear about the details and even big zones of our own hierarchy of ends. That is why often we have a very hard time making up our minds as to which of the alternative courses of action or forms of life we like best or want most. But we are clear about the hierarchic character of the complex of our ends and about some parts of it. On many occasions we are quite confident about our next action and know what we really want. No doubt, the ranking can be changed. Then we have a personal crisis or revolution, if the rearrangement of ends affects those of first magnitude.

It is also possible that in the general, vague hierarchic outline of the complex of ends that we subscribe to, we come to detect an inconsistency or an impossibility of the joint fulfillment of several ends. In such cases, we modify our hierarchy of ends – at least when we are rational enough to face squarely the need for a change and to give up some cherished ideal or goal. Indeed, part of what we mean by "man is a rational animal" concerns precisely our uneasiness before a clear contradiction and our readiness to revise our concepts and ideals in order to remove it.

Consider two men X and Y at a certain time t. We have, then, two hierarchical complexes of the ends they subscribe to at t, say, C_X and C_Y. There is, of course, no guarantee that C_X and C_Y are harmonious or consistent, i.e., that they can be jointly attained. Indeed, X and Y may both deeply and urgently desire the exclusive use or possession of a given object or person. In such a case C_X and C_Y are disharmonious. But there are always several complexes C'_X and C'_Y which are harmonious and are, respectively, revisions of C_X and C_Y. Of course, there is no guarantee that there are such complexes C'_X and C'_Y as would be endorsed by X and Y instead of C_X and C_Y, respectively. Nevertheless, we may consider *ideal harmonizations* of complexes C_X and C_Y such that: (i) C_X is revised to H_X, which differs from C_X as little as is possible in its highest ranks; (ii) C_Y is revised to H_Y, which differs from C_Y as little as is possible in the highest ranks; (iii) H_X and H_Y are harmonious. Obviously, there may very well be many ideal harmonizations of C_X and C_Y. Furthermore, these harmonizations may be incompatible. Let $H*_X$ be the part common to all ideal harmonizations H_X, and similarly for $H*_Y$. Since $H*_X$ and $H*_Y$ are consistent, let us consider their junction and call it *the total ideal hierarchic complex of ends* subscribed to by X and Y, and let us represent it by $H*_{X,Y}$. If C_X and C_Y are consistent, we let $H*_{X,Y}$ be the junction of C_X and C_Y.

In general, let $H*_\alpha$ be the total ideal hierarchic complex of ends subscribed to by all the members of a set α of agents.

Who is an agent is an empirical question we cannot investigate here. Formally, we are at this juncture characterizing agents as creatures who propose to themselves ends and are subjects of mandates and prescriptions. As we discussed in Chapter 2, §7, if animism is true, many entities that we normally take to be non-agents are in fact agents. Now, however, we are concerned with a more specialized concept of agent or person, namely, with the concept of a being whom another considers as entering with him in partnership for determining total ideal hierarchic complexes of ends. Patently, a man can treat other men in an *anti-animist* way, so to speak: he can treat them as creatures housing several kinds of causal powers, but not as capable of making plans or reaching decisions. Yet a man can treat a man as an agent, but not as a *co-person*. At a given time, whether fully aware of it or not, a man takes himself to be a member of a very special community of persons, namely, those persons in a set α that determines a hierarchy $H*_\alpha$ which he endorses.

In general, at any given time t each agent X determines a set $\alpha(X, t)$ of those persons whose ends X is prepared to accept, with revisions if necessary. Let us call $\alpha(X, t)$ *X's kingdom of co-persons at time t*. Of course, $\alpha(X, t)$ is most likely a stratified set, i.e., a genuine kingdom with X as a king and other persons as privy councillors and others as high dukes and others as earls, and so on down to a large crowd that constitutes the peasantry of $\alpha(X, t)$. In short, $\alpha(X, t)$ is the stratified kingdom of everybody whom at t X cares about in at least some minimal way. *Caring* is, of course, not a matter of having something before consciousness, but of a network of dispositions, propensities and readinesses to alter one's trains of action and thoughts once one is aware of how one's actions affect, or may affect, the people in question. (See Chapter 10, §3.)

At any time t an agent X determines a kingdom of co-persons $\alpha(X, t)$. This kingdom determines many harmonizations H_α acceptable to X at t. But many, pershaps all, of them are unacceptable to some, or all, other members of $\alpha(X, t)$. Consider the total ideal hierarchic complexes of the ends to which the members of α would subscribe if they were to modify their own motivational hierarchies as little as possible at the higher ranks and yet preserve the stratification of $\alpha(X, t)$. Let K_α be the harmonious partial hierarchy common to all such total ideal hierarchic complexes. Let us call K_α the *absolute context of X, qua member of α, at time t*.

Consider now two men X and Y and let their corresponding kingdoms of copersons at a time t be α and β. Each determines the two absolute contexts K_α and K_β of X and Y, *qua* members of α and β, respectively, at time t. Again, more likely than not, K_α and K_β are not harmonious But we can form in the usual way the *absolute context* $K*(X, Y)$, which is the partial hierarchy common to all harmonizations of K_α and K_β such that the least disturbance is introduced either in the higher ranks of K_α, or in the higher ranks of $K\beta$, and the stratifications of α and β are preserved. The absolute context includes the total history of the world up to time t.

In the case of a set A with more than two persons, we represent their absolute context by $K_*(A)$. And now we can formulate other central principles of Legitimacy values:

(L*)   The value of prescriptions, analogous to truth, that is involved both in the ordinary issuance of mandates and their inferential use is a Legitimacy in an absolute context $K(A)$, where the agents of the mandates in question and the issuer himself are members of A.

(E.P*)   If at a time t a person X endorses an imperative I, then at t X takes I to be Legitimate-in-the-absolute-context-$K_*(A)$ at t, where A includes X and the agents of I.

The latter principle is a counterpart of principle (T.9) governing belief discussed in Chapter 3, §2. We pointed out the difference between believing a proposition and believing that the proposition is true. Likewise, there is a difference between endorsing a prescription and believing that the prescription is Legitimate. (E.P*) is about the former.

There is a very important relativity still present in absolute contexts, and, therefore, present in our endorsement and issuance of imperatives. There is always the relativity to a set A of agents, among whom we are ourselves. Thus, there is an unavoidable egocentricity in practical thinking. This is fine. Practical thinking is concerned with one's own survival. It is the ideal of morality that extends the set A to all human beings or even all rational agents.[5]

Principle (E.P*) does not mean that the commander or requester or adviser has examined the whole life and character of the person he is addressing to and has "seen" in detail what are all the ends that person subscribes to. (E.P*) only means that in normal commanding, requesting, etc., the speaker is telling the contemplated agent to perform a certain act or class of acts, under the *implicit assumption* that a consideration of everything pertaining to both of them would uncover no reason against the agent's doing that act or class of acts, i.e., under the implicit assumption that a consideration of all the facts, and at least of all the higher ends and procedural conventions each of them subscribes to, will show the imperative to be Legitimate (orthotic) in the relevant absolute context.

NOTES TO CHAPTER 5

[1] My Legitimacy-values have some kinship with Alf Ross' 'Objective Validity', in *Philosophy of Science* 11 (1944): 30–46. Perhaps the main departures are (a) that I characterize them in terms of ends, conventions, and causal connections, and (b) that he was convinced that objective validity is a chimera. They also resemble Everett Hall's legitimacy-values of both imperatives and 'ought'-sentences. The main differences are: (1) I characterize them in terms of ends, whereas Hall had in mind some ultimate metaphysical or quasi-metaphysical property of assertions about values; (2) my Legitimacy-values do not apply to norms or to 'ought'-sentences; (3) Hall's values are at least three. Cf. his *What is Value?* (London: Routledge & Kegan Paul, 1952), pp. 154, 238n, *et al.*

[2] Failure to see this difference vitiates Milton Fisk's criticism of an earlier version of a thesis that appears in Chapter 8 §1 below. In a friendly review of *Morality and the Language of Conduct*, in *Natural Law Forum*, Vol. 9 (1964), Fisk wrote of 'Imperatives, Decisions, and Oughts: A Logico-Metaphysical Investigation': 'Castaneda himself holds that "X ought to do A" implies and is implied by the metalinguistic claim "The Imperative 'X, do A!' is [necessarily – left out by Fisk] justified",... Yet this analysis seems to run up against the fact that there can be duties where imperatives are unjustified. Gentle persuasion, not raw imperative is needed in bringing many people around to do their duty... [1] "Peter ought to tell the truth" is true. But John's telling [my italics] Peter to tell the truth...' so [2] "The imperative 'Peter, tell the truth' is justified" is false. (p. 174). Fisk is of course, correct in speaking, in an ordinary sense of 'justify', of not being justified in telling Peter to tell the truth. But this not the use of 'justified' I explained as analogous to 'true', that predicates a semantical property of mandates, the one property preserved in implication – *not* a property of acts. Fisk does not show that [1] is true and [2] is false; his example shows that perhaps [1] can be true even if [3] "The imperative 'John, tell Peter to tell the truth' is justified" is false. But [2] does not imply [3]. In earlier writings including *The Structure of Morality*, the term 'Justified' is synonymous with 'orthotic'. Keith Lehrer suggested the switch to 'Legitimacy' because 'Justifiedness' suggests, not the analogue of truth, but the analogue of the justifiedness of belief – which can obtain even if the belief is false proposition.

[3] This point was not only ignored by Fisk, as noted in the preceding note, but also by Kai Nielsen who also wrote a perceptive review of 'Morality and the Language of Conduct' in *The Philosophical Review* 75 (1966). In a relevant part he says: "[On Castañeda's view] complex metalinguistic assertions about resolutives and imperatives could replace the corresponding normatives. This last challenging thesis does not seem to me to be adequately sustained, for in his metalinguistic statements about resolutives and imperatives Castaneda ascribes to the imperatives or resolutives the semantical properties of justifiedness, nonjustifiedness, and unjustifiedness. But then we have not succeeded in dispensing with normatives, for they are used in our metalanguage". (pp. 238f.) Nielsen did not heed the remark that justifiedness and nonjustifiedness are semantical values, analogous to truth and falsity. Thus, the statement *Imperative *X, do A* is justified* is not in that book a normative statement; it is not normative in exactly the way in which the statement *The proposition *The Earth is roundish* is true* is not normative, or even a geological statement.

[4] This crucial distinction is one seriously absent from David Lyon's discussions of several important issues in his *Utilitarianism: Its Forms and Limits* (Oxford, England: Clarendon Press, 1965), e.g., the sense of *caeteris-paribus* clauses (pp. 44 ff), criticism

of Stout) (pp. 112ff), and his arguments for the material equivalence of acts and rule-utilitarianism (Chapter 4).

[5] For the universality of morality and a total analysis of its complex structure, see H-N. Castañeda, *The Structure of Morality*. For a quick glance at the structure of morality, see Castañeda, 'The Good Society and the Complexity of the Structure of Morality', *The Philosophic Exchange* (1975).

CHAPTER 6

INTENTIONS AND INTENDING

In this chapter we continue the study of intentions began in Chapter 2, §5. Recall that an intention is in this book *what* a person intends, not a state of intending. We tackle the question raised there whether intentions are actions or propositions. We argue that they are neither. Obviously, they are not prescriptions or mandates. Intentions and prescriptions exhaust the category of practitions. We show that intentions have a two-valued logical structure in a way exactly parallel to that of prescriptions, studied in Chapter 4. We need again Meta-theorem I of Chapter 3, §14. Similarly we have the problem of elucidating the designated value of intentions involved in implication. Maintaining the principle of the unity of reason, since prescriptions and intentions are complementary basic units of content of practical thinking, we adopt the view that that value is very much the same as the Legitimacy of prescriptions. Thus, we built on Chapter 5 an account of the Legitimacy values of intentions. The causal role of intending is discussed in Chapter 10.

1. WHAT IS INTENDED IS NOT AN ACTION

The word 'intend' appears in different syntactical constructions, for instance:

(1)   John intends to leave;
(2)   John intends Mary to go;
(3)   John intends that his son should behave decently toward others.

A simple reflection shows that constructions (2) and (3) are semantically very different from (1). They ascribe to John not an intention to do, as (1) does, but an attitude involving the prescription *Mary to go* and the deontic judgment *His son should behave decently to others.* This attitude is one that can be a content before consciousness in the episodes of thinking in which the attitude of intending is exercised. A scrutiny of

such episodes reveals that intentions are either propositions, or proposition-like structures. Yet a look back at statement (1) above suggests,
differently, that the psychological relationship of intending stands, not
between John and a proposition-like structure, but between John and the
action of leaving. This is patently only a grammatical appearance. Here
is a case in which we must be emphatically careful in separating linguistic
features from features that belong to the contents of thought.

Consider closely the case of John when, in accordance with statement
(1) above, he intends to leave. Let him exercise his attitude of intending.
He rehearses, then, his practical thought of his intention to leave. What
does he think in such rehearsals? Obviously, he thinks of the action of
leaving. But this action is an abstract entity, a universal, a property, that
can be instantiated by several agents. Equally obviously, John does not
merely think of the action of leaving. He thinks of it as *his* action: his
intending to leave is his determination *to leave himself,* i.e., the particu-
larized action consisting of *the universal action as done (as instantiated)
by him.* When John has occurrent thoughts that exercise his attitude of
intending, he has before his consciousness a predicative structure having
the action of leaving as predicate and his first-person conception as
subject. This is exactly what he expresses when he expresses his intention:
then he says "I shall come". Thus, in general, a simple intention is either
a proposition or a complex like a proposition in that it has a subject,
namely, an agent conceived in the first-person way, and a predicate,
namely, an action.

Propositions like (1) of the form *X intends to A* are, to put it philosophically more perspicuously, of the form *X intends that he (himself)
A*, where the pronoun 'he (himself)' is a *quasi-indicator,* the same one
appearing in 'X believes that he (himself) is a millionaire'. Quasi-indicators
are expressions such that: (i) they occur in *oratio obliqua,* i.e., are subordinated to verbs expressing psychological attitudes; (ii) they are not
indicators or demonstratives because they have an antecedent, which in
the case of sentence (1) above is the name 'John'; (iii) the antecedent is not
in the *oratio obliqua* of the quasi-indicator, and (iv) the quasi-indicator
is used both to represent the positions of indexical or demonstrative
references and to attribute such references. In the case of (1) above, 'he
(himself)' represents first-person (indexical) references by John.[1] Naturally,
we are not advocating that we change ordinary language and replace in

sentences like (1) the infinitive 'to A' with the subjunctive clause 'that he (himself) A'. (See Chapter 1, §4). Indeed, in the light of our arguments in §2 next, to the effect that intentions are not propositions, the inventors of ordinary language performed an admirable invention in introducing the infinitive construction illustrated by sentence (1). The subjunctive clause 'that he (himself) A' as a formulation of an intention in 'X intends that he (himself) A' could easily suggest that the intention in question is a proposition, the same one expressed by it in the sentence 'X believes that it is possible that he (himself) A'. Thus, the normal infinitive construction has the great philosophical virtue of signaling the fundamental hiatus between propositions and intentions. Furthermore the infinitive construction, as (1) illustrates, is economical in the number of words. It is also unambiguous, for clearly it is the first-person concept of the intender which is the subject of the intention. In brief, the invention of the infinitive construction as a means of expressing intentions as noemata of intendings is an admirable invention! It must be maintained – in practical daily language.

Some philosophers, nevertheless, hold that *what* is intended is an action. As far as I can make out, the reasons for that feed on too close a fusion of philosophical analysis and analysis of surface grammar of ordinary English sentences. This is tersely illustrated by Annette Baier's defense of the view that the full *what*, or content, of an intending is an action.[2]

Baier insists that intentions are first-personal, yet she contends that intentions are actions:

Now it appears that... [there is] a dummy agent, or rather agent-patient, since the "I" who is intending always figures in his own intentions. Is this objectionable, or is it a mark of that necessary truth mentioned earlier, that I can intend only *my* doings?... if I intend to speak, this is not to intend me to speak... we drop off our intentions [i.e., intendings], they are simply intentions [i.e., intendings] to do. (*Op. cit.*, p. 658.)

Baier's conclusion seems to be that the noema, or what is before a man's mind, when he comes to intend to speak is simply the action to speak. Yet she claims that one can only intend *one's* doing's. This is interesting. For it seems that the only way of guaranteeing that a man never even in principle takes anything but *his* own doings as intentions is by requiring an intention to have as a constituent a first-person subject. Thus, Baier seems to be committed to requiring that the idea of oneself as agent be part of each of one's intentions. This is difficult to reconcile with her official view that intentions are actions. The reason she gives for that view is that the sentence 'I intend to speak' is not in ordinary language an abbreviation of 'I intend me to speak'. This linguistic point is, of course, absolutely correct. There is no formal speech or writing that requires 'I intend me to speak' as unabbreviated form in the way in which 'it's' must yield to 'it is' in formal non-abbreviated language. Yet this grammatical fact cannot establish that one does not have to *think* of oneself as agent in order to intend to do something. Consider, for proper perspective, that the sentence 'I shaved' is not in ordinary English an abbreviation of the sentence 'I shaved me'; yet this fact does not have the tendency to show that shaving is not a dyadic relation that is reflexively instantiated when a person shaves.

A man who intends to speak may very well express his intention, i.e., the full content of his intending, by saying "I shall [or will, depending on his dialect] speak". We have here in *oratio recta* that the first-person reference is part and parcel of a man's intention, even though 'John intends to speak' contains no explicit first-person reference as part of what John intends. This conflict in the data is, nevertheless, *not* an impasse. It is a "conflict" between a piece of *oratio obliqua* in a larger context, where elisions of iterations are natural, and a whole simpler *oratio recta*. Undoubtedly, the *oratio recta* is more revealing than its corresponding *oratio obliqua* of the structure of what they both express. This conclusively nails down the view that an intention is a proposition-like structure, which in the simplest case has as subject an agent conceived in the first-person way and an action as predicate.

Baier has replied to my principle that in the conflict between the deliverances of *oratio obliqua* constructions and the deliverances of *oratio recta* constructions we must choose the latter. She attempts to turn the tables by proposing to take the *oratio recta* constructions as originating in a simple requirement of surface grammar:

One might equally well explain away the *occurrence* of the pronoun ['I'] in the intention expression ['I shall...'] by noting that the syntactical rules demand that we speak in complete sentences, even when no confusion results from our failure to do so. Suppose that I have been brooding, then announce *I have reached a decision.* [My italics.] When asked what I intend, I reply "to go". No one would mistake my meaning, thinking perhaps that I meant *he* was to go. I agree with Castañeda that we should not be bullied by surface grammar, and I am ready, as he is not, to drop the requirement that we speak in complete sentences.[3]

I am, however, still unpersuaded. First, whether anyone hearing Mrs. Baier's "to go" mistakes her meaning or not is not the issue at hand. The issue is: *what is the structure of a certain thought content,* namely, Mrs. Baier's intention? Her audience got it right. Fine. But *what* did they understand her to be saying? Merely to be naming the action to go, or to be expressing this action as a predicate, connected in the intentional form of copulation to her conception of herself in the first-person way? I go beyond Mrs. Baier concerning the requirement that we speak in complete sentences. We in fact already relax this requirement in dialogue, and in telegraphic communication reaping both efficiency of conveyance and monetary savings. But, as noted in Chapter 3, §§6–7, the interests of efficient communication often run counter to the interests of philosophy. However our need for possessing a language in order to think may be, language is primarily a means of communication. No wonder, therefore, that many a linguistic rule conforms to the interests of efficient communication rather than to the interests of ontological analysis. Yet the requirement of speaking at least in formal speech in complete sentences has a deeper ontological foundation than Mrs. Baier recognizes in the above quotation. Thus, while I am more than prepared to follow her in giving it up in daily life, I should see it reinstated temporarily in the context of philosophical discussion.

Mrs. Baier offers an excellent example of speech using incomplete sentences. The effect is, however, illusory. Her dialogue really has the sentence: 'I have reached a *decision* [,namely]: to go'; that is, her utterance "to go" places this infinitive in *oratio obliqua* under the main clause 'I have reached a decision'. But this is how we began: in *oratio obliqua* we delete the deep grammatical subject 'he (himself)' and replace the subjunctive with the infinitive.

I conclude, therefore, that as things now stand with the ordinary syntax of English, in the case of an apparent conflict between an *oratio obliqua* construction and its corresponding *oratio recta* construction, concerning the structure of the noema they both express, the *oratio recta* construction provides the *better* (or clearer) guidance. I further conclude that neither the syntactical fact of, nor the fact of communication by incomplete sentences in dialogue, adduced by Annette Baier, furnishes evidence in favor of the view that the full contents of intending are mere actions.

2. WHAT IS INTENDED IS NOT A PROPOSITION: GENERAL ARGUMENT

Our view is that intentions (i.e., the *what's* of intendings to do) are not propositions. This view, like any other philosophical view, cannot be proven by a foolproof deductive argument. That view, like all philosophical and scientific views, is supported by an argument, namely, the argument that it accounts for some data. The more diversified and complex the data, the stronger the argument is. Theorization is not deduction. It is the creation of a point of view that illuminates given data through a system of principles that fit, organize, refine and harmonize the data, these appearing before the theorization disorganized, conflicting, and even paradoxical. The role of deductive arguments in philosophy is central only in the development of perplexities from the data and in the development of a theory. All of these remarks apply, of course, to the theories developed in the other chapters of this book. But they are especially crucial for the theories of this chapter and for those in Chapter 7. They are valid for Chapters 4 and 5, but very few people have had the temptation to think that mandates or prescriptions are propositions. On the other hand, this temptation is widespread in the case of intentions.[4] In Chapter 7 the temptation we will fight is the temptation to take deontic judgments as built on propositions, not on practitions, as we claim.

The view that intentions are not propositions illuminates a large collection of data both about practical thinking, and about practical language. It would be a serious error to concentrate just on simple intentions and then develop a purely local theory of intentions. We seek after a theory of intentions that fits in with a larger theory of practical thinking. Specifically, we aim at a theory of intentions (i.e., what is intended) embeddable in a theory that can accommodate, *inter alia,* the following types of data (A)–(L).

(A)   The fundamental practical questions *Shall I do A?* and *What shall I do?*, without loss of self-identity, allow of two types of answer complementary to each other. The first type is the *prescriptive* answer that another may give: *Do A* or

Don't do A. The second answer is the *intentional* one, the one that the agent himself must give: *I shall do A* or *I shan't do A*.

This suggests that prescriptions and intentions belong in one practical category, differing only in "grammatical" person. Since prescriptions are not propositions, that suggests that intentions are not propositions either. Here we find a profound principle of harmony and elucidation: the unity of practical thinking is immediately accounted for by taking prescriptions and intentions as complementing each other in one category of practitions vis-à-vis the category of propositions.

(B) The differences of "grammatical" person are irreducible, as we have argued elsewhere and briefly discuss in §1 above and in §3 below.

Thus, the view that intentions are first-person practitions does *not* reduce them to commands to oneself, or to first-person prescriptions. There are *no* first-person prescriptions. One can, of course, command oneself to do something. But such commands involve second-person prescriptions (or even third-person ones). The following command is to myself, only because I believe that I am the second-person addressee of the command: *You, [looking at myself in a mirror], or Hector [without looking at myself], do that*. The point of (B) is to reinforce the need of locating the first-person counterpart of prescriptions.

(C) The contrast drawn in Chapter 5, §1 between the Future Framework and the Future Zone of Indeterminacy applies to intentions as well as to prescriptions. If we consider the case of a domain A of agents that has only one agent, the contrast is more significant when the practical actions determined by a context $C(A, E, S, \alpha, t)$ are taken to determine primary intentions than it is if taken to determine primary prescriptions.

This datum is simply a deeper manifestation of the profound underlying unity of practical reason, which any theory of practical thinking has to account for.

(D) Intentions do not appear to be true or false. This datum can, naturally, be suppressed by introducing a broad sense of 'truth' and 'falsity'. But it will re-appear if one proceeds, as one should, to characterize the "truth"-conditions of intentions. It is a powerful datum.

(E)   Sentences formulating complex intentions of an agent contain a structural duality of subordinate clauses. And the intentions themselves contain a duality of component noemata. Such duality is very perplexing if we take all the subordinate clauses to be formulations of propositions. For example, consider the noema *I shall do the following: Open the window unless I happen to open the door, and call George if I come before 10 p.m.*. Patently, the agent in question has an intention that focuses, so to speak, on (i) *his opening the window* and on (ii) *his calling George,* but not on (iii) his opening the door or on (iv) his coming before 10 p.m. This is a semantical point about the sentence, and the syntax signals it beautifully by dropping the subject 'I' before the focus clauses. The four items (i)–(iv) are clearly different, and they are all *inside* the scope of *I shall do the following.*

This datum goes hand in hand with (A)–(D). Items (i) and (ii) belong in the Future Zone of Indeterminacy, whereas items (iii) and (iv) pertain in the Future Framework.

(F)   The duality of the elements mentioned in (D) grounds a duality of implicational properties.

(G)   The duality mentioned in (E) and (F) is correlated with a duality of components inside propositions ascribing intentions to some person or other.

(H)   The dualities mentioned in (E)–(F) and (G) are correlated with a similar duality in deontic judgments, as we shall see in Chapter 7, §§7–12.

(I)   The view that the dualities of elements in (E)–(H) are manifestations of one and the same duality proposition-practition has helped solve *even before* they were discovered for other systems of deontic logic proposed by Von Wright and others, the so-called paradox of the Good-Samaritan and Chisholm's "paradox" of contrary-to-duty imperatives. We shall see this in Chapter 7, §§10–11.

(J)   The view outlined in (I) can also solve other "paradoxes",
           like the time-of-duty "paradox" as we shall see in Chapter 7,
           § 12.

Data (I) and (J) are interesting. When I first conceived the view I did not
have them in mind. Thus, that the theory satisfies (I) and (J) is a clear case
of a theory that when applied to new data shows its fertility and non-ad-
hocness.

(K)   The view outlined in (I) explains certain dualities and per-
           plexities present in the combination of quantification and
           deontic concepts, as we shall see in Chapter 7, § 13 and § 15.
(L)   The extensionality and referential transparency of deontic
           judgments, to be discussed in Chapter 7, § 15 and § 16, depends
           in part on the duality of components in complex deontic
           judgments.

We have discussed data (A) in Chapter 2, and data (C) in Chapter 5.
Data (H)–(L) will be presented in Chapter 7. We consider the remaining
data in this chapter.

3. WHAT IS INTENDED IS NOT A NON-FIRST-PERSON PROPOSITION

In this section we consider data of type (B) above. Since the issue of
demonstrative reference is a very profound one, we can only scratch its
surface. We must stress, however, that the comprehensive theory of
action we are aiming at has to link up with the theory of demonstrative
reference.

Now, it is tempting to suppose that the difference between a woman
intending to go (to pursue Annette Baier's example) and the same woman
believing that in fact she will go is not a difference between two noemata,
but a difference between two psychological states or attitudes. To be sure,
there is a charming ontological simplicity in the view that unifies the
thought contents involved, and treats both intending and believing as just
different propositional attitudes. Furthermore, a concrete reinforcement
of that temptation comes about from statements like this: *When a
woman expresses her intention to do something, and a man predicts that
she will do it, they are both talking about the *same* thing; and what

fulfills the man's prediction, namely, its truth, is precisely what fulfills the woman's intention*. Doubtless, the sameness spoken of in this statement would be perfectly guaranteed if the man's prediction were exactly the same proposition as the woman's intention. (Chapter 2, § 2 is relevant here). In correspondence P. T. Geach has called that sameness *Frege's point.*

Yet, a moment's reflection suffices to see that the sameness involved in a prediction and in an intention cannot be the sameness of *propositional* content. The woman's intention is a first-person thought content, while the man's prediction is most likely a third-person noema. The intention is of the form *I shall A*, whereas the predicted proposition is of the form *The woman such-and-such will A*. Clearly, the first-person way of referring to herself that enters as constituent in the woman's intention is not a constituent of the man's prediction. This would be true even if the woman's intention were a proposition. For, in general, first-person propositions are not reducible to third- or second-person propositions. To see this consider the proposition

(1)   The Editor of *Soul* believes that he (himself) is a millionaire.

Here we have again the quasi-indicator 'he (himself)' that represents in this case the first-person way of referring by the Editor to himself. The subordinate clause 'he (himself) is a millionaire' expresses the same first-person proposition the Editor would express by saying "I am a millionaire". Let this proposition be *I [=the Editor of *Soul*] am a millionaire*. Evidently, proposition (1) is not the same proposition as the proposition

(2)   The Editor of *Soul* believes that the Editor of *Soul* is a millionaire.

This follows from the fact that neither (1) implies (2) nor (2) implies (1). The Editor may believe, even know, that the Editor of *Soul* is a millionaire without believing that he himself is a millionaire, and on good evidence, if he has seen a probated will that bequeaths a million dollars to the Editor of *Soul*, whoever he may be, and he does not know that he has recently been appointed to such Editorship. Likewise, a very rich Editor may know (and believe) that he himself is a millionaire while believing that the Editor of *Soul*, whom he takes to be a well-known penniless fellow, is not a millionaire. Patently, any other description of the

Editor that replaces the phrase 'the Editor of *Soul*' in sentence (2) would express a different proposition from the one expressed by sentence (1). The Editor may very well fail to believe that he has the property mentioned in the description in question.

The Editor of *Soul* may believe that he (himself) is a millionaire, without believing that a person he is pointing to and referring to demonstratively, who happens to be himself, is a millionaire. For instance, while believing that he is a millionaire the Editor may see a man in a mirror, and point to him (i.e., to himself unknowingly), and think *That man is not a millionaire*. In general, then, *proposition (1) may be true even though every third-person proposition about the Editor of Soul, even a third-person demonstrative proposition to the effect that he is a millionaire, is not believed by him*. Thus, if proposition (1) is true, i.e., if the Editor of *Soul* believes the proposition *I [=the Editor of *Soul*] am a millionaire*, the proposition he believes is different from every third-person proposition about him, and, of course, different from any third-person proposition about anything else.[5]

To sum up, when a man predicts that a certain woman's intention will come true, there is something identical that she intends to do and he predicts that she will do. But that identical thing is not a proposition. It is simply the *action*, and perhaps, that the action will be performed by a certain agent. Thus, *if* the woman's intention is a proposition, it is, not identical with, but materially equivalent to, and *factually coincident with*, the proposition that is the man's prediction. The woman's intention is a first-person future-tense noema.

4. WHAT IS INTENDED IS NOT A FIRST-PERSON FUTURE-TENSE PROPOSITION

It is very tempting to hold that a woman's intention is identical with the woman's corresponding prediction. Both are certainly first-person future-tense noemata, and both share the same subjects and the same actions as predicates. For instance, the woman's intention *I [=the woman of the example] shall go to visit Smith* and her prediction *I [=the woman of the example] will go to visit Smith* do look very like the same noema. Let us refer to this view as *the view that identifies intentions with their intimately corresponding propositions*. Since the view is very tempting, seeing that it does not illuminate some crucial data is to gain a deeper insight into the structure of practical thinking. And since the view is only too tempting, we must marshall all the relevant data and pay close attention to their subtleties and complexities. We proceed now to consider data (E)–(G) listed above in §2, but the reader must remember that *all* the data discussed in the preceding chapters and in Chapter 7 converge on the examination of that view.

Let us take up data (E). Our preliminary discussion in §2 shows that some intentions are mixed in that they are compounds of two different types of components, those of one type being propositions and those of the other looking like pure intentions. To develop that duality further consider the following two intentions, either of which Arthur may adopt, depending on the circumstances:

(1)   I shall press button A, unless I jump.
(2)   Unless I press button A, I shall jump.

Undoubtedly, each of these sentences can be used by an English speaker to express one and the same intention, namely, the disjunctive intention:

(3)   (Either) I shall press button A, or I shall jump,

in which each disjunct is a pure intention. Our point here is not about how the sentences can be used, but about how the sentences may naturally be used, given their grammar, to express different noemata. Sentences (1) and (2) are especially designed to contrast both with each other and with sentence (3). Those are the contrasts we want to exploit.

If sentences (1) and (2) are used perspicuously in full exploitation of their syntactic form, they would express different intentions. These are the intentions we are assuming Arthur capable of expressing. Both intentions are disjunctions, and both seem to be mixed containing a disjunctive circumstance and a pure intention. They differ in that the circumstance of one is the intimately corresponding proposition of the pure intention of the other. Clearly, if the pure intention and its corresponding proposition were identical, then the disjunctive intentions expressed by sentences (1)–(3) would be the same.

The difference between intentions (1) and (2) is the difference between a pure intention and its intimately corresponding proposition. Suppose Arthur is subjecting himself to some experiments. If he is, say, experiment-

ing with a drug that can make him jump, he may adopt at a time T intention (1): his jumping, if it happens, will be only a *circumstance* for him to
act. In the terminology of Chapter 5, §1, his jumping belongs to his
Future Framework at time T, while his pressing button A belongs to his
Future Zone of Indeterminacy at T. Exactly the reverse is the case in connection with Arthur's intention (2). The difference is not only of great
significance concerning the setup and the interpretation of Arthur's
experiments. It is of great significance for normative judgments and
punitive action. If the experiments are performed by another person,
rather than by Arthur himself, Arthur will not be worthy of reward or
commendation, and will not be responsible, liable, punishable, or the
like by the obtaining of the circumstance, even though it is his own action.
He will be responsible, liable, punishable, etc. only for his doings that
fall within the purview of his intentions, i.e., within his Future Zone of
Indeterminacy. Palpably, intentions (1) and (2) differ from intention (3)
in that the latter contains no admixture of circumstances. In the case of
(3) Arthur will be worthy of praise, liable, punishable, etc. for whatever
of the two disjuncts he performs, since both are within his Future Zone
of Indeterminacy. Clearly, then, a theory that forces the collapse of
intentions (1) and (2) into intention (3) would have very disastrous consequences.

The disparity of the disjuncts *I shall press button A* and *I (will)
press button A* in (1) and (2) is, therefore, evident. That disparity rules
out the view that the intentional character of (1) and (2) is external to,
and superimposed on, a basic homogenous disjunction. If such were the
case, the differences among (1)–(3) would vanish. We must, therefore,
hold fast to the different roles of the disjuncts in (1) and (2).

An isolated consideration of intentions (1)–(3) is, of course, capable
of suggesting different local views. One such view is this: The type of
disjunction expressed by 'unless' is different from the one expressed by
'or': for instance, the former is, while the latter is not, non-commutative.
At this local level it can be argued that the contrast between (1) and (2) is
evidence for the non-commutativity of the unless-disjunction. But matters cannot be left just like that. We do not have here a theory yet. We
merely have a suggestion of a theory that can be treated seriously only
after it includes an account of non-commutative disjunctions. We will not
argue here that such a theory looks too complicated. On the contrary, we

urge anybody interested in developing the suggestion to do so. The more theories there are the better our understanding of the structure and functions of practical thinking will be. We must emphasize, however, that the local suggestion about the unless-disjunction is worthless, unless both it grows into a theory and, by taking into account all of the relevant data (A)–(L), it grows into a comprehensive theory.

Part of the data of type (E) is the fact that the disjunction (1) and (2) *do* behave like ordinary disjunctions in crucial respects. They obey principles of implication and equivalence that govern ordinary disjunction, except for the heterogeneity of their disjuncts. The data here are, in a way, opposite to the one collected under type (F). This shows, once again, the need for a comprehensive theory. To illustrate, intention (1), *I shall press button A, unless I jump* and the premise that the circumstance will not be realized, namely *I will not jump*, imply together the pure intention*I shall press button A*. Intention (1) implies both the conditional intention *If I do not jump, I shall press button A* and the conditional *I shan't press button A, only if I jump*. Furthermore, intention (1) implies the negative mixed-conjunctive intention *I shan't do the following: not press button A while it is the case that I will not jump*. And so on. In §7 we shall *strengthen* this set of data by a systematic collection of implication principles governing intentions.

It should not be thought that the difference in the disjuncts of (1) and (2) consists of their time differences, the circumstance being the earlier action. In Arthur's experiments described above the times were supposed to be the same. But this is immaterial. The circumstance *may* be later than the action lying in the Future Zone of Indeterminacy. If Arthur knows that the later circumstance will not obtain he may realize his disjunctive intention at the proper earlier time.

Our difference between an action considered as a circumstance and an action considered as within the Future Zone of Indeterminacy suggests another local view: The difference between intentions (1) and (2) involves Arthur's jumping as a *happening* to him and Arthur's jumping as his *doing*. Thus, it might be proposed that intention (1) be analyzed as:

(1A)   I will do the pressing of button A unless it happens that I jump;

or perhaps as:

(1B)   My doing of the pressing of button A will occur, unless the happening of my jumping occurs.

Neither (1A) nor (1B) are helpful without some commentary. We still have the problem of distinguishing the heterogeneous disjunction (1) and (2) from the homogeneous intention (3) and from the homogeneous prediction

(4)   I will press button A, or I will jump.

We must, therefore, understand the contrast between *doing* and *happening* in the appropriate way. The view that this suggests is that the former is an operator that yields intentions, and the latter is one that yields propositions. But on what do they operate? If they operate on the set of elements entering in an intention and its intimately corresponding proposition, we may construe the operators as copulae. This, of course, is fine.

Another suggestion would be to say that an intention *I shall do A* is the future-tense proposition *I will do A intentionally*. But this seems circular. *I will do A intentionally* being *I will do A because I intend to do A*, i.e., *I will do A because of my intention: I shall do A*.

In short, the heterogeneity of the disjuncts in (1) and (2) is *internal* to the disjunction: it cannot be wholly located in a mental state or attitude operating on the disjunction as a whole. Furthermore, that heterogeneity does *not* consist of any of the parameters that distinguish one proposition from another. This suggest immediately that the difference between an intention and its intimately corresponding proposition is one that introduces a new, non-propositional element – like a copula or an operator on predicates or subjects. (In Chapter 10, §3 we analyze this element as a copula operator.)

Let us consider some evidence of type (F). Examine the case of Alfonso who made the following decisions:

(11)   *If* Joan comes early from school, I shall drive her to the shopping center.
(12)   I shall buy Mary a purse, *if and only if* I drive Joan to the shopping center.

Alfonso's intentions (11) and (12) are mutually compatible. The former is just a conditional intention, but the latter is a biconditional. That is to say, (12) does bind Alfonso not to buy Mary a purse if he does not drive Joan to the shopping center. And this is what he wants. He is protecting his flank, so to speak, and he is protecting his flank to Mary regardless of his intention concerning Joan. Now, if intentions were identical with their intimately corresponding propositions, Alfonso would not be protected from buying Mary a purse regardless of his intention to Joan. Suppose that:

(13)   Joan comes early from school, and
(14)   Alfonso does not drive Joan to the shopping center.

On the identity view, Alfonso's conditioned intention *I shall drive Joan to the shopping center* in (11) is the same as the condition *I drive Joan to the shopping center* in (12). Both would be propositions. Hence, (11) and (13) would imply the proposition-intention.

(15)   I shall buy Mary a purse.

On the other hand, (14) and (12) imply in any case Alfonso's intention (*not* intending, of course):

(16)   I shan't buy Mary a purse.

Thus, on the identity view the set {(11), (12), (13), (14)} would be contradictory, and Alfonso would be committed to buy Mary a purse even if he does not drive Joan to the shopping center!

Clearly, the situation is this. By the truth of (13) and (14) Alfonso has violated his intention (11) concerning Joan, but has automatically *relieved* himself of his *bi*conditioned commitment concerning Mary (whether Mary knows of it or not is irrelevant). That is, Alfonso does not violate his intention (12) concerning Mary. Since he is bound by (12) as a whole, then his non-violation of (12) is due only to his not being committed to *I shall buy Mary a purse*. Thus, intentions (11) and (12) do *not* imply:

(17)   If Joan comes early from school, I shall buy Mary a purse.

Hence, unless we are going to give up the transitivity of conditionality, we must hold that the *intention* *I shall drive Joan to the shopping center* in (11) is not even implied by the *proposition* *I (will) drive Joan to the shopping center* in (12). *A fortiori,* they are not equivalent, much less identical with each other.

There are many other implications, e.g., modus ponens, that depend on the heterogeneity of the components of certain compound intentions. We will just consider one simple and interesting case. Examine the following intention:

(21)   I shall go home, if and only if I go home.

This intention may also be formulated thus:

(21A)   I shall do the following: go home, just in case I go home.

It is a very peculiar intention. It formulates an intention that has both as sufficient and as necessary condition the truth of the intimately corresponding proposition. Reflection reveals that it is odd, but perfectly all right. It is an intention that rules out the agent's merely happening to go home. If the agent goes home, he will have performed a doing, in the terminology of some paragraphs above. In other words, the agent's action is either realized intentionally, or it is not realized, but then he had no intention of performing it. Patently, the biconditioned intention (21), or (21A), is not logically valid: it is *contingently valid,* or contingently committing, upon its own realization. Yet the view that identifies an intention with its intimately corresponding proposition makes intention (21) a trivial tautology. (Of course, sentence (21) can express a tautological proposition. But this is beside the point.)

Let us discuss now some evidence of type (G). Consider the proposition

(31)   Martin intends to: sell the house he will inherit tomorrow.

As we have argued in §1 above, there is an implicit quasi-indicator 'he', which is the subject of the verb 'sell'. The pronoun 'he' in sentence (31) is also a quasi-indicator. That is, the whole subordinate infinitive clause 'sell the house he will inherit tomorrow' expresses the intention *I [=Martin] shall sell the house that I will inherit tomorrow*. As the infinitive construction emphatically signals, Martin's acts of selling and of inheriting enter in that intention in a very different way. His act of selling is part of his Future Zone of Indeterminacy at the time in question, whereas his act of inhering is a circumstance, a part of his Future Framework at that time. This difference determines a further difference. The circumstance is something pertaining to believing, not to pure intending. Here we find another instance of the phenomenon described in Chapter 1, namely, that practical reason includes pure reason. Intending is a practical generalization of believing, but, *intending is not believing.* The propositional elements of a compound intention are items of belief, and in some combinations are believed. This is the case with (31), which is of the form:

(31A)   Martin intends: $\exists x(x$ is a house and he will inherit x and he to sell x).

It follows from (31A), and from (31), that:

(32)   Martin believes that $\exists x(x$ is a house and he will inherit x).

But it does *not* follow from (31A), or from (31), that:

(33)   Martin intends that: $\exists x(x$ is a house and he will inherit x).

Of course, it may be right that Martin intends to inherit the house he will inherit. But it need not be true: his intending may be a happening not at all under his control. At any rate, whether his inheriting is something he can intend or not, the point is that *in* (31) Martin's inheriting is a *circumstance,* not a practical action.

Here we are confronting a very important principle of rational psychology (See Chapter 1, §3 and Chapter 10, §1–§2) to wit:

(IB.1)   *X intends to do the following: to A while it is the case that $p*$ *implies* *X believes that p and X intends to A*.

Another very important principle connecting intending and believing is this:

(IB.2)   *[X is rational with respect to his intentions, and] X intends [intention] i, and X believes that intention i implies intention $j*$ implies *X intends $j*$.

Some philosophers hold that the first conjunct of (IB.2), within brackets, is deletable. We will do so here, but the reader may assume, if he so wishes, that the person X is rational with respect to his intentions.

Now, principle (IB.2) does not fit the view that intentions are propositions, nor does it fit the view already rejected in §1 above that intentions are mere actions. If intentions were identical with their intimately corresponding propositions, (IB.2) would be the same as:

(B−)   *X intends (the proposition) that X will do A, and X believes
         that (the proposition) that X will do A implies (the proposition) that X will do B* *implies* *X intends (the proposition)
         that X will do B*.

But (B−) is false, precisely because it ignores the internal duality of elements that appears in the complex contents of some intendings. We proceed to show this by deriving from intending an analogue of the so-called Good-Samaritan paradox of deontic calculi, which is part of our data (I) mentioned in §2 above, and which we shall study in Chapter 7, §10.

Consider the case of our friend Corliss, who knows that he is driven to hurt the feelings of people with whom he comes in contact when there is a full moon. His friend Marco will visit him for two weeks and on the 10th day of the visit there will be a full moon. Corlis is worried about his behavior on the 10th day. Very carefully and deliberately Corliss reveals his problem to Marco, and frames an intention:

(41)   Corliss intends to do something special for Marco on the
         11th day when he recognizes that he has wholly unintentionally
         hurt Marco's feelings on the 10th day.

Clearly,

(42)   (The proposition) that Corliss will do something special for
         Marco on the 11th day when he recognizes that he has wholly
         unintentionally hurt Marco's feelings on the 10th day,
         implies (the proposition) that Corliss will hurt Marco's
         feelings on the 10th day.

We assume Corliss to be bright enough, so that:

(43)   Corliss believes (42).

Then, by (B−), it would follow from (41) and (43) that:

(44)   Corliss intends (the proposition) that he will hurt Marco's
         feelings on the 10th day,

which, according to the view identifying intentions with their intimately corresponding propositions, is formulated in idiomatic English as follows:

(45)   Corliss intends to hurt Marco's feelings on the 10th day.

On the other hand, (41) implies:

(46)   Corliss does not intend to hurt Marco's feelings on the 10th day.

Therefore, we must reject either some of the assumptions or $(-B)$ together with the identity view behind it. We opt for the second alternative. The reason is, again, that in Corliss' intention (41), both the action of hurting Marco's feelings, and the proposition *I [=Corliss] will hurt Marco's feelings*, enter as circumstances, i.e., as parts of Corliss' Future Framework, not as practical parts of the Future Zone of Indeterminacy.

The reader will note that the Corliss example is also a counter-example to revisions of $(B-)$ that include any combination of the following conditions on action B: (i) the agent X can perform B, (ii) X can initiate his doing B, (iii) X can intentionally perform B, (iv) X does not intend not to do B. All conditions (i)–(iv) are satisfied by Corliss and his hurting Marco's feelings. So, if (IB.2) is true, these conditions, added to the proposition Corliss would express by saying "I will hurt Marco's feelings", do not suffice to produce a propositional analysis of the intention pertaining to, although not endorsed or adopted by, Corliss: namely, to hurt (himself) Marco's feelings.

5. Intentions to bring about

It may be thought that an intention is a proposition and that the state of intending is more perspicuously expressed by the locutions 'intends to bring it about that' or 'intention to bring it about that'. It may be contended that

(1)   Jones' intention is to open the door

should be understood as:

(2)   Jones intends [or his intention is] to bring it about that he opens the door.

No doubt, we can use the two sentences to make exactly the same statement. Yet, given the primary semantical rules governing them, they can be used properly to formulate different propositions. The difference we have in mind is essentially the difference illustrated above in the Corliss example, but now the situation is more delicate.

In the Corliss example Corliss' action of hurting Marco's feelings is a pre-future, or future-perfect circumstance within Corliss' intention to do something special for Marco. In the case of Jones in (2), Jones' action of opening the door in question is a post-future circumstance within Jones' intention. According to (2) Jones intends to do some action, not specified, which fits in with his other purposes and goals, so that as a consequence of that action of his he will be in a state that will cause his opening of the door. Patently, Jones may cause his opening of the door by persuading a hypnotist to put him in a hypnotic trance and order him to open the door, or to perform some other action that will inevitably lead Jones to open the door unintentionally and unaware. Clearly, Jones' causing that it be the case that he opens the door is different from Jones' opening the door: he can do the former without *in* doing it open the door. Thus, his intending the former, which is what he intends when he intends to bring it about that he opens the door, is *not* the same as his intending to open the door.

Bringing-about is, therefore, not a feature characteristic of the state of intending, but an element that enters as a constituent of *some* intentions. Furthermore, an intention of the form *I shall do A* is different from the corresponding intention of the form *I shall bring it about that I do A*, and neither of these is identical with their corresponding proposition of the form *I will bring it about that I (will) do A*.

6. INTENTIONS AS FIRST-PERSON PRACTITIONS

According to the preceding argumentation we need a theory of intentions that identifies them neither with proposition nor with actions. We have seen that an intention contains a first-person subject expressed by an absent quasi-indicator 'he (himself)' within either of the larger contexts 'X intends [himself] to come' and 'John's intention is [himself] to come'. We also noted that intentions are primarily formulated by future-tense sentences of the form 'I shall [will] do A'. Now, it appears entirely natural to think that what John fully intends in the above example is the same as what he would express, had he *decided* to come, by saying "I shall come". We exalt this natural identification as a *theoretical thesis,* namely: *the very same thought content that is a decision. or resolution, is also an intention.* Whether an intention is a decision or not, then, depends solely on whether a psychological process of deciding or deliberating has the intention as its ending element. Partial support for this thesis is furnished by the wide-spread view that decisions are neither true nor false, i.e., are not propositions.

The fundamental ontological theory of intentions we adopt is, as noted in §2, the intentional copulation view. According to it, a basic or simple intention has, *inter alia,* the following important features: (i) an intention is a propositional-like content in that it has as constituents both a subject and an attribute which is an action; (ii) like a proposition, a decision or intention does not have the person, who is the agent, himself as a constituent, as can be seen from the fact that in the above example John may fail to believe that he himself is John; (iii) an intention does have as subject constituent the conception of an agent in the first person way, i.e., the sense (to speak a la Frege) or the individual concept (to speak a la Carnap and Church) of the agent's first-person references;[6] (iv) the attribute constituent of an atomic intention is an actional one (see Chapter 11), precisely the same attribute entering in the corresponding performance proposition, but (v) this attribute is linked to its subject, the agent concept, by means of a *different copula,* which will be analyzed in Chapter 10, §3.

The intentional copula is, or contains, an irreducible ingredient that characterizes, together with the prescriptional copula, introduced in Chapter 4, §1 and §8, the autonomy of practical thinking. At any rate, we have two crucial contrasts on our hands.

(A) The contrast between the two propositions:
(1)   John intends to come;
(2)   John believes that he (himself) will come.

(B) The contrast between intention (3) and proposition (4) below, which are the contents of the intending of (1) and the believing of (2):

(3)   I [=John] to come
(4)   I [=John] will come.

Here the parenthetical '[=John]' is an index on the first-person pronoun signaling a comment *by us* on, and external to, intention (3) and proposition (4). This comment is intended to help identify the intention and the proposition, respectively, that are expressed by the subordinate clauses in (1) and (2).

We have dwelt upon contrast (B). In Chapter 10 we shall say more about contrast (A). Intending is, in the exercise of practico-theoretical reason, the engulfing counterpart of believing. But intending and believing differ not only in terms of the noemata they take as contents, but also as mental states, involving different dispositions or propensities.

Intentions or decisions (noemata, that is) belong with pieces of advice, requests, orders, commands, and, in general, with the contents of assertive-like and deliberate acts of telling a person what to do. We have used before the word *'mandate'* as the generic term to group all the contents of such acts, and the word 'prescription' to refer to the structure common to a family of mandates that demand of the same agents the doing of the same actions in exactly the same circumstances. For example, the order *Peter, go home*, the request *Peter, please go home*, and the advice *Peter, you better go home* (assuming, of course, that we have the same Peter and the same time throughout), have as underlying structure the prescription *Peter to go home*, in the notation introduced in Chapter 2, §4. Prescriptions are characterized by: (i) being neither true nor false, and (ii) not being the contents of believings or knowings-that. The atomic ones are constituted by an agent concept tied to an actional attribute by means of a special copula. Prescriptions are not necessarily second-person contents. Mandates are, of course, second-person contents. But a prescription like *Peter to go home* is a third-person prescription. As discussed in Chapter 2, §3, to issue a prescription is to issue it embellished as, or clothed under the guise of, a mandate of one type or another. Issuing a prescription (or mandate) is the linguistic act counterpart of stating a proposition.

Thus, the logico-ontological parsing of

(1)   John intends to come

may be represented as:

(1a)   John intends-to (I [=John] to come),

where *I [=John] to come* is the first-person practition corresponding to the second-person prescription *You [=John] to come*.

The first-person noema *I [=Peter] to go home*, which we no longer call a prescription, we propose to identify with the intention *I [=Peter] shall go home*. Thus, at this juncture our crucial thesis is this: *intentions are the first-person counterpart and complement of prescriptions:* more specifically, *the intentional copula is exactly the same as the prescriptional copula.* As explained in Chapter 2, §6, we call prescriptions and intentions *practitions.* Our view rules out the identification of intentions with a subset of mandates. Therefore, intentions are not first-person mandates. There is, however, in the case of intentions a duality like the one between mandates and prescriptions. Formulations of decisions and intentions are the first-person counterpart of mandates, and just as mandates are embellishments of prescriptions, such formulations are embellishments of underlying first-person practitions. We could use the words 'intention' and 'decision' to refer to first-person contents of acts of deciding or intending conceived as analogous to ordering, entreating, advising, requesting and commanding.

In any case, the fundamental contrast we are dealing with is not the contrast between intentions and propositions, but the one between practitions and propositions. Thus, the operations of the mind divide into those addressed to propositions, the propositional or purely contemplative attitudes or acts, and those addressed to practitions, the practico-cognitive or practico-theoretical, or simply practitional attitudes or acts. *The propositional operations yield propositions out of propositions; the practitional operation yield propositions out of practitions.* This is one of the fundamental laws of rational psychology. (See Chapter 10 for additional discussion of topics in the rational psychology of action).

7. THE BASIC STRUCTURE OF INTENTIONS

Like propositions (as studied in Chapter 3, §§12–13) and prescriptions (as studied in Chapter 4, §§3ff), intentions have a "natural" partial ordering related to the unreasonableness of an agent's failure to endorse, or his unreasonableness to endorse, an intention, given that he endorses certain other propositions or intentions. Since intentions are on our theory the first-person counterpart of prescriptions, we are committed to view intentions as having the same implicational structure of prescriptions. Conversely, finding out that intentions do have the same implicational structure of prescriptions does provide evidence for the adequacy of our theory. In the light of the parallelism between prescriptional and propositional implications established in Chapter 4, §§3–5, the implicational structure of intentions is, then, parallel to that of propositions. We must parallel our examination of prescriptional implication offered in Chapter 4, §§2–7 in our study of intentional implication. But we shall only furnish the outline of the study here.

Intentions combine with other intentions by means of the regular propositional connectives. There are, thus, denials, conjunctions, conditionalizations and biconditionalizations of intentions. For example: a negative intention is expressed by 'I [=John] won't go home', when this sentence expresses or is used to rehearse a decision; a conjunctive intention is expressed by the infinite clause '[John] to go home and study' *in* 'John intends to go home and study'. Some philosophers have argued, and others will undoubtedly argue, that the words 'not', 'and', 'but', and 'or' do not express the same connection in examples like the preceding ones. Their reason is that since decisions have no truth-values the English connectives cannot be governed by the ordinary truth-tables when they link sentences or clauses expressing decisions. This argument is in one sense absolutely sound. If the *truth*-tables fully characterize the meaning of 'not', 'and', and 'or', then these words are used in a different sense in the above examples. But so are they when they are used in examples like 'Someone is not here' and 'Someone is tall or heavy', in which the connectives 'not' and 'or' express a connection of properties or propositional functions, *not* propositions. In short, as in the case of prescriptions and mandates discussed in Chapter 4, §2, it is an uninteresting verbal matter whether we say or not that intentions are compounded in the same ways propositions are. A fortiori, it is also a verbal matter whether we say or not that intentions (prescriptions) stand in the same relationship of implication in which propositions stand. What is important is the fact that intentions parallel propositions both in their way of composition and in their formal structure. If the reader wishes, we again "extend" the sense of the English connectives and speak of the same forms of composition and of the same rules of implication characterizing each connection or content structure – with just one restriction: *to be compossible* (i.e., disjoinable, conjoinable, etc.) *two intentions must have first-person references to the very same agent.* This is rather, a first-person thinkability requirement.

Intentions combine with propositions. For example, John's intention may be *I [=John] shall go home before it is dark*, where the sentence 'it is dark' expresses a proposition, i.e., a truth-valued noema. The combination expressed by the word 'before' is a complex involving quantifiers and conjunction: going home at some time t and t being earlier than the time at which it is dark. Thus, intentions and propositions also combine with each other by means of the regular connections. What type of noemata are such mixed combinations? Clearly, the above compound example "feels" like an intention. Likewise, conditional compounds like *If he comes, I will (shall) go home* and disjunctives like *I will go, unless she comes soon* all "feel" intentional. In other cases, however, it is not completely clear how one should classify the complex noema. If a man says "It is getting dark, and I am going home", his token of 'and' links a sentence that expresses an intention; but there is no compulsion to say either that the compound is an intention or that it is a proposition. Doubtlessly, one can develop a theory that allows some compounds to be intentions, others to be propositions, and others to be neither. But the general idea that propositions and, hence, noemata are closed under the logical connections would demand a complicated bookkeeping. For more details on this issue see Chapter 4, §4–§5. Thus, we propose, not as a generalization of what one is inclined to say, but as a theoretical principle, that *mixed connective compounds of intentions and propositions are intentions.* This principle maintains the closure of propositions and of intentions, making propositionhood a recessive character.

The preceding terminological decisions and principles allow us to show that intentions have a simple basic deducibility structure, namely, the one captured by the principles of implicational partial ordering given below, which exhibit the corresponding principles of composition. Let α be a set of noemata, i.e., propositions and/or intentions; let 'i' and 'j' represent intentions; let 'X' and 'Y' be any noemata, whether propositions or intentions; let 'not-X' represent the negation of noema X, and let '(X & Y)' represent the conjunction of noemata X and Y. As in Chapters 3 and 4 we say that noemata as well as sets of noemata imply. Thus, the basic implicational structure of intentions is, *assuming compossibility,* characterized by:

I.1.   If *i* is a member of α, then α implies *i*.

I.2.   If α implies *i*, then α implies not-not-*i*.
         Example: *I [=John] shall A* implies *I [=John] shall not
         fail to A*.

I.3.   If α implies not-*i*, then α implies not-(*i* & X).
         Example: whatever implies *I [=John] shall not A* implies
         *I [=John] shall not do the following: A while it is the
         case that *p**.

I.4.   If α implies not-*i*, then α implies not-(X & *i*).
         Example: whatever implies *I [=John] shall not A* implies
         I [=John] shall not both B and A.

I.5.   If α implies *i*, and α also implies *j*, then α implies (*i* & *j*).
         Example: If endorsing a set α of noemata makes unreasonable
         for John to refuse to endorse *I [=John] shall do A* as well
         as to refuse to endorse *I [=John] shall do B*, then it is
         unreasonable for John to refuse to endorse *I [=John] shall
         do both A and B*.

I.6.   If α and *i* imply *j*, and α and not-*i* also imply *j*, then α by itself
         implies *j*.

I.7.   If α implies not-(X & not-*i*), then α and X imply *i*.

I.8.   If α implies not-(*i* & not-X), then α and *i* imply X.

These principles are formally the same as the principles D*1–D*7 discussed in Chapter 4, §5. They characterize the most elementary structure of negation and conjunction. We leave it to the reader to satisfy himself by the examination of specific examples that I.1–I.7 all hold for some non-empty class α of noemata that contains intentions only, or contains intentions and propositions.

Principles I.1–I.7 govern propositions and intentions. They say absolutely nothing about the linguistic mechanisms employed or employable to express negation or conjunction, as we discussed in Chapter 3, §§6–7 and §15. This is of utmost importance. The fact that a sentence having a future-tense clause after the word 'if' cannot grammatically express a decision does not show, for instance, that there are no pure conditionalizations of intentions. If conditionalization is reducible to the negation of a conjunction, then pure conditionalizations of intentions are expressible in ways that do not include the use of 'if' or 'only if'. If conditionalization is a primitive connection, not reducible to negation of a conjunction, then we can *at most* say that certain compounds are not expressible in ordinary language. But from this it does not follow that they cannot be thought, and much less that they do not occupy their positions in the logical space of intentions and propositions, which space is partially ordered by principles D∗1–D∗10 of Chapter 4, §5. Indeed, if we interpret the asterisked letters in the formulations of D∗1–D∗10 to represent propositions as well as practitions, whether prescriptions or intentions, D∗1–D∗10 have as special cases our principles I.1–I.7.

The principles of quantification formulated in Chapter 4, §8 also generalize to intentions. Again, we shall simply assume that that section, like most of Chapter 4, can be read replacing the words 'prescription', 'imperative', and 'mandate' with the word 'practition', or even with the word 'intention'. Thus, the theory of *intentional functions* and *intentional quantification* is all there.

8. THE LEGITIMACY-VALUES OF INTENTIONS

By reasoning exactly parallel to the one developed in Chapter 4, §6 we must conclude that a two-valued implicational structure frames the class of intentions that abide by I.1–I.7 above. We erect this result as a theory, i.e., we adopt the view that every class of intentions abides by I.1–I.7. Naturally, this commits us to analyzing away all value gaps that seem to violate the two-valued structure. But we should avail ourselves of the techniques already in use for the case of two-valued propositional logical theory.

There are, therefore, two intentional values analogous to truth and falsity. One is a designated value, like truth, in that both it is preserved in implication and it is the polar star of intending. We do not call it "truth", for it necessarily lacks the requisite correspondence with fact. We call it *Legitimacy* or *orthotes*. The other value we call *Nonlegitimacy* or *anorthotes*. The crucial task is now to furnish an account of intentional orthotes.

Since intentions are the first-person counterpart of prescriptions, the Legitimacy of an intention corresponds point by point to the Legitimacy of its corresponding prescriptions, i.e., the prescriptions that demand the very same action of the same agent in exactly the same circumstances.

Thus, the Legitimacy-values of intentions come in an infinity of pairs, depending on the contexts of ends (purposes and goals) and of the agents that belong in the agent's kingdom of co-persons. In short, then, we adopt the view that the Legitimacy-values of prescriptions are the same Legitimacy-values of all practitions. At this juncture we assume the accounts of the Legitimacy-values of prescriptions given in Chapter 5.

Now, the values of compound intentions are governed by the same generalized tables for logical connections introduced in Chapter 4, §6. Hence, we need be concerned only with primary intentions. And we analyze their Legitimacy-values as follows, building on Chapter 5:

(J.*i*)   A primary intention of the form *I [=X] shall A* is Legitimate in context C of ends E and kingdom α of co-persons, if and only if the corresponding prescription of the form *X to A* is Legitimate in context C of ends E and kingdom α of co-persons, where X is in α.

(N.*i*)   A primary intention of the form *I [=X] shall A* is Non-legitimate in a context C, if and only if it is not Legitimate in C.

NOTE: In (J.*i*) and (N.*i*), C is either a limited context or an absolute context for a domain of agents at a given time.

NOTES TO CHAPTER 6

[1] For an examination of quasi-indexical reference and its crucial role in the conception of other minds, see Hector-Neri Castañeda's papers: (i) 'He: A Study in the Logic of Self-Consciousness', *Ratio* 8 (1966): 130–157; (ii) 'Indicators and Quasi-indicators', *American Philosophical Quarterly* 4 (1967): 85–100; (iii) 'On the Logic of Attributions of Self-Knowledge to Others', *The Journal of Philosophy* 65 (1968): 439–456.

[2] See Annetet C. Baier, 'Act and Intent', *The Journal of Philosophy* 67 (1970): 648–658. Jack W. Meiland in his *The Nature of Intention* (London: Methuen & Co., Ltd. 1970) also holds that the "objects of intention" are actions (p. 43). This book has some interesting discussions on the nature of intending. Baier's paper is part of a symposium on intentions. The other papers are: Roderick M. Chisholm, 'The Structure of Intention', *Ibid.*: 633–647; and George Pitcher, '"In Intending" and Side Effects', *Ibid.*: 659–668. H-N. Castañeda has examined critically the symposium in 'Intentions and the Structure of Intending', *The Journal of Philosophy* 68 (1971): 453–466.

[3] This is from a reply by Annette Baier to Castañeda's paper mentioned in note 2 above.

[4] This is the view advocated by Alvin Goldman in his comments on H-N. Castañeda's, 'Purpose and Action' presented at the 1974 Oberlin Philosophy Colloquium (forthcoming). It seems to be the view that Bruce Aune advocates in his 'Sellars' Theory of Practical Reason' in H-N. Castañeda, ed., *Knowledge, Action, and Reality: Critical Studies in the Philosophy of Wilfrid Sellars* (Indianapolis: Bobbs-Merrill, 1975). Sellars

also seems to hold that view in *Science and Metaphysics* (London: Routledge & Kegan Paul, New York: Humanities Press, 1967). See H.N Castañeda 'Some Reflections on Sellars' Theory of Intentions', also in *Knowledge, Action and Reality*. Relevant papers are William Todd, 'Intentions and Programs', *Philosophy of Science* **38** (1971): 530-541; Robert Audi, 'Intending', *The Journal of Philosophy* **70** (1973): 387–403; K. W. Rankin, 'The Non-Causal Selffulfilment of Intentions', *American Philosophical Quarterly* **9** (1972): 279–289; Donald Gustafson, 'The Range of Intentions', *Inquiry* (1975), 83–95.
[5] For more detailed argumentation in support of the claim that first-person propositions are different from, and irreducible to, second- and third-person propositions, see Hector-Neri Castañeda, 'On the Phenomeno-Logic of the I', *Proceedings of the XIVth International Congress of Philosophy*, Vol. III (Vienna, Austria: Herder, 1969): 260–266. See also 'Indicators and Quasi-Indicators' and 'On the Logic of Attributions of Self-Knowledge to Others', mentioned in note 1 above.
[6] Here we come to the border of larger issues in ontology. On the view I prefer primary intentions do not have exactly Fregean first-person senses, but only similar primary individuals called *concrete individuals* in H-N. Castañeda, 'Thinking and the Structure of the World', *Philosophia* **4** (1974): 3–40, and called *ontological guises* in Castañeda's 'Identity and Sameness', *Philosophia* **5** (1975): 121–150. See Chapter 12 §5.

CHAPTER 7

DEONTIC JUDGMENTS AND THEIR
IMPLICATIONAL STRUCTURE

In this chapter we continue the study of deontic noemata began in Chapter 2, §7. As in the preceding studies of prescriptions and intentions, our initial concern here is a careful collection of fruitful and rich data concerning the internal nature of, and the implicational structure of, deontic judgments. We gather deontic principles *Deon.* 1 through *Deon.* 29. In Chapter 9 we braid together all the strands developed in the preceding chapters as well as in this one into a formal theory of the basic logic of all the practical noemata. This is supplemented by the theories of intendings, needs, and wants outlined in Chapter 10 and the theory of ideal wants developed in Chapter 11.

In particular, we collect evidence for these general theses: (1) deontic noemata are propositions; (2) the primary or atomic deontic noemata are the result of deontic operations operating on practitions (i.e., prescriptions or intentions); (3) rightness, wrongness, oughtness, and the like are not genuine properties of either persons or events, but are modal connections or modalities, that transform practitions into propositions; (4) deontic modalities are different from ordinary propositional modalities in that *ought* and obligation do not create referentially-opaque or non-extensional contexts. We also discuss the most fundamental principles of deontic implication.

1. DEONTIC JUDGMENTS ARE PROPOSITIONS

As we pointed out in Chapter 2, imperatives (or mandates), and intentions and prescriptions are not the only practical noemata, i.e., noemata characteristically suited for the guidance of conduct. There are, in fact, hosts of noemata that are practical, and yet are not practitions, namely, deontic judgments. We have already explained in Chapter 2, §7, how they differ from prescriptions and intentions with respect to negation. But for the time being let us concentrate on their rich and bewildering multiplicity. The following are just *some* of the most obvious types:

(1) assertions to the effect that certain general types of action are unconstitutional, i.e., violate the Constitution of one's own country;

(2) assertions to the effect that given actions are, more specifically, legally permissible, or forbidden, or mandatory, i.e., violate or fail to violate the laws of one's own country;

(3) assertions to the effect that given actions are not allowed by municipal or local ordinances;

(4) noemata to the effect that certain courses of action are prohibited, or enjoined, by the statutes or regulations of certain institutions;

(5) noemata to the effect that a certain social or institutional role or office is constituted by a certain list of duties;

(6) noemata to the effect that the rules of a club or association make it imperative that something be done, or left undone;

(7) judgments to the effect that in a certain game, or in a certain play of a game, certain moves must be done, or avoided;

(8) assertions to the effect that given certain ends, goals, or purposes, as well as the circumstances of the case, a certain person ought, or ought not, to perform certain actions;

(9) judgments to the effect that certain actions are morally wrong, or morally right;

(10) judgments made in deliberation to the effect that, everything being considered, one ought to do, or not to do, such and such, or that one may do or may leave undone a certain action.

The differences between any two of the above types of noema are very important. It cannot be stressed enough that such differences *must* not be obliterated. Here we have: general principles (e.g., of morality), fundamental precepts of constitutional law, basic legal statutes, regulations, ordinances, norms, prescriptions, conclusions of law, results of deliberation, and rules of all sorts. The large variety of words to refer to the noemata of the above types is a valuable asset of ordinary language that helps us to keep track of the crucial differences among the noemata in question, and, thus, to find our way in the world. The same is true of the large variety of words that are used in ordinary language to formulate those noemata: 'duty', 'obligation', 'ought', 'may', 'right', 'wrong', 'must', 'have (has) to', 'is required', 'allow', 'disallow', 'correct', 'permitted', 'permissible', 'unlawful', etc. Each of these words has special functions of its own that must be studied and classified in detail, if we are to have a complete understanding of practical language and thinking. The differences among the meanings and functions of these words are clues to the differences among the types of the assertion made with their aid. These differences are so enormous that there is not one, but several disciplines that study the above types of noema. Some of those types are studied by jurisprudence and the philosophy of law, others by moral philosophy, others by the experts in certain games; others by anthropology and sociology; and some subtypes of those types are the specialty of highly professional fields like constitutional law or penology. See Ch. 1 §1.

However, there are several features that pervade the above ten types of noema, setting them apart as a general category, which we have called the category of *deontic judgments* or *deontic noemata*. To begin with, they share four fundamental features. On the one hand, deontic judgments are like mandates in that:

(i) they formulate courses of action whose performance or non-performance by certain agents is demanded, and perhaps desired, or hoped for, or favored, or approved of; but

(ii) they do not, in general, imply that such actions are, or have been, or will ever be, performed by the agents in question: a deontic statement, just as much as a mandate, can be unfulfilled or even disobeyed.

On the other hand, deontic assertions differ from mandates in that:

(iii) each of them *appears* to ascribe to an agent's doing a certain action what looks like a condition or property of a sort; for instance, a statement of the form *Jones's doing A is obligatory (required, a duty, right, wrong, unlawful, incorrect)* appears to ascribe to Jones's doing A what may be called the property or condition of obligatoriness (requiredness, dutifulness, rightness, wrongness, unlawfulness, incorrectness);

(iv) sometimes *expressing* assertively a deontic judgment is to tell the addressee what to do, but a deontic judgment itself is not simply the formulation of what a person is *meant to do*. For instance, when merely posing a conflict of duties one says "You ought, inasmuch as you promised, to do A; yet doing A is illegal", before deciding whether the oughtness (of the promise) or the illegality in question is the overriding or weightier deontic feature; neither of the two statements tells the hearer what he is really to do. Compare Antigone's conflict of duties in Chapter 2.

Deontic judgments appear to have the traits characteristic of propositions. As we discussed in Chapter 2, §2 and in Chapter 3, §2, propositions are characterized by: (a) being true or false; (b) being contents or *whats* of believing, conjecturing, assuming, knowing and all other propositional attitudes; and (c) being constituents of "larger" noemata by means of logical connections, in particular, the strictly propositional modalities like *Necessarily* and *It is possible that*. Deontic judgments appear to have these three traits. This appearance comes from the natural and pedestrian linguistic fact that sentences expressing deontic judgments of any type, e.g., of the ten types illustrated above, can fit nicely and comfortably in each of the blanks of the following sentence frames:

(F) (1) It is true that _____
         It is false that _____
     (2) John believes that _____
         Antigone knows that _____
         Ismene doubts that _____
         Creon is sure that _____
         Napoleon conjectured that _____
         Hitler supposed that _____
     (3) It is the case that _____
         It is necessary that _____
         It is possible (or possibly the case) that _____

To begin with, deontic noemata are properly spoken of as true or false. For instance: it is true that in the United States one must drive on the right-hand side of the road; it is true that residents of Detroit have to pay an income tax to the City of Detroit; it is true that at Wayne State University an assistant professor has a right to apply for the Wayne State Fund Recognition Award; it is true that in chess one cannot move a pawn more than two places at a time; it is true that once when this writer played checkers with his youngest son no player was allowed to move a piece if the move involved jumping another of his own pieces; it is false that one ought, morally, to inflict pain just for the mere enjoyment of its manifestations.

Every one of the noemata said in the preceding paragraph to be true, or false, can be said to be believed, known, doubted, etc. Furthermore, they can also be said to be the case, not to be necessarily the case, etc.

The fact that all three types of sentence frames of (F), which characteristically express propositional forms, apply to sentences or clauses expressing deontic judgments is impressive. None of the sentences evidences that it no longer expresses a strictly propositional form when it precedes a sentence or clause that expresses a deontic judgment. What are we to do? Are we to say that deontic judgments *are* true or false? Are they true or false in exactly the same sense in which ordinary propositions are true or false?

Undoubtedly, there are procedures of verification for deontic judgments. Some of them allow of complete verification. For instance, when Secundus promises Privatus to teach him English, Secundus knows conclusively that he has a duty to teach Privatus English. Some legal obligations can be fully ascertained by consulting the law books. Nevertheless, there is a difference between mathematical and scientific verification procedures and all the piocedures for verifying deontic judgments. The difference is, roughly, that many a deontic truth seems to depend intimately on legislative procedures, so that deontic truth seems manmade in a way in which scientific and mathematical truths are not manmade. This is a very large issue whose bulk falls outside the scope of our present investigation. Here we will deal with its structure only. Some philosophers have tried to minimize that difference. On the other hand, other philosophers have stressed the difference and have claimed that deontic noemata are not really true or false, that they are not really believed or known, are not really possible or necessary. Some have argued even that they are neither implied nor implying. This issue is not entirely verbal. It is like the issue we tackled in Chapter 4, §2, namely, whether there is imperative logic or not.

I propose to deal with the issue whether deontic judgments are propositions or not in the same way we dealt with the issue about the existence of imperative logic in Chapter 4, §2. We *can* agree that the words 'truth' and 'false', 'believe', 'know', 'assume' and the like, as well as the words 'necessary', 'possible' and 'impossible' do mean something different when they appear in frames like (F) above, depending upon whether the blank '_____' is occupied by a sentence expressing an (ordinary) proposition or by a sentence expressing a deontic judgment. We can introduce the prefix 'sh' to refer or to express the latter meaning. Thus, we contrast truth with sh-truth, believing with sh-believing, knowledge with sh-knowledge, necessary with sh-necessary, and propositions with sh-propositions (i.e., deontic noemata). The crucial thing that must be seized upon very firmly is that the philosophical problem about the elucidation of the sh-concepts *remains* unaffected.

As in Chapter 4, §2, we can for convenience introduce new words, to wit: the italicized *'proposition'*, *'truth'*, *'falsity'*, *'believe'*, *'know'*, *'assume'*, *'possible'*, *'necessary'*, etc. Each of these words has the *one* meaning of expressing generically either what its corresponding unitalicized word expresses or what is expressed by its corresponding sh-word. Thus, in one and the same meaning we can say that ordinary propositions and deontic noemata are both *propositions*, are either *true* or *false*, are *believed* or not, etc.

Now, who is to say and prove that the ordinary English words are the unitalicized words of two paragraphs back or our italicized ones? Hereafter we shall just drop the italics.

But it does not matter. If the italicized words constitute an innovation, this innovation is philosophically worthwhile. The generalization of our discussion of propositions in Chapter 2, §2 and in Chapter 3 to deontic judgments is a marvellous stroke of simplification. First, we accommodate the data involving sentence Forms (F). Second, we avail ourselves of a nice theory of the mind, for we do not have to split the powers and states of the mind into the propositional ones and the sh-propositional powers and states. Of course, we throw away the problems about the connections between the two sets of powers and states. Third, we enjoy the ontological simplicity of not having to postulate sh-propositions in contradistinction to propositions, which would require some special structures. Fourth, we rejoice at our fast enrichment of logical theory. Since deontic judgments are propositions, every principle of truth (T.10)-(T.16) discussed in Chapter 3 automatically applies to deontic judgments.

In short, there is explanatory advantage, and evidence in support of this thesis:

> *Deon.* 1. Deontic judgments are propositions (or statements), and deontic functions and forms are propositional functions and propositional forms, respectively.

As a consequence of *Deon.* 1, we have that:

> *Deon.* 2. All the logical principles formulated in Chapter 3 apply, as special cases, to deontic judgments, to deontic functions and to quantifications of deontic functions.

2. Deontic Properties

The rightness, obligatoriness, oughtnesses, forbiddennesses, and the like that enter into deontic judgments will be (provisionally) called *deontic properties*. We must emphasize that the phrase 'deontic property' is here only a convenient technical term that does *not* imply any metaphysical status for the rightness or wrongness of an action. Indeed we shall argue in Chapter 13 that there are no deontic properties *in rerum naturae*. In this chapter we shall see that deontic properties are not genuine properties but operators like negation.

The ten kinds of deontic proposition or statement illustrated in §1 above, show that there are many deontic properties. Such properties can, however, be grouped into families, primarily by means of the following three criteria:

(1) geographical jurisdiction,
(2) social or group jurisdiction, and
(3) enactment.

The geographical jurisdiction of a set of rules, laws, regulations, ordinances, is the geographical region in which those rules, laws, regulations, ordinances, have an unrestricted and immediate application. Deontic statements with different geographical jurisdiction attribute to the actions they are about different deontic properties. Thus, for example, an action forbidden by a French law, has a different forbiddenness from one which is forbidden by an American or German law. Similarly, the obligatoriness that an ordinance of the City of Detroit, Michigan, bestows upon the actions it makes obligatory for Detroiters, is a different deontic property from the obligatoriness that an ordinance of the City of Austin, Texas, bestows upon the actions it prescribe for the residents of Austin. In the same way, the moral wrongness of an action is a different deontic property from each legal wrongness of a given action. The latter wrongnesses have a geographical jurisdiction normally coincident with some national or regional borders, while the former flows through all national or regional demarcations.

The social or group jurisdiction of a deontic statement is the class or kind of persons for which the deontic statement prescribes courses of actions to be done, or left undone. Laws of two different countries, states, or cities, ascribe different deontic properties to the actions they make obligatory or forbidden, even if the two countries, states, or cities occupy exactly the same geographical territory. For example, the forbiddenness of criminal actions in accordance with the laws of Julius Caesar's city of Rome is a different deontic property from the forbiddenness of criminal actions in accordance with the fascist laws of Mussolini's Rome. In the same fashion, moral principles ascribe to certain actions deontic properties which differ from the deontic properties ascribed, perhaps, to the same actions by some legal system: moral principles have presumably the whole of humanity as their group jurisdiction. Finally, the oughtness that a person deliberating about some crucial decision in his life ascribes to the actions he concludes that he ought, everything being considered, to do is a different deontic property from any legal, or moral, deontic property: the oughtness that person ascribes to such actions has as its group jurisdiction the group whose only member is that person himself.

In ordinary life we tend to speak of enactment primarily in connection with those legal or statutory processes that culminate in legislation. Legislating is, however, simply a special case of formulating principles of action to be taken into account by a domain of persons in a certain social jurisdiction. Befitting the generality of our study, we shall say that the *enactment* of a set of deontic statements is an act or chain of acts that culminates in the deontic statements of the set in question being formulated as new principles of action or practical premises to be taken into account by a certain group of persons. Thus, an enactment of a set of deontic statements is not merely the formulation of deontic statements that follow as logical consequences from previously known deontic statements. An enactment either creates new obligations, duties, or the like, or creates new rights, or permissions, or freedoms to act. Another characteristic feature of an enactment is that it means to add practical premises to be considered together with some of the principles of action already held by the agents in the social jurisdiction of the new practical premises. Even in the case of an enactment that cancels certain deontic statements previously held, the substitute deontic statements it introduces are meant to be added as true practical premises to the remaining set of held principles of action. (The concept of enactment is elucidated further in §4 below and in Chapters 10 and 11.)

There are both generic and specific deontic properties, just as there are generic and specific nondeontic properties. Note for contrast that we distinguish the generic property redness from the specific color properties which are the specific shades of red, like red vermillion and apple red. Similarly, we have the shape property of triangularity as a genus under which fall specific triangularities, for instance, triangularity-with-angles-measuring-60°, -100°, and -20°. In the same fashion, there are many *legal deontic properties*. We have both the generic deontic property of Congressional-obligatoriness and the less generic deontic property of 78th-Congress-Congressional-obligatoriness and the even less generic one of 1964-Congressional obligatoriness; the former is possessed by all actions made obligatory by acts passed by the 78th Congress of the United States and possessed by all actions made obligatory by some act passed by Congress during 1964. Furthermore, all of these three deontic properties must be distinguished from the specific deontic properties of being obligatory by the MacCarran Act, or being obligatory by Article 12 of the MacCarran Act.

The very idea of enactment is, of course, imprecise. In general we have certain distinct processes that can each be called the enactment of a law or act. But what counts as the enactment of a certain law can be broken down into enactments of several parts of the law. Thus, we have more and more specific deontic properties, the smaller the parts we consider of a given law.

This proliferation of generic and specific deontic properties is not peculiar to legal deontic properties. *Games* illustrate this proliferation just as well. Consider the chessly deontic properties pertaining to the game of chess. There is a generic set of deontic properties: being disallowed in chess, being mandatory in chess, being allowed in chess. Here the enacted rules can be found everywhere in instructions accompanying most sets for sale. Tournament chess is a different game characterized by its own set of generic deontic properties. Each play of the game of chess determines a unique set of specific deontic properties. In general, if White can stop a check only by interposing his black bishop he is required chessly to do so; on the other hand, while in a given play on P. C. Jones' chess board here called play No. 1, D. C. Smith played White and was required to interpose his black bishop in order to stop a check by Jones, in another play, this time on Smith's chessboard, and here called No. 2, D. C. Smith, who again played White, was never required to move his black bishop at all: he lost the game before he was even in a position to move his black bishop. Here we have three different requiredness. The first one, which we may call chessly-requiredness, or requiredness-in-chess-in-general, is a generic deontic property that has the other two, requiredness-in-play-No.-1-of-chess and requiredness-in-play-No.-2-of-chess, as species. To nail down the distinction, note first that the two plays have a social jurisdiction limited to the class of persons whose only members are D. C. Smith and P. C. Jones, so that they are different from generic chessly-requiredness; and note, secondly, that the "geographical" jurisdiction of requiredness-in-play-No.-1-of-chess is precisely Jones' chess board, while requiredness-in-play-No.-2-of-chess has as "geographical" jurisdiction Smith's chessboard.

Consider *promises*. There is a set of generic deontic properties determined by the general practice of making and keeping promises. These deontic properties are the counterpart of the generic deontic properties corresponding to games (in general). On the other hand, each individual event of promising is the realization of some specific deontic properties, which are the counterparts of the specific deontic properties determined by a given play of a game. *Each act of promising is an act of the same type as an act or process of enactment of a law.*

Finally, there seems to be a general principle that if a person x has an end or purpose E and some action A is a necessary means for E, and x can perform A, then x must, or ought *ceteris paribus* (that is, everything else being equal) to, do A. This principle, however hard it may be to state it correctly, is clearly a practical principle. It is not merely a verbose statement to the effect that action A is a necessary condition for the realization of E. The principle is the statement that it is rational for x to do A if he wants E to obtain, provided that there are no stronger reasons for his not doing A. Thus, to do justice to the idea behind this principle we shall consider that for a person x to adopt an end E is to do something which may be taken as his enactment of a special deontic statement of the form *X ought$_E$ (ceteris paribus) to do A*. Here again, the adoptions of different ends are different adoptions, and different enactments of different deontic noemata; if a certain complex and E includes a specific end E', we shall say that the deontic properties determined by the adoption of E, or by the enactment of the corresponding deontic statement *X ought$_E$ to do A*, are more generic than the deontic properties determined by the adoption of E', which is tantamount to the enactment of the correspond-ing statement $*X$ ought$_E$, to do A$*$. (See Chapter 11, §3.)

To sum up,

> *Deon.* 3. For each process, or act, of enactment of a set of deontic statements there is a unique characteristic family of deontic prop-erties;
>
> *Deon.* 4. Each enactment of a set of deontic statements is the determination of some actions as possessors of the deontic properties characteristic of the enactment.

So far we have been engaged in proliferating deontic properties right and left. We shall proceed now to order and classify them. To start with, a simple reflection establishes that all deontic properties naturally group in several categories that cut across their differences in type or family, as follows:

> (*A*) Deontic properties that one attributes to an action by saying that the action in question is *obligatory, required, a duty,* one that *ought to, must,* or *has to,* be done;
>
> (*B*) Deontic properties that one attributes to an action A by saying that A is *wrong, prohibited, disallowed, unlawful, illegal, incorrect, improper, out of order, out of place, invalid*;
>
> (*C*) Deontic properties that one attributes to an action A by saying that: if one ought to do A, then it is *right* for one to do A, or one *may* do A; or by saying that: if one must (has to, is required to, is obligated to, has an obligation to) do A, one is *let* (*allowed to, permitted to*) do A.
>
> (*D*) Deontic properties that one attributes to an action A by saying that both one *may, can,* do A and one *may, can,* omit, or refrain from doing A; or by saying that both the doing of A and the not doing of A are *right, permissible, legal, allowed, proper, correct,* or by saying that one has *a right* to do A as well as *a right* not to do A.

Ordinary language has no general terminology to talk about the categories (*A*)–(*D*). But given our task here, we simply have to have some set of terms to expedite our study:

> *Convention.* We shall employ the italicized words *'obligatory'*, *'forbidden'*, *'permitted'*, and *'optional'* to express the generic deontic properties of types (*A*), (*B*), (*C*), and (*D*) respectively.

Our italicized deontic words are technical terms that, without obliterating the differences in meaning, sense, reference, and function of the ordinary deontic words of each type, allow us to refer to the categories (*A*)–(*D*) directly. They are simply schematic words. Thus, a sentence of the form 'It is *obligatory* that Jones pay Smith' does not really formulate a deontic statement. It really is a sentence schema, which formulates the statemental core common to all deontic statements that ascribe a property of category (*A*), regardless of type (legal, moral, institutional, of game, etc.), to the action Jones-paying-Smith. That schema yields a sentence formulating a deontic statement once a deontic word or phrase is substituted for 'obligatory'. Likewise, we shall speak of the deontic properties *obligatoriness*, *permittedness*, *forbiddenness*, and *optionalness* to refer to, without specifying it, some deontic property of the corresponding category, regardless of type.

We shall often use subscripts to indicate clearly that we are discussing very specific deontic properties of a given family. We shall write, for instance, 'It is *obligatory$_i$* that x do A', or 'x is *obligated$_i$* to do A', to formulate the statement to the effect that the doing of A by the agent referred to by 'x' has the specific *obligatoriness* determined by enactment i, or institution i, as explained in Chapter 1, §1.

> *Deon.* 5. A simple deontic proposition (as contrasted with deontic propositional form) has, *inter alia*, two characteristic constituents: (i) a generic deontic property, namely, either *obligatoriness*, or *forbiddenness*, or *permittedness*, or *optionalness*, and (ii) the specification, or qualification, of that property as of a certain family. A perspicuous expression of the full-fledged deontic property that enters in a deontic noema is an adverbial locution of the forms *'obligatory$_i$'*, *'forbidden$_i$'*, *'permitted$_i$'*, and *'optional$_i$'*, where the adverbial subscript 'i' expresses the specification (ii).

Undoubtedly, deontic judgments presuppose the agent's freedom to choose in the sense in which practical thinking presupposes it – as explained in Chapter 4 §1.

3. Deontic Propositions and Mandates

Now we can discuss some of the basic kinships between deontic statements and mandates that link them together as practical noemata, in definite contrast with statements not concerned with the guidance of conduct, but rather with a mere contemplation or inventorization of truths. In §4 coming next we shall discuss the crucial differences between deontic propositions and imperatives or mandates.

As noted in Chapter 2, §7, a distinctive feature of obligatoriness is that a deontic statement of the form *It is obligatory that x do A* can be naturally related to the mandate *x, do A* by an inferential link, while an obligatoriness first-person deontic statement, say, *I ought to do A* can be naturally reinforced by the intention or resolution *I do A*. For instance, it is in the nature of the case for a father to advise and urge his son to study as follows: "But it is your duty as a student to study, *hence* study!" Similarly, a man may reinforce his advice by saying "X, you ought to go home, *therefore*, go home". Obviously, it is not necessary that the *obligatoriness* statement and the corresponding mandate be so inferentially linked. In a case of a conflict of duties a person is *obligated$_i$* to do some action A as well as *obligated$_h$* to do some action B, and he cannot physically or logically do both A and B. (Note that there need not be a contradiction, since '*obligated$_i$*' and '*obligated$_h$*' may denote different deontic properties.) In such a case, before a solution to the person's conflict is found one cannot consistently assert "You are *obligated$_i$* to do A; hence do A; and since you are *obligated$_h$* to do B, and if you do B you don't do A, don't do A". In any case, a deontic statement of the form *x is *obligated* to do A* can, in the absence of a conflict of duties, be made to distill, so to speak, its practical or conduct guiding role by serving as the *ground* for the mandate *x, do A*. On the other hand, it *cannot* serve as the proper ground for the mandate *x, don't do A*, unless one issues the latter as a form of rejection of the obligation statement.

Similarly, a distinctive feature of forbiddenness is that a deontic statement of the form *x is forbidden to do A* can be reinforced in its conduct-guiding role by being inferentially linked to the corresponding mandate of the form *x don't do A*, while the first-person *forbiddenness* deontic statements of the form *It is *forbidden* that I do A* *can* naturally by inferentially reinforced be the corresponding negative resolution *I won't do A*. On the other hand, *x, you are *forbidden* to do A* *cannot* be the proper ground of the mandate *x, do A*, unless one means to reject the forbiddance statement.

A deontic statement of the form *It is *optional* for you, x, to do A* has a conduct-guiding role which consists in the statements's demarcating an area of complete freedom for the person x in question. Such statement can only be inferentially reinforced by the null mandate *With respect to A, x, do as you please*.

Finally, a deontic statement of the form *x is *permitted* to do A* has a more complex role in the guidance of conduct. It has no mandate that can naturally be attached to it by an inferential link in order to reinforce its conduct-guiding power. A statement *x is *permitted* to do A* is, in part, the articulation of a certain inapplicability of the corresponding mandate *x, don't do A*. This is precisely why *It is *optional* for x to do A*, which is the conjunction of the corresponding statements *x is *permitted* to do A* and *x is *permitted* to leave A undone*, can be the ground of *With respect to A, x, do as you please*. The conduct-guiding role of *permittedness* is more apparent through the logical relations between *permittedness* and the other deontic properties, than through a direct relationship between *permittedness* and mandates.

Intuitively, the inferential reinforceability of *A is *obligatory$_i$* by *Do A* and *A is *forbidden$_i$* by *Don't do A* does distinguish *obligatoriness$_i$* from *forbiddenness$_i$*. Yet this notion of reinforceability, already used in Chapter 2 §7, is in need of clarification. We clarify it in §6 below.

The relationships just discussed between mandates and deontic noemata reveal that deontic statements are not merely statements that quote other persons', or tribes', or nations' commitments. For example, a missionary to Frugandia may very well assert "By Frugandian laws (or morality) one ought to kill one's parents when they reach the age of 50", without in the least suggesting either that he himself holds that it is indeed morally right to kill one's parents when they reach the age of 50, he may hold only that it is really right, *caeteris paribus*, for the Frugandians to kill their own parents when they reach the age of 50 – denying that the other circumstances are ever *paribus*. The missionary's statement is *not* a quotational statement that can be put more clearly as follows: "The Frugandians hold and practice the rule *One ought to kill one's parents when they reach the age of 50*". The missionary's statement *is* a practical assertion. Yet we must note very carefully that expressions like 'by law L', 'according to rule (regulation, ordinance, statute, law, constitution) L', and even 'law (rule, regulation, ordinance, by-law) L requires (demands, says)' can be naturally used to make a purely quotational statement, as well as a genuine deontic statement. A deciding test is, of course, whether or not the statements made with the help of those expressions relate to mandates in the ways above discussed; another test, which is at bottom tantamount to the previous one, is the attitude the speaker means to be part of his assertion. If he approves, or favors doings of the kind mentioned in his statement, even if only qualifiedly, and this approval or favor is expressed in his assertion, then it is a deontic statement. This attitude need not be strong enough to move him to reinforce his statement with the corresponding mandate, but it must be such that if there were no conflict of duties he would be prepared to assert, for instance, "The law says...; hence, *do*...."

Another important feature of kinship between deontic statements and mandates is the following. Simple deontic statements are statements ascribing to certain actions certain deontic properties; but they are not statements that ascribe realization or performance to the actions in question. For example, *Jones is *obligated* to do A* leaves it entirely open, just as much as the mandate *Jones, do A*, whether or not Jones has or will perform A. Summing up then:

> *Deon.* 6. A deontic statement of the form *x is *obligated$_i$* to do A* demands action A and is a sufficient ground in some contexts for the valid inference of its corresponding mandate *x, do A*; deontic statements of the form *x is *forbidden$_i$* to do A* demand the not-doing of A and in some contexts are sufficient ground for the valid inference of the corresponding mandate *x don't do A*.

Deon. 6 raises the problem of the elucidation of the sense in which a deontic judgment is a ground, relative to a context, for a mandate. The problem itself is an important datum concerning the connections between mandates and ought- or deontic judgments that any adequate theory of the structure of practical thinking must satisfy. We anticipate that on the theory being developed in this chapter and in the next, *Deon.* 6 is complied with very nicely by the following explication of the way in which a deontic judgment is a ground for its corresponding imperative: a deontic judgment of the form $*x$ is *obligated$_i$* to do A$*$ implies that the corresponding practition $*x$ to do A$*$ is Legitimate in context C_i, where C_i is any context that is determined by enactment i. (See §6 below and Chapter 8, as well as Chapter 5, §1.)

4. ENACTMENT

Now we can provide an analysis of the enactment of a set of deontic statements which dissolves any trace of circularity that may appear in principles *Deon.* 3 and *Deon.* 4. It might seem circular to claim both than an enactment determines a unique family of deontic properties and that an enactment is precisely the endorsement of statements to the effect that certain actions possess those properties. But that there is no circularity becomes apparent when we fasten to the fact that an enactment is the act, ceremony or event of coming to endorse a set of practitions. Here we build an analysis of enactment on the discussion of endorsement of practitions in Chapter 5, §2. In general, on the present analysis from the point of view of a person who *makes* deontic statements:

> *Deon.* 7. An enactment is, fundamentally, (i) an act of giving qualified endorsement to a set of practitions; derivatively it is (ii) the creation of the realization of a unique set of deontic properties, namely, those ascribed to the actions involved in those practitions; an enactment is, also derivatively, (iii) the acceptance of the truth of the deontic statements ascribing to such actions such unique deontic properties.

By *Deon.* 7 a law, a statute and every set of rules that apply to a person must each be viewed fundamentally as a set of practitions (or mandates, if desired) restrictedly endorsed by the person in question. This is so regardless of the words actually appearing in the texts formulating the law or the rules. By *Deon.* 7, then, aside from legal definitions, the more basic language of the law, or of every normative system, is the language of practitions. The language of imperatives is more common. Rules are often formulated as lists of $*$Do$*$s and $*$Don't$*$s. Given the limitations, discussed in Chapter 4, §§4–5, of the imperative mood we find words like 'shall' and 'duty' and 'must', employed where an imperative sentence is grammatically incorrect, e.g., in subordinate clauses. But because of (iii) of

Deon. 7, it is perfectly correct for a law or a rule to be formulated by means of deontic language. We shall show in the next section that each promise is a full normative or deontic system. Each act of promising is, as already noted, an enactment of a normative system.

We say that the enactments of practitions that give rise to types of deontic propositions (and properties) are qualified, because it is the nature of deontic propositions that conflicts of duties are possible. Thus, to acknowledge that one is *obligated$_i$* by a certain rule R to do some action A is qualifiedly to endorse one's intention *I shall do A*. Roughly, the qualification is that in the case of a conflict of obligations one may be overridingly required to decide not to A instead. Let us discuss this in more detail.

5. CONFLICTS OF DUTIES AND THE NATURE OF PROMISES

The qualification of an enactment connects directly with the crucial difference between mandates or formulations of intention and deontic propositions. Mandates, it will be recalled from Chapter 4, §1 and §3, are units of thought content for acts of issuance. They articulate what certain agents are to do in a categorical or absolute way, so to speak. A person issuing a mandate of the form *You, x, do A* is unmistakably telling the agent what to do; his utterance formulates what exactly he expects or hopes that agent will do regardless of any consideration, or after everything relevant has been considered. On the other hand, the corresponding deontic statements of the form *x, you are obligated$_i$ to do A* may be simply asserted by a person in the middle of a deliberation whose ultimate conclusion may very well be *Therefore, everything (relevant) being considered, x, don't do A (after all)*. That is, the deontic statements of the form *x, you are obligated$_i$ to do A* do *not* tell the agent what to do, but only tell him that if certain considerations alone are operative then he is to do A; that is, in the terminology of Chapter 5, §1 and Chapter 6, §5, *x, you are obligated$_i$ to do A* merely indicates or signals that if certain things alone were considered, the corresponding mandates *x, do A* or prescriptions *x to do A* would be unquestionably orthotic or Legitimate in the contexts determined by those things considered. This contrast in assertive strength between deontic statements and mandates becomes crystal clear in the case of both a conflict of duties and a deliberation that finds a solution to the conflict. We have already had an inkling of this in Chapter 2 §1, but now we can, and must, see the relativity of deontic judgments to contexts of Legitimacy grow under our philosophical microscopes.

Consider, for instance, the following train of deliberative advice given, say, by Gaskon to his friend Secundus:

(1)   Secundus, inasmuch as you promised Jones to wait for his friend, you ought to wait for Jones' friend.

(2)   But inasmuch as both you promised your wife not to wait for Peter, and it has turned out that Peter is Jones' friend, you ought not to wait for Jones' friend.

(3)   You have no other duties in conflict.

(4)   In this case you *must* keep your promise to your wife.

(5)   Therefore, you *must* not wait for Jones' friend;

(6)   Hence, Secundus, don't wait for him!

Here is a normal sample of the sort of reasoning one may go through if one is asked to give advice. Secundus faces a conflict of duties and there are certain facts and principles from which Gaskon derives a solution. Clearly, an assertion formulating the whole situation (the conflict, the facts, the principles and the solution) is self-consistent. Thus, the two statements (1) and (2) form a consistent pair. This is precisely the pair that formulates the conflict, but, not, of course, a self-contradiction. From statement (1) Gaskon may correctly deduce:

(7)   Secundus, you ought to wait for Jones' friend.

Similarly, from (2) Gaskon may deduce:

(8)   Secundus, you ought not to wait for Jones' friend.

Since the set (1)–(6) is consistent, (7) and (8) are not each other's contradictory. What happens is, of course, simply that the ought to which (7) refers is different from the ought to which (8) refers. Statement (7) is at bottom statement

(7a)   Secundus has *a* duty$_i$ (an *obligation$_i$*) to wait for Jones' friend.

And (8) is the statement:

(8a)   Secundus has *a* duty$_j$ (an *obligation$_j$*) not to wait for Jones' friend.

Obviously, (7a) is not the contradictory of (8a). From them together we cannot deduce the self-contradiction *Secundus has a duty (an *obligation*) both to wait and not to wait for Jones' friend*. In order to make this deduction we need the additional premise *The dutifulness referred to in (7a) is identical with the dutifulness referred to in (8a)* or *The oughtness referred to in (7) = the oughtness referred to in (8)*. But this premise is not available in the present case.

Premises (1) and (2) show quite clearly that we are dealing in (1)–(6) with different oughtness or obligatoriness. This difference is signaled by the subordinate clauses of the form 'inasmuch as...'. This locution performs in sentences (1) and (2) the double role of expressing logical conjunction and of signaling the type or kind of oughtness involved in the deontic statement expressed by the main clause. The analysis of (1) and (2) are, respectively:

(1a)   Secundus, you made to Jones a promise, call it "*j*", that you would wait for his friend, and you ought$_j$ to wait for him;

(2a)   Secundus, you made a promise, call it "*h*", to your wife that you would not wait for Peter [hence you ought$_h$ not to wait for Peter], and it has turned out that Peter is Jones' friend [hence], you ought$_h$ not to wait for Jones' friend.

The locution 'inasmuch as' implicitly attaches a subscript to 'ought'; but we must refrain from taking this as evidence that the word 'ought' has different meanings in sentences (1) and (2). On the one hand, given that Gaskon and Secundus are dealing with a conflict of duties, the word 'ought' is used by Gaskon in the sense in which this word expresses a general deontic property of what we call type (*A*) in §2. On the other hand, the two total subscripted locutions 'ought$_j$' and 'ought$_h$' do have different meanings, for they express specific *obligatorinesses*. Thus, these subscripted words are really phrases of the form 'ought' plus subscript – as we already noted in *Deon.* 5. Thus, here is a corroboration of *Deon.* 5.

The preceding unveiling of two specific obligatorinesses is in perfect consonance with our multiplication of deontic properties in §2. We may, thus, list an interesting result concerning the analysis of promises:

Principle of promise-oughts: Each consistent promise P determines, and is characterized by, a unique *ought$_p$* or *obligatoriness$_p$*.

There is an ancient dispute, by no means dead, concerning the duty to keep promises. The problem is usually put as whether there is a moral duty to keep promises, and as whether that is analytically so or not. Given our vantage position here reached, we can shed light on that dispute. Since each promise *i* is a normative system, each promise is *analytically* characterized by duty$_i$ or *obligatoriness$_i$*, in accordance with the above principle. Thus, the sentence 'Promises ought, necessarily, to be kept' may very well, and naturally, express the analytic proposition which is our principle of promise-oughts. This is, of course, *not* a moral principle, but a second order proposition that articulates part of the nature of promises. Now, morality is an institution that sanctions or passes judgments upon all non-moral normative systems, i.e., upon non-moral *obligations*. Thus, there is the moral principle *What one ought$_i$ (i.e., has an *obligation$_i$*) to do one ought morally to do if there is no conflict of duties*. This principle is not analytic. It is a first-order principle that introduces moral duties. It is a principle constituting morality in the way in which the rule *You must in chess move your bishops diagonally* is constitutive of the general normative system which is the game of chess. But there is no moral principle that one ought morally to keep every promise. The preceding deliberation refutes this.

There are, of course, other principles of morality absorbing promisory *obligations* in the case of conflicts of duties; but we cannot discuss them here.[1]

6. THE UNQUALIFIED OUGHT

Let us continue our examination of the preceding deliberation. Evidently, neither (7a) [*Secundus has *a* duty to wait for Jones' friend*] nor (8a) [*Secundus has a duty not to wait for Jones' friend*] are, or include, mandates. Likewise, neither (7) nor (8), nor (1) [i.e., *Secundus, inasmuch as you promised Jones to wait for his friend, you ought to wait for Jones' friend*] nor (2) [i.e., *Inasmuch as you promised your wife not to wait for Peter, and it has turned out that Peter is Jones' friend, you ought not to wait for Jones' friend*] are or include mandates. At any rate, it is clear that both the ought-statement in (1) and the whole of (1) fail to be noemata that *tell* Secundus *to* wait for Jones' friend. Moreover, *here we have proof that at least one genuine deontic statement fails to entail its corresponding imperative or prescription.*

Suppose that every statement of the foim *x ought to do A* entailed its *corresponding* imperative *x, do A*. Then, since from (1), [i.e., *Inasmuch as you, Secundus promised Jones to wait for his friend, you ought to wait for Jones' friend*] we can deduce (7) [*Secundus, you ought to wait for Jones' friend*], we could derive from (1), the mandate *Secundus, wait for Jones' friend*. Similarly, from (8) and (2) we could derive the mandate *Secundus, don't wait for Jones' friend*. But then, we could derive from (1) and (2) a contradictory pair of imperatives. Hence, if every ought-statement entailed its corresponding imperative, our set (1)–(6) would entail a self-contradiction. Therefore, at least one of the two ought-statements (1) and (2), or (7) and (8) fails to entail its corresponding imperative. Actually, neither statement entails its corresponding imperative. Hence,

> *Deon.* 8. It is *not* characteristic of unnegated deontic propositions (or ought-statements) to entail their corresponding imperatives or prescriptions, i.e., the imperatives and prescriptions that demand the same actions from the same agents in exactly the same circumstances.

Elsewhere[2] we have examined in detail a view that analyzes ought-judgments as implying imperatives. That examination provides further support for *Deon.* 8.

A look at our conflict of duties (1)–(6) above shows that besides the conflicting *obligatorinesses* of (1) and (2), there is also the higher *obligatorinesses* of (4) and (5) [*You *must* not wait for Jones' friend*], expressed by '*must*', which solves the conflict. This *obligatoriness* is patently quite different form the *obligatoriness* mentioned in premise (2). It is deontic statement (5), *not* (2), from which Gaskon derives mandate (6) [*Secundus, dont wait for Jones' friend*]. While Gaskon claims premise (2) to be true because he and Secundus qualifiedly endorse prescription *Secundus not to wait for Jones' friend*, Gaskon claims conclusion (and premise) (5) to be true because at that juncture he sees that he and Secundus unrestrictedly, as well, endorse the very same prescription. The qualification of the endorsement pertaining to premise (2) [*Inasmuch as both you promised your wife not to wait for Peter and it has turned out that Peter is Jones' friend, you ought not to wait for Jones' friend∗] is precisely the fact that the *obligatoriness* ascribed by (2) to Secundus' not waiting for Jones' friend arises from a promise. On the other hand, the unqualifiedness of the endorsement pertaining to premise (5) [∗You must not wait for Jones' friend∗] is precisely the fact that the *obligatoriness* ascribed by (5) to that prescription emanates from a higher-order principle not in conflict, together with all the circumstances taken to be relevant. This unqualifiedness of premise (5) makes (5) absolutely assertive, like a mandate. That is exactly why Gaskon is justified in deriving the mandate ∗Secundus, don't wait for Jones' friend∗ from (5).

Summing up, we have the important datum for any theory of *obligatoriness*:

> *Deon.* 9. In every conflict of duties there is a deontic property *obligatoriness*$_1$, that:
> (i) enters in the conflict in order to delineate the way to the solution of the conflict;
> (ii) is determined not by a specific consideration of ground like a given promise, a certain law, or rule, a given purpose, or a certain performance; but
> (iii) is determined by higher deontic principles and *all* the facts relevant to all the duties in conflict;
> (iv) is, because of (iii), determined by an unqualified endorsement;
> (v) is such that a deontic statement of the form ∗It is *obligatory*$_1$ that x do A∗ implies the corresponding practition ∗x to do A∗.

> *Convention.* We shall speak of the deontic property *obligatoriness*$_1$ described in *Deon.* 9, as well as of its corresponding deontic properties *permittedness*$_1$, *forbiddenness*$_1$ and *optionalness*$_1$ as unqualified or *overriding* deontic properties.

Now we are in a position to clarify the notion of a deontic statement being reinforceable by an imperative that we discussed, both in Chapter 2, §7 and above in §3. This reinforcement is in part a matter of how a deontic statement implies its corresponding practition, i.e., *Deon.* 9 above and *Deon.* 10 and *Deon.* 11 below.

> *Deon.* 10. A non-overriding deontic statement of the form ∗It is

*obligatory*ⱼ that x do A* and the statement *There is for x no other *obligation** entail together the practition *x to do A*.

As we discussed in Chapter 4, a mandate has the entailments of the prescription constituting it. Yet it is not a matter of indifference which mandate a person issues. Particularly, by *Deon*. 9 an overriding statement of the form *It is *obligatory*₁ that x do A* implies the prescription *x to do A*. Nevertheless, a person who truly asserts the former is not entitled to issue any mandate whatever embodying *x to do A*. For instance, in our example of Gaskon advising Secundus, Gaskon may be entitled to issue the advice *Secundus, don't wait for Jones' friend*, but he may not be entitled to issue the corresponding order or command. Thus,

> *Deon*. 11. If an overriding deontic statement D implies prescription X, then which mandate constituted by X is an asserter Y of D entitled to issue in order to inferentially reinforce D is determined by Y's context or circumstance of issuance.

7. DEONTIC PROPOSITIONS AND PRACTITIONS

We have discussed some important relationships between deontic statements and mandates. In particular, we have noted that exactly the same things which are commanded, ordered, requested or entreated are said to be obligatory, permitted, forbidden, right or wrong. Those things are normally said to be actions. But we must now look into this matter more carefully. Consider, to begin with, the order

(1)   Peter, do the following: if it rains, close the windows if and only if the awnings are not up, and if it does not rain, turn on circulator A if and only if you didn't turn on circulator B.

This mandate is an order to Peter and demands of him the performance of a rather intricate action. But, as we discussed in Chapter 4, §1, the whole of mandate (1) is nothing more than the embellishment under the form of an order of the prescription

(2)   If it rains, [Peter] close the windows if and only if the awnings are not up, and if it does not rain [Peter] turn on circulator A if and only if [Peter] did not turn on circulator B.

Thus, we also say that what order (1) orders or demands is that Peter do the action in question. In this sense, what a mandate demands or, better, prescribes is the whole prescription: the complex of agent and action copulated in the peculiar way that characterizes prescriptions.

Now, some deontic propositions demand of Peter the performance of exactly the same action demanded by order (1), and, again the deontic properties involved in such propositions apply also to a whole complex of agent and action. This is evident in the deontic proposition:

(3)   The following is *obligatory$_i$*: that if it rains, Peter close the windows if an only if the awnings are not up, and if it does not rain Peter turn on circulator A if and only if Peter did not turn on circulator B.

Apparently, deontic proposition (3) is the application or ascription of obligatoriness$_i$ to the very same prescription (2) that makes up order (1). This is an important point revealed by (3), for at a naive level of reflection it is not obvious that deontic properties should apply to prescriptions, and not to propositions.

But there is no room for doubt here: *obligatoriness$_i$ applies to prescription* (2), and *not* to the proposition corresponding to (2):

(4)   If it rains, Peter will close the windows if and only if the awnings are not up, and if it does not rain Peter will turn on circulator A if and only if he did not turn on circulator B.

There is an important grammatical clue in the sentence expressing proposition (3) that signals that (3) applies *obligatoriness$_i$* to prescription (2), not to proposition (4). This clue is not merely the fact that the very same clause expressing prescription (2) appears in the sentence expressing proposition (3). The clue is, more specifically, that the clause expressing that to which *obligatoriness$_i$* applies must contain some verbs in the subjunctive mood – exactly as the clause expressing prescription (2). The verbs here are 'close' and 'turn on'. These verbs contrast very neatly, but not only, with the other verbs in the clause expressing prescription (2), namely, 'rains', 'are', 'does not rain', and 'did not turn on'; they also contrast with their indicative counterparts 'will close' and 'will turn on' in the sentence expressing proposition (4).

Yet the grammatical differences just discussed are only clues. The real matter lies on the fact that that to which *obligatoriness$_i$* applies in deontic proposition (3) is a complex of elements some of which are propositions, and some prescriptions. The former are *it rains*, *the awnings are not up*, *it does not rain*, and *Peter did not turn on circulator B*. Evidently, the elements *Peter close the windows* and *Peter turn on circulator A* are prescriptions. Within the total unitary complex to which *obligatoriness$_i$* applies in proposition (3) the propositions function as conditions for the elementary actions demanded of Peter. Clearly, Peter is not demanded to produce rain or the condition of the awnings or to do anything to circulator B. What he is demanded depends on whether these conditions obtain or not. This is the crucial fact about proposition (3): it applies *obligatoriness$_i$* to a complex structure of mixed components. We already know from Chapter 4, §4 that a mixed prescription-proposition compound is a prescription. On the other hand, proposition (4) is a homogeneous complex, as it must be in order to be a proposition.

We have spoken rather vaguely of the deontic property *obligatoriness$_i$* being applied in (or by) proposition (3) to prescription (2). This is due to the need for distinguishing between two kinds of propositions related to prescriptions. On the one hand, there are propositions like (3) of the form *It is *obligatory$_i$* (*permitted$_i$*, *right$_i$*, *wrong$_i$*) that p*. These propositions are literally made up of the prescriptions represented by '*p*': they are, like negatives, compounds of one prescription as component subjected to a deontic form of composition. These propositions are first-order propositions about the same subject-matter, i.e., agents and actions, their constituting prescriptions are about. On the other hand, the proposition *The proposition *2+2=5* is false*, is not a compound one having as component the proposition *2+2=5*. The proposition *The proposition *2+2=5* is false* is a second-order proposition, not about numbers, but about the proposition *2+2=5*. Likewise, there are second-order propositions about prescriptions, that predicate of prescriptions some property or other. For instance, the proposition *The prescription *John to go* is not fulfilled* is a second-order proposition predicating non-fulfillment of a prescription. Clearly, our proposition (3) above [namely, *It is *obligatory$_i$* that: if it rains, Peter close the windows if and only if the awnings are not up, and if it does rain he turn on circulator A if and only if he did not turn circulator B*] is a *first-order* proposition about Peter and his actions in certain circumstances, exactly as it is the case with prescription (2) [i.e., *If it rains Peter to close the windows if and only if the awnings are not up, and if it does not rain Peter to turn on circulator A if and only if he did not turn on circulator B*]. Hence, proposition (3) does *not* apply *obligatoriness$_i$* to prescription (2) in the sense of predicating *obligatoriness$_i$* to prescription (2), but in the sense in which negation is applied to a proposition (or prescription) by its corresponding negative proposition (or prescription).

Naturally, what we have said about prescription (2) applies to the corresponding intention, if we consider the first-person counterpart of proposition (1). In general, then:

> *Deon.* 12. Deontic properties are *operations* that yield first-order deontic propositions from practitions, i.e., prescriptions and intentions.

> *Deon.* 13. Deontic propositions attribute deontic properties to actions only in the sense that deontic propositions are the results or values of deontic properties operating on practitions that involve the actions in question.

To clarify things further we must not only distinguish the way in which *obligatoriness$_i$* applies to prescription (2) in proposition (3), namely, as an operation, from the way in which orthotes, as a predicate, enters in the second-order proposition

(5)   Prescription (2) is orthotic.

We must also contrast the relationships between prescription (2) and propositions (3) and (5) with the relationships between (2) and mandates like (1). They can be summarized as follows:

a. Prescription (2) makes up order (1), but order (1) is not a logical compound of prescription (2) in a certain form of composition. The ordering embellishment that (1) adds to (2) is simply a mere psychological overall wrapping that imposed on (2) produces no whole that alters the logical properties of prescription (2).

b. Prescription (2) is a logical component of proposition (3). This proposition is a new logical unit that both lacks some of the implications that (2) has and possesses new implications of its own.

c. Prescription (2) is not a constituent of proposition (5), just as

Napoleon's fifth male child is not a constituent of the proposition *Napoleon's fifth male child was crowned king of Budapest*. Proposition (5) has as a constituent a conception that includes reference to prescription (2): the sentence expressing proposition (5), in its turn, has as a part a name of prescription (2), namely 'prescription (2)' but not prescription (2) itself.[3]

An immediate consequence of *Deon.* 12 is

Deon. 14. There are no deontic propositions with genuine iterated deontic operations.

That is to say, inasmuch as the operation *It is *obligatory$_i$* (*permitted$_i$*, *forbidden$_i$*, *optional$_i$*) that* applies to a practition and yields a proposition, that operation cannot apply to a deontic proposition and yield a proposition, say, *It is *obligatory$_i$* that it is *permitted$_i$* that Peter close the window*. By *Deon.* 12 simply there cannot be such a doubly deontic proposition.

Needless to say, there are deontic propositions of the form *It is *obligatory$_i$* that x make it the case that it is *permitted$_j$* that y do A*. Here, of course, there is a practition for *It is *obligatory$_i$* that* to operate on, to wit: *x to make it the case that it is *permitted$_j$* that y do A*. Now, in keeping with our emphasis on the distinction between a sentence or clause and the noema expressed with the sentence or clause in question, we must agree that it is conceivable that a person may use the sentence 'it is *obligatory$_i$* that it is (be) *obligatory$_i$* that Peter close the window', not to express a non-existing doubly deontic proposition, but as a verbose expression of the proposition *It is *obligatory$_i$* that Peter close the window*.

We have given sufficient evidence for *Deon.* 12, i.e., that so-called deontic properties are really operators that transform practitions into propositions. We shall see later on that a deontic proposition like (3), in which a deontic operation applies to a connective compound of intentions and propositions, is equivalent to a deontic judgment in which the latter propositions are not in the scope of a deontic operation. Thus, (3) is equivalent to:

(3a)   If it rains, Peter is *obligated$_i$* to close the windows if and only if the awnings are not up, and if it does not rain Peter is *obligated$_i$* to turn circulator A if and only if he did not turn circulator B.

Patently, proposition (3) is *not* the same as proposition (3a). The former has just one deontic operator; (3a) has two. Therefore, the equivalence between (3) and (3a) cannot be correctly used to argue that deontic operators apply not to practitions, but to propositions, or something else.

The treatment of quantified deontic judgments requires the recognition of deontic propositional functions. It also requires a generalization of *Deon.* 12:

> *Deon* 12g. Deontic properties are operations that yield first-order propositions from practitions, and first-order propositional functions from practitional functions.

Given *Deon.* 12 the step to *Deon.* 12g is trivial. We have substantiated *Deon.* 12 and we will furnish additional evidence in §9. We have undermined any attack against *Deon.* 12 that may come from the fact that in purely connective deontic compounds propositions may be, preserving equivalence, brought out of the scope of a deontic operator. Interestingly enough, *Deon.* 12g crushes such attacks in the bud.[4] There are cases in which a propositional function in the scope of a deontic operator cannot, preserving equivalence, be brought outside that scope. To see this consider deontic propositions of the form:

(13)   It is *permitted$_i$* that everybody who did (does) B do A.

Here the propositional function expressed by the clause 'who did (does) B' cannot be brought out of the operator ∗it is permitted that∗. The statements normally made with a sentence of form (13) are not equivalent to the statements normally made with the corresponding sentences of the form

(14)   Everybody who did (does) B is *permitted$_i$* to do A.

The statements made with a sentence of form (13) entail, but are not entailed by, the statements made with the corresponding sentence of form (14). Suppose that our statements of form (13) are about a club that has only two members say, *a* and *b*. Hence, (13) would amount to:

(13a)   It is *permitted$_i$* that both if *a* did (does) B, he do A and if *b* did (does) B, he do A.

On the other hand, (14) would amount to:

(14a)   If *a* did (does) B, he is *permitted$_i$* to do A, and if *b* did (does) B, he is *permitted$_i$* to do A.

Clearly, (13a) entails (14a). But (14a) does not entail (13a): each person can have a right or permission to do something while lacking a right or permission to do it jointly.

Thus, the act B or the doing of B appears in (13) and in (13a) *inelimina-bly* in the scope of the deontic operator *it is *permitted$_i$* that*, in spite of the fact that it does not occur essentially, so to speak, in such a scope. In a statement made with sentence (13), or (13a), doing B is conceived of only as a circumstance, not as an act in that peculiar sense in which acts are the subject matter of deontic considerations, or, as we shall say, as an act prescriptively or practitionally considered.

8. DEONTIC PROPOSITIONS AND OUGHT-TO-BE

The deontic propositions whose structure we have been analyzing must be carefully distinguished from other propositions that are often expressed also with sentences containing deontic words. In traditional terminology, former philosophers distinguished between the Ought-to-do and the Ought-to-be. Our deontic propositions belong in the Ought-to-do. Our deontic propositions are the result of operations on practitions: they require a logical subject that plays the role of an agent and an action that is related to an agent not as a mere propositional predicate but in the prescriptional and intentional form of copulation. On the other hand, the Ought-to-be does not involve agents or actions: it merely applies to states of affairs independently of anybody having an obligation to bring it about or not. For instance, the sentence 'There ought to be no illnesses' can be, and is often, used to make a statement that demands no action of anyone. The statement is merely the formulation of a condition the realization of which would make the world a better world. The oughtness in question is *not* a deontic property in the sense characterized in §2 above. The statement in question is not reinforceable with an imperative of the form *x, destroy all the illnesses*, nor could it have been reinforced before the world was created by a mandate of the form *x, create no illness*. The oughtness involved in that statement is a positive value, i.e., an *axiological* property of there being no illnesses. We must distinguish

very carefully that oughtness from the one involved in a deontic proposition *God ought not to have created a world with illness*. This proposition takes God as an agent and demands of him an action: it has a
deontic oughtness that applies to a prescription. Very likely, the past tense
'have created' expresses in that sentence the proposition *God created illnesses*; hence, the whole deontic proposition is perhaps a mixed conjunction: *God created illnesses at a certain time t and God ought not
to create any illness at t*.

   Since axiological oughtness does not involve agents, it seems as if
statements about what ought-to-be apply axiological oughtness to propositions. In the axiological statement *There ought to be no illnesses*, for
example, the oughtness in question seems to apply to the proposition
There are no illnesses. There certainly is an axiological proposition
There ought to be persons who ought to do something or other, which
formulates the *desirability* of the existence of persons with obligations of
some sort. But we shall not investigate what exactly are the items on
which axiological oughtness operates to yield propositions about the
Ought-to-be.[5]

   Here all we need to keep in mind is that

   Deon. 15. Deontic propositions, by involving agents and demands
   on agents, are propositions about the Ought-to-do, and must be
   carefully distinguished from the axiological propositions about the
   Ought-to-be, which ascribe desirability or value, or absence of these,
   to states of affairs, or propositions.

9. ACTIONS, CIRCUMSTANCES AND IDENTIFIERS

We have emphasized that practitions and deontic propositions both deal
with agents and actions in a special link between them. Evidently, there
are many propositions that deal with agents and actions, as, for instance,
the proposition *Peter came late yesterday*. In general, all propositions
formulating the performance of an action by an agent deal with agents and
actions. Thus, what distinguishes, say, *Peter will come late* and *Peter,
come late* is, as we said in Chapter 4 §1, the different way in which Peter
is conceived as agent and the way the agent and the action of coming late
are linked, i.e., the different way of *copulation* of agent and action. Thus,

we have distinguished between the propositional and the practitional copulas. We shall say that the action of coming late is practically considered in the prescription *Peter to come late*.

In general, we define thus:

DEFINITION 1. An action A is *practically considered* in an intention, or a mandate or prescription X if and only if A appears in X in the scope of the prescriptional copula, i.e., A is linked in X to an agent or a practitional function by means of the practitional copula. An action A is practically considered in a deontic proposition D if and only if A is practically considered in a practition which is a constituent or component of D.

As we know, a practition can be a mixed compound of practitions and propositions. Thus, by the above definition, one and the same action can be considered practically as well as not in the very same practition. For instance, examine the order:

(1)   Peter, do the following: if it rains, *close the windows*, and if you-close-the-windows uncover the skylight.

In the above sentence we have italicized the expression of the prescription *Peter to close the windows* and hyphenated the expression of the proposition *Peter closes the windows*. Clearly, the action of closing the windows appears both practically considered and not practically considered in the total prescription constituting mandate (1). Similarly, it is considered in the same two ways in the deontic proposition:

(2)   Peter *ought$_i$* to do the following: if it rains to close the windows, and if he closes the windows to uncover the skylight.

We shall say the action of closing the windows, or of Peter's closing the windows, is considered as a circumstance in prescription (1) and in deontic proposition (2), in its occurrence in the latter as part of the proposition *Peter closes the windows*. But we shall not say that every action or proposition which occurs in a prescription X, without being practically considered in X, is ipso facto considered as a circumstance in X. For instance, the prescription constituting mandate

(3)   Peter, return to Jones the book you stole from him;

does not contain the action of stealing practically considered, for it is linked by the propositional copula to Peter as well as to both the book in question and Jones. Yet we shall not say that the action of stealing is considered as a circumstance in (3). Instead, we shall say that the action of stealing, as well as the actions of stealing a book, stealing a book from Jones, stealing from Jones, and the proposition that Peter stole a book from Jones, are all considered as *identifiers* in (3). The point is that all these actions and this proposition enter as constituents of the reference to a certain book, i.e., they characterize the object whose return is demanded of Peter. Linguistically, the expressions of the actions and the proposition are part and parcel of the noun 'the book you stole from him' which is in this context like a proper name referring or purporting to refer to just one thing. Thus, we define as follows:

DEFINITION 2. An action A is *considered as a circumstance* in a practition X [deontic proposition D], if and only if both A occurs in X [D] but is not practically considered in X [D] and A appears in X [D] in the scope of connectives and quantifiers, but not as a part of a reference to, or characterization of, some entity or entities.

DEFINITION 3. A proposition X is considered as a *circumstance* in a practition Y [deontic proposition D], if and only if X appears in Y [D] in the scope of quantifiers or connectives, but not as a part of a reference to some entity.

The actions and propositions which function as identifiers in references to individual entities are implicationally speaking only *apparently* in the scope of a deontic property. They are neutral with respect to all deontic properties. Thus, the identifier *Peter stole a book from Jones*, which is part of the reference to a certain book in mandate (3), behaves in exactly the same way as it does in (3) in the following deontic propositions:

(4)   It is *obligatory$_i$* that Peter return to Jones the book he stole from him;

(5)   It is *forbidden$_i$* that Peter return to Jones the book that he stole from him;

(6)   It is *right$_i$* that Peter return to Jones the book he stole from him.

All three (4)–(6) imply *Peter stole a book from Jones*, so that this proposition is not affected by the difference in deontic properties appearing in (4)–(6). Structurally this proposition is in the scope of those deontic properties; but implicationally it is without that scope, enjoying in the scope of all deontic properties, so to speak, its own implicational immunity.

On the other hand, an action or a proposition considered as a circumstance in a deontic statement does not enjoy implicational immunity in the scope of deontic properties. To see this examine the oft quoted proposition

(7)   It is wrong to kiss and tell.[6]

At first sight (7) seems to be of the logical form *It is wrong both to A and to B*, where *both* actions A and B are on the same footing, i.e., prescriptively considered. This form is characterized by the fact that it implies *Either it is wrong to A or it is wrong to B*: *the conjunctive action is wrong if and only if at least one conjunct is wrong.* Furthermore, *It is wrong both to A and to B* (where both actions A-ing and B-ing are practically considered) implies neither that if you A, it is wrong for you to B, nor that if you B it is wrong for you to A. The wrongness of the conjunctive act is not contingent upon the performance of one or the other conjunct, i.e., upon the proposition articulating that performance. Finally, *It is wrong both to A and to B* does not imply that any A-ing has been performed.

In contrast, the ordinary statement (7) demands something contingent upon a performance of one conjunct. Statement (7) is simply equivalent to

(7a)   If you kiss, it is wrong for you to tell.

Proposition (7) assigns different roles to the actions of kissing and telling: (7) is *not* equivalent to *If you tell, it is wrong to kiss*. Yet the assymmetry of the roles assigned by (7) to the two actions is not one that affects the commutativity of conjunction. Clearly, (7) is the same as *It is wrong to tell and kiss*. It will be recalled that the action of stealing a book from Jones which occurs as an identifier in propositions (4)–(6) above is such that these propositions imply that the action has been performed. In contradistinction, *It is wrong to kiss and tell* does not imply that kissing has occurred.

There is, then, a problem of ambiguity in ordinary sentences of the

grammatical form 'It is wrong to...and _____'. The context of discussion must determine whether the actions mentioned in the verbs filling
the blanks are both practically considered or whether one is practically
considered and the other is considered as a circumstance. Naturally
enough, that problem of ambiguity is not equally present in the case of
sentences of the form 'It is right to...and _____'. In this case, the natural
interpretation is to have both actions as practically considered. Compare,
for instance, 'It is right to kiss and tell'. This sentence does not normally
express the *right*-proposition corresponding to (7). It expresses one that
implies both *It is right to kiss* and *It is right to tell*. The same holds
for sentences of the form 'One ought to...and _____'.

Once again we face here the need for distinguishing with the utmost
care between the logical analysis of a proposition and the grammatical
analysis of the sentences expressing such a proposition. But here the
different semantical behavior of the deontic words is a clue to the lack of
implicational immunity of a circumstance in the scope of a deontic
operation. The very same circumstance possesses different implicational
properties in the scope of different deontic operations. Consider, to
begin with:

(8)   It is *forbidden_i* for Jones to do the following: that while it is
         the case that it rains at 3 p.m. he fertilize the lawn at 4 p.m.

Interdiction (8) demands from Jones the nonfulfillment of a mixed conjunctive prescription. Clearly, Jones is in the position of having satisfied
the demand if and only if either the propositional conjunct of the conjunctive prescription is false, or, that conjunct being true, he fails to fulfill
the prescriptive conjunct. Thus, the mere demand of nonfulfillment of the
mixed prescription leaves it open whether the propositional conjunct is
true or not. Because of this, interdiction (8) is equivalent to:

(8a)   If it is the case that it rains at 3 p.m., it is *forbidden_i* that Jones
         fertilize the lawn at 4 p.m.

Now consider:

(9)   It is *obligatory_i* that Jones do the following: that while it is the
         case that it will rain at 3 p.m. he fertilize the lawn at 4 p.m.

Here (9) demands from Jones the fulfillment of the same mixed conjunctive prescription whose nonfulfillment is demanded by (8). Jones satisfies (9) if and only if both the propositional conjunct *It will rain at 3 p.m.* is true and he fulfills the prescriptive conjunct *Jones fertilize the lawn at 4 p.m.*. Thus, in the sense in which obligations are fulfillable, i.e., in the sense in which an incapactity to perform an action makes the action non-obligatory, the truth of (9) requires that the propositional conjunct be true. That is, deontic proposition (9) implies

(9a)   It will rain at 3 p.m. and it is *obligatory$_i$* that Jones fertilize the lawn at 4 p.m.

To sum up, therefore:

Deon. 16. Circumstances are entirely different from identifiers.
The latter enjoy their own implicational jurisdiction and have a scope that includes the scope of the deontic operations appearing to include them. The former are constituents of the practitions to which deontic operations apply and have a scope within the scope of such operations. But, we must insist, there is no mechanical grammatical rule to ascertain whether a proposition or an action functions as a circumstance or as an identifier in the scope of a deontic operation.

Many a proposition is expressed as a *parenthetical statement* by a clause in a sentence that makes it *appear* that the proposition lies in the scope of a deontic operation, without this being actually the case. For example, the sentence 'It is obligatory (forbidden, right, wrong) that Jones, *who came in late today*, work next Saturday' includes as a subordinate clause 'who came in late today', yet the proposition *Jones came in late today* is *not* at all in the scope of the deontic operation expressed by the prefix 'it is obligatory (forbidden, right, wrong)'. The proposition normally expressible with the total sentence is really a conjunction:

(10)   Jones came in late today, and it is obligatory (forbidden, wrong, right) that he work next Saturday.

Of course, in (10) Jones' action of coming in late is not prescriptively considered; and *Jones came in late today* is a circumstance that may be moved, so to speak, into the scope of the deontic operation. That is to say, each of the propositions appearing in (10) is equivalent to a proposition having *Jones came in late today* in the scope of its deontic operation. But we must distinguish this equivalence between propositions from a grammatical rule that both preserves meaning and allows moving the sentence 'Jones came in late today' so that it precedes, or follows, the prefix 'It is obligatory (forbidden, wrong, right) that'. That latter rule is *not* the simple one: replace 'be' with 'Jones', put after 'Jones' the clause 'who came in late today', and delete the first six words. The fact is that the grammatical rule in question has to treat each deontic operation separately.

10. THE GOOD-SAMARITAN PARADOX

The distinction between acts practically considered and acts considered as circumstances or as identifiers is of great intrinsic importance. But it also has valuable uses. It provides an elegant way of organizing the system of deontic implications.

We all assume a principle of deontic logic naturally, though obscurely, put as follows:

(P)   If X's doing A entails Y's doing B, then that X's doing A is
        _____ly obligatory entails that Y' doing B is _____ly
        obligatory,

where the blanks are to be filled with exactly the same appropriate adjective, e.g., 'moral' and 'legal'. (See Chapter 1 §1.) The first obscurity of (P) lies in 'doing': if doings are events they do not have entailments or implications. The phrases 'X's doing A' and 'Y's doing B' must, then, formulate in (P) statements or something like statements. Thus, it is natural to interpret (P) as

(P')   If *X performs A* entails *Y performs B*, then *X is
        obligated$_i$ to do A* entails *Y is *obligated$_i$* to do B*, where
        'i' stands for an adverb denoting type of *obligation*.

But (P') leads immediately to the so-called Good-Samaritan paradox. Suppose, for example, both that Arthur is today legally (morally) obligated to bandage his employer, Jones, and that a week from today Arthur will murder Jones. (It makes no difference whether Arthur or Jones knows today that the former will murder the latter.) In this case, Arthur is legally (morally) obligated to perform the act, call it C, of bandaging the man he will murder a week hence. Clearly, Arthur's doing C entails his doing the act of murdering a man a week hence. So, if (P') were true, Arthur would be legally (morally) obligated to murder a man a week hence. Thus, (P') is false and if (P) is true it is *not* interpretable as (P').

The preceding example shows that the Good-Samaritan paradox cannot be resolved by insisting that (P) must hold only for one and the same agent, or for future actions, etc. The difficulty has nothing to do with distinctions of agents, patients, times, or places.[7] The difficulty arises, on our view, solely from taking the implicational links between deontic statements as patterned on the implication lines between the corresponding statements of fact, rather than on those between the corresponding practitions. Specifically, in our example, the trouble is this: in *Arthur is legally (morally) obligated to bandage the man he will murder a week hence*, the act of bandaging is practically considered, while the act of murdering is considered as a circumstance. Thus, the principle that (P) hides is, on our view:

> *Deon.* 17 = (P*). If practition *X to do A* entails practition *Y to do B*, then *It is *obligatory$_i$* that X do A* entails *It is *obligatory$_i$* that Y do B*.

Let us check the "paradox" against (P*). On the one hand, the prescription *Smith to bandage the man he will murder a week hence* does entail the *statement* *Smith will murder a man a week hence*. But we cannot apply (P*) to it: the operator *It is obligatory that* applies to practitions only. Hence, by this route we cannot derive *It is obligatory that Smith murder a man a week hence*. On the other hand, the prescription *Smith to bandage the man he will murder a week hence* does *not* entail the prescription *Smith to murder a man a week hence*. Thus, even though we do have the materials to infer *It is obligatory that Smith murder a man a week hence*, we do not have the appropriate premise. So, there is really no Good-Samaritan paradox. And there is a nice, simple principle, namely (P*), that bridges the gap between practitional and deontic implication. (See Chapter 1 §5.)

There are other solutions to the so-called paradox of the Good-Samaritan. Many of them are too awkward. Actually, in some cases the "paradox" can be solved by forcing distinctions in the scope of deontic operators. For instance, in our example above, we can interpret the

sentence 'Arthur has a duty to bandage a man he will kill' as expressing
(1) below, where '*a*' abbreviates 'Arthur':

(1)   (∃x) (*a* will kill *x* & *a* has a duty to bandage *x*),

and not as:

(2)   (∃x) (*a* has a duty to (bandage (*X* & kill *x*)).

It does not follow from (2) by (P') that Arthur has a duty to kill, since
the part *a has a duty to bandage x* of (2) implies nothing about killing.

There is, however, a reply to the preceding scope solution of the Good-
Samaritan "paradox". It requires that (1) does not imply (3):

(3)   There is a man such that Arthur has a duty to do the follow-
           ing: to bandage him while it is the case that Arthur will kill
           him.

In other words, as (3) evidences the conjunct *a will kill x* may be moved
in and out of the scope of the deontic operator *Arthur has a duty to do
the following*. Of course, (3) cannot be represented in a system that does
not distinguish propositions (and propositional functions) from practitions (and practitional functions). In brief, the scope solution does dis-
solve the paradoxicality of certain examples; but it does that at the cost of
the incapacitation for understanding the logical form of propositions like
(3), and like the ones discussed in earlier sections, and, *a fortiori*, at the
cost of proscribing the implication, indeed, equivalence, between propositions like (1) and those like (3).

Several of the cases that have been proposed as variants of the Good-
Samaritan "paradox" can be analyzed, castrating though it is, as involving
confusions on the scope of the deontic operators at issue, or of a definite
description: but not all.[8] A beautiful case that cannot be analyzed away
by scope distinctions is Åqvist's "paradox" of the Knower, in "Good
Samaritans, Contrary-to-Duty Imperatives, and Epistemic Obligations",
pages 366ff.[9] Consider the case of a man, say Jones, whose job, in accordance with the rules R of the office in which he works, is to know what
is done wrong, in accordance with the same rules, by other people in the
same office. Suppose that Smith did A, which is wrong by the rules of the
office. Thus, *It is wrong$_R$ that Smith do A* and *Jones ought$_R$ to know
that Smith (does) did A* are both true. Since *Jones knows that Smith

(does) did A∗ implies ∗Smith (does) did A∗, by (P′) it follows, then, that ∗Smith ought$_R$ to do (have done) A∗, which contradicts the hypothesis that it is wrong$_R$ for Smith to do A. Here the scope distinction does not help.

For one thing, there is apparently no satisfactory analysis of knowledge so that we can take, in the model of (5a), some conjuncts of the analysis outside the scope of the deontic operator ∗ought$_R$∗. But suppose that we can analyze ∗Jones knows that p∗ as ∗p and Jones believes that p and Jones has excellent evidence for that p∗. Then the scope analysis, patterned after (2), of ∗Jones ought$_R$ to know that Smith did A∗ yields ∗Smith did A and Jones ought$_R$ to both believe that Smith did A and have evidence for this∗. But the fact is that a duty to know is not the same as a duty to believe and have evidence: surely one can have the latter without having the former.

There are psychological attitudes that one must acquire, or psychological acts that one must perform that imply that something that happens to be wrong has occurred. Such cases give rise to troubles for (P′). The trouble is compounded in those cases in which there is no purely psychological content, that can be extracted, in the way believing is the pure psychological core of knowing. For instance, there is no purely psychological core that can be really *obligatory$_i$* when one is said to be *obligated$_i$* to repent, to lament, or to apologize for, having done some action A which it is wrong$_i$ to do.

Åqvist's proposed solution consisted of distinguishing different types of duties. But his proposal was shown by Lawrence Powers, in 'Some Deontic Logicians', pages 384–388, not to be at all adequate.[9] Of course, we do not object to distinguishing types of duties: we have done so in our phenomenological examination of conflicts of duties in the preceding sections and in Chapter 1, §1. But we do not have to resort to this to solve the Repenter paradox. In fact, we have already found, independently of (P), that deontic operators apply to practitions. Thus, we can, with simplicity, recognize in (P) a practitional principle, not a propositional one, namely, (P∗) above.

(P∗) provides an immediate, sharp and unified solution to all the forms of the Good-Samaritan "paradox". In the Åqvist-type example above:

(4)   It is *obligatory$_R$* that Jones know that Smith did A.

This contains the prescription ∗Jones know that Smith did A∗. This prescription implies neither the proposition *Jones knows that Smith did A* nor the prescription *Jones to do A*. Hence, from (4) by (P*) we cannot derive that it is *obligatory*$_R$ for Smith to do (have done) A. Thus, we may properly and consistently accept that the system of rules governing the tasks of all the people in Jones' office, including Jones, are all duties *in exactly the same sense*, and even of the same type, expressed by the subscript 'R'.

11. CONTRARY-TO-DUTY NORMATIVES

Consider:

(1)   John ought$_i$ to do the following: not to gamble or to get a highly-paying job.

This clearly implies:

(2)   If John ought$_i$ to gamble, then he ought$_i$ to get a highly-paying job.

Here we have the problem discussed in Chapter 3 §7 about the thematic roles of the conditioning words 'if', 'only if', and their relatives. Having that discussion in mind, we are suspicious of formulating (1) as:

(3)   John ought$_i$ to do the following: if he gambles to get a highly-paying job.

But, recalling that '⊃' is a pure logical connective with none of the thematic and dialectical properties of 'if' and 'only if', we can formulate (1) as:

(1a)   John ought$_i$ to do the following: (he) to gamble ⊃ (he) to get a highly-paying job.

This suggests that the following principle of implication governs deontic judgments:

> *Deon.* 18: *It is *obligatory*$_i$ (A⊃B)* implies *It is *obligatory*$_i$ A ⊃ it is *obligatory*$_i$ B*.

But we must be careful to note that the first '⊃' *cannot* be read by means of an ordinary conditioning particle.

The so-called Chisholm's paradox[10] of contrary-to-duty imperatives is just another variation of the problems created by the failure to see that deontic operators sometimes operate on practitions that have both propositions and simpler practitions as components. To illustrate consider the case of a university that has rules r governing commencements, and Nameprofessorships, such that:

(11)   Mellon Professor Goldsmith ought to attend the June commencement,

(12)   Goldsmith ought, do the following: wear academic regalia if he attends commencement; and

(13)   Since the only academic ceremony in June is the commencement, if Goldsmith does not attend it, it's not the case that he ought, to wear academic regalia in June.

If we do not distinguish between propositions and practitions, and take (D.1) above to have A and B as expressions of propositions, ignoring our warning about 'if' and ' $\supset$ ', we would derive (14) from (12) with the help of (D.1):

(14)   If Goldsmith ought, to attend the June commencement, he ought, to wear academic regalia in June.

From (11) and (14) we may derive:

(15)   Goldsmith ought, to wear academic regalia in June.

Suppose that being tired of commencements

(16)   Goldsmith does not attend the June commencement.

From (16) and (13), we can infer:

(17)   It is not the case that (15).

Obviously, we cannot have (15) and (17). Rejecting (D.1) would leave the implications illustrated by (1) and (2) unaccounted for. We cannot any longer ignore the heterogeneity of the elements in (12). Thus, the simplest and more elucidatory course is to insist on that heterogeneity and insist that it is present in (D.1), in which the components A and B are practitions, not propositions. This view also fits in harmonisouly with our separation in Chapter 3, §5–§7 of the roles of the ordinary language connectives. It also harmonizes with the data of type (F) discussed in Chapter 6, §4.

Keeping in mind that A and B in (D.1) are practitions, not propositions, we must conclude that (D.1) does not apply to (12), which is of the form:

(12a)   Goldsmith ought, to do the following: $(p \supset B)$,

where 'p' stands for the proposition *Goldsmith attends the June commencement* and 'B' for the practition *Goldsmith to wear academic regalia in June*. Hence, (12) does *not* imply (14). And with this we cannot derive (15), leaving (17) as true.

12. THE TENSELESSNESS OF OBLIGATORINESS

Further evidence for our thesis that actions practically considered must be distinguished from actions considered as circumstances, as well as for the further thesis that it is the former that belong essentially and primarily in deontic judgments, comes from a consideration of the involvement of obligation and time. Examine the case of a person, or a group of persons, who are considering what to do during a certain period of time. It does not matter what sort of requiredness is involved in their considerations. For specificity we may suppose that they are operating under some type of utiliterian system u, and that they have, correctly, determined that there are several courses of action, pairwise incompatible, that would bring about the greatest value or utility:

$$A_1, A_2, A_3, \ldots$$
$$B_1, B_2, B_3, \ldots$$
$$C_1, C_2, C_3, \ldots .$$

But things are not so simple that one course of these three is superior to the others at all times in all circumstances. The superior course, let us suppose, is the A-course, provided that every single A_i is performed in time. Suppose that as soon as one A-action A_i is not performed, then the agent ought$_u$ to shift to the B-series, and as soon as an action B_j is not performed, he ought$_u$ to shift to the C-series, and so on. This suggests that:

(1)   The agents ought$_u$ to do A_1 & A_2 & A_3 & ...

Hence,

(2)   The agents ought$_u$ to do A_2 at time t_2.

Suppose that

(3)   The agents fail to do A_1.

Then:

(4)   At time t_2 the agents ought$_u$ to do B_2, not A_2.

Here is another "paradox" that can tempt a philosopher to take some drastic measures, for instance: (A) to reject the principle that *X ought$_i$ to do A & B* implies *X ought$_i$ to do B*, which is implied by *Deon.* 19; or (B) to adopt the view that deontic operators have temporal parameters. View (A) would reject the derivation of (2) from (1) right away. But the view is *ad-hoc*, i.e., purely local, and barren. We will say no more about it. View (B) is, on the other hand, intriguing and open-ended. It requires

(1a)   The agents ought$_u$-at-time-t_1 to do A & B & C & ...
(2a)   The agents ought$_u$-at-time-t_2 to do A.

And the view would reject the derivation of (2a) from (1a).

View (B) deserves to be developed in full detail, but we will not do so here. The view can be attached to the main theories put forward in this book. Indeed, that development could be a deepening of those theories. We must note, however, that the cases under consideration do *not* demand the tensification of 'ought' or the renunciation of *Deon.* 19. We can solve the "paradox" with materials already in hand, suggested by other data. To see this is to see that our views about the practition-proposition contrast and about the mixed nature of deontic operators possess elucidatory fruitfulness.

Propositions (1) and (2) do not describe the situation of our agents. Let us examine the situation more slowly. What happens is this:

(11)   The A-series has more value *in toto* than the B-series, and
        (perhaps) the B-series has more value *in toto* than the C-series.
(12)   The agents *obligation$_u$* is the following:
        (a) (*to do A_1 at t_1*) & (*to do A_2 at t_2*, if they have done A_1
        at t_1) & (*to do A_3 at t_3*, if they have done A_1 at t_1 and A_2
        at t_2) & ...

(b) (*to do B$_2$ at t$_2$*, if they have not done A$_1$ at t$_1$) & (*to do B$_3$ at t$_3$*, if they have not done A$_2$ at t$_2$ but have done A$_1$ at t$_1$) & ...

(c) (*to do C$_3$ at t$_3$*, if they have not done B$_2$ at t$_2$ but have done A$_1$ at t$_1$) & ....

In sentence (12) the italicized infinitive clauses formulate practitions, i.e., *actions practically considered*; the non-italicized indicative clauses formulate propositions, i.e., *circumstances*. It is perfectly clear that (2) does not follow from (12). But given the pairwise incompatibility of the courses of action, (4) does follow from (12) and (3). Evidently, then, there is no paradox, and there is no need to construe *obligatoriness$_u$* as a generic one that is instantiated or specified differently at different times. At any rate, even if there are powerful reasons to temporalize the obligatorinessess determined by normative systems, we must describe the situation of our agents as in (12), distinguishing between the actions that are required, and are, hence, practically considered, from the circumstances of that requiredness. This is precisely the distinction that cannot be maintained if we take deontic operators to operate on propositions. For if in (12) every clause expresses a proposition, (12) becomes self-contradictory, and (12) (a) becomes equivalent to (1). Clearly, *p & (if p, q)* is equivalent to *p & q*.

Our ultimate point here is, then, that proposition (12) (a) is *not* equivalent to (1). Hence, the duality of noemata expressed in (12) (a) by the contrast between subjectless infinitive clauses and full indicative clauses is an irreducible one. We theorize that it is the same duality practition-proposition we argued for in Chapter 6, §2–§6.

According to (12) the temporal parameters t_1, t_2, ... belong with the actions A$_1$, B$_1$,...; A$_2$, B$_2$,.... *Obligatoriness$_u$* is timeless. This timelessness is on a par with the timelessness of the possession by an object of a temporal property, e.g., being blue at 3 p.m. today. It is true, however, that deontic sentences do include a tensed verb in their expressions of deontic operators, for instance:

(21)   John was required by the rules to retire at 65.

(22)   It was obligatory$_i$ that some men stayed behind.

They suggest that obligations come and go. Yet this need not be any different from the way in which colors and shapes come and go leaving predication, on some views in any case, as timeless. In this respect, the English verb 'ought', inflexible and selfsame in all its constructions, seems to be philosophically the most perspicuous of all deontic words. Thus, (21) and (22) are better taken as:

(21a)   John *ought*by the rules to have retired at 65.
(22a)   It *ought$_i$* to have been that some men stayed behind.

Perhaps we ought to distinguish the time of an action and the time of its *obligatoriness$_i$*. But we need more persuasive evidence than the mere grammatical phenomenon of tense agreement registered in (21) and (22).

13. CONJUNCTIVE AND QUANTIFIED DEONTIC PROPOSITIONS

Since deontic operations are practitional-propositional modalities, we can expect to take advantage of the work done by modal logicians in order to systematize the implications of deontic noemata. We have already collected some important principles of deontic implication. In particular, we must recall *Deon.* 2 of §2 (which applies the principles of Chapter 3 to deontic judgments), *Deon.* 8 and *Deon.* 9 (iv) of §6 (which determine the implications of prescriptions by their corresponding deontic noemata), *Deon.* 14 of §7 (which shows deontic operators as not iterative), and *Deon.* 17 of §10 (which transfers the implicational relationships between practitions to the latter's corresponding deontic noemata). We need explore the implications relating deontic operations and conjunction. This will determine to which system of modal logic is the system of deontic implications more akin. Given the results obtained by modal logicians we need consider just two cases.

Examination of examples shows that

Deon. 19. ∗It is *obligatory$_i$* that X do A & B∗ is equivalent to ∗It is *obligatory$_i$* that X do A, & it is *obligatory$_i$* that X do B∗.

We have here put '&' instead of 'and', because, as we explained in Chapter 3 §6, 'and' does not always mean logical conjunction. Some counterparts of *Deon.* 19 for other logical relations expressed by 'and' are false. As often in philosophy, an ambiguity of a word has caused unjustified objections to a sound principle of entailment.[11] Now, if X is *obligated$_i$* to do A & B, then he fails to do his obligation if he fails to do A and also if he fails to do B. Thus, the extent to which, and the reasons for which, the truth of *X is *obligated$_i$ to do A & B* impose a restriction on X's freedom to act, are precisely the extent to which and the reasons for which *X is *obligated$_i$* to do A, & X is *obligated$_i$* to do B* imposes a restriction on X's freedom to act.

Analogously to *Deon.* 18 we have:

> *Deon.* 20. *It is *obligatory$_i$* that (X do A & *p*)* is equivalent to *p* & it is *obligatory$_i$* that X do A*.

Here the expression '(X do A & *p*)' formulates a complex practition in which the statemental component represented by '*p*' is considered as a mere conjunctive *circumstance*, not as an identifier or as a parenthetical remark. In this case '&' is read in English, *inter alia*, as 'while it is the case that' or 'it being the case that'. The former reading was used in example (9) of §9, where the equivalence between (9) and (9a) illustrates *Deon.* 20. Note the structural parellelism between *Deon.* 20 above and principle (IB.1) governing intending and intention, formulated in Chapter 6 §4. In Chapter 11 §3 we discuss it from the point of view of the production of action by practical thinking, and explain how *Deon.* 20 is partially grounded on (IB.1).

The form *(X do A & *p*)* is also found in existentially quantified prescriptions. Consider

(1)   Someone who chaired a meeting last year preside over the entire committee this year.

It is the core of deontic statement

(2)   It is obligatory that someone who chaired a meeting last year preside over the entire committee this year.

Let us abbreviate as follows, where as in Chapter 4 §8 parentheses signal propositional copulation and square brackets signal practitional copulation;

C(*x*): *x* chaired a meeting last year,
P[*x*]: *x* to preside over the entire committee this year.

Then prescription (1) is *∃*x*(C(*x*) & P[*x*])*, while statement (2) is

Obligatory$_i$ $\exists x$(C(x) & P[x]). This is an obligation that applies to the whole class of relevant agents. Those who have never chaired any meeting last year, i.e., who lack the property C(x), are of course free from the duty imposed by (2). On the other hand, those who have that property C(x) are collectively under a duty to preside over the entire committee this year; but the duty is a *disjunctive* one: if one man who has the property C(x) presides over the entire committee this year all of last year's meeting chairmen comply with their duty. Clearly, there is nothing anybody can do about having been a meeting chairman last year or not. But if anybody is to comply with the duty that (2) demands, then property C(x) must be possessed by some of the relevant agents. For if *Obligatory$_i$ $\exists x$(C(x) & & P[x])* is both true and fulfilled, then *$\exists x$(C(x) & P(x))* is true; i.e., somebody both has *already* in fact chaired a meeting last year and presided this year over the entire committee; that is, somebody has already property C(x). Thus, if *Obligatory$_i$ $\exists x$(C(x) & P[x])* is fulfillable, i.e., prescribes no empty duty, *$\exists x$(C(x))* is true.

In brief, *Deon.* 20 is required by the principle that Ought implies Can, provided that this Can is understood in a sense that includes the sense in which one cannot change the facts of the case, particularly the past. *Deon.* 19 explains in part how (2), *It is *obligatory$_i$* (required) that someone who chaired a meeting last year preside over the entire committee this year*', entails *Someone chaired a meeting last year*.

Now, with the establishment of the consistency principle *Deon.* 21 in the next section, we will have established that the basic layer of deontic implication is a weak non-iterative modal logic resembling the standard logic of quantifiers. This is all spelled out in Chapters 8 and 9.

14. CONSISTENCY OF NORMATIVE SYSTEMS

By *Deon.* 7 of §4 the enactment of a normative system is the setting aside of a set of practitions for the qualified endorsement of a domain of agents. It is also the setting aside for endorsement of the set of deontic statements corresponding, and embodying, those practitions. Thus, the enactment of a normative system is the postulation of the truth of the statements in question as practical premises, to be joined to any other practical premises that we may already have. This involves the implicit claim that the set of deontic statements we enact in a given enactment is consistent, that is, that it does not imply both a noema x and the latter's negation $\sim x$. Yet it is quite easy to conceive of a law-issuing body deliberately to formulate a self-contradictory bill, i.e., one which implies some prescription *X to do A* and the negation *X to do not A*. It is easy, for more specificity, to imagine a tyrant, set on destroying a political foe with some appearance of legality, have his rubber-stamp congress pass a self-contradictory law, so that in a very legalistic trial his opponent is found guilty of doing something unlawful. However, in a situation such as the one described, it is doubtful whether the tyrant himself or anyone of his henchmen does really endorse the self-contradictory command, i.e., takes it in his heart to be Legitimate, or orthotic. For most people, in any case, the very deliberateness of the proceedings makes them a shameful legal farce.

Doubtless, a self-contradictory bill can be passed through the official machinery of legislation of a county. Of course, one can have a concept of obligation that allows self-contradictory obligations. But if we have such a concept, we also have the weaker concept, which is like the self-contradictory one in every other respect except that it allows no contradictory obligations. This is the concept governed by the principle

> *Deon.* 21. The deontic judgment *It is *obligatory$_i$* that X do A* implies that practition *X to do A* is selfconsistent.

Deon. 21 is part of our version of what is usually referred to as Kant's axiom and as the principle that Ought implies Can. Here we are interested in elucidating the concept of obligation that conforms to *Deon.* 21. Therefore, we must provide an analysis of the normative situation that ensues from self-contradictory bills processed through an official law-making procedure.

In normal countries with normal legislative procedures an obvious startling self-contradictory act does not get through, or if it gets through, the self-contradiction would be taken to be a voiding condition of either the whole law or of at least the self-contradictory part. Some persons would prefer to say that it is not a law at all, while others may want to say that a self-contradictory law is perfectly all right as a law, although it may be immoral, or even difficult to apply. What we say here depends on how widely we want to use the word 'law'. Without prejudging the issue as to the best way of using this word, we shall here adopt the view that *if a self-contradictory set of practical noemata is properly issued as one law or normative system by a legislative body or office, then it is either not a law, or it is ipso facto void as a whole.* But we must emphasize that because a law, or a so-called law is void as whole, it does not follow that a certain part of it is also void. In fact, a law void as a whole because of a self-contradiction may be taken to be automatically split into several parts, each consistent, which enter into a conflict. That is, the enactment of a self-contradictory bill is the enactment of a set of laws in conflict. (Recall our discussion of generic and specific deontic properties in §2 above.)

This view of self-contradictory laws applies very nicely to the not far-fetched case of a legislative body passing, wholly inadvertently, a bill containing subtle self-contradictions. It may very well be the case that only after the law has been applied rather widely that the contradiction comes to light. It may happen that in such a case for a law court to declare the totality of the act void would be to bring about a national catastrophe. Logically, in such a case it is open to the law courts to do many different things. We can only describe the problem and show how our concept of enactment sheds light on the logic of the situation. Suppose, then, that there is the enactment of a self-contradictory bill, i.e., the restricted endorsement of a set of practitions, among which there are, say, a prescription A and its corresponding negation $\sim A$. This is the enactment that at the time the contradiction is revealed we say to be cancelled, or voided. There is, however, the enactment, call it j, consisting of the restricted endorsement of the same set of practitions minus A; and there is the enactment, call it h, consisting of the restricted endorsement of the first set of practitions minus $\sim A$. Thus, A is *obligatory$_j$*, and also $\sim A$ is *obligatory$_h$*. Since neither j nor h are automatically cancelled, or voided, we have here two true deontic statements in conflict, but not in contradiction. Naturally, the conflict must be resolved, and this is what some law court, or some legislative body, or even some other public servant will have to do by either cancelling one enactment of the two in conflict, or by cancelling both, or by giving some priority to one over the other. But this is a matter of the existing legislation for solving conflicts of laws, traditions, and purposes, needs, and facts, that goes beyond the logic of the mere formulation of a conflict of duties.

Every specific normative system is, in our terminology, a system of deontic noemata governed by *Deon.* 21, i.e., a system characterized by a specific *obligatoriness$_i$*. Furthermore, a specific normative system cannot both demand the doing and the not doing of one and the same action. This is also part of the principle that Ought implies Can. For obviously, if one and the same action A were both enjoined and interdicted, either the injunction or the interdiction would have to be left unfulfilled. Thus, specific normative systems are self-consistent systems of deontic judgments that conform to

> *Deon* 22. ∗It is *obligatory$_i$* that X do A∗ implies ∗It is not *obligatory$_i$* that X not do A∗.

On the other hand, generic obligatorinesses, which do not belong in a system of norms, but supervenes to systems of systems of norms, do not abide by *Deon.* 21 or *Deon.* 22.

15. DEONTIC QUANTIFICATION IS EXTENSIONAL

By *Deon.* 1 and *Deon.* 2 of §1, the principles of quantification studied in Chapter 3, §18 are also valid for deontic judgments. There are now, however, two types of propositions that must be carefully distinguished. There are those propositions that do, and those that do not, result from the application of a quantifier to a deontic function. We have already discussed some examples of this type in §7 in connection with *Deon.* 12*g*. Consider deontic propositions of the form:

(1)   It is *obligatory$_i$* for everybody to A.

Here the propositional function is ∗it is *obligatory$_i$* (that) to A∗, or, if you wish, ∗it is *obligatory$_i$* (that) for x to A∗. This function contains the practitional function ∗to A∗ or ∗x to A∗. Propositions of form (1) contrast with the corresponding propositions of the form

(2)   It is *obligatory$_i$* that everybody A.

These propositions result from the application of the deontic operator ∗it is *obligatory$_i$* that∗ to the universally quantified prescription ∗Everybody (to) A∗. What is the difference between (1) and (2)?

Reflexion does not reveal any difference in what (1) and (2) demand. They appear to be equivalent. In the case of a finite domain of agents they are both tantamount to a conjunction of the form ∗agent 1 to do A & agent 2 to do A...∗.

Propositions of forms (1) and (2) are alike in that both deal with allegedly real, not merely possible obligations. Real obligations belong, naturally, to real agents and demand real actions on (to, with, by, ...) real objects and patients. Thus, corresponding propositions of forms (1) and (2) deal with the same domain of agents. There is no reason at all to suppose that the exchange of the quantifier and the deontic operator, when we move from (1) to (2), or vice versa, alters the domain of agents.

Here is a very important point in which deontic operators differ from ordinary propositional modalities like necessity and possibility. A proposition of the form *Everybody is necessarily P* is clearly about all existing people, but the corresponding proposition of the form *Necessarily, everybody is P*, or better, *It is necessarily the case that everybody be P* is not clearly just about all existing persons; rather, it is about all *possible* persons. Thus, the interchange of modality and quantifier does in this case reveal a change in the domain of the quantifier.

Consider a proposition of the form, like (1), *∀xM(x is P)*, and the corresponding proposition of the form, like (2) *M∀x(x is P)*, where the quantifier has a different domain, depending on whether it precedes or follows the modality M. Then a subtle ambiguity appears in the sentential function 'M(x is P)'. If 'x' represents values of the external quantifier in *∀xM(x is P)*, then the propositional function *M(x is P)*, as well as any of its instances *M(a is P)*, implies the existentially quantified proposition *∃xM(x is P)*. But if the free occurrence of 'x' in 'M(x is P)' represents a value of the inside quantifier of *M∀x(x is P)*, then the existential implication is ruled out.

Now, there is *no* such ambiguity in the case of sentential functions of the form 'it is *obligatory$_i$* that x do A'. Given the normal semantical conventions of English, that sentence schema expresses a propositional function from which, and from whose instances, we can derive the proposition *There is someone for whom it is *obligatory$_i$* that he do A*, i.e., more idiomatically, *It is *obligatory$_i$* for someone to do A*. Therefore, deontic operators do not in any way affect the range of the quantifiers. Furthermore, there are no two kinds of positions in a deontic function, namely, those that allow existential generalization and those that do not allow it. In technical jargon, we summarize all these points, by saying that:

Deon. 23. Deontic propositional functions are extensional with respect to quantification.

Naturally, deontic logic does not preclude people from dying or getting born. At different times in the history of each institution there may be different sets of agents who have the corresponding institutional obligations or duties. This by itself imposes no need to alter the conception of quantification we developed in Chapter 3 §§ 18ff. The phenomena of death and birth can be handled by either discussing the obligations of a type i at a given time, when the domain of agents is fixed, or by doing what is customarily done in the general theory of quantification, namely, to consider in the domain of a quantifier any entity that at some time or other exists. Thus, the fundamental theory of quantificational deontic implicacation only needs the addition of

> *Deon.* 24. Propositions of form (1) are equivalent to their corresponding propositions of form (2).

16. IDENTITY AND THE EXTENSIONALITY OF DEONTIC JUDGMENTS

Identity statements are statements; therefore, they cannot give rise to deontic judgments. Thus, the only question about identity in deontic logic is whether the standard principle of substitutivity of identity holds unrestrictedly for deontic propositions. This principle is:

> (Id.) If a sentence of the form '$a = b$' expresses a true proposition and so does a sentence S, containing occurrences of the individual symbol a, then the sentence S' obtained from S by replacing some (free) occurrences of a in S with (free) occurrences of b in S also expresses a true proposition.

This principle fails in so-called intensional, or non-extensional, contexts, among which are sentences containing words expressive of the ordinary propositional modalities and sentences expressive of psychological attitudes that involve belief or cognition. Thus, 'Anthony believes that Napoleon was defeated at Waterloo' may express a truth while 'Anthony believes that Josephine's divorced husband was defeated at Waterloo' expresses a falsehood.[12]

Obligation contexts are *not* intensional. While a man is the referent of another man's beliefs under some characterization or other, a man's obligations are *his* regardless of his characterizations, once he has got them. To be sure, obligations accrue to a man *because* of his circumstances and relationships to other people, but once they accrue they belong to the whole of him, so to speak. For example, let 'P' be any adjective such that Richard M. Nixon is the one and only one man who in 1925 was P; then the sentence 'The man who in 1925 was P ought to finish the Viet Nam war in 1971' is as true, or as false, as the sentence 'Richard M. Nixon ought to finish the Viet Nam war in 1971'. The same happens with the patients of the actions that are *obligatory$_i$*. If a man has a duty to do action A to a person or thing c, then that man has the same duty to do action A to entity d, if $c=d$. In short:

> *Deon.* 25. Deontic propositional functions are extensional with respect to identity.

Palpably, the extensionality of deontic propositional functions with respect to quantification is intimately bound up with their extensionality with respect to identity. The fundamental thing is that the positions (represented by individual variables) in deontic functions are just of one type, namely, the type that allows quantification. Thus, a unique characterization of an individual inside the scope of a deontic operator is not prevented by that scope to refer to the entity it purports to refer. That is to say,

> *Deon.* 26. Unique characterizations (i.e., what are expressed by uniquely referring descriptions) are not bound by the scope of the deontic operators in which they lie. More precisely, $*Obligatory_i \{\phi(\alpha)\}_\alpha *$ is equivalent to $*\{Obligatory_i\ \phi(\alpha)\}_\alpha$, where '$\{\ \}_\alpha$' indicates the scope of α, a being only in extensional positions in ϕ.

For instance, the three propositions below are equivalent:

(1)   It is *obligatory$_i$* that the one man who came late withdraw.
(2)   The following is *obligatory$_i$*: that it being the case that just one man came late he withdraw.
(3)   It is the case that just one man came late and it is *obligatory$_i$* that he withdraw.

The pairwise equivalence of (1)–(3) is obviously dependent upon the fact that a unique characterization of an individual is a propositional complex, not a practitional one. Thus,

Deon. 27. The extensionality of deontic propositional functions depends on the fundamental distinction between propositions and practitions as well as on the laws governing their transactions.

17. THE DEFEASIBILITY CONDITIONS OF OBLIGATION

Many philosophers have rightly worried about the defeasibility of obligation claims. L. Powers, in the paper mentioned earlier, has discussed a case that has been adduced in support of a so-called dyadic or conditional deontic logic. The idea of a special conditional has been strongly suggested by causal statement. Powers' example has been celebrated because it connects causality and obligation. Here is the example:

(1)   John Doe has impregnated Susy Mae; so, he ought to marry her. But John kills Susy Mae and then it is not the case that he ought to marry her.

The conditional approach to deontic logic is so-called because it builds the logic of *ought* on a special *if* connective called "conditional", which is not an extensional connective. In particular that connective is not governed by the principle

(C)   *If p, then it is obligatory that A* implies *If p and q, then it is obligatory that A*.

But the situation is more complicated. First, it has been too quickly assumed that John Doe's killing Susy Mae automatically cancels his obligation to marry her – if he has one to start with. It is not out of order to suppose that some laws that demand marriage upon impregnation continue to require that the marriage be consummated with the dead Susy Mae, so that she goes away without the capital sin in question. The situation I am considering is in substance not different from the American practice of promoting George Washington posthumously to whatever may be the highest rank in the American Army at the time, the latest one being to the rank of a five-star general when this rank was created during World War II. Note also that Susy Mae must be unmarried, unless we allow polyandria. It may be said that this quibbling is irrelevant, so that as long as *some* laws do not require John to marry a dead Susy, (C) fails. But this is not what the example establishes. The example with our commentary establishes that

Deon. 28A. *Different* normative systems may have *different* conditions for the "cancellation" of obligations.

Now the question is: How are we to represent Deon. 28A in general deontic logic? Undoubtedly, the claim that (C) is false is one way, and it has several advantages.

Yet the denial of (C) is a negative solution that looks like overkill and leaves a converse problem unsolved. It tampers with the extensionality of ought discussed above. And it leaves no account for the fact that only in *very* few cases we *seem* to have the situation of an obligation cancelled by the addition of another circumstance. The denial of (G) is a drastic reaction to the *exceptional* cases. Just consider that if John Doe ought really to marry Susy Mae because he got her pregnant, then he obviously ought to marry her regardless of most of what happens to them. For practically anything one can think of (C) holds obviously. *This too has to be explained.*

The loss of the extensionality is serious. A careful attention to Powers' example suggests that the 'if' in (1) is more like the expression of a material conditional. For instance, it is governed by transposition: *Only if John didn't impregnate Susy, is it not the case that he ought to marry her* is equivalent to it. It also implies *(Either) John didn't impregnate Susy Mae, or he ought to marry her*.

In general, since rules and norms are for the most part arbitrary stipulations, there is *no* relevant or logical connection between conditions of obligation and obligatory actions. More deeply: the assumed freedom of practical thinking, which is presupposed in the creation of normative systems and institutions, suggests very strongly that the conditionality of rules and norms is an arbitrary and stipulative conditionality, one that can be fully grounded on the unrestricted conditionality of *material implication*. Normative "necessity" is to a large extent stipulative. And this is the profound rationale for the extensionality of the deontic operators.

The "conditional" approach to deontic logic, which treats *ought*-ness as a form of alethic or intensional necessity, ignores the crucial principle on which we have built our study of the foundations of institutions, namely, that *deontic judgments belong into systems*. But, as noted, this systematicity is not a connective linking two propositions. Each system is an arrangement from a certain point of view, as described above, of *all* propositions and *all* practitions. The "conditional" approach seems to equate conditions for obligation with the qualification of qualified obligation.[14]

In consonance with all the previous findings about practical thinking we submit, then, that:

> *Deon.* 28. Each deontic operator D_i is paired with a characteristic set C_i of necessary conditions for *ought$_i$*-ness.

Thus, *in* the normative system *j* that Powers is considering, where nobody marries dead people,

> (1a)   At time *t* John Doe impregnated Susy Mae, and at time *t* (and later at t_1) John Doe *ought$_j$* to marry Susy Mae *only if* Susy Mae is alive at *t* (or t_1).

We find no need to leave the normal unproblematie cases unelucidated. Hence,

> *Deon.* 29. Deontic operators are governed by (C).

The analogy between causality and obligation deserve a comment. Causality in science is a very obscure concept, and many conditions are left unspecified, but since we tend to think of a general concept of causality the denial of (C) seems tempting. Now, in the case of obligation we deal with the different *specific* obligatorinesses of the varied specific normative systems. In such systems things need be specified and *are* specified arbitrarily. Especially in criminal law and in serious matters we want clearcut lines of responsibility. Given our conception of ourselves and the world we fix conditions that are required for obligatoriness to hold. Since in many cases we depend on the causal participation of an agent, we have in fact impregnated the notion of cause with normative seeds, so that deontic logic should be a model for causality, not the other way around! When we speak of causality in the abstract, independently of a set of normative considerations we are dealing with a schematic concept that is too anemic to provide a healthy model for deontic logic.

The preceding does not, of course, imply that the characteristic obligatoriness "cancellation" conditions C_i of a normative system N_i are always very simple and fully spelled out in some text publicly available and easy to read. In the very important case of a legal system there are wholly appropriately provisions that establish a fixed and clear procedure for determining the pervasive necessary conditions C_L of a given obligatoriness$_L$, without the procedure specifying in advance exactly what they are. For instance, judges or certain administrative officers have as one of their primary roles to determine some of the conditions C_L of obligatoriness$_L$. But the law, or the statutes of an institution, make the procedure final at a certain point. Obviously, there is no such finality in the abstract general conception of causality. And the law of the land and the by-laws of institutions are more efficient by having both an open-ended set C_L of necessary conditions of obligatoriness$_L$ and a precise procedure for determining with *finality* certain elements of C_L. They can cope with changes in circumstances.

18. A PAUSE AND A CAUTION

We come to the end of our phenomenological investigation of the internal structure of deontic judgments. We have also uncovered the fundamental laws governing the basic layers of deontic implication. We have found, again and again, how deontic implication rests both (i) on structural connections between deontic judgments and practitions, and (ii) on implicational relations within practitions and on those between practitions and propositions.

We have crystalized phenomenological results *Deon.* 1–*Deon.* 29. These are laws governing deontic noemata. Many of them are somewhat vague, so that they need further elucidation. They are criteria of adequacy for any meta-ethical theory that analyzes deontic concepts. They are criteria of adequacy for any theory of morality, as well as for theories of normative systems, whatever they may be, including legal systems.

Deon. 1–*Deon.* 29 are also the foundations for the elucidation of deontic truth. This is precisely what we attempt to accomplish in the next chapter.

NOTES TO CHAPTER 7

[1] For the complex structure of morality and the formulation of the fundamental principles of each of its layers, see Hector-Neri Castañeda, *The Structure of Morality.*
[2] See H-N. Castañeda, 'Imperatives, Decisions, and Oughts', in H-N. Castañeda and G. Nakhnikian, *Morality and the Language of Conduct* (Detroit, Michigan: Wayne State University Press, 1963), pp. 225–243.

³ Here we touch on general problems in metaphysics and epistemology that are beyond our present scope. For a fitting theory of names, definite descriptions, and the constitution of objects, see H-N. Castañeda, 'Thinking and the Structure of the World', *Philosophia* **4** (1974): 3–40, and 'Identity and Sameness', *Philosophia* **5** (1975).

⁴ In his 'Some Deontic Logicians', *Nous* **1** (1967): 361–400, Lawrence Powers objected to the way the distinction between actions considered prescriptively and actions considered as circumstances is drawn in Hector-Neri Castañeda, 'Acts, the Logic of Obligation, and Deontic Calculi', *Crítica* **1** (1967): 77–99, and *Philosophical Studies* **20** (1968): 13–26. Powers' objections attack some of the examples, which were indeed inadequate partly because the *Crítica* paper failed to distinguish actions considered as circumstances from parenthetical remarks and from identifiers, as is done here in §9 and was done, before Powers' objections, in Hector-Neri Castañeda, 'Acts, Imperatives, and Obligations', *Aristotelian Society Proceedings* **68** (1967–68): 25–48. Powers, however, did not consider the example in the *Crítica* paper, reproduced here, that involves a mixture of universal quantification and the deontic modality of permittedness. The *Crítica* paper said that examples such as that one provide "to my mind the clinching proof of the distinction between the two ways of considering actions", namely, as circumstances and as practical actions.

⁵ A distinction between two types of goodnesses, one that applies to propositions (or states of affairs) and another to intentions, has been defended in Hector-Neri Castañeda, 'Goodness, Intentions, and Propositions', in Paul Welsh (ed.), *Facts, Value, and Perception* (Durham, North Carolina: Duke University Press, 1975).

⁶ This beautiful example of a mixed conjunctive prescription expressed by 'and' was provided by Robert Fogelin in a first draft of comments on H-N. Castañeda, 'Ethics and Logic: Stevensonian Emotivism Revisited', *The Journal of Philosophy* **64** (1967): 671–683.

⁷ Such solutions have been suggested, for instance, by H. P. Rickman, 'Escapism: The Logical Basis for Ethics', *Mind*, n.s., **72** (1963): 273–274, and John Robison, 'Who, What, Where, and When: A Note on Deontic Logic', *Philosophical Studies* **15** (1964): 89–91. P. H. Nowell-Smith and E. J. Lemmon wrote a nice discussion of the good-samaritan paradox in connection with a standard deontic calculus of Alan R. Anderson, in 'Escapism: The Logical Basis of Ethics', *Mind*, n.s., **69** (1960): 289–300. Their solution is examined in the *Crítica* paper mentioned in note 2. In brief, their solution consists in relativizing the deontic modalities to agents. Thus, they introduce an operator Ox, which is to be read as 'it is obligatory-for-x that'. This is not completely adequate for the case in which the Good-samaritan is himself the wrongdoer. Another obvious difficulty with their method is this: in their calculus we cannot express statements of the form *It is *obligatory* that somebody do A*. Such statements have a deontic operator, not relativized to any agent, applied to a quantified noema, not to a noematic function or a singular noema. It is, on our view, of form *$O(\exists x A \lfloor x \rfloor)$*. On Nowell-Smith and Lemmon's calculus it cannot be represented by that formula or by '$Ox(\exists xp)$', for neither is a well-formed formula in their calculus: the latter has a free variable 'x' which is not free in '$(\exists xp)$'. The non-relativity to agents of deontic modalities will be clearer from our discussion of the extensionality of deontic propositions in §15 and §16 below in this chapter.

⁸ For discussion of proposals to solve the Good-samaritan paradox see H-N. Castañeda 'Acts, the Logic of Obligation, and Deontic Calculi', mentioned in note 4 above; W. Sellars, 'Reflections on Contrary-to-Duty Imperatives', *Nous* **1** (1967): 303–344; L. Åqvist, 'Good Samaritans, Contrary-to-Duty Imperatives, and Epistemic

Obligations', *Ibid.*: 361–379; and L. Powers, 'Some Deontic Logicians'.
⁹ See preceding note 8.
¹⁰ R. Chisholm first discussed this "paradox" in 'Contrary-to-Duty Imperatives and Deontic Logic', *Analysis* **23** (1963): 33–36. He correctly noted that Castañeda's systems of deontic logic were not affected by the "paradox". See Sellars' paper mentioned in note 8.
¹¹ For a recent exchange on the distributivity of *obligatoriness*ᵢ through conjunction see: (1) H. G. Von Wright, *Norm and Action* (New York: The Humanities Press, 1963), pp. 182ff.; ⟨2) H-N. Castañeda, 'The Logic of Change, Action, and Norms', *The Journal of Philosophy* **62** (1965): 333–344; (3) David Sidorski, 'A Note on Three Criticisms of Von Wright', *Ibid.*: 739–742; and (4) H-N. Castañeda, 'A Note on Deontic Logic (A Rejoinder)', *The Journal of Philosophy* **63** (1966): 231–234.
¹² For a general theory of reference that deals with the problem of opacity, the papers mentioned in note 3 above. Some philosophers have assumed that because deontic judgments are modal judgments they are referentially opaque. This is an error. See Lou Goble 'Opacity and the Ought-to-Be', *Nous* **7** (1973): 407–412, and 'Corrigenda' in *Nous* **8** (1974): 200.
¹³ See, for instance, Robert Stalnaker, 'A Theory of Conditionals', in N. Rescher, ed., *Studies in Logical Theory* (Oxford, England: Blackwell's, 1968), who argues that conditionals do not obey (C), contraposition, and other standard laws.
¹⁴ For other difficulties with the dyadic treatment of deontic logic, see H.-N. Castañeda, 'The Logic of Change, Action, and Norms', *The Journal of Philosophy* **62** (1965): 333–344, which is a critical study of H. G. Von Wright, *Norm and Action* (New York: The Humanities Press, 1963), who is the founder of treatment, and does it in an impressive and large scale in this book. N. Rescher applied the "conditional" approach to imperatives in his *The Logic of Commands* (London, England: Routledge & Kegan Paul, 1966). For difficulties with this work see H.-N. Castañeda's review of it in *The Philosophical Review* **19** (1970): 439–446. Some of these difficulties apply also to the conditional approach to deontic logic. A nice study of earlier "conditional" systems of deontic logic by Von Wright and Rescher is Bengt Hansson, 'An Analysis of Some Deontic Logics', *Nous* **3** (1969); 373–398.

CHAPTER 8

DEONTIC TRUTH

In the preceding chapter we examined both the ontological and the logical structures of deontic judgments. We argued that they are propositions so that their implicational structure is partly a special case of the implicational structure studied in Chapter 3. In developing the special additional principles that govern deontic implication we proceeded, essentially, along the inferential approach. Given the coincidence of the inferential and the semantical approaches to implication discussed in Chapter 3, §17 and §22, there must be some principles of deontic truth that provide a semantical underpinning for the inferential deontic principles gathered in Chapter 7. In this chapter, building on Chapter 5, we discuss several ways of underpinning semantically those principles of implication. Naturally, these ways are coincident or "equivalent" to one another as well as to the inferential system erected in Chapter 7. These coincidences are discussed in Chapter 9, which contains a cumulative formal theory of the logical structure of all the practical noemata we have been studying since Chapter 1.

This chapter contains an analysis of deontic truth, in that sets of conditions that are both necessary and sufficient for a deontic judgment to be true are formulated. But this chapter does *not* contain an analysis of deontic judgments. Indeed, as we shall explain in Chapter 13 we endorse the thesis that deontic judgments are not reducible to, or analyzable into, non-deontic judgments.

1. DEONTIC TRUTH AS NECESSARY LEGITIMACY

In Chapter 7 we ended up by developing an inferential system of deontic implication. But as we explained in Chapter 3, §12, the inferential approach to implication has to be grounded on a semantical approach. That is, implication is founded on a structure of principles of truth. Thus, the inferential system of Chapter 7 has to be mounted on a structure of deontic truth.

We have studied in Chapter 7 how a deontic statement is constituted by a core practition and a qualification that signals the type of consideration of a systemic character of the deontic statement in question. That consideration is precisely a context of Legitimacy for the core practition. When a deontic judgment is true its core practition is Legitimate in the context correlated with the systemic character of the judgment. But a practition may be Legitimate in the same context even when the deontic judgment having it as its core is not true. This connection between deontic truth and the Legitimacy-values of practitions must be described in full detail.

There is a tremendously important difference between the semantical values of propositions, i.e., those involved in implication, namely truth and falsity, and the semantical values of practitions. The former are just *two* absolute values in the sense that a proposition has its value once and for all tenselessly and regardless of how large a segment of the actual universe we consider. If a proposition is true in a segment of the universe, then, as we explained in Chapter 3, §2, it is true in any other segment of the universe, as well as in the whole universe. On the other hand, the semantical values of practitions are many and depend intimately on segments of the universe. They pertain to the Legitimization of the commands, orders, requests, pieces of advice, or petitions, or resolutions, they formulate. As before and always, mandates are the *contents* of speech acts and of psychological attitudes and must be distinguished from the acts of ordering, requesting, begging, etc. As will be recalled from Chapter 5, whenever we speak of the semantical values of mandates we are dealing with the sense of the word 'right' in which we often say of a person: "*What* he said was the right thing to say, but it was wrong of him *to say it*". Here the word 'right' expresses a porperty of a content or a *what* of a speech act; and the property is clearly analogous to truth, it being a designated or preferred property of such contents. On the other hand, the word 'wrong' expresses a deontic property of the man's *act* of saying something. The contrast between the two properties is very great. We are concerned with the former and, as in Chapter 5, shall capitalize the initial of the word 'Legitimate' to avoid confusion.

As we discussed in Chapter 5, §§1–3, a mandate is *Legitimate* in relation to some specific end or purpose and on account of a set of facts of the situation, and often in regard to procedural conventions and decisions to which the speaker and the agent, among others, subscribe. Each set of ends, facts, conventional procedures, and decisions determines a context for Legitimacy-values of certain imperatives and resolutives. Thus, an imperative has as many Legitimacy-values as one cares to parcel out contexts. An imperative may be Legitimate in one context and Non-legitimate in another in view of the possible conflicts of ends as well as of procedures. But the Legitimacy or Non-legitimacy of an imperative relative to a certain context constituted by a set of facts, ends, procedural conventions and decisions would be useless unless the conflict were resolved in a larger context. In cases of conflict, life itself forces us to make choices and produce a balance, so that we may speak of a total context, in which we regard the ends and procedural conventions as hierarchically organized, even if that organization is rough and revisable, and even if its structure and outline are only dimly conceived (as it may well be, especially in the case of a conflict.) In Chapter 5, §3 we developed in detail the idea of an absolute context that covers a domain of agents.

The distinction between the relative and the absolute contexts of Legitimacy of an imperative is connected with that between the qualified and unqualified uses of ought as well as with the fact that imperatives are always used assertively. We explain this fact by the view that: (i) imperatives are always used against the total background of ends, facts, and decisions, i.e., with the implicit claim that they are *Legitimate* in the absolute context; (ii) a normative with an unqualified ought is true or false, depending on whatever the facts, ends, etc. of the absolute context make its core practition *Legitimate*, and (iii) a normative with a qualified ought is true or false depending on whether the facts, ends, etc. of the context determined by its qualification makes its core practition *Legitimate*. This threefold view accounts for some of the exciting data uncovered earlier in Chapters 4 and 7, already adumbrated in Chapter 2: (1) mandates are not used in deliberation as means of presenting courses of action for mere consideration; (2) qualified normatives do that very nicely; (3) qualified normatives are not used motivationally and fail to imply their corresponding imperatives; (4) the unqualified normatives are used motivationally or imperatively and imply imperatives.

We may say that a noema *points to* each of the noemata different from it but equivalent to it. This relation of pointing to holds, then, between *This is an equiangular Euclidean triangle* and *This [referring to the same thing] is an equilateral Euclidean triangle∗. Adopting a similar use of the term 'express' by Reichenbach we say that a proposition P containing a certain structure *expresses* the structure, without referring to it, and *expresses* a second-order proposition in which the structure is predicatively referred to as possessed by P. Thus, as we view the general systematic structure of practical discourse, one of the fundamental links between ∗X ought (*unqualifiedly*) to do A∗ and ∗X, do A∗ is that the former expresses, or points to, the *Legitimacy* of the latter in the absolute or total context of ends, facts, conventions, and decisions; but it does not formulate what these are. Indeed, it does not even articulate that the imperative is *Legitimate*. A statement of the form ∗X ought (unqualifiedly) to do A∗ formulates in its own way in the object-language, i.e., in the material mode of speech (to use Carnap's helpful term, but without its old sting) what the corresponding second-order statement of the form ∗The practition ∗X to do A∗ is necessarily Legitimate in the absolute context of ends, etc.∗ formulates in the metalanguage of the language of action. But the two statements, though equivalent in content, are different. They belong to different conceptual contexts: the normative, to that in which we are directly engaged in guiding behavior; the second-order statement, to that in which we discuss propositions and evaluate inferences. The latter context presupposes the former and may include it. The two statements entail one another in the latter context but not in the former, i.e., specific implications that bridge the two contexts are needed for the entailment. This makes it incorrect to regard the second-order statement as the analysis of the meaning of the term 'ought (unqualifiedly)', or as the analysis of the whole normative. Since imperatives are only used assertively, the manner in which we can talk about actions and their reasons without stepping into the metalanguage in which imperatives are mentioned but not used, is to use normatives. Thus, the division of functions between normatives and imperatives allows each type of noema greater efficacy.

There is an analogous relationship between normatives of the form ∗X ought (unqualifiedly) not to do A∗ or ∗It is wrong (unqualifiedly) for X to do A∗, and the second-order statement ∗The practition ∗X to not do A∗ is *necessarily Legitimate* in the absolute context of facts, ends, conventions, and decisions∗. On the other hand, ∗X may (unqualifiedly) do A∗ is the image in the material mode of speech of the second-order statement ∗The practition *X not to do A* is not *necessarily Legitimate* in the absolute context*.

A qualified use of a normative of the ought-type, on the other hand, points to and *expresses* the *necessary Legitimacy* of the corresponding practition in the context determined by the qualification. The same holds, *mutatis mutandis*, for the other types of normative. Thus, if a normative with a qualification is not used motivationally, the normative expresses that the whole hierarchical complex of ends, conventions, and decisions is not necessarily considered in ascribing a relative *Legitimacy*-value to its corresponding practition. Thus, a different value may be ascribed to the imperative in a final examination.

To sum up, let C_1 be the absolute context determined by the relevant domain of agents, as discussed in Chapter 5, §3, and let C_i be any context of Legitimacy, including C_1. Let 'X' represent first-, second- or third-person ways of reference to agents. Then, the semantical thesis we are advocating, which establishes the implicational unity throughout the whole of the structures of practical thinking, is this:

S.T.1. SEMANTICAL THESIS NO. 1:
  (For terminology, see *Convention* and *Deon.* 5 in Chapter 7, §2.)

  (i) A deontic judgment of the form *It is *obligatory$_i$* that X do A* is true, if and only if its corresponding second-order proposition of the form *The practition *X to do A* is necessarily Legitimate (orthotic) in context C_i* is true.

  (ii) A deontic proposition of the form *It is *forbidden$_i$* that X do A* is true, if and only if its corresponding second-order proposition of the form *The practition *X not to do A* is necessarily Legitimate (orthotic) in context C_i* is true.

  (iii) A deontic proposition of the form *It is *permitted$_i$* to do A* is true, if and only if its corresponding second-order proposition of the form *The practition *X to do A* is not necessarily Legitimate (orthotic) in context C_i* is true.

  (iv) A deontic judgment of the form *It is *completely optional$_i$* that X do A* is true, if and only if its corresponding second-order propositions of the forms *The practition *X to do A* is not necessarily Legitimate in context C_i* and *The practition *X not to do A* is not necessarily Legitimate in context C_i* are both true.

This thesis produces the first step of an analysis of deontic truth in terms of second-order statements about practitions and their orthotic values.[2] A second step is needed in order to elucidate the necessity of which so much is made in the above semantical thesis.

In order to take the step that elucidates the necessity involved in our semantical thesis let us look back at our analysis of orthotic values in Chapter 5, §1 and §3, and Chapter 6, §8. There we find that, roughly, a primary practition P is Legitimate in context C_i if and only if it satisfies one of three conditions: (a) the corresponding performance proposition $c(P)$ is *implied* by a set C_i^+ of propositions whose members are: propositions that formulate the situation of a segment of the world, propositions that formulate the ends determining context C_i, and propositions that formulate that those ends (perhaps contrary to fact) are fulfilled; (b) neither $c(P)$ nor $\sim c(P)$ is implied by C_i^+, but P is endorsed by some, while $\sim P$ is not endorsed by any, of the agents characterizing C_i; (c) neither P nor $\sim P$ satisfy condition (a) or condition (b), but P is fulfilled, i.e., $c(P)$ is true.

The only condition that involves a necessity of some kind is condition (a). What is implied by a set of noemata is necessarily connected with the set in question. On the other hand, conditions (b) and (c) are strictly contingent. The satisfaction of condition (b) is contingent upon the desires or whims or purposes of the agents determining context C_i that are not part and parcel of C_i. The fulfillment of condition (c) is contingent on the empirical course of the history of the universe, including, again, the whims of the agents under consideration.

Consequently, we must view condition (a) for the Legitimacy in a context C_i of a practition as the analysis of the necessity involved in our semantical thesis. That is to say, *condition (a) provides an analysis of the necessity which is the guts of all deontic operators of the ∗obligatory∗ type.*

S.T.2. SEMANTICAL THESIS NO. 2:
    (i) A deontic judgment of the form ∗It is *obligatory*$_i$ that P∗ is true, if and only if C_i^+ implies $c(P)$.
    (ii) A deontic judgment of the form ∗It is *forbidden*$_i$ that P∗ is true, if and only if C_i^+ implies $-c(P)$.
    (iii) A deontic judgment of the form ∗It is *permitted*$_i$ that P∗ is true, if and only if C_i^+ does not imply $c(P)$.

(iv) A deontic judgment of the form *It is (completely) *optional$_i$* that P* is true, if and only if C_i^+ implies neither $c(P)$ nor $\sim c(P)$.

Here is a theory that connects deontic judgments with practitions in two ways: (i) by putting a practition at the core of each deontic judgment, and (ii) by analyzing the truth conditions of deontic judgments in terms of the semantical values of practitions. Furthermore, the theory explains the necessity of an ought or obligation in terms of implication. This implication holds ultimately between a certain characterization of a part of the actual world conjoined to a characterization of a possible future that may never be actualized, and a proposition attributing the doing of actions to certain agents. Thus, *deontic propositions have truth-values that depend ultimately on nothing but non-deontic empirical propositions and non-deontic implications.* Yet the truth of a deontic judgment that is true but not logically true is in general non-inferrable from a set of true non-deontic propositions.

This analysis of deontic truth must, naturally, be tested against the crucial data *Deon.* 1–*Deon.* 29 carefully gathered in Chapter 7. In particular, we must test our Semantical Thesis No. 2 against the principles of implication spread out through Chapter 7. We leave this test to the reader, aside from the following illustrative cases.

In Chapter 7, §10 we argued for principle (P*), which is *Deon.* 17, namely: that if a practition P implies practition Q, then that it is *obligatory$_i$* that P implies that it is *obligatory$_i$* that Q. This is satisfied by our Semantical Thesis No. 2. Clearly, if P implies Q and C_i^+ implies P, then C_i^+ implies Q.

We found in Chapter 7, §12 that the presupposition of consistency underlying normative systems requires that *It is *obligatory$_i$* that P* imply *It is not *obligatory$_i$* that $\sim$P*. Since set C_i^+ is consistent, that C_i^+ implies P in its turn implies that C_i^+ does not imply $\sim$P*.

In Chapter 7, §11 we found that *It is *obligatory$_i$* that P & Q* implies *It is *obligatory$_i$* that P & it is *obligatory$_i$* that Q*. This implication, as well as the converse implication, are delivered with by our Semantical Thesis No. 2. If C_i^+ implies P & Q, then C_i^+ implies P and C_i^+ implies Q. Conversely, if C^+ implies P and C_i^+ implies Q, then C_i^+ implies P & Q.

2. DEONTIC TRUTH AS PRACTITIONAL IMPLICATION

The analysis of deontic truth furnished in the preceding section is metaphysically more profound, for, as we pointed out there, it reduces deontic truth ultimately to special implications between propositions. We will build on it in Chapter 12. On the other hand, epistemologically it is a very complicated analysis. It is extremely hard to trace every deontic judgment of type i to the set C_i^+ of facts that determine its truth-value. For practical and other more mundane purposes we can often determine the truth-value of a deontic judgment more easily by remaining at the level of practitions, without attempting to reduce the Legitimacy of such practitions to the underlying set C_i^+ of propositions. We have, therefore, a practitional semantics of deontic statements. Though this wants the deeper philosophical foundation of the set C_i^+, it is nevertheless exciting by itself. We are in any case to locate the nature of deontic truth, or that part of its nature that can reveal itself in the contemplation of deontic or normative systems. These must be able to present the holistic or systemic character of deontic judgments, i.e., the character that ultimately leads to a set C_i^+.

As we have repeatedly seen, legislating or rule-making is essentially the setting up of a system of endorsed practitions. This operation of setting up a system of legislation involves, among others, four points of utmost importance:

(A) Each system of legislation or norms, i.e., of endorsed practitions, is set up by the selection of a set of practitions from which the system is generated, it being the generating set together with its logical consequences;

(B) Each system is determined by a set of considerations or grounds;

(C) Each system limits the freedom of the agents in its universe of discourse in several respects:

    (a) the agents' freedom to choose policies or courses of actions pertaining to the considerations or grounds of the system;

    (b) the agents' freedom to demand from other agents actions pertaining to the ground of the system;

(D) Each system of norms is calculated to guide action so that the future trains of events in and facts of the world have a certain character; but in general systems of norms by themselves do not determine the shape of the world of the future. *What is implied in a system of norms is valid regardless of whether the norms are fulfilled (or obeyed) or not.* (See Chapter 5, §1).

We have in Chapter 7 found a large multiplicity of *obligatory$_i$*-nesses, one for each normative system. We found, *inter alia*, some features of great significance: (a) every deontic statement is characterized by a practition, which also characterizes a manifold of mandates; (b) each deontic statement we take to be true presents us with a practition in whose fulfillment we have an interest, perhaps not an overriding interest, but an interest nonetheless; (c) a given *obligatory$_i$*-ness we deal with determines a set of deontic statements attributing *obligatory$_i$*-ness to a set of practitions. Thus, each obligatory$_i$-ness we deal with is characterizable as a set of practitions in whose fulfillment we are interested. More specifically, *to adopt ought$_i$ – or obligatory$_i$ principles is to endorse a set B_i of practitions and to be ready to endorse the logical consequences of both B_i and the facts of the universe on the assumption that B_i is both self-consistent and compatible with whatever facts there may be.* This is the fundamental insight we are to develop as the view that deontic truth is practitional implication. In order to prepare the way for our new semantical claim, let us both remind ourselves of some logical points (D1 and D2) below and introduce some helpful concepts (D3 and D4).

D1. A set B of noemata *implies* a noema Z, if and only if some members of B imply Z.

D2. A set B of noemata is *consistent* if and only if B does not imply both Z and the denial of Z for some noema Z whatever.

D3. A set C is a *proposition-extension* of a set B of practitions if and only if C is the union of B and a set (perhaps empty) of propositions.

D4. A set B of noemata is *true*, if and only if every proposition implied by B is true.

For example, consider a set $B = \{p, q, p \supset R, P\}$, where the capital letters represent practitions and the small letters propositions. A proposition-extension of B is B itself, since B is the union of B and the empty set of propositions. Another proposition-extension of B is $B' = \{p, q, p \supset R, P, s \& r\}$. The set C = {*Columbus to discover America*, *Columbus to discover America≡Isabella does not help him∗} is not true, for it implies the false proposition ∗Isabella does not help Columbus∗.

A set of noemata is true if and only if its implicational closure is true. Furthermore, a true set A (and, a fortiori, a true extension of a set B) is consistent.

Let B_i be a set of practitions endorsed by a set of agents α such that the union of B_i with any set whatever of true statements is a true proposition-extension of B. Then B_i determines a type i of deontic operators which enter in deontic judgments, characterized by the following:

S.T.3. SEMANTICAL THESIS NO. 3:

(i) A statement of the form ∗It is *obligatory$_i$* that A∗ is true, if and only if there is a true proposition-extension of B_i that implies the practition A.

(ii) A statement of the form ∗It is *forbidden$_i$* (*wrong$_i$*) that A∗ is true, if and only if some true proposition-extension of B_i implies the practition A.

(iii) A statement of the form ∗It is *permissible$_i$* (*right$_i$*) that A∗ is true, if and only if no true proposition-extension of B_i implies the practition A.

(iv) A statement of the form ∗It is (completely) *optional$_i$* that A∗ is true, if and only if no true proposition-extension of B_i implies the practition A, and no true extension of B_i implies $\sim$A.

(v) If B_i is not endorsed by α and A is a non-tautologous practition in B_i, then both ∗O_iA∗ and ∗$O_i\sim$A∗ are false.

In the case of the overriding ought$_1$, the practitions in B_1 are unqualified premises held by the members of α.

The above principles of deontic truth determine a system of propositional entailments that conform with the entailments piecemeal arrived at above in Chapter 7. We also leave the testing of this claim to the reader.

3. ALTERNATIVE DEONTIC WORLDS: SET THEORETICAL MODELS FOR DEONTIC TRUTH

It is nowadays fashionable to illuminate the implicational structure of modal systems by means of set-theoretical systems, often called formal-semantical models.[3] In our case there is a special value in such modeling. It allows us to see the view, discussed in the preceding section, of deontic truth as practitional implication in a different light. It provides a formal account of implication. Yet it does not go deeply enough to produce an analysis of Legitimacy-values as we did in Chapter 5, nor does it go deeply enough to reveal what constitutes deontic truth. Thus, we here unravel the *formal* structure of deontic implication, not, so to speak, its content, i.e., here we do not reach down to the underpinnings of deontic truth or of practitional orthotes.

Let us, once again, consider our generalized conception of the common structure underlying all processes of legislating or rule-making, regardless of whether they go on continuously in high legislative chambers of nations, or in pompous meetings of legislative bodies of institutions, or in pedestrian discussions of procedures by the members of informal groups or clubs. A formal analysis of the general underlying structure of rule-making, whatever its kind, is this: (i) a framework of facts and laws of nature governing the facts is recognized; (ii) a set B of practitions is adopted or endorsed (subject to overriding considerations in cases of conflicts); (iii) the set B limits the freedom of action, decision and command, of the agents that are the subjects of the practitions in B. Thus, *a piece of rule-making creates a confrontation between the real world, with its facts and laws of nature, and other possible practical worlds in which the fixed set of the same facts and laws of nature and the same Past hold, but different decisions and orders and free actions take place*: the enacting of a set of rules is, at bottom, nothing more (on this analysis) than the adoption of a system S_B of alternative *practical* worlds which share both the same Future Framework and the same set B of practitions that, in the terminology of Chapter 5 §1, purport to fix *through free action* at least part of the Future Zone of Indeterminacy. A contingent practition or command (with respect to S_B) is one that holds in some worlds but fails to hold in other worlds of S_B. What is obligatory with respect to the legislating or enacting of B, i.e., what is *obligatory$_B$* is what is "commanded" in every world of S_B. What is *obligatory* is, thus, in a sense, what is necessarily prescribed or intended.

The introduction of the deontic judgments of a normative system amounts to the recognition that for practical thinking, given the hierarchical nature of the agents' motivational powers, the Future is divided into:

(i) the Framework, which, even if not fully determined by the Past and the Present, is assumed not to be under the agents' control; (ii) the Central Future Zone of Indeterminacy, which is under the agents' control, but it is expected to be taken as acceptable to all agents, and (iii) the Outer Future Zone of Indeterminacy, where each agent or subset of agents can go its own way. As stressed in Chapter 5, §1, we are dealing with the presupposition of freedom on which practical thinking rests. But as Kant saw, the fact that practical thinking presupposes freedom as part of its content in no way provides a firm premise for claiming that freedom is a metaphysical reality. There is here no enrichment of pure or theoretical knowledge.

The preceding is a crude statement of the intuition behind our approach to deontic logic in terms of the alternative world formulation. It is non-standard with respect to the ideal-world analysis that other philosophers have developed. The standard approach to deontic logic conceives of deontic expressions ('it is obligatory that', 'it is permissible that', 'it is forbidden that', 'it is wrong that', 'it is right that', 'it ought to be the case that', etc.) as expressing operators that have the same domain and range: the domain of propositions (or states of affairs) and properties. Linguistically, on this standard approach deontic expressions are operators whose domain and range are the domain of propositional functions and sentences, i.e., the domain of well-formed formulas (wffs). Thus, on the standard approach if D is a deontic expression and f is a wff, Df is a wff of the same general kind f is. Semantically, the idea is that Df is true in a given possible world W if and only if f is true (or false, depending on D) in some (or every) possible world which is ideal with respect to W. Here a possible world W' is ideal with respect to W if and only if all obligations belonging to W both are also obligations belonging to W' and are fulfilled in W'. The intuition behind this analysis of the truth-conditions for Df is straightforward: what makes our world have genuine, non-empty obligations is nothing but its falling short of an ideal in some respects, i.e., its having something false which is true in an ideal world; but since the realization of certain ideals may prevent others from being realized, we must consider not only one ideal world but a set of them, not necessarily arranged in a linear sequence of perfection: there may be alternative roads to perfection. Thus, the primary contrast in the standard approach to deontic logic is the contrast between what is and what ought to be.

On this approach a deontic statement formulates a necessary lack in our universe. It does *not* demand any action from any agent and does not distinguish between actions that are circumstances and actions that are practical. (See Chapter 5, §1.) Such statements of the Ought-to-be type are essentially pure value judgments, rather than genuine judgments that demand action from specified agents.

Let us deploy our non-standard alternative-world view. Each non-deontic or *natural world* W may be conceived to be a maximal consistent set of non-deontic propositions, i.e., a consistent set that for every non-deontic proposition p either has p or has $\sim p$. Then W generates systems of deontic possible worlds, as follows: Let P be a maximal consistent set of practitions. Then the union C of both W and P is a *practical possible world*, provided that C is consistent. Let us suppose that D is a practical possible world. Let B_i be a set of practitions in D closed under implication, i.e., such that whatever practition is implied by members of B_i is also in B_i. Then any maximal consistent set M of both practitions and non-deontic statements which also has W and B_i as subsets is a practical world compossible with C. Each of these practical worlds M yields deontic alternatives D_j by adjoining to M deontic judgments that preserve for D maximality and consistency. Thus, the problem of the structure of deontic implication is the problem of how to extend each world M to a deontic alternative D_j. The key idea is that *It is *obligatory*$_i$ that X* is (true) in a world D_j if and only if the practition X belongs to every deontic alternative to D_j. In general, a proposition is true in a world if it is in that world, and a practition A is Legitimate$_i$ in a world W in a system S_i of worlds, if A belongs to W.

We proceed now to articulate the above concepts in an analysis of deontic truth. We shall not assume that we are dealing with maximal consistent sets of propositions and practitions. We assume that there is a non-empty set S_i of non-empty sets D_h of propositions and practitions that satisfy the conditions listed below. There is a set D_h, namely D_o, called the *actual world*. We use '$p*$', '$q*$', to represent any noemata whatever; we use 'p' to represent propositions, 'A' and 'B' to represent practitions, 'F*' to represent propositional or practitional functions. As usual '$\in$' abbreviates 'belongs to'; '$O_1(\ )$' is short for 'It is unqualifiedly (and) overridingly *obligatory* that', and '$O_i(\ )$' is short for 'It is *obligatory*$_i$ that'. We drop quotation marks for convenience and let D'_h be a world in our system S_i of worlds not identical with D_o.

DS.1. $p* \in D_h$, if and only if $\sim p* \in D_h$.

DS.2. $(p* \ \& \ q*) \in D_h$, if and only if both $p* \in D_h$ and $q* \in D_h$.

DS.3.   If $p \in D_h$, then $p \in D_j$, for every deontic world D_j belonging to S_i.

DS.4. $O_i(A) \in D_h$, if and only if $A \in D'_h$, for every D'_h in S_i.

DS.4a. $O_1(A) \in D_h$, if and only if $A \in D'_h$ and $A \in D_o$ for every D'_h in S_i.

DS.5. $(x)(F*(x)) \in D_h$, if and only if $F*(a) \in D_h$ for every object a in the domain of objects of D_h.

Rules DS.1 and DS.2 are exactly the two rules given in our generalized value table for negation and conjunction in Chapter 4, §6. According to DS.3, every fact (or true proposition) in one deontic world is a fact (or true proposition) in every deontic world compossible with the former. According to DS.4, *X ought$_i$ to do A* is true in one deontic world D_h if and only if the practitions *X to do A* is designated, i.e., Legitimate in context C_i, in every deontic world compossible with D_h.

A *logical deontic truth* is a proposition which is true in the real world D_o of every system S_i of deontic possible worlds. We can show that a certain proposition p is logically true by showing that there is no system of deontic possible worlds in which $\sim p$ is true in D_o. A proposition p implies deontically a proposition q if in every system of deontic worlds if world D_o contains p it contains q. By way of illustration as well as by way of confirmation we consider some of the entailments discussed in Chapter 7.

1. *Deon.* 18. $O_i(A \ \& \ B)$ implies $O_i(A) \ \& \ O_i(B)$, and vice versa.

Proof. Consider a system S_i of deontic worlds such that world D_o is in S_i and $O_i(A \ \& \ B) \in D_o$. Then, by rule DS.4 for every D'_h in S_i: $(A \ \& \ B) \in D'_h$. By rule DS.2 $A \in D'_h$ and $B \in D'_h$ for whatever D'_h is in S_i. Hence by rule DS.4 $O_i(A) \in D_o$ and $O_i(B) \in D_o$. Hence, the first part of *Deon.* 18 holds by DS.2. The vice-versa part holds, too.

2. *Deon.* 19. $O_i(p \ \& \ A)$ implies $p \ \& \ O_i(A)$, and vice versa.

Proof. Consider any system S_i of deontic worlds in which the real world D_o contains $O_i(p \ \& \ A)$. Then for every world D'_h in S_i: $(p \ \& \ A) \in D'_h$, by DS.4. Then by DS.2 both $p \in D'_h$ and $A \in D'_h$. Hence by DS.3 $p \in D_o$, and $O_i(A) \in D_o$ by DS.4. By DS.2, $p \ \& \ O_i(A) \in D_o$. Hence the first part of *Deon.* 19 holds.

Consider now a deontic world D_o containing $p \ \& \ O_i(A)$. Then by DS.2,

$p \in D_o$ and $O_i(A) \in D_o$. Hence by DS.3, p belongs to every world D'_h in S_i, and so does A by DS.4. Hence, by DS.2 every world D'_h contains p & A. Hence by DS.4, $O_i(p$ & A$)$ is in D_o. Hence, the vice-versa part holds.

3. *Deon.* 21. $O_i(A)$ implies $\sim O_i(\sim A)$.

Proof. Consider a world D_o in S_i and $O_i(A)$ in D_o. Then, by DS.4 in every world D'_h in S_i: $A \in D'_h$. Hence by DS.1 for every world D'_h: $\sim A$ is not in D'_h. Hence, by DS.4, $O_i(\sim A)$ is not in D_o; by DS.1, $\sim O_i(\sim A) \in D_o$.

4. Principle (P*), i.e., *Deon.* 17, of Ch. 7 §10 holds quite palpably.

5. DS.4a. amounts to the principle that *It is *obligatory* (unqualifiedly) that X* implies X, i.e., to *Deon.* 9 (iv).

In brief, our deontic semantics tallies very neatly with the deontic entailments we encountered in Chapter 7. This is excellent evidence of adequacy.

NOTES TO CHAPTER 8

[1] Hans Reichenbach, *Elements of Symbolic Logic* (New York: The Macmillan Company, 1947), pp. 319ff. He calls a term expressive on a given use if it does not on that use "stand in the place of an argument variable, or a functional variable, or a propositional variable" (p. 319). He explains how the copulative term 'is' is expressive in his sense in the sentence 'Peter is tall', and shows how the copula can be referred to by means of a relational term. For instance, in 'Peter has the argument-function relation with respect to tallness' the term 'argument-function relation' denotes the copula, which is also expressed by the verb 'has' (p. 322). The copula is thus in need of being expressed, even when denoted or referred to. Thus, too, the word 'is' is a merely expressive term. Reichenbach characterizes a logical term as one which "is merely expressive and indispensable, or [as one that] is definable by means of such terms" (p. 323): logical terms "produce certain sign structures and thus do something; but they do not say something. They can only *express* features existing outside the realm of signs" (p. 322). Reichenbach's characterization of logical terms is insightful. Whether it is sufficient or not to make a term logical, it sheds light on the nature of words expressing deontic operators (regardless of whether one calls them logical or not). Thus the terms 'ought' and 'it is obligatory that' are expressive in Reichenbach's sense; they express a structure, outside the realm of signs, that propositions like *John ought to go* and *It is obligatory that Mary work* have. They do not *predicate* that structure of the latter propositions – much less of the sentences expressing the propositions. Furthermore, the transposition of Reichenbach's insight to propositions allows us to see why propositions of the form *a is A* are different from the corresponding propositions of the form *a exemplifies A-ness*.

[2] This is one of my oldest theses. It goes back to 1952 when I wrote 'An Essay on the Logic of Commands and Norms', presented as an M.A. thesis to the Graduate School of the University of Minnesota.

The implicational analysis, discussed below in §2, as Semantical Thesis No. 3, was published about 12 years belatedly in 'Actions, Imperatives, and Obligations', *Aristotelian Society Proceedings*, October, 1967, **68** (1967–68): 25–48. On the other hand,

Semantical Thesis No. 2 had to wait until the erroneous analyses of Legitimacy values given in 'Imperative Reasonings', *Philosophy and Phenomenological Research* **21** (1960), pp. 37ff., were corrected. The set-theoretical system of §3 had to wait the developments contained in the papers mentioned in note 3 below.

[3] Among the principal originators of the set-theoretical elucidation of modal logic are: (1) Stig Kanger, *Provability in Logic* (Stockholm: Almquist & Wiksell, 1957); 'A Note on Quantification and Modalities', and 'On the Characterization of Modalities', both in *Theoria* **23** (1957); (2) Saul Kripke, 'A Completeness Theorem in Modal Logic', *The Journal of Symbolic Logic* **24** (1959), and 'Semantical Analysis of Modal Logic I', *Zeitschrift für mathematische Logik und Grundlagen der Mathematik* **9** (1963); (3) Jaakko Hintikka, 'Modality and Quantification', *Theoria* **27** (1961), and 'The Modes of Modality', in *Acta Philosophica Fennica* **XVI** (1963) devoted to Modal and Many-Valued Logics; (4) Richard Montague, 'Logical Necessity, Physical Necessity, Ethics, and Quantifiers', *Inquiry* **3** (1960).

CHAPTER 9

A FORMAL SYSTEM FOR THE QUANTIFICATIONAL LOGIC WITH IDENTITY OF PROPOSITIONS, PRACTITIONS, AND DEONTIC JUDGMENTS

This chapter summarizes and systematizes the phenomenological investigation and the theoretical proposals contained in the foregoing chapters. Its purpose is to impose some rigor and precision on the basic distinctions and principles of implication found in the preceding chapters. To this effect we shall construct an axiomatic formal calculus, whose primary intended interpretation is as a general system of propositions and practitions involving connectives, quantifiers, and identity. This calculus is more comprehensive than most deontic calculi discussed in the philosophical journals in several respects. First, it represents not only implication among deontic judgments themselves, but also implications among deontic judgments and practitions. Second, it represents the structural relationships between deontic judgments and practitions. Third, it includes a treatment of implications involving quantifiers and identity.

The formal system formulated here represents both all the ontological and all the logical distinctions and principles arrived at in the eight previous chapters. Hence, its adequacy for its subject-matter is palpable.

1. CRUCIAL FACTS ABOUT PRACTICAL LANGUAGES

In the preceding chapters we have examined in detail the fundamental relationships among the basic practical noemata. We have found that the contents before the consciousness constituting practical thinking divide naturally into several types, whose implicational and psychological units are: (1) propositions, (2) intentions, (3) prescriptions, and (4) deontic judgments. In Chapter 2 we fully characterized these four types of noemata. We have found that neither intentions nor prescriptions are propositions, although they have a logical structure parallel to that of propositions. We call intentions and prescriptions practitions.

Deontic judgments we found to be propositions, the atomic or basic deontic judgments being the result of deontic operations on practitions. This fundamental ontological relationship between deontic judgments and practitions marks our approach to deontic logic as nonstandard. Let us briefly explain this.

Prescriptions

As we did in Chapter 4, we call commands, orders, petitions, requests, pieces of advice, entreaties, and suggestions *mandates*. Clearly mandates belong into families. One and the same imperative sentence, e.g., 'Karl, go home at 3 p.m.', may express an order, a command, a piece of advice, a petition, a request, etc. What all these have in common is a structure consisting of a conception of an entity referred to with the name 'Karl' and the predicative action going-home-at-3-p.m. This structure we call a *prescription*. It is like a proposition or statement; but in this simple or atomic case it differs from the corresponding proposition expressed with the sentences 'Karl goes home at 3 p.m.' and 'Karl will go home at 3 p.m.' in the copulation of subject and predicate. In ordinary language this prescription is expressed by the subjunctive clause 'Karl go home at 3 p.m.' or by the infinitive clause 'Karl to go home at 3 p.m.' In any case, simple prescriptions are, then, abstractions from families of mandates that disregard not only the modality of the mandates, but also the time, the place, and circumstances of issuance, as well as the issuer.

An important structural property of prescriptions and mandates is this: mixed compounds of prescriptions (or mandates) and propositions are prescriptions (or mandates). Consider, for instance:

(1)   Karl, do the following: if you come late, close the windows if and only if you-raise-the-awnings, but *do raise the awnings* if it is raining.

Here we have the mandate operator 'Karl, do the following' followed by the subjunctive sentence expressing the prescription that is the core of mandate (1). This is a complex prescription having as components the proposition *You [Karl] came late* and the prescription *Karl close the windows*, as well as both the proposition *You [Karl] raise the awnings* and the prescription *Karl raise the awnings*.

In Chapter 4 we showed that a class of prescriptions and mandates have a two-valued logic parallel to the logic of propositions. Then we theorized that all mandates and prescriptions have a two-valued logical structure. In Chapter 5 we provided an analysis of the two prescriptional values.

Intentions

In Chapter 6 we showed that intentions are not propositions and placed them together with prescriptions in the category of practitions. We argued that the same copula that differentiates prescriptions from their corresponding performance propositions differentiates intentions from their corresponding propositions. Intentions are simply first-person practitions, while prescriptions are second- and third-person practitions, the differences in person being irreducible and ultimate.

We also argued and theorized in Chapter 6 that the logic of intentions is two-valued. We extended the analysis of prescriptional values in Chapter 5 to the analysis of the intentional values involved in implication.

Deontic judgments

We are concerned with genuine deontic judgments, i.e., judgments that prescribe or connect with action through practitions. See Chapter 5, §10. This makes our approach to deontic logic non-standard. As explained in Chapters 2 and 7, our approach focusses on agential ought-statements and on the processes of legislating or rule-making. As summarized in Chapter 8, §3, the formal analysis of the general underlying structure of rule-making, whatever its kind, includes: (i) a framework of fixed circumstances, which includes assumed facts and laws of nature; (ii) a set β of practitions adopted or endorsed (subject to overriding considerations) by the rule-makers for domain of agents; (iii) a zone of indeterminacy where individual freedom is allowed by β to operate. The adoption of a normative system is nothing more than the endorsement of a system S_β of alternative practical worlds that share both the same circumstances and the same set β of practitons. A contingent prescription or command (with respect to S_β) is one that holds in some worlds but fails to hold in other worlds of S_β. What is *obligatory$_\beta$* is, roughly, what is commanded or decided in every world of S_β. What is obligatory is, thus, in a sense, what is necessarily intended or prescribed. Chapter 8 is *not*, however, concerned with the analysis of ought-statements themselves, but only with the analysis of the *truth-conditions* of ought-statements. In Chapter 12 we contend that at least one deontic operator is unanalyzable.

The main structural and implicational properties of deontic judgments appear formulated throughout Chapter 7 as principles Deon. 1–Deon. 29. Among them are:

D°.1. Deontic operators of the Ought-to-do type are operators on practitions.

D°.2. Deontic operators of the Ought-to-do type yield propositions or statements.

D°.3. Deontic operators of the Ought-to-do type are not iterative.

A helpful illustration of D°.1 is:

(2)   It is permitted that Karl do the following: if it rains, *close the windows* if and only if the awnings are not up, and if it hails, *turn circulator A on* if and only if circulator B is off.

In this example we see a complex hybrid practition, made up of both propositions and prescriptions, in the scope of the deontic operator *It is permitted*.

As we discussed in Chapter 2, §1 and Chapter 7, §§5–6, there is a general and fundamental concept of *ought* or *duty* that appears both in conflicting duties and in overriding, conflict-solving duties. That it is the same concept is required for the practical relevance of the conflict. But obviously not all *ought*'s or obligations are overriding and only the overriding ones are overwhelmingly action-guiding. Thus,

D°.4. While the overriding ought in *X ought to do A* may be said to imply or fully support the imperative *X, do A*, the prima-facie oughts in conflict do not imply or fully support their corresponding imperative.

We shall indicate each type or kind of *ought* by means of a subscript. We shall let 'ought$_i$', and 'obligatory$_i$', represent the overriding *ought* or obligatoriness.

In Chapter 7, §§10–12, we discussed the so-called Good-Samaritan paradox, the contrary-to-duty paradox, the time paradox, and showed that they originate in part from a failure to distinguish in deontic judgments the role of circumstances (i.e., propositions) from that of actions practically considered. We were able to extirpate the "paradoxes" by holding fast to the following principles:

D°.5. Where 'and' expresses merely logical conjunction, statements of the form: *It is obligatory that p and A* imply the corresponding statement that p, where 'p' stands for a proposition and 'A' for a practition.

D°.6. If practition A implies practition B,
then: (1) *It is obligatory$_i$ that A* implies *It is obligatory$_i$ that B*, and (2) *It is wrong$_i$ that B* implies *It is wrong$_i$ that A*.

In Chapter 7, §§ 10–16, we discussed some principles of deontic implication. With D°.1–D°.6 some of those principles constitute a complete systematization of basic deontic logic. They are principles that, in the terminology of Chapter 3, Section 4, result from the inferential approach to deontic implication. As discussed in Chapter 3, § 16, § 17, and § 22, the semantical, the inferential, and the analytic approaches to implication yield essentially the same system of logically valid noemata and logically valid reasonings. This must, of course, be proven. In any case, from the perspective of the analytic approach, the investigation carried out in Chapters 3–7 yields a set of logically valid noemata that can be taken as axioms in an axiomatization of basic deontic logic. Thus, the purely logical results of our discussion in Chapters 3–7 of the basic logic of obligation- or ought-judgments with respect to negation, conjunction, quantification, and identity, can be summarized in the following axiomatic informal system:

A. *General axioms for connectives,* whether in propositions or in practitions.
B. *Axioms for quantifiers,* whether in propositions or in practitions.
C. *Propositional axiom for identity:* *Everything is self-identical*.
D. *Axioms for deontic logic,* as follows, where 'A' and 'B' represent practitions, '*p*' represents propositions, 'and' expresses logical conjunction, and 'not' and 'It is not the case that' express negation, and '... ⊃ ...' is short for 'not (... and not ...)' and can often be unofficially read as 'if' (see Chapter 3, § 7):
   (1) It is obligatory$_i$ that A ⊃ it is not obligatory$_i$ that not-A.
   (2) It is obligatory$_i$ that A and it is obligatory$_i$ that B ⊃ it is obligatory$_i$ that A and B.
   (3) It is the case that *p* and it is obligatory$_i$ that A ⊃ it is obligatory$_i$ that A while-it-is-the-case-that-*p*.
   (4) For anybody it is obligatory$_i$ that he A ⊃ it is obligatory$_i$ that everybody A.
E. *Rules of inference:* where '*p**' and '*q**' represent propositions or

practitions, as the case may be:

(1) If $p*$ and $p* \supset q*$ are logically valid, so is $q*$.

(2) If $p*$ is logically valid, so is "Everybody $p*$".

(3) If $A \supset B$ is logically valid, so is $*$It is obligatory$_i$ that $A \supset$ it is obligatory$_i$ that $B*$.

(4) If $p \supset A$ is logically valid without reference to the D-axioms, then "$p \supset$ it is obligatory$_i$ that A" is logically valid.

The system just formulated satisfies the main results of Chapters 3–7, particularly the important theses *Deon*. 1–*Deon*. 29 established in Chapter 7. We shall not stop to show this. We proceed, however, to formulate a formal calculus that contains the above system and has a neat symmetric structure.

2. BASIC DEONTIC LANGUAGES D_i*

We adopt here the customary procedure of studying the logic of a certain family of noemata through the construction of formal languages. Thus, we pass to describe the syntactical structure of purely deontic languages. We start by constructing a large number of such syntactical structures, one for each prima facie obligatoriness and one for the overriding ought. These languages will be called D_i*, for $i = 1, 2, 3, ...$, where D_1* is the language of the pure overriding ought.

Primitive signs: Individual constants; individual variables; predicate constants; the connectives '$\sim$' and '&' expressing negation ('it is not the case') and logical conjunction ('and', 'but', 'although'), respectively; the square brackets '['and']' which paired constitute the sign of practical copulation; the sign 'O_i' of oughtness$_i$ or obligatoriness$_i$; the identity sign '$=$', and the parentheses '('and')', which are both signs of grouping as well as of propositional copulation.

Rules of Formation: We use Quine's corners implicity throughout. Let the small letters 'p', 'q', 'r', range over *indicatives* (i.e., expressions of propositions or propositional functions); let the capital letters 'A' and 'B' range over *practitives* (i.e., expressions of practitions or practitional functions); let '$p*$' and '$q*$' range over both indicatives and practitives; let 'C' range over predicates and 'x' and 'y' with subscripts or not range over individual variables, unless otherwise specified.

(a) The *indicatives* of D_i* are the sequences of signs of D_i* having one of the forms:

(1) $C(x_1, ..., x_n)$, where C is an *n*-adic predicate and each x_i is an individual constant or variable;

(2) $(\sim p)$;   (3) $(p \& q)$;

(4) $((x) p)$;   (5) $(O_i A)$;

(6) $(x_i = x_j)$, where each of x_i and x_j is an individual constant or an individual variable.

(b) *Practitives* or *imperative-resolutives* of D_i* are the sequences of signs of D_i* having one of the following forms:

(1) $C[x_1, ..., x_n]$, where C is an *n*-adic predicate, each x_i is an individual variable or constant;

(2) $(\sim B)$;   (3) $(p \& B)$;

(4) $(B \& p)$;   (5) $(B \& A)$;

(6) $((x) B)$.

(c) The indicatives and the practitives of D_i* are all the wffs of D_i*.

Definitions

We adopt the usual definitions of 'bound variable' and the definitions of the other connectives and the existential quantifier but we generalize them so as to cover practitives. The occurrence of an individual variable x in a wff $p*$ is *bound* in $p*$ if and only if it is an occurrence in a wff which is a part of $p*$ and is of the form $(x) q*$. An occurrence of an individual variable x in a wff $p*$ is *free* if and only if it is not bound in $p*$. The *bound* [free] *variables* of a wff $p*$ are the variables which have bound [free] occurrences in $p*$.

Def. 1 $(p* \vee q*) = (\sim((\sim p*) \& (\sim q*)))$
Def. 2 $(p* \supset q*) = (\sim(p* \& (\sim q*)))$
Def. 3 $(p* \equiv q*) = ((p* \& q*) \vee ((\sim p*) \& (\sim q*)))$
Def. 4 $((\exists x) p*) = (\sim((x) (\sim p*)))$

We introduce the following deontic definitions:

Def. 11 $(P_i A) = (\sim(O_i(\sim A)))$
         It is permitted$_i$ that A if and only if it is not obligatory$_i$ that not-A.

Def. 12 $(W_iA) = (O_i(\sim A))$

It is wrong$_i$ that A if and only if it is obligatory$_i$ that not-A.

Def. 13 $(L_iA) = ((\sim(O_i(\sim A))) \& (\sim(O_iA)))$

It is optional$_i$ (or there is a liberty$_i$ that A) if and only if neither is it obligatory$_i$ that not-A nor is it obligatory$_i$ that A.

We adopt the standard conventions on parentheses introduced in Chapter 3: (1) we drop the pair of outermost parentheses of each wff; (2) we associate chains of conjunctions, or disjunctions, to the left: e.g. p∗ ∨ q∗ ∨ r∗ stands for (p∗ ∨ q∗) ∨ r∗; (3) we rank the connectives in the following order of increasing scope or bindingness: deontic operators and quantifiers; $\sim$; &; ∨; ⊃; ≡.

The desired interpretation for each language D_i* is this: (1) indicatives should express propositions; (2) practitives should express practitions; (3) predicates should express properties or conditions. Patently, each language D_i* satisfies some crucial data: (i) the difference between atomic propositions and corresponding atomic practitions is represented by the difference between the two expressions of copulation: '(...)' and '[...]'; (ii) deontic judgments are represented as propositions; (iii) mixed indicative-practitive compounds are practitive; (iv) the deontic operators expressed by 'O_i', 'P_i', 'W_i', and 'L_i' apply to practitions, not to propositions; (v) there are no iterations of deontic operators. For convenience we have omitted the distinction between agent and non-agent constants, and between actional and non-actional predicates. They are easy to introduce. See Chapter 4, §8 for the mechanics of their introduction.

The part of each language D_i* that includes neither quantifiers nor identity will be called, D_i^c*. That is, D_i^c* is D_i* without the wffs determined by rules (a4), (a6), or (b6).

3. THE AXIOMATIC DEONTIC SYSTEMS D_i**

We build on each deontic language D_i* and axiomatic system D_i**, which is constituted by the axioms and rules of derivation enunciated below. We shall take advantage of the above definitions and conventions on parentheses. We shall also use the following convention. Let X be a wff. Then an expression of the form '$X(a \mid b)$' stands for any wff resulting from X by replacing some occurrences of a in X with occurrences of b, where all occurrences in question of a or b (or both) are free if a or b (or both) are variables. $X(a \parallel b)$ is the wff $X(a \mid b)$ that results when *all* occurrences of a in X are replaced with occurrences of b. S_i is an indicative of D_i^*.

Axioms
The axioms of D_i** are all and only the wffs of D_i* that have at least one of the following forms:

A0. $O_iA \supset S_i$, where S_i are the defeasibility conditions characteristic of O_i.

A1. $p*$, if $p*$ has the form of a truth-table tautology.

A11. $O_iA \supset \sim O_iA$

A11a. $O_1A \supset A$

A111. $(x) p* \supset p*(x \parallel y)$

A1111. $(\exists y)(x=y)$.

Note: A11a replace A11 in the system $O_1 (D_1*)$ for the overriding *ought*$_1$. We adopt the standard definitions of 'proof' and 'theorem':

1. A *proof* of D_i** is a sequence of wffs of D_i* such that each member of it is either (i) an axiom of D_i** or (ii) a wff derivable from previous members of the sequence by one application of the derivation rules R1, R11, R111, or R1111 of D_i**, formulated below.

2. A *theorem of* D_i** is the last member of a proof of D_i**. We write '$\vdash_iX$' to abbreviate 'X is a theorem of D_i**'. We write '$\vdash_{i-a}X$' as short for 'X is a theorem of D_i** provable without axiom A11a.

3. $p_1*, p_2*, ..., p_n* \vdash_i q*$, if and only if $\vdash_i p_1* \& p_2* \& ... \& p_n* \supset q*$.

Rules of Derivation. The rules of derivation of D_i** are:

R1.   *Modus ponens:* From $p*$ and $p* \supset q*$, derive $q*$.

R11.   OG: If $\vdash_{i-a}(p \& A_1 \& ... \& A_n \supset B)$, then $\vdash_i(x)(p \& O_i A_1 \& ... \& O_iA_n) \supset O_i(x) B \& (x) O_iB$, where $n \geqslant 0$.

R111.   UG: If $\vdash_i p* \supset q*$, then $\vdash_i p* \supset (x) q*$, provided that $p*$ has no free occurrences of x.

R1111. ID: If $\vdash_i p* \supset q*$, then $\vdash_i x= y \supset (p* \supset q*(x \mid y))$.

The axioms and the rules are labeled so that each pair $\{A_m, R_m\}$ characterizes one layer of implication:

1. $\{A_1, R_1\}$ is the *basic noematic calculus*, i.e., the propositional

calculus of Chapter 3 generalized to all practitions in Chapter 4, §6 and Chapter 6, §4.

2. $\{A_1, A_{11}, R_1, R'_{11}\}$, where R'11 is R11 without quantifiers, is the *basic propositional-practitional deontic calculus.*

3. $\{A_1, A_{111}, R_1, R_{111}\}$ is the *calculus of quantification generalized to practitions.*

4. R11 is restricted to theorems not depending on A11a in order to allow the basic logic of conflicts of duties to be represented by the union D** of deontic calculi D_i**. As explained in Chapter 7, Section 5, a conflict of duties is the truth of a conjunction of the form "O_iA & O_jB", where A and B are at least causally incompatible and $i \neq j$. The solution to the conflict brings in the overriding *ought$_1$* so that we come to discover, or postulate, the truth of a conjunction of the form "O_iA & O_jB & O_1A & $\sim O_1B$". Thus, in general "$O_1A \supset O_iA$" is not a logical truth. This dreadful consequence would follow if we drop the restriction of R11 to $(i-a)$-theorems, thus:

1. $\vdash_i O_1A \supset A$ A11a
2. $\vdash_i O_1A \supset O_iA$ 1; DR11.2 below.

From the preceding axioms by means of rules R_1–R_{111} we can derive the following theorems and derived rules:

Th.1. $\vdash_i O_iA$ & $O_iB \supset O_i(A$ & $B)$
Th.2. $\vdash_i p$ & $O_iB \supset O_i(p$ & $B)$
Th.3. $\vdash_i (x) O_iA \supset O_i(x) A$
DR11.1. If $\vdash_i A \supset B$, then $\vdash_i O_iA \supset O_iB$
DR11.2. If $\vdash_i p \supset B$, then $\vdash_i p \supset O_iB$.

These are the deontic axioms and rules stated at the end of §1 above. They together with A1, A11, A1111, R1, R111, and R1111 constitute a realization of the informal axiomatization discussed in §1.

The axiomatic system D_i^c** is the subsystem of D_i** built on deontic language D_i* constituted by axioms A1, A11, and rules R1 and R'11. It is decidable, e.g., by the techniques Quine has developed by monadic quantification with propositional variables.[1] We will not discuss this further here.

4. Models for the systems D_i**

The deontic systems D_i** have as appropriate semantical models those discussed in Chapter 8, §3.

1. D_i^c**. A model M for a system D_i^c* is an ordered triple $\langle W_o, W, I \rangle$, where W is a nonempty set of entities called *possible deontic worlds*, or just worlds, for short; W_o is a member of W and is called the *real* or *designated world*, and I is a two-argument function that assigns to each pair of a world and a wff of D_i^c* one element of the set $\{1, 2\}$, in accordance with the following rules, where W_j is a member of W.

R1. $I(p*, W_j) = 1$ or 2, if $p*$ is atomic, i.e., $p*$ is a wff of D_i* by formation rule (a1) or (b1).

R2. $I(\sim p*, W_j) = 1$, if and only if $I(p*, W_j) = 2$; otherwise $I(\sim p*, W_j) = 2$.

R3. $I((p* \& q*), W_j) = 1$, if and only if both $I(p*, W_j) = 1$ and $I(q*, W_j) = 1$; otherwise, $I((p* \& q*), W_j) = 2$.

R4.   If there is a world W_j such that $I(p, W_j) = 1$, then for every world W_h: $I(p, W_h) = 1$.

R5a. $I(O_iA, W_o) = 1$, if and only if for every world W_j in W different from W_o: $I(A, W_j) = 1$.

R5b. $I(O_1A, W_o) = 1$, if and only if for every world W_j in W: $I(A, W_j) = 1$.

We define: $p*$ is *valid* in D_i^c*, $\vDash_{ic} p*$, if and only if for every model M, $I(p*, W_o) = 1$, for I and W_o in M. And $p*$ has a model if and only if for some model M, $I(p*, W_o) = 1$, for I, and W_o in M.

It is a simple thing to show that

MT1.   If $\vdash_{ic} p*$, then $\vDash_{ic} p*$.

And the proof of the following proceeds along the lines of all proofs of Henkin completeness:

MT2.   If $p*$ is consistent, $p*$ has a model.

Outline of proof. By standard procedures it can be shown that the set of wffs of D_i^c* is denumerable and that every consistent set can be extended to a maximal consistent set. Take any maximal consistent set of wffs of D_i^c* that includes $p*$, and call it W_o. Take as W the set of maximal consistent sets W_j generated by W_o as follows: every indicative p of W_o is in W_j, and for every indicative of the form O_iA in W_o, A is in W_j; in the latter case A is also in W_o if we are dealing with O_1A. We let l be the function such that $l(p*, W_j)=1$ if $p*$ belongs to W_j. It is clear from the construction that $\langle W_o, W, l\rangle$ is a model for $p*$. We have, therefore, from MT1 and MT2, by standard reasoning, that:

MT3. $\vdash_{ic}p*$, if and only if $\vDash_{ic}p*$.

2. D_i**. The models for the full systems D_i** are ordered septuples $\langle W_o, W, D, P, V, \pi, l\rangle$, where W_o and W are as above, D is a domain of persons and objects, V is a function assigning members of D to the primitive signs of D_i*, π is a function assigning members of P to the primitive predicates of D_i*, and l is as before except for conditions assigning **1** or **2** to quantified formulas. See the end of the penultimate paragraph of §2. P should be a domain of properties, both practical and contemplative, taking the *practical* copula as an operator on primitive predicates. We shall adopt an extensional model, taking P as a set of "practitional" objects and D as a subset of P. In modal propositional logic it is of great importance not to assume that the objects in the universe are necessarily fixed once and for all, i.e., regardless of the objects it has we must allow that the universe may have had more, or fewer, objects. On the other hand, for pure deontic logic we may assume without damage that the agents and objects are constant across all the practical worlds in W – if we are dealing with a system of duties and interdictions at a given time. This amounts to assigning D to each world in W. We need the following semantical rules:

V1. $V(x)$ is a member of D, for every individual constant or individual variable x of D_i*.

V2. $V(A^n)$ is a set of ordered n-tuples of D for every primitive n-adic A^n predicate of $D*$.

π1. $\pi(A^n, W_h)$ is a set of ordered n-tuples of P, for every primitive n-adic predicate A^n of D_i*. Clearly $V(A^n)$ may turn out to be identical with $\pi(A, W_h)$ not only for some, but for all worlds W_h in W.

R6. $l(A^n(x_1,..., x_n), W_h)=1$, if and only if $\langle V(x_1),..., V(x_n)\rangle \in V(A^n)$.

R7. $I(A[x_1, ..., x_n], W_h) = 1$, if and only if $\langle V(x_1), ..., V(x_n)] \rangle$ $\in \pi(A^n, W_h)$.

By means of a standard Henkin-type proof it can be shown that

MT4. $\vdash_i p*$, if and only if $\models_i p*$.

5. THE ADEQUACY, ESPECIALLY THE EXTENSIONALITY, OF D**

System D** and its subsystems D_i** satisfy the criteria of adequacy for the logic of imperatives, intentions, and deontic judgments developed in the earlier sections of this chapter, as well as those gathered in Chapters 2–8. In particular the system represents the proposition-practition duality, the parallelism between the logic of propositions and the logic of practitions, the dominance of practitionhood in mixed compounds, and the twenty-nine criteria for deontic judgments *Deon.* 1–*Deon.* 29 deployed in Chapter 7. D** and its subsystems D_i** are, therefore, an adequate formal representation of the basic logico-ontological structure of the Representational Image of practical thinking.

We have already pointed out how some of the criteria are complied with by D** and the D_i**. But we will not, except for the case of *Deon.* 27, engage in the straightforward exercise of showing how the criteria of adequacy are satisfied.

In Chapter 7, §15 we showed that deontic contexts are extensional in the sense that if a man has an obligation or a permission to do an action A to someone, he has the obligation or permission to do A to that someone, regardless of how he or that someone is conceived of, or described. That is to say, the following argument form is valid.

(1)   *a* ought$_i$ to do A to *b*

        $a = c$ [*b* does not occur in the scope of intensional connectives in A]

        $b = d$

    Therefore, *c* ought$_i$ to do A to *d*.

We also saw that the scope-solutions to the so-called Good-Samaritan paradox run afoul of the validity of (1).

Now, a crucial condition of adequacy of our axiomatic system D_i** as a formal model for deontic logic is that each system D_i** preserves the validity of (1). I proceed now to show that this is the case. More specifically, if definite descriptions are analyzed in the way Bertrand Russell proposed, then there is no need to worry about the scope of a description in an *ought*$_i$ context, because all formulas that differ only in scope are deductively equivalent. Let us write '$[\ \ ]_a$' to express that the formula inside the brackets is in the scope of the description a. Thus, we want to show that

$$\vdash_i O_i [\varphi a]_a \equiv [O_i \varphi a]_a, \text{ where } \varphi a \text{ is a practitive of } D_i^*$$

If a is the definite description *the A*, then φa is analyzable in Russell's style as follows:

(2) $\varphi a = (\exists x)\, (Ax\, \&\, (y)\, (Ay \supset x = y)\, \&\, \varphi x)$.

Then the extensionality of *ought*$_i$ is established by the following theorem.

THEOREM. $O(\exists x)\, ((y)\, (p(y) \supset x=y)\, \&\, p(y \parallel x)\, \&\, (B(x))) \equiv$
$(\exists x)((y)\, (p(y) \supset x=y)\, \&\, p(y \parallel x)\, \&\, OB(x))$.

Proof. I will use 'PC' to signal a set of applications of A1 and R1. The sign '$\vdash$' is deleted before each formula for convenience. We take variables x and z that do not occur free in p(y), so that p(y $\parallel$ x $\parallel$ z) is p(y $\parallel$ z).

(1) $(y)\, (p(y) \supset x = y) \supset (p(y \parallel z) \supset x = z)$ A111

(2) $((y)\, (p(y) \supset x = y)\, \&\, p(y \parallel x)\, \&$
$B(x)) \supset (p(y \parallel z) \supset x = z)$ 1; PC

(3) $((y)\, (p(y) \supset x = y)\, \&\, p(y \parallel x)\, \&$
$B(x)) \supset ((y)\, (p(y) \supset x = y)\, \&$
$p(y \parallel x)\, \&\, B(x))$ A1

(4) $x = z \supset ((y)\, (p(y) \supset x = y)\, \&\, p(y \parallel x)\, \&$
$B(x) \supset (y)\, (p(y) \supset z = y)\, \&$
$p(y \parallel z)\, \&\, B(x \parallel z))$ 3; R1111

(5) $(y)\, (p(y) \supset x = y)\, \&\, p(y \parallel x)\, \&\, B(x) \supset$
$(p(y \parallel z) \supset ((y)\, (p(y) \supset z = y)\, \&$
$p(y \parallel z)\, \&\, B(x \parallel z)))$ 2, 4; PC

(6) $\sim (p(y \parallel z) \supset ((y)\, (p(y) \supset z = y)\, \&$
$p(y \parallel z)\, \&\, B(x \parallel z))) \supset$

$(x) \sim (y)(p(y) \supset x = y) \,\&\, p(y \parallel x) \,\&\,$
$B(x))$ 5; PC; R111

(7) $(\exists x)((y)(p(y) \supset x = y) \,\&\, p(y \parallel x) \,\&\,$
$B(x)) \supset (p(y \parallel z) \supset ((y)(p(y) \supset$
$z = y) \,\&\, p(y \parallel z) \,\&\, B(x \parallel z)))$ 6; PC; Def 4

(8) $p(y \parallel z) \,\&\, (\exists x)((y)(p(y) \supset x = y) \,\&\,$
$p(y \parallel x) \,\&\, B(x)) \supset ((y)(p(y) \supset$
$z = y) \,\&\, p(y \parallel z) \,\&\, B(x \parallel z))$ 7; PC

(9) $p(y \parallel z) \,\&\, O(\exists x)((y)(p(y) \supset x = y) \,\&\,$
$p(y \parallel x) \,\&\, B(x)) \supset O((y)(p(y) \supset$
$z = y) \,\&\, p(y \parallel z) \,\&\, B(x \parallel z))$ 8; R11, R111, PC

(10) $(x)\,[9]$ 9; PC, R111

(11) $(\exists x)(p(y \parallel x) \,\&\, O(\exists x)((y)(p(y) \supset$
$x = y) \,\&\, p(y \parallel x) \,\&\, B(x)) \supset$
$(\exists x)\,O((y)(p(y) \supset x = y) \,\&\, p(y \parallel x) \,\&\,$
$B(x))$ 10; PC, R111, Def 4

(12) $(\exists x)(p(y \parallel x) \,\&\, O(\exists x)((y)(p(y) \supset$
$x = y) \,\&\, p(y \parallel x) \,\&\, B(x)) \supset$
$(\exists x)\,O((y)(p(y) \supset x = y) \,\&\, p(y \parallel x) \,\&\,$
$B(x))$ 11; PC, R111, Def 4

(13) $\sim (\exists x)(p(y \parallel x) \supset \sim (\exists x)((y)(p(y) \supset$
$x = y) \,\&\, p(y \parallel x) \,\&\, B(x))$ PC, R111, Def 4

(14) $\sim (\exists x)(p(y \parallel x) \supset O \sim (\exists x)((y)(p(y) \supset$
$x = y) \,\&\, p(y \parallel x) \,\&\, B(x))$ 13; R11, (n = 0)
                                                                                        PC, Def 4

(15) $O \sim (\exists x)((y)(p(y) \supset x = y) \,\&\,$
$p(y \parallel x) \,\&\, B(x)) \supset \sim O \sim \sim (\exists x)$
$((y)(p(y) \supset x = y) \,\&\, p(y \parallel x) \,\&\,$
$B(x))$ A11

(16) $O(\exists x)((y)(p(y) \supset x = y) \,\&\, p(y \parallel x) \,\&\,$
$B(x)) \supset (\exists x)(p(y \parallel x) \,\&\, O(\exists x)$
$((y)(p(y) \supset x = y) \,\&\, p(y \parallel x) \,\&\,$
$B(x))$ 15, 14; PC

(17) $O(\exists x)((y)(p(y) \supset x = y) \,\&\, p(y \parallel x) \,\&\,$
$B(x)) \supset (\exists x)\,O((y)(p(y) \supset x = y) \,\&\,$
$p(y \parallel x) \,\&\, B(x))$ 12, 16; PC

(18) $O((y)(p(y) \supset x = y) \,\&\, p(y \parallel x) \,\&\,$

$$B(x)) \supset ((y)\,(p\,(y) \supset x = y)\ \&$$
$$p\,(y \parallel x))\ \&\ O\,B\,(x) \qquad\qquad 3;\ R11,\ R111,\ PC$$

(19) $(\exists x)\ O\,((y)\,(p\,(y) \supset x = y)\ \&\ p\,(y \parallel x)\ \&$
$$B(x)) \supset (\exists x)\,((y)\,(p\,(y) \supset x = y)\ \&$$
$$p\,(y \parallel x)\ \&\ O\,B\,(x)) \qquad\qquad 18;\ R111,\ PC,\ Def\ 4$$

*(20) $O\,(\exists x)\,((y)\,(p\,(y) \supset x = y)\ \&\ p\,(y \parallel x)\ \&$
$$B(x)) \supset (\exists x)\,((y)\,(p\,(y) \supset x = y)\ \&$$
$$p\,(y \parallel x)\ \&\ O\ B\,(x)) \qquad\qquad 17,\ 19;\ PC$$

(21) $(y)\,(p\,(y) \supset x = y)\ \&\ p\,(y \parallel x)\ \&\ B\,(x) \supset$
$$(\exists x)\,((y)\,(p\,(y) \supset x = y)\ \&\ p\,(y \parallel x)\ \&$$
$$B(x)) \qquad\qquad A111,\ PC,\ Def\ 4$$

(22) $((y)\,(p\,(y) \supset x = y)\ \&\ p\,(y \parallel x))\ \&$
$$O\,B\,(x) \supset O\,(\exists x)\,((y)\,(p\,(y) \supset x = y)\ \&$$
$$p\,(y \parallel x)\ \&\ B\,(x)) \qquad\qquad 21;\ R11,\ R111,\ PC$$

*(23) $(\exists x)\,((y)\,(p\,(y) \supset x = y)\ \&\ p\,(y \parallel x)\ \&$
$$O\ B\,(x)) \supset O\,(\exists x)\ y\,(p\,(y) \supset x = y)\ \&$$
$$p\,(y \parallel x)\ \&\ B\,(x)) \qquad\qquad 22;\ R111,\ PC,\ Def\ 4$$

(24) Theorem follows from 20 and 23 by **PC**.

NOTES TO CHAPTER 9

[1] See W. V. O. Quine, *Methods of Logic* (New York: Holt, Rinehart, and Winston, revised ed., 1963), pp. 116f.

PART II

THE META-PSYCHOLOGY OF
PRACTICAL THINKING:
THE ACTION SCHEMA

CHAPTER 10

THE INTERNAL CAUSALITY OF
PRACTICAL THINKING

In Part I we dealt with the contents, or noemata, of practical thinking. In this chapter and in the next we deal with practical thinking itself. We discuss the practicality of practical thinking, i.e., the general schema of the way in which the thinking of a practition or a deontic judgment leads to action. We ground the practical action schema on an account of needs, desires, and wants. The contents of the schema belong to empirical psychology. The ultimacy of practical thinking *in* the Representational System, as we saw in Part I, lies in the practitional copula. In this chapter we elucidate the role of that copula and, therefore, the sense of the infinitive, imperative and future-tense first-person constructions expressive of practitions. In Chapter 11 we will discuss the connection between deontic operators and action.

1. PRACTICAL OR PRACTITIONAL STATES OF MIND

Just as comtemplative thinking is the manifestation of a variety of propositional attitudes, practical thinking is the manifestation of a variety of practitional attitudes. Just as propositions provide the unity of content for the former, practitions provide the unity of content for the latter. Deontic judgments being, as expected from Chapter 7, a mixed type of thinking, it is propositional thinking that gets hold of the practition at the core of a deontic judgment. There is, as one would expect, a thorough-going parallelism between the propositional and the practitional attitudes, as is illustrated in the following chart:

Propositional thinking	*Practitional thinking*
Proposition: (that) p	*First-person Practition:* [I] to A
believing that p	intending to A
conjecturing that p	aiming to A, purposing to A, planning to A
presupposing that p	being predisposed to A

coming to believe that p	deciding to A
being inclined to believe that p	wanting to A
considering whether p or not	considering whether to A or not
remembering that p	remembering to A
knowing that p	knowing what to do, namely, to A.

Notes. (1) The lists above are not complete. (2) The psychological vocabulary is not completely precise, so that there are no perfect differentiations between many pairs of members of either list, on the one hand, and, on the other, there is no perfect fit between the propositional and the practitional counterparts. My claim is that in some central uses of the terms listed the parallelism is roughly present. Alternatively, the parallelism holds for the states of mind, even if we do not have precise parallel terminology to express it. (3) The verb 'intending' is the most general practical term that corresponds to the verb 'believing'. In generality it contrasts with the verbs 'aiming', 'planning', and 'purposing' and others of the same ilk. These terms are somewhat special in that they emphasize the breadth or comprehensiveness of what is intended; often they suggest a distant state of affairs in whose actualization means of different sorts can be involved. But aside from this more specific suggestion about the intended practition, these verbs can be used sometimes not to emphasize a firm determination in the pursuit, just because of the very general character and comprehensiveness of the goal. In this respect they are the counterparts of 'conjecturing'. At any rate the difference between conjecturing and believing is also a subtle one. (4) The verb 'wanting' is a difficult one. Sometimes it is used to refer to intendings and purposings. Perhaps the most general sense of 'wanting' can be characterized briefly as the practitional counterpart of the disjunction 'believing or being inclined to believe or presupposing.'

It is very interesting that, as contrasted with doxastic or belief-type verbs, like 'consider' ('investigate', 'examine', 'study', 'determine'), the epistemic verbs 'know' and 'remember' apply to both practitions and propositions. This is understandable given that they emphasize the "objectivity" of the contents of thinking and the reasons for holding the relevant propositional, or practitional, attitude.

The propositional attitudes differ from one another, not characteristically by the propositions they have as contents, but by their degrees of firmness, so to speak; likewise, preliminarily, the practitional attitudes differ from each other, again, not by the practitions they have characteristically as their contents, but by their degrees of firmness. A noema can be: considered or entertained, assumed, adopted as a matter of course (i.e., taken for granted), adopted temporarily while some deliberation is going on, adopted just in case, or endorsed firmly and fully as in the case of a firm belief and a fully determinate intending. But what are these differences which can naturally but metaphorically be described as differences in firmness?

This difference in firmness between two propositional, or practitional, attitudes oriented toward the same noema is nothing but a difference in the causal networks that constitute the different attitudes. As a psychological reality an attitude is a bundle of propensities or dispositions, unless it is a mental act. A mental act is either the appearance of something to consciousness, or the disappearance of something from consciousness, or the holding of something before consciousness, or the onsetting of a propensity, or the disappearance of a propensity, or the re-arrangement of the hierarchical system of propensities that constitutes a thinker. Thus, the difference between two propositional, or practitional, attitudes or acts is at bottom nothing more than one of the items just mentioned or a combination of several of them.

Believing is the central propositional state and intending is the central practitional state. Coming to believe is to undergo a re-arrangement of propensities, and so is coming to intend. And just as one rehearses his states of belief one also rehearses his states of intending. Both can be rehearsed contemplatively, so to speak, as when one draws conclusions from propositions, or from practitions. But practical thinking has a peculiar aspect: it is practical: it is connected with action in a very special way. And this requires that there be very special rehearsals of one's intending. Let us examine the state of intending and its special rehearsals.

2. INTENDING AS A BUNDLE OF PROPENSITIES

Succintly put, intending in its primary sense is the endorsement of a first-person practition. An act of coming to endorse a noema, whether practition or proposition, is the act of creation of a unified bundle of

propensities and dispositions. A state of endorsement is the sustainance
of such a bundle. Degrees of endorsement can in principle be measured
by the complexity of the bundle of propensities. In the case of intending
as in the case of believing we are dealing with total endorsement. For an
agent Jones to totally endorse at time t a first-person practition of the
form $*I_{[= \text{Jones at } t]}$ do A$*$ is for him to cause the re-arrangement of his
system of propensities and dispositions, so as to: (i) accommodate a bundle
pertaining to that practition, and (ii) to assign a place to it in the hierarchical structure of the system of propensities constituting the personality of
the agent.

   Consider the propensities and dispositions that Jones acquires at time t
and maintains when he intends to A later on. Some propensities are purely
mental. For instance, he has the propensity to think or consider the
practition $*I_{[= \text{Jones at } t']}$ to A$*$ at times t' later than t. He has the propensity
to use this practition as a premise in practical deliberations. He has the
propensity to resist endorsement of practitions that he believes to be
incompatible with it. This includes resistance to adopting certain plans,
or goals, which are simply especialized broad practitions. Since totally
endorsing a practition involves having certain beliefs, Jones is also in the
possession of propensities linking his thinking of that practition to his
thinking of certain propositions. Jones' whole purview of the world has,
even if slightly, been affected by his intending to A. Also his intending of
the practition in question strengthens somewhat his inclination to believe
certain things rather than others.

   In addition to the propensities to think and to believe and endorse in
general which constitute Jones' intending to A, there are also other mixed
propensities that depend on his powers of action. Jones' intending to A
may be qualitatively different from another person's intending to A in that
each agent may have different powers of action. Intending to A *qua*
intending, irrespective of the agent's individual powers of action, has a
certain characteristic actional quality that we must bring into the open.

   An agent's intending at time t to do an action A at time t', much later
than t, is essentially nothing but a matter of a *re-arrangement* of his dispositions and propensities so as to prepare himself for performing A at t'.
The thinking propensities that go with the intending are propensities that
either help to enhance that preparation for eventually performing A at t',
or at least do not disturb whatever preparation is present at the time of

thinking something between t and t'. Undoubtedly, an agent can engage in intendings that conflict. But this reveals only that the re-arrangement of propensities and dispositions that coming to intend introduces within an agent is limited by certain properties of the existing arrangement. Also an agent can change his mind, as we say in ordinary English, and this is a most felicitous phrase. Changing one's mind about doing something is exactly that: a literal changing of the arrangement of propensities to think and to act.

Now, the fundamental phenomenon of practical thinking is intending to do something *then*[1] at the very time of the rehearsal of the intending. The thought contents of such rehearsals are present-tense intentions of the form *I shall A now*. The fundamental phenomenon of practical thinking is, then, the direct totally endorsing thinking of a first-person present-tense practition. (As we explained in Chapter 2, §5, intentions are not sentences, so that we leave it entirely open whether to rehearse an intention requires tokening indexical sentences or not.) Such episodes of endorsing thinking are what used to be called *volitions*.

Volitions are the fundamental phenomenon of practical thinking in that the propensities and dispositions involved in long-range intendings, or in very complex intendings that can be fulfilled piecemeal only, depend in an important way on the direct totally endorsing thinking of a first-person present-tense practition. The dependence lies in part in that the propensities of remote or complex intendings are only weakly connected with action, while those fundamental thinkings connect with action more intimately and immediately. The idea is obvious and simple. Complex and remote plans can be carried out because of complex connections of all sorts of things to actions than an agent can perform *at will*. These are the fundamental actions that constitute practical thinking *par excellence*. The rest of practical thinking is genuinely practical only because of their relations to practical thinking *par excellence*, both through the relations of shared aspects between noemata thought of, and through the causal relations between propensities and dispositions involved in the re-arrangement of propensities to action. We will say more about volitions in §3.

In brief, an agent does some action A literally at will precisely when he is the theater of the immediate causality of his totally endorsing thinking of the first-person present-tense practition *I to do A now*. These are the thinkings that bring an intending to complete fruition.

At the *core* of every intending lies a propensity to engage in such type of thinkings, i.e., in volitions. That some thinkings cannot be like that is not the fault of the intending or of its practition, so to speak, but the fault of the world. It is only because the world is on the whole inhospitable that we can do so few things at will. The core propensity in every intending is a propensity to issue in causal thinking when the agent *thinks* that it is then[1] the time for acting. This propensity to activate the mechanisms of action by the pair of a propositional thinking about time identity (and circumstances) and the practitional belief-counterpart about an action, can be spread about by inference to other practitions and actions. Thus, huge plans that require lots of actions deployed through a long interval of time lend their intendingness to their required actions or plan parts. These gain then corresponding core propensities, and can in their turn lend intendingness to other smaller parts, which then gain their core propensities, and so on and so forth, until we find the actions the agent can perform at will.

The preceding is straightforward. What needs emphasis is perhaps only that the inferential inheritance of intendingness, with what this involves in terms of the psychological reality, presupposes a theory of the logical structure of practitions like the one developed in Chapter 6, §7 and Chapter 9 above. Naturally, when an agent engages in practitional inference, his inferences may be invalid, yet his conclusions, if endorsed, inherit the appropriate bundle of propensities constituting the agent's intendingness for it at that time.

On the other hand, some propositions to the effect that an agent intends to do an action A imply other propositions to the effect that the agent intends to do some action B. When these implications hold, the agent does not infer and transfer intendingness to his intention to do B by an inferential feat: the agent automatically undergoes the proper re-arrangement of propensities and dispositions corresponding to his intending to do B as part of the rearrangement he undergoes by coming to intend to do A.

At this juncture we should go into the system of implications of propositions about intending. This is a very obscure subject which we cannot deal with in full here, partly because we have not developed the logic of indexical and quasi-indexical reference, and partly because we need the logic of propositional attitudes.[2] We limit ourselves to formulating some fundamental principles that have direct relevance to our ensuing discussion. The following are self-evident:

Int. 1. *At time *t* X intends to do A & B* *implies* *At time *t* X intends to do A and at *t* X intends to do B*.

Int. 2. *At time *t* X intends to do the following: to do A while it is the case that *p** *implies* *At time *t* X intends to do A, and at time *t* X believes that *p**.

*Int.** *X intends to A and *X to A* implies *X to B** does *not* generally imply *X intends to B*.

An example of *Int.* 2 is *Jones intends to visit Paris in the summer, when his father will be there*, which implies *John believes his father will be in Paris next summer*. *Int** is a special case of the general fact of the finitude of the mind. *No* propositional attitude and *no* practitional attitude is closed under logical implication. That is, there is no attitude A such that one has A toward all the consequences of a noema toward which one has A. *This* principle of finitude *must be kept in mind particularly when we are dealing with practical thinking.*

There are principles of intending inheritance that provide the balance required by *Int* *. Some of them are the following, where 'X is rational at *t*' is short for 'at time *t* X is paying attention to his intentions involving actions A and B and to his beliefs about the possible effects of his doing A and to proposition that *p*':

Int. 3. *X is rational at *t*, and *at* *t* X both intends to A and intends to B* *implies* *At *t* X intends both to A and to B*.

Int. 4. *X is rational at *t*, at *t* X intends to A, and at *t* X believes that *p** *implies* *At *t* X intends to (A while it is the case that *p*)*

Int. 5. *X is rational at *t*, at *t* X intends to A, and at *t* X believes that *$I_{[=X \text{ at } t]}$ to A* implies *$I_{[=X \text{ at } t]}$ to B** *implies* *At *t* X intends to B*.

Int. 6. *X is rational at *t*, at *t* X believes that *p*, and at *t* X intends to (do A if *p*)* *implies* *At *t* X intends to A*.

The *state* of intending determined by a true proposition *p* of the form *X intends to A* is a pair $\langle I_p, P_p \rangle$, where I_p is the set of dispositions and propensities X has because of the truth of *p* and P_p are the practitions *I[=X] to B* such that *p* implies *X intends to B*.

3. THE PRACTITIONAL COPULA AND VOLITIONS

We are now in a position to say something about the practitional copula. As discussed in Chapter 6, a practition is a thought content that presents to the mind in the primary cases: an agent as subject and an action as a predicate combined in a very special way. The form of combination cannot be the form of proposition combination for two general reasons: (i) because a subject-predicate proposition combines the subject and the predicate in a way suitable for possession of truth, for membership in the world of facts; (ii) because a practition combines its subject and its predicate in a way suitable for action. Characteristically, when an agent is considering what to do he considers complex propositions, some components of which are already known to be true and others can be anticipated to be true given the known regularities of nature. But the whole point of considering the complex proposition for action lies in that some constituents, i.e., some constituent predications are, as we explained in Chapter 5, §1, *open*, i.e., are in so far as the agent is concerned indeterminate. An agent who is contemplating what to do at a given time sees the future of the world from that time on branching out into many alternatives, and he also sees that those alternatives can be tied to the past by *his* making certain instantiations true. Those selected instantiations become special just by their being selected: they are the junctions at which the agent's causality can connect the future containing the truth of the complex proposition to the given past. Thus, *a practitional copula is at bottom the ordinary propositional copula with a signal of its practical or causal openness.* Here is a profound unity of predication.

The practitional copula is then a complex of the ordinary copula and a practitional operator. We can, then, analyze primary practitions as follows:

(1)   X to A: A[X]:   A($\underline{X}$),

where the $*[\ ]*$ and $*(\ )*$ are the practitional and the propositional copula, taken as primitive in Chapters 4–9, and the underlining in $*(\ )*$ is the ultimate practitional operator. We must underscore that a copula operator is in the Representational System an unconceptualized component of a noema. It is the unconceptualized representation of the internal causality of the rehearsal of intendings.

To give concretion to the preceding analysis consider the case of Jones who intends to paint the chair brought by Mary. The practition which is the content of Peter's intending is:

(1) $\exists x$ (x is the chair brought by Mary & $I_{[=\text{Peter at } t]}$ to paint x).

If Peter thinks of this practition, he is *ipso facto* thinking, in the sense of entertaining or considering, the complex proposition

(2) $\exists x$ (x is the chair brought by Mary & $I_{[=\text{Peter at } t]}$ will paint x).

Now, his thinking endorsingly of practition (1) is *not* Peter's endorsingly thinking of proposition (2). Peter may come to intend (1) without coming to believe (2). But having before his consciousness practition (1) is at once his having *before* his consciousness proposition (2), behind, so to speak, the practitional copula represented by the infinitive construction in sentence (1). It is the truth of proposition (2) what is at stake in Peter's considering what he is to do at time t. But proposition (2) by itself does not present the component $*I_{[=\text{Peter at } t]}$ will paint $x*$ as one needing Peter's intervention. It is a future proposition all right, but many, indeed most, future propositions will be true by the power of the regularities of nature without Peter's intervention as a storehouse of actions that emanate from the contents of his thinkings. In other words, Peter's contemplation of proposition (2) does not reveal anything special to him. His power of inner causality has nothing that can activate it in that proposition.

If Peter's thinking of an intention N is to set off his action mechanisms by virtue of being a thinking of N itself, then there must be in N some aspect that can by its contemplation in an act of endorsing thinking set off those action mechanisms. It must be an aspect of N that has that role. But it must have *only* that role, since it must be possible for Peter to think the future-tense proposition $c(N)$ corresponding to N as a mere happening, since $c(N)$ and N both have, like (1) and (2) above, all their categorematic elements in common. That aspect is then a formal aspect that accrues to different propositions. This is precisely what the practitional copula does. It is a *focussing mechanism* that spots the relevant parts of a proposition where the agent's thinking causality can connect the proposition whose truth he is attempting to bring about with the mechanisms that carry out the attempt. That spotting role is the "sense" of the practitional copula-operator.

To nail down both the role of the practitional copula-operator and the need of practical thinking for such a formal mechanism of internal causality let us examine a case of voluntary action and contrast it with a case of external causality of contemplative thinking. We want to highlight the contrast between a first-person future-tense intention I and its corresponding first-person future-tense proposition, $c(I)$, which formulates a happening.

Consider a case of deliberation. You weigh the pros and cons for doing some action A. You decide to do A. You do A deliberately, fully intentionally. You set yourself to do A at time t, and after a certain time interval during which you single-mindedly pursue the doing of A you finish doing A. Clearly, your doing A is not intentional or deliberate, if there is no intimate causal connection between your thinking to do A and your doing A. Compare an agent's intentional action with the case of a man who is now at 2:30 p.m. contemplating his jumping at 3 p.m., who believes that he will jump at 3 p.m., not because he intends to do it, but because he believes that the causal powers of his environment will cause him to jump at 3 p.m. He is now rehearsing his belief, he is firmly predicting that he will jump at 3 p.m., *refusing* to frame an intention to jump. But there is a causal circuit that can be activated by his thinking, by his predicting, that he will jump at 3 p.m., and the circuit is such that it will make him jump at 3 p.m. The man knows something about the mechanism, so that now at 2:30 p.m. he thinks:

(3)   I will jump at 3 p.m. and my thinking this is activating a causal mechanism, that, by including my causal powers of action, will make me jump at 3 p.m.

Obviously, (3) is not the man's intention:

(4)   I shall jump at 3 p.m.

The man's thinking (3) is not his thinking (4). Therefore, intentions are not the same as their corresponding (4)-type propositions. What is their difference? The difference lies solely in the special causality of the thinking of (4). But how special? It is more intimately connected with the fulfillment of (4) than the thinking of (3) is connected with the fulfillment of (3). But how intimately? – that's the question. And the answer involves the following steps:

(i)   The causality of the thinking of (4) is internal: it connects the effects of thinking with the elements of (4).

(ii) The causality of the thinking of (4) is not a mere accidental matter; even if the agent's acting with intention (4) is unsuccessful, one's rehearsal of intendings are *necessarily* thinkings that purport to cause what is thought in them.

(iii) The causality of the thinking of (4) does not attach to the first-person reference or to the concept jump: or to their propositional combination: the agent must be able to think sometimes that he will jump at 3 p.m. without his thinking being causally oriented toward his jumping at 3 p.m. and, of course, he must be able to think of himself and of jumps without being inclined to jump.

(iv) That causality lies on the *shall* then

(v)   That causality has to be formal, i.e., must attach to a formal aspect of a noema, so that it can be necessary; i.e., endorsingly thinking a noema having it is always causal, and it can be universal, i.e., it can attach to any action, making this action practical.

(vi) Thus, that internal causality lies at the connection between the agent and the action, and the *shall* of intention (4) is, then, in part the "opening" in (4) where that causality enters (4) linking it to the action powers of the agent.

(vii) To think (4) endorsingly is to have before one's mind the burst of the causality that the thinking of (4) exercises in the world.

(viii) But that internal causality cannot guarantee the success of the action. Its success depends on the friendliness of the world. All it can secure is a tendency or readiness to act.

In sum, the mind is presented with propositions. But sometimes the mind is so set that it "marks" or "spots", as we said above, certain components of those propositions; these "spotted" propositions are practitions, and the mind apprehends them. This explains how the complexes of propositions and practitions are practitions. The practitional copula is, therefore, a modality of consciousness and has no external ontological status. (This is so on our account even if propositions are mind-independent entities.[3]) But by attaching piecemeal to each of several occurrences of the propositional copula, the practitional operator becomes a

definite, though still syncategorematic and unconceptualized, item before
consciousness. This makes practical consciousness flexible and efficient –
a powerful tool for survival.

Let us discuss briefly *being inclined to intend*. Wantings are characteristically inclinations to intend, although intendings themselves are often
called wantings. However, the word 'want' is a very delicate one. It has a
wide spectrum of connotations. At the other extreme from intendings lie
those uses of the word in which the emphasis is upon needs and lacks of
different sorts. There is, of course, a good reason for this. Our intendings
are bundles of propensities, but these propensities rest on the larger pool
of propensities to intend, i.e., in propensities to acquire the specific
intending-constituting propensities. Those deeper and more general propensities undoubtedly rest on the needs and basic powers of the agent. We
deliberately refrain at this juncture from speaking of the needs and powers
of man, because we are dealing with the general structure of agency, which
transcends the peculiar characteristics of *homo sapiens*. We are not doing
here, in Kant's term, anthropology, or applied philosophy of human action. We are concerned here with discussing the underlying theory of
rational action, whether human or not, in the sense of action involving
intentions, deliberations, etc. The general philosophical theory of action
cannot assume anything about the specific human needs. It can only assume that inclinations to intend *do* rest on other inclinations and powers,
and that some of these rest on needs, whatever their content and character.

4. Needs and Desires:
their minimal logical structure

We must talk about needs in any case. We cannot give here a full analysis
of the structure of needs, but we must relate them to wants. Customarily
we talk of needs in the context of living organims, although we extend the
use of the term to systems or gadgets in whose workings we are interested.
We can make a general assumption to this effect, so that the structure we
are going to discuss is only a necessary condition in the analysis of needs.

A need is typically a causal structure involving the circumstances of an
individual at a given time, a certain future state the individual may be in,
and a necessary causal condition for the individual reaching that future
state. Ordinarily the future states have to do with states of pleasure or

satisfaction and with states in which the individual has the power to engage in certain activities, including in the case of human beings, the activities of formulating plans and carrying them out. In any case, needs are primarily causal structures in which thinking and its contents are *not* at issue. This is important. A *desire* is often simply the complex of a need and the awareness of it, or an inclination to be in some state together with the awareness of the inclination.

Let 'N $[\alpha, x, C]$_____' express: x needs, with respect to some state in
set α, in his circumstances C, that_____.

Then the most general structure of needs includes the following laws:

N1. $(N[\alpha, x, C]p \ \& \ N[\alpha, x, C](p \supset q)) \supset N[\alpha, x, C]q$.

N2. $N[\alpha, x, C](\sim N[\alpha, x, C]p) \supset \sim N[\alpha, x, C]p$

N3. $N[\alpha, x, C](N[\alpha, x, C]p) \supset N[\alpha, x, C]p$

N4. $\sim N[\alpha, x, C] \sim p \supset N[\alpha, x, C](\sim N[\alpha, x, C] \sim p)$.

We may for convenience introduce as a trivial need for everybody a need for tautological states of affairs. If so, we can add two more laws:

R1.   From p, and $p \supset q$, infer q

R2.   If p is a logical truth, then $N[\alpha, x, C]q$ is also a logical truth.

This general structure of needs allows for contradictory needs with respect to a set α of desirable states. Indeed, α itself may be contradictory. There is no reason to deny contradictory needs. They cannot be fulfilled, and a creature with contradictory needs may likely go insane or die. Thus, in order to provide a machinery for understanding some forms of insanity and some forms of death we must provide a logical structure for needs that are contradictory.

In Chapter 11 we will be concerned with reasonable action, which deals with consistent systems of actions or with how to erradicate inconsistency. In the end we must be concerned with consistent needs.

A consistent need has a set α of states and an associated network of causal regularities that ensure the following conceptual law:

No. $N[\alpha, x, C]p \supset \sim N[\alpha, x, C](\sim p)$.

Clearly, given a set S of desirable states for x and given different circumstances C (including time), there will be many states of affairs p_j that can satisfy x's needs in α. Thus we can define:

The *content* of a need n_i is a set N_i of ordered quadruples of the form $\langle x, C_j, S_j, p_j \rangle$, where N_i is closed under implication, i.e., if $\langle x, C_j, S_j, p_j \rangle$ is in N_i, and being in C_j implies being in C_k, and being in state S_j implies being in state S_k, and that p_j implies that p_k, then $\langle x, C_k, S_k, p_k \rangle$ is in N_i.

If need n_i is consistent, it will not have in N_i quadruples with their fourth elements p_j incompatible with the fourth element p_k of any other quadruple, unless their respective second elements C_j and C_k are also incompatible.

The property that needs have of being closed under logical implication makes them infinite in content. *This is a general property of reality*, that contrasts with the principle of finitude we found in the contents of intendings.[4]

It falls outside the scope of our present topic and purpose to discuss needs in more detail. We assume, of course, that living creatures as well as sentient and (embodied) thinking creatures have at every time a set of viable needs they can be in. We also assume that such creatures may have other inclinations or tendencies to change their states, which need not be inclinations or tendencies to acquire states that satify needs.

5. WANTS: TYPES AND MINIMAL LOGICAL STRUCTURE

A creature that lives in a cozy, fully hospitable environment can have its needs satisfied without the expense of energy and action. But if the environment is not fully hospitable a creature with needs must exercise some action, and if the creature is to survive it will normally have to possess a set of inclinations to act so as to attain the states that satisfy its needs. We must distinguish two types of inclinations: (a) *blind inclinations*, which are purely causal mechanisms that do not require that the creature think and come to intend to do anything; (b) non-blind *wants* which are inclinations to intend, some of which can be inclinations merely to have the core propensities of the acts the agent can perform at will, but others are inclinations to intend plans of different complexity and breadth.

Having a blind inclination consists at bottom in being in a state that implies that other states will ensue with a high degree of probability depending on circumstances. We will not examine this probability core of inclinations here. We note, however, that inclinations may conflict, but there is no inconsistency in there being in a creature conflicting inclinations. Hence, we must understand the structure of inclinations so as to allow conflicts without implying a contradiction. Inclinations are, like needs, causal structures, and their contents can be said to be sets of ordered quadruples of the form $\langle x, C_i, A_i, t \rangle$, where x is an agent, C_i is a set of circumstances, A_i is a state of action, and t is a time, so that x in C_i at t tends to get in state A_i. *Blind inclinations are closed under logical implication*, so that a clause like the one above for needs applies to inclinations too.

Non-blind wants are practical inclinations, i.e., inclinations to engage in thinking that includes the thinking of some practitions. Wants in the sense or type we are considering here are endorsements of sets of practitions, but these sets are *not* closed under implication. Wants differ in the strength of endorsement those practitions receive, and, as we explained above, this degree of endorsement is a matter of the complexity of the bundle of the propensities to think as well as a matter of whether the propensities are propensities to adopt practitions or to consider them in certain ways.

A want w_i has a *content* that consists of a pair of sets: $\langle I_i, P_i \rangle$, where I_i is the set that is the content of the inclination-bundle composing w_i, and P_i is the set of practitions attached to w_i. The members of I_i have as third components certain action states A_i, these are in the case of w_i states of thinking, states of inferring, states of acquiring inclinations to reject propositions or practitions, etc., and these states of thinking are particularly thinkings of the practitions in P_i with certain degree of commitment which is appropriate to w_i. The actions that are not mental acts to whose origination a want w_i contributes are the actions appearing as predicates in the practitions in P_i. The causal structure of mental acts included in the members of I_i is *qua* psychological reality rather indistinctive. The essentially differentiating content of non-blind wants lie, therefore, in their associated content sets P_i of practitions. Even though these are internal to the mental acts in I_i they are precisely the contents that both take the want w_i outside the agent's mind and spread their causal force about in the environment.

The differentiating feature as well as the causally external aspect of a want is precisely its most internal component. This is why we know so little about the workings of wants as psychological reality, but know a lot about them by the practitions characterizing them.

The development of non-blind wants in the history of the universe is an extraordinary phenomenon. The insertion of practitional awareness in the equipment of a creature *both* enhances the survival value of the creature's equipment and weakens inclinations with a somewhat indirect mechanism as just explained, but because of the indirectness of the action mechanism wants gain in power in a larger area of space and time: they are remote-control mechanisms that can be moved also. Furthermore, non-blind wants gain power of breath and scope. On the other hand, wants by not being blind lose some power of content. A thinking being that acts through thinking does not automatically transfer his energy from implicans to implicate, or from equivalent to equivalent. Thus, practical action is seriously limited to the practitions that the agent can think.

The crucial principle to remember is this:

(W*) The set P of practitions that is a constituent of a want w_i is *not* closed under logical implication.

There are inconsistent wants, but we have to pay special attention to the consistent ones. These wants have the basic structure determined by the following laws:

Let '$W_{ixt}A$' abbreviate: x wants$_i$ at t A, where 'A' stands for a practition. That is to say, '$W_{ixt}A$' can also be read as: at t x has want w_i whose set P_i includes A. Here 'A' stands for either a first-person practition, e.g., $*I_{[=x \text{ at } t]}$ to go home* or for a second-person practition like $*You_{[=Peter \text{ at } t]}$ to engage in revolution* or for a third-person practition, e.g., *The tallest philosopher to read 'Indicators and Quasi-indicators'*. Then the basic laws for consistent wants are, where 'A' and 'B' stand for practitions and 'p' for a proposition, and 'B_{xt}' for 'x believes at t that':

W1. $W_{ixt}A \supset \sim W_{ixt} \sim A.$
W2. $W_{ixt}(A \ \& \ B) \supset (W_{ixt}A \ \& \ W_{ixt}B)$
W3a. $W_{ixt}(p \ \& \ A) \supset (B_{xt}p \ \& \ W_{ixt}A)$
W3b. $W_{ixt}(A \ \& \ p) \supset (W_{ixt}A \ \& \ B_{xt}p)$

R1.   Modus ponens: From p∗ ⊃ q∗ and *p*∗ infer q∗, where asteristed variables have both propositions and practitions as values.

Consistent wants, and inconsistent wants, too, of course, *like all other mental states exhibited in consciousness,* do *not* abide by the following closure rules:

W.R2.   If A is logically valid, then $W_{ixt}A$ is logically valid.
W.R3.   If A ⊃ B is logically valid, then so is $W_{ixt}A ⊃ W_{ixt}B$.
W.R4.   If $p ⊃ A$ is logically valid, so is $p ⊃ W_{ixt}A$.
W.R5.   If A and B are logically equivalent, so are $W_{ixt}A$ and $W_{ixt}B$.

We will not bother here to develop this little calculus of consistent wants precisely, nor will we bother to device set-theoretical models to show it consistent and complete in some sense. The point is that whatever completeness calculi for propositional and practitional attitudes may have, that completeness cannot, if adequacy is maintained, be such as to include closure under logical implication or under logical equivalence.

We have discussed the practitional interpretation of ordinary sentences of the form 'X wants Y to A', where 'Y' can be the null symbol (representing the quasi-indicator' himself' discussed in Chapter 6 §3⁵). There are two comments, or apparent criticisms, that can be made.

First, it may be adduced that there are sentences of the form 'X wants Y to A' that do not express a practition in their infinitive clause. For example, the sentence 'Jones wants the rain to fall' does not express the practition ∗Rain to fall∗, which would be embedded in commands or requests. That is, what the sentence expresses may be true, so, Jones wants the rain to fall, even though he is not prepared to issue an order or a request to the rain to fall. Of course, Jones might be an animist and might indeed be prepared to issue such a request. (See Chapter 2, §7.) In such a case our analysis would apply. But we must grant that our modern Jones need not be an animist, so that whoever knowingly uses the sentence 'Jones wants the rain to fall' may be using it to make a true statement without his utterance of 'the rain to fall' expressing ∗Rain to fall∗. What this shows is that once again we cannot follow ordinary speech naively when doing conceptual analysis. What the speaker wants to say about our non-animist Jones is that Jones wants that it rain. Conversely, given the hazyness of the psychological constructions, some people say something like "Jones wants that Peter come(s)" to mean by 'Peter come(s)' the practition *Peter to come*.

Second, we do say things like "Jones wants that the rains come early this year", where there is nothing that Jones can do to bring the rains early this year, not even asking them to come early because he is no animist. If there is really nothing that Jones can have in mind so as to help the rains to come early this year, then it seems that the sentence attributes to Jones a mere *wish*, not a genuine want – certainly not a want as we characterized wants above, in which a want is an inclination to intend, i.e., to cause action through thinking. As noted in §1, the word 'want' is very promiscuous, and we have simply selected one most important phenomenon often described by means of the word 'want'.

Perhaps wishes are practitional attitudes, a sort of limiting case in which not only the core propensity to intend but also all the peripheral ones are absent, there remaining only a propensity to find satisfaction in the unhoped-for fulfillment of the envisioned practition. A two-sorted noematic theory of the contents of wishings also seems appropriate. Such a theory would open the problem of explaining the *optative* copula, to give it a name, not only formally in terms of a syntactical mechanism that expresses it, but ontologically, in terms of what it does in terms of the role it plays in consciousness. We assume here without more ado that an optative copula is, like the practitional copula, not an ontological tie somehow linking subject and properties out there in the world, regardless of minds, but a way of conceiving. What way? This question must eventually be answered if we are to gain a fuller understanding of wishing. And perhaps the causal thinking of practitions that is intending does connect with needs and with those aspects of the mind that would enter compactly, surreptitiously and unanalyzed in the optative copula. But here we can only mention it.

Now, many a time a sentence of the form '*X* wants that *p*' does not formulate a wish, being a natural abbreviation of something like '*X* wants to (help) bring it about [or, make it the case] that p'. The latter sentence contains obvious verbs that the dynamism of ordinary language naturally leaves tacit. The context makes it clear whether X wants to bring it about that *p* all by himself, or whether he merely wants to help the realization of that *p*. Evidently, the abbreviational, not merely desiderative, uses of 'X want that *p*' fall within our elucidation. (See the dialectical principles discussed in Chapter 3, §§6f.)

The verb 'want' sometimes takes nouns, rather than clauses as direct complements. We often say something like "Anthony wants that apple". Such constructions are effective economical devices that facilitate communication by not mentioning the evident. Such sentences have a clause whose verb is determined by the context of speech. In this example the full sentence may be *Anthony wants to paint (to buy, to give away, to cut up, to peel, to throw at the moving clay donkey, etc.) that apple*. Hence, there is here not a philosophical problem, but a problem about the contextual rules governing speech deletions, i.e., a problem in the theory of the surface grammar of English and in the theory of communication.

6. THE CAUSALITY OF PRESCRIPTIONAL THINKING

In some circumstances the utterance of an imperative sentence in an appropriate tone of voice acts as a stimulus upon hearing which a person (or a dog) reacts. Military drills are almost of that sort. In the extreme case the imperative sentence need not convey a mandate (see Chapter 2, §3) to the addressed entity. Minimally, commands are rational means of guiding behavior when the hearer is required at least to understand the commands being issued to him, even if his response is automatic. The point is that as long as he understands the issued mandate his behavior includes among its causes a use of reason. Characteristically, however, mandates are rational means of guiding conduct in a second, deeper sense, viz., in that their legitimacy is assumed to be relevant. (See Chapter 5.)

In their primary use prescriptions are issued on the expectation or hope that the person or persons addressed to will perform the actions mentioned in that issuance. But neither prescriptions, nor mandates, nor acts of issuance of prescriptions or mandates are in general complete causes. It is in the nature of an imperative presenting a course of action that it may remain unfulfilled or disobeyed. Typically, the point of using imperatives, be it in commands, requests, pieces of advice, etc., is only to help the listener to act, to give him a "push" of some sort. The use of an imperative carries with it the idea or intention that the imperative is to participate, however small this participation may be, in a causal chain of events which will terminate with the agent's doing the action in question. We shall refer to this typical feature of imperatives as the *causal intention* or the *pushing aspect* of issued imperatives. How strong the pushing aspect is in fact depends on the circumstances or context of utterance and on the sort of person the agent is, as well as on the variety of prescriptive discourse being discharged by the imperative, i.e., whether the latter is an imperative which formulates a command, a request, a piece of advice, etc.

Whatever the degree of the pushing aspect of the issuance of a mandate, in the deeper sense in which mandates are rational means for the guidance of conduct, they have a causality that depends on the internal causality of intentions. In such cases the agent, if he endorses the prescription, translates it into its corresponding intention, and then we have the practicality of the first-person discussed in §2–3 above. See also Chapter 5, especially §3.

NOTES TO CHAPTER 10

[1] This 'then' is a quasi-indicator. See the materials mentioned in note 5 to Chapter 6.

[2] See the materials referred to in note 1 above and those mentioned in note 6 to Chapter 6.

[3] For a view that identifies states of affairs, which are supposed to be mind-independent, with propositions and identifies further facts with true propositions, see H.-N. Castañeda, 'Thinking and the Structure of the World', *Philosophia* **4** (1974): 3–40.

[4] For a full treatment of the infinity of reality and the finitude of the contents of the mind see the paper mentioned in note 3 above.

[5] See the papers referred to in note 1 above. For a recent nice discussion of volitions see, Hugh McCann, 'Volition and Basic Action', *Philosophical Review* **83** (1974): 451–473.

CHAPTER 11

OUGHTS AND THE REASONABLENESS OF ACTION

In this chapter we discuss the causal links between thinking that one ought to do an action A and what one thinks. There are two types of phenomena here: the connections between wants and oughts, and the internalization of normative systems. In both cases the causality or practicality of normative thinking is derivative from the practicality of practitional thinking. Normative thinking is, as we saw in Chapter 7, deeply involved with the reasonableness of actions.

1. RATIONAL AND REASONABLE ACTION

In Chapter 10 we have offered a general characterization of the psychological reality of intending and being inclined to intend. That characterization depends on the formal structure of practitions given in Chapters 3–6. Altogether we have the picture of a creature that is a rational agent in the sense that his reason is an internal mechanism of action in that the causality of thinking depends necessarily on a formal aspect of what is thought. An agent is, then, rational in the minimal sense that he has the power of affecting the future by his endorsingly thinking of intentions. Doubtless, the bio-chemical nature of that creature determines a good deal, or all, for that matter, of his purposes and wants and intentions. An agent is rational, then, in the sophisticated sense that his beliefs about his needs and about his environment and about the causal regularities of the world determine the Legitimacy of practitions in which he is interested. The rational agent in the preceding sense is rational in a more sophisticated sense if he has the power not only of getting beliefs but also of getting many true beliefs. In that case his rational actions have survival value and they are rational with respect to this value.

Yet even in possession of true beliefs, a rational agent may die or may barely maintain survival. His needs are of different sorts, and of different degrees, and many of them cannot always be jointly fulfilled, or fulfilled to the same high degree. The satisfaction of some of his needs is perhaps indispensable for the agent's survival, but the satisfaction of others is indispensable for his remaining stable, healthy, relaxed, and capable of engaging in variegated plans of activities. An agent has, in short, a hierarchy of needs and possible satisfactions from the point of view of his survival and his well-being. This hierarchy may be completely unknown to the agent – and in such a case his chances of survival in a not fully hospitable environment are minimal. The hierarchy of needs and possible satisfactions, to be called from now on the agent's *motivational hierarchy*, is partially known to him, even if to some very small degree. This is powerful knowledge. Even if the agent's needs are all consistent and all the inclinations supporting them are also consistent, many inclinations may conflict, and the only way to solve the conflict is for the agent to keep at least one need unsatisfied. This state of dissatisfaction may be serious enough to threaten survival, or it may not. This is what the agent better knows in order to sacrifice his lesser satisfaction. This is the crucial problem of rational action in its highest value sense. To avoid confusions, we shall speak of *reasonable actions* to refer to the actions that an agent ought to perform in order to minimize the internal conflict of his inclinations and needs. This is for the agent the problem of determining, not merely what intentions are Legitimate with respect to this or that context, but what intentions are Legitimate in the Absolute context he is operating in at the time in question. (See Chapter 5, §1 and §3.)

Here we are concerned with practical thinking and reasonable action in general. Moral obligations and political and legal obligations, as well as other institutional obligations, cannot be relevant to an agent's problem of what to do in certain circumstances, *unless* those obligations manage to appear to his consciousness as courses of action that have positions in his motivational hierarchy, i.e., unless those obligations are actions to which he is not wholly indifferent, so that his performing them or his refraining from performing them would provide him with some satisfaction, or dissatisfaction, or a mixture of both. The external obligations must be at least partially internalized if they are to be taken into account by an agent. Internalization here is the process of adopting at least some of the practitions characteristic of a normative system, and, hence, creating in us dispositions to rehearse them in the endorsing causal way discussed in Chapter 10. How we internalize the rules of the different institutions we belong to is a very complex matter that falls wholly outside the scope of our present study. The fact is that different institutions are internalized differently, and that part and parcel of being a rational agent – let alone a reasonable one – is to learn how to internalize a normative system *qua* system through the adoption of some characteristic practitions or rules. The unity of the mind is involved here. That is, to become an agent is to acquire a disposition to modify one's motivational hierarchy so as to be inclined to adopt the logical consequences of the rules one has adopted. This is *only* an inclination, since the mind, as we have emphasized in Chapter 10, is finite. But the inclination is exercised when one comes to believe that certain deontic judgments or practitions are logical consequences of both the rules one has adopted and the propositions one takes to be true. Like believing, endorsing practitions and rules has, in spite of its finitude and openness, a *tendency to closure*. This is the unity of rationality.

In general, the requirements impinging upon an agent are of three sources. *First*, there are those which issue from the agent's biological and physico-chemical nature and from his psychological make-up. *Second*, there are the goals, purposes, and intentions the agent adopts on his own, with no sense of commitment to others. *Third*, there are the requirements resulting from the agent's internalization of his institutional involvements, ranging from morality and the laws of his country to the ordinary institutions to his agreements and promises. From the point of view of the mechanism of action it is immaterial whether these institutional internalizations have been freely brought about by the agent, or whether they have been induced by others, as in the case of morality, through preaching and example, or whether they have been imposed by force and threats as in the case of morality, the law, and some institutions that control our lives.

2. THE FIRST TWO STEPS TOWARD REASONABLENESS

We continue our examination of practical thinking by considering, for convenience, a lone agent, to be called *Agens*, engaged in thinking about his corner of the world, himself, and how to act so as to maximize his satisfactions – which implies that he survives. Moral, legal, institutional obligations can be assumed to be internalized, so that he has a whole array of inclinations to act in order to bring conformance of his life to the obligations of each type. Depending on his upbringing and bio-chemical properties of his body, our agent derives certain satisfactions from doing what he believes is demanded by this or that system of norms. This means that he has given some degree of endorsement to the systems of rules that bind him. This endorsement has, therefore, created some needs in him. These needs have their supporting inclinations.

The inclinational profile of an agent or his motivational hierarchy is, then: (1) the pristine inclinations and propensities to act that are part and parcel of the agent's bio-chemical nature; (ii) the acquired inclinations and propensities to act that have arisen from his transactions with the physical environment by virtue of some powers of his that have been developed, as well as by virtue of those that have been weakened or atrophied; (iii) the inclinations and propensities that he has created in himself by his adoption of ends, goals, purposes and other intentions; (iv) the complex bundles of inclinations that he has acquired through transactions with other agents, *qua* sources of friendly as well as unfriendly powers, without the intervention of conventions or rules; and (v) the complex bundles of inclinations wrought by the adoption of conventions, norms, and agreements.

Our paradigm agent *Agens* has then a rich motivational hierarchy. He also has an underlying inclination to maximize his total satisfaction and his highest satisfactions. To attain this he has to know a lot about the world and about himself, but he has to reason about the possible futures of the world. He has to consider himself objectively from an eternal point of view. Our agent has to see his inclinations to act as extending all the way so as to cover *all* possible actions. This step is required so that he can contemplate the possible conflicts among his inclinations. But the agent, being limited to his beliefs, must transcend somehow his predicament by projecting his beliefs as facts. These are the two fundamental steps in reasoning about one's inclinations. The result is, so to speak, the conception of *an ideal complete and consistent and objective want*. Of course, this is not really a want: *it is more like an ought*, a prima facie ought, to use W. D. Ross' old terminology.[1] *Ideal wants are proto-oughts,* and provide the link between ordinary real wants and genuine prima facie oughts. Let us explain this.

3. Oughts

Recall that the content of a want w_i was analyzed as a pair $\langle I_i, P_i \rangle$ of a set I_i of inclinations to engage in certain psychological acts and a set P_i of first-person future-tense practitions. Recall that the set P_i is not closed under logical implication. Consider for the moment the set P_i^0 which is the closure of P_i under logical implication. Naturally, given the implication principles given in Part I, P_i^0 contains most likely some propositions, namely, those which are implied by practitions in P_i^0. By principles W3a and W3b in Chapter 10, §5, those propositions in P_i^0 are believed by the agent endorsing the practitions in P_i. Consider those propositions as true, and collect them in the set P_i^T. Now, the content of ideal want W_i corresponding to want w_i is constituted by the pair $\langle P_i^0, P_i^T \rangle$. Corresponding to this ideal want and, hence, to w_i there is a concept of ought, which is, *roughly*, the concept of the reasonableness of W_i. It is governed by certain laws, the basic ones being those discussed throughout Chapters 7 and 9.

As in Chapter 9, let A and B be practitions, first- or second- or third-person ones, as the case may be. Let p be a proposition, p∗ a proposition or a practition, and let the usual connectives be interpreted in their customary way. Then we have the following ought$_i$ laws, already discussed in Chapter 9, and derivable in the system D∗ outlined in Chapter 9, §3:

O1.　　p∗, if p∗ has the form of a truth-table tautology.

O2.　　$O_i A \supset {\sim} O_i {\sim} A$.

O3.　　$(O_i A \,\&\, O_i B) \supset O_i (A \,\&\, B)$.

R2.　　If $A \supset B$ is logically valid, so is $O_i A \supset O_i B$.

R3.　　If $p \supset A$ is logically valid, so is $p \supset O_i A$.

T11.　　$O_i (A \,\&\, B) \supset (O_i A \,\&\, O_i B)$.

T12.　　$O_i (p \,\&\, A) \supset (p \,\&\, O_i A)$.

Axiom O2 for *ought$_i$'s* corresponds literally to axiom W1 for consistent wants. *Ought$_i$* theorem T12 corresponds to *want* axioms W3a and W3b, and to *intending* law *Int.* 2 of Chapter 10, §2, but with a crucial difference. The former allows a proposition to fall out of an obligation into reality, so to speak, while the latter allows a proposition to fall out of a want, or out of a state of intending, of the agent into his beliefs. This is part and parcel of the objectivity of ought$_i$'s: they derive from ideal wants. Another part of this objectivity comes from principles R2 and R3, whose counterparts do not hold for wants, as we carefully emphasized at the end of Chapter 10. Principles R2 and R3 demand that the practitions in the scope of ought$_i$ form a set that is closed under logical implication. Since the logical implication of practitions is, by the principles formulated in Chapters 4 and 6, parallel to the logical implication of propositions, the closure of a set of *ought$_i$* practitions requires principles O1 and O3, which have no *want* counterparts. In brief, the system D_i* of implication principles, developed in Chapter 9, §§3–6, realizes in full the objectification of ideal wants. Each want w_i determines a prima facie *ought$_i$* having the structure D_i*.

The content of an *ought$_i$* is precisely the set P_i^0 of the ideal want W_i corresponding to the real want w_i. This fundamental connection illuminates the way in which the endorsement of a part of a normative system involves a deontic commitment to the whole of a normative system. A *normative system* is a set P_i^0 closed under logical implication, i.e., a system constituted by both a context of obligation$_i$ or ought$_i$ and a set of practitions that conform to the structure D_i*. An enactment of a normative system consists either in the proposal of a norm-creating body that a domain of agents endorse, or of the endorsement by the agents in question of, a generating set of practitions, i.e., a set α of practitions that extended to a set β by the adjunction of true propositions yields a set γ of propositions and practitions that is closed under logical implication. (See Chapter 8, §2.)

The preceding connection between *oughts* and *wants* does not yield a reductive analysis of *ought* in terms of *want*. In fact, the contrast made above between the subjectivity and finitude of wants and the objectivity and logical closedness of oughts stands in the way of any such reduction. More generally, we hold that deontic concepts are not reducible to non-deontic ones. (See Chapter 13.)

4. HYPOTHETICAL 'IMPERATIVES'

The thesis of the irreducibility of each ought$_i$ does not preclude ought$_i$-propositions from standing in implication relationships with other types of propositions. This is a point to which many philosophers have been blinded by the dogma of the so-called Naturalistic fallacy or Hume's guillotine. We will not attack this dogma here.[2] The essential thing is that the very unity of the world and of our experience of the world requires that there be *bridging* implications connecting different types of concepts and noemata to each other. In particular, there must be bridging implications connecting wants and oughts, which arise out of the way in which the practitional content or realm of each ought-ness is precisely the content of an ideal want. We revealed the structure D_{i*} of an ought$_i$ so as to bring forth this correspondence, but we still need to make explicit some implication principles that bridge the gap between real wants, on the one hand, and oughts and ideal wants, on the other. Perhaps the most important bridging implication of this sort is what Kant called hypothetical imperatives. The form of the relevant paradigm arguments in English is this:

(1) x wants that p,
          if p, then x performs A at time t (where this 'if' is an effect-cause 'if', not cause-effect 'if')
          x can perform A at t;
          Hence, x ought to (must) perform A at t.

This is a valid schema connecting wants, causal connections, and oughts, *if* it is interpreted as having the following logical form:

(1A)   1. x wants$_i$ $I_{(x, t'-t)}$ to (help) bring it about that p,
          2. If p, then   _____ (x to A at t)
          3. x can P (x to do A at t)
          Hence, x ought$_i$ to A at t,

where $*P$ (x to do A at t)$*$ is again the performance proposition corresponding to the practition $*x$ to do A at $t*$, and it is like the latter except for containing the propositional copula where $*x$ to do A at $t*$ contains the practitional copula not in the scope of a propositional-forming operator, e.g., not in the scope of an ought$_i$.

Another valid schema closely related to (1A) is this:

(2)   1. x wants$_i$ to do A at t,
          2. If $_{effect}x$ performs A at t, then $_{causal\ factor}x$ performs B at t',
          3. x can perform B at t';
          Hence, x ought$_i$ to perform B at t',

which must be understood along the lines of (1A). The subscripts attached to 'if-then' in the second premises of both schemata are crucial. *The want$_i$ goes with the effect and the ought$_i$ with the causal factor.* Reversing the direction of conditionality can make the argument invalid as is clearly shown by this example:

(3)   1. x wants$_i$ not to water the plants.
        2. If $_{causal\ factor}x$ does not water the plants, then $_{effect}x$ kills the plants,
        3. x can fail to water the plants
        Hence, x ought$_i$ to kill the plants.

In (1), (1A), and in (2) the second premise is a causal proposition. Both it and premise 3 require a performance proposition corresponding to a practition, rather than the latter, for practitions themselves can be involved in causal connections *only* indirectly and internally, as explained in Chapter 10, §3, i.e., only by being the contents of fully endorsing thinkings, the thinkings in question being the psycho-logical reality directly involved in causal connections. Schema (1A) has an ought$_i$-conclusion, which introduces the ideal want corresponding to the real want$_i$. It is a beautiful schema that provides a conceptualization of the inclinations and needs connected with want w_i and relates them to rational and reasonable action.

5. KANT'S ANALYTICITY OF HYPOTHETICAL IMPERATIVES

We have always admired Kant's profound insights on the workings of practical thinking.[3] He seems, however, to have committed a subtle error, which is important to clarify. Kant claims that

(K.1)   [The proposition] whoever wills the end, so far as reason has decisive influence on his action, wills also the indispensably necessary means to it that lie in his power ... in what concerns the will, is analytic (417).[4]

He goes on to explain why:

(K.2)   for, in willing an object as my effect, my causality as an acting subject, i.e., the use of the means, is already thought (417).

And Kant summarizes his discussion, after mentioning examples, thus:

(K.3)   that if I know that only through such an action can the thought of effect happen, then if I fully will the effect, I will the action too is an analytic proposition (417).

The subtle error that Kant makes in his transition from (K.1) to (K.3) is precisely the confusion of ideal wants with real wants, and the confusion of rational action in the non-value senses explained above in §1 with reasonable action.

In (K.1) we can take the phrase 'in so far as reason has decisive influence on his action' as meaning that the action is reasonable and rational. Then, Kant is saying that "The agent has reasonable inclinations and wills end E and knows that his doing A is necessary for E being achieved and he can do A, then the agent wills to do A" is analytic. This is not felicitous, but 'reasonable inclination' can be understood so as to get the desired analyticity. Kant's claim that the proposition is analytic with respect to the will amounts then to the claim that the state of willingness described in the conclusion obtains as a matter of course, so that thinking ought-propositions of that form has no conduct-guiding or propensity-creating power: endorsing one such proposition does nothing to one's action mechanisms.

Now, one can read the preceding interpretation of (K.1) as being about an ideal agent who is reasonable and has ideal wants. Then (K.1) can be taken to contain schema (1A) in §4 above. But we must hurry to emphasize that this interpretation, which does make schema (1A) analytically valid, does *not* make it analytic that an ordinary finite agent who does not have ideal wants automatically wills what he knows to be a necessary means for an effect, upon merely willing the effect. Interestingly enough, Kant knew this, and said so just a few pages earlier:

(K.4)   All imperatives are expressed by an *ought* and thereby indicate the relation of an objective law of reason to a will which is not necessarily determined by its subjective constitution to conform with it [the law]. [This is] constraint (413).

Here Kant sees how the whole point of the concept *ought* is to have, like our practitional copula above, an internal causality. Endorsingly thinking an *ought* proposition, according to (K.4), is to think a certain content, a law, together with an aspect, or concept, or representation (to use Kant's favorite term for what appears to consciousness), namely, *ought*, which by being thought with that law or proposition constrains the will – and this will is one that may not have, and perhaps does not have, a pre-existing inclination to act in accordance with that law. The constraint

Kant talks about in (K.4) is only a generalization of what he called *respect* some pages earlier and described in one of the most beautiful passages in the whole history of the philosophy of action:

(K.5)   What I recognize directly as a law for myself I recognize with respect, which means merely the consciousness of the submission of my will to a law without the intervention of other influences on my mind. The direct determination of the will by the law and the consciousness of this determination is respect (401n).

Kant, then, was clear that for finite agents whose wants are not ideal and who are imperfect, i.e., whose actions and inclinations are not automatically reasonable, thinking true ought-propositions is the means to introduce some reasonableness both in their actions and in their inclinations. But for this to be the case it is necessary that the ought-proposition, whose being thought at a certain time by an agent is to rearrange the agent's inclinations and even lead him to action, be *nonanalytic with respect to the will*. Thus, while a perfect agent needs no oughts because he analytically moves from wanting effects to wanting the necessary means, a finite imperfect agent needs oughts which by revealing the analytic nature of a perfect agent projected from him can *synthetically*, by thinking an ought-proposition, approximate somewhat his perfect projection by acquiring an inclination to adopt the necessary means.

We agree happily with this view. That is why we are not happy with the natural and apparent interpretation of (K.3), which makes it unnecessary for an agent to think an ought$_i$-proposition. (K.3) seems to say that one's knowing the causal connection between the ends and the means suffices for one's willingness to (help) bring about the end to generate automatically one's willingness to do the means in question. Kant speaks in the first-person suggesting that he has in mind imperfect finite agents. Kant is actually contradicting himself if this interpretation of (K.3) is correct. On grounds of charity, we prefer the hypothesis that Kant was careless by not explicitly putting in (K.3) his restriction to perfect agents, and that he was negligent by not adding a paragraph explaining the transition from the perfect agent to the imperfect one, so that it becomes clear how the wants of the former are the oughts of the latter. This is after all the view that Kant is adumbrating.[5]

6. CONFLICTS OF OUGHTS AND THE OVERRIDING OUGHT

We have explained how needs are supported by inclinations, how wants are inclinations, how practical or conscious wants are inclinations to intend, how intendings have first-person practitions as contents, and how real practical wants yield ideal wants, which yield prima facie oughts. This chain of structures, biological at the base, but ideal-normative at the end, provides the fundamental connection between the prima facie reasonableness of actions, which appears to practical consciousness as the constraint of an ought, and the bio-chemical foundation of that prima facie reasonableness. But there is more to this practical story. The missing element is the hierarchy of needs that yields a hierarchy of inclinations, this in its turn yielding a hierarchy of prima facie oughts with both their degrees of constraint and their degrees of reasonableness. The significance of these hierarchies lies in the possibilities of conflicts of inclinations, which in the case of those that appear to the agent's consciousness as amenable to his (at least apparent) free action, appear as conflicts of oughts. Such conflicts the agent is deeply inclined to solve in favor of those inclinations that are higher in his motivational hierarchy, i.e., those inclinations that are more comprehensive and furnish more long-lasting and more deeply-seated satisfactions. The general details of a motivational hierarchy and the general characterization of satisfactions and their degrees are problems that lie outside our present purview. Here all we need is the fundamental principle that all of an agent's inclinations form a motivational and emotional hierarchy, which appears to practical consciousness, to the extent that it appears at all, as a hierarchy of claims or prima facie oughts, and the principle that the direction of that hierarchy is the direction of the agent's deep preference for the solution of his conflicts of oughts (or inclinations). This is, of course, not to say that the agent knows at any given time what his deep preferential ranking of inclinations is. Finding relevant fragments of his motivational hierarchy is precisely the whole point of his deliberations.

The agent, then, has a pervasive deep formal inclination to solve his conflicts of oughts in terms of his mostly unknown motivational hierarchy.

This *formal* inclination appears to his consciousness as his *overriding ought*. Since this is essentially a super-inclination, a formal, or meta-inclination, it is actually easy to be aware of it – what is not easy is to see how one's motivational hierarchy ranks one's concrete and primary inclinations. Correspondingly, the overriding ought is essentially formal, both assuming a ranking of all other, prima facie, oughts and demanding compliance with the one that comes higher in the ranking. Furthermore, given the formal nature of an agent's overriding ought, there need not be any harm in holding that the overriding ought for one man is the overriding ought of everybody else. Thus *the overriding ought, or the general structure of all individual overriding oughts, is a fundamental feature of reason*. But one must avoid Kant's and Prichard's and Hare's identification of the moral oughts with the overriding ought.[6]

The overriding ought, let us call it $ought_l$, like every other $ought_i$, conforms to the ought-laws formulated above in Chapters 7 and 9. But it has a very special law of its own:

$$O_l*. \qquad O_lA \supset A. \qquad \text{[See axiom A11a on page 263.]}$$

This means that if an action is one that the agent overridingly ought to perform, then the corresponding practition is Legitimate for him in his absolute context, as characterized in Chapter 5, §3. This law justifies an agent's inferences of the form:

$(O_l\text{–I})$ I ought overridingly to do A
           Hence, I shall do A.

To think firmly that one ought overridingly to do A is in fact to endorse the practition to do A. Kant's passage (K.5) is indeed particularly true of the overriding ought. As Kant correctly saw, all "imperatives", i.e., all affirmative ought-propositions, are such that their endorsement subdues the will in the sense that an inclination is created or reinforced, which inclination presents a constraint on the will. But he tended to ignore this general principle when he concentrated on the moral law which he, wrongly, equated with the categorical imperative. Categorical imperatives, understood as overriding-ought propositions, subdue the will in a much stronger way, namely, they quash all inclinations that run counter to the inclinations to doing the action santioned by, i.e., within the domain of, the agent's overriding ought. This is really the reverence for the law – the overriding ought – that Kant has in mind in (K.5).

The preceding suggests that the restrictive influence on the will, i.e., on the agent's motivational nature, that the prima facie ought have is derived from the reverence (to use Kant's term) of the overriding ought. Moreover, the preceding suggests that we should, developing further the view of deontic judgments of Chapter 7, construe each $ought_i$ as a complex of $ought$ and i, where $ought$ pure and simple is the overriding $ought_i$. This provides the clear unity of practical thinking that we want to find. Thus, each prima facie ought is, then, a *qualified* ought, restricting the overriding ought both in content and in reverence. The qualification signaled by each subscript i indicates the restrictive content we are attaching to the overriding ought. And that content provides a special reason for endorsing a given practition. But this special reason, precisely because it is special, is only a part of the totality of reasons, namely, the *whole* motivational hierarchy of the agent. Hence, the prima-facie-ought proposition of the form $*X$ ought$_i$ to do A$*$ can only yield a limited endorsement of the practition $*X$ to do A$*$ and, therefore, can only create a bundle of weak inclinations of the type that ought-thinking creates.

NOTES TO CHAPTER 11

[1] W. D. Ross, *The Right and The Good* (Oxford, England: The Clarendon Press, 1930), pp. 19ff.
[2] See H-N. Castañeda, 'On the Conceptual Antonomy of Morality', *Nous* 7 (1973): 67–77, and the glimpse into the issue in Chapter 13, §1.
[3] Kant has influenced my understanding of the working of practical thinking both directly and through Wilfrid Sellars and David Falk. My conception of the motivational role of *ought*, i.e., the overriding ought, was developed during the 1950's partly in an attempt to understand the latter's insightful papers on *ought* and action, to wit: W. Sellars, 'Obligation and Motivation', in W. Sellars and J. Hospers, eds., *Readings in Ethical Theory* (New York: Appleton-Century-Crofts, Inc. 1st ed., 1952): 511–417, David Falk, "'Ought' and 'Motivation'", *Proceedings of the Aristotlian Society* **48** (1947–48), reprinted in Sellars and Hospers, *op. cit.*, 492–510.
[4] I. Kant, *Foundations of the Metaphysics of Morals*, in Vol. IV of the Prussian Academy edition of Kant's works. We follow, with some departures, the translation by Lewis White Beck in I. Kant, *Critique of Practical Reason and Other Writings in Moral Philosophy* (Chicago: University of Chicago Press, 1949). The numbers in parentheses refer to Vol. 4 of the Academy edition.
[5] Hare has interpreted Kant as holding that *all* hypothetical imperatives are analytic *qua* imperatives in his *The Language of Morals* (Oxford, England: The Clarendon Press, 1952), p. 37. This is what (K.3) suggests. The thesis is examined in H-N. Castañeda,

The Structure of Morality (Springfield, Illinois: Charles Thomas Publisher, 1974), Chapter 6. That thesis is central to Hare's views on the nature of deontic judgments. See *op. cit.* Chapter 3. Hare's views on ought are examined in H-N. Castañeda, 'Imperatives, Decisions, and Oughts', in H-N. Castañeda and G. Nakhnikian, eds. *Morality and the Language of Conduct* (Detroit, Wayne State University Press, 1965), pp. 225–243.

[6] See H-N. Castañeda, 'Imperatives,Oughts, and Moral Oughts', *Australasian Journal of Philosophy* **44** (1966): 277–300, and *The Structure of Morality*, Chapter 7.

PART III

THE METAPHYSICS OF PRACTICAL
THINKING:
THE REALITY OF DOING AND OF
DEONTIC PROPERTIES

EVENTS AND THE STRUCTURE OF DOING

In Part I of this book we carried out a thorough investigation of the basic structure of the contents of practical thinking, and in Part II we studied practical thinking as a psychological phenomenon characterized by a peculiar form of internal causality. In Part III we take our inquiries further into the world and consider the involvement of practical thinking with reality. In Chapter 12 we examine the structure of the effects wrought out by practical thinking, and in Chapter 13 we consider the degree of reality, i.e., the place in the whole fabric of reality, of practical noemata and their elements.

In this chapter we continue the investigation developed in Chapter 10. There we discuss the practical action schema through which practical thinking exercises its internal causality. Here we study the structure of the efficient exercise of that action schema in intentional action. Here more than ever before in these investigations we must deal with the specific problems of practical thinking, making sure that we bring the "local" issues up to where they presuppose solutions to the general problems in ontology and metaphysics.

1. THE STRUCTURE OF DOING: ITS BASIC LAWS

As we explained in Chapters 10 and 11, the core of practical thinking is from the point of view of action intentional thinking, and the kernel of that core is the thinking of an intention about a present action, namely, the thinking which consists of deciding or intending to do something *right now*. Episodes of such thinking have been called *volitions*, and we can call them so without commitments to any theory on the nature of the mental. In Chapter 10, §3 we explained the action schema of volitions. A volition is an endorsingly rehearsing thinking of an intention, i.e., the fully endorsing episode of thinking of a thought content of the form *I shall A*, which is *not* a proposition (as we argued at length in Chapter 6). So far as Chapter 10 reached, the activation of the practical action schema by a volition need *not* be effective. In fact, as we well know, it is often ineffective. Too many of our resolutions are never realized. But many others are realized, and when they are we *do* something. In short, as we are using the words 'volition' and 'doing' here, and explain below in Def. 1–Def. 7, *volitions are not doings.* If the reader wants to speak of mental acts, then volitions are acts, but they are still not doings. In §2 we shall say more about actions and we will see how ambiguous and treacherous the word 'action' is.

Consider the case of an agent Agens who has just resolved to do an action B right away (e.g., the action of killing Smith) by means of doing another action A (e.g., by shooting Smith, Agens already having a gun in his hand). In this case Agens has a rather complex intention in mind. But now we are not interested in the meta-psychological phenomenon of Agens' volition or in the internal causality of his thinking. Suppose that Agens succeeds in his project. We have then:

(1)   At time *t* Agens decides to kill Smith there then *by shooting him with the gun in his* hand[1].

Agens' actions constitute a typical case of intentional doing. We want to examine the structure of this doing of Agens. In this section whenever we speak of *doing* we are treating intentional doing, which is the primary or paradigmatic sense of 'doing'. In §2 we discuss generic doing. Now, the principal elements of Agens' doing can be pictured in Figure 1, which is meant to represent the three-dimensional ontological "space" of intentional action.

As the diagram indicates, there are very many serious problems pertaining to the elucidation of the total nature of action. Some of those problems are among the most difficult and important in philosophy, and all we can do here is to make sure that whatever view we propose about our "local" problems is embeddable in a larger philosophical theory.

There are three problems that go together as special instances of the mind-body relationship: (i) the connection between volition V and its physical counterpart V_φ (if any); (ii) the causation of the primordial stage P by volition V; (iii) the connection between P and V_φ. We cannot deal with these problems here. But we can see how powerful is the metaphysical perspective suggested by natural science. If in fact there are volitions in a mental dimension, then the laws of physics and chemistry suffer a dramatic

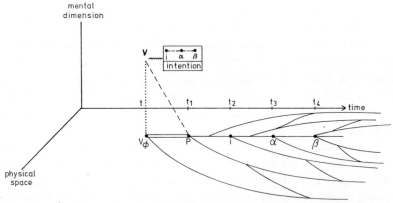

Fig. 1.

V   is Agens' volition to kill Smith by shooting him right there then. The top part of
    the box next to 'V' represents Agens' belief about the causal chain leading from
    his pressing the trigger to the shooting and on to the death of Smith. The lower
    part should contain the representation of Agens' intention to shoot and kill.

V_φ is the physical counterpart of V (if any; on some views $V = V_\varphi$).

P   is the state of Agens' body which is immediately "caused" by V and is thus the
    primordial stage of Agens' doing at time t: P is in the case of human beings a brain
    state.

i is the *initial stage* of Agens' doing: it is the state of Agens' fingers and hand at the
    moment when he just finished pulling the trigger of his gun.

α is the state of Agens' gun at the moment when it finishes firing: in this example it is
    an *intermediary stage* of Agens' doing.

β is the state of Smith at the moment of just having become dead: it is the *terminal
    stage* of Agens' doing.

The solid line segments linking state P to other states as well as the line segments is-
    suing from those states or their links represent the flow of causality or energy in
    physical space.

The heavier segments in the box next to 'V' indicate the small sections of the causal
    chain that Agens conceives, the lighter segments being segments of the causal path
    that he merely hypothesizes to exist.

The fainter causal lines issuing from states P, i, α, and β or from their causal links are
    causal lines in which we are not interested. They are only a few of the very many
    causal paths that issue from every spacetime point. Probably from P there issues a
    continuum or at least an infinity of causal routes; but only very few of them are of
    practical interest to the agent, to his critics, and to the makers of rules affecting the
    agent.

The dashed line from V to P represents the psycho-physical causality (if any) linking
    volitions to physical changes.

The dotted line from V_φ to V represents the possible physical causation end of volitions,
    or profound identity of volitions and physical events.

The double line linking V_φ to P indicates the controversial causation of P by V_φ,
    rather than by V, which materialists and physicalists defend.

exception at those places, like our brains, where volitions cause physical changes. It would be much "simpler" to have a world which exhausts itself in the ordinary physical spacetime and in which the laws of physics and chemistry reign, uninterrupted by mental exceptions, throughout space-time. One feels an urge to wipe out the whole dimension of the mental. But here we shall make no assumptions either way. We record the existence of that urge. And we also record the crucial fact that to the consciousness of an agent making deliberations: (i) he appears to be free to choose from alternative courses of causation; (ii) his choices appear to be uncaused; (iii) his apparent free choice appears not to be a physical event, and (iv) his free choosings or volitions appear to be efficient in causing physical changes in his body and in his environment. Whatever the ultimate metaphysical reality of these appearances may be, they are part and parcel of the data that any adequate theory of the mind has both to take into account and to illuminate.

Let us consider P, the *primordial* stage in Agens' doing at time *t*. P is a state of readiness in Agens' brain. It would appear to Agens, if he is sophisticated enough to have some idea of how his body has a brain that controls the functioning of his body, that P is caused by his volition. But since it is not open to inspection, P is a hypothesized state. More importantly, P is not the sort of state that enters an agent's mind when he brings to consciousness his beliefs about his circumstances and rehearses his intendings to act. That is why it is not registered in the top of the box of noemata next to V in Figure 1. There is too little one can say about P at the present state of knowledge.

Agens' intention (i.e., the content of Agens' intending, see Chapter 2, §5), or his intending, to kill Smith does not involve the primordial state P, but involves the *initial* state *i*. In our example (1) Agens does not consider at all the further consequences of Smith's death. But as we said, the flow of causality will probably not be interrupted with Smith's death but will continue beyond and will mix with the flow in other paths and will spread about in different paths issued from later space-time points. All sorts of states of different objects will be in a direct causal chain linking them to Smith's death and to states β, α, i, and P. Many of such states will be of no interest to Agens or the members of his community. But some of those states will interest some persons, and Agens may be declared responsible for them by reference to certain rules or laws that establish a *conventional* normative link between them and the initial stage i of Agens' doing at time t. Such states for which Agens may be declared responsible by such conventional laws or rules are *not*, however, states that Agens' intentionally brings about. For Agens to bring about some state γ intentionally it is necessary that he believes at the time of his volition V that there is a causal link between this initial stage i of his doing and γ.

The chief points we want to establish are these:

(D.1)   The initial stage of an agent's intentional doing is the state that he envisions as one that he can bring into existence simply by willing it.

(D.2)   The initial state i of an agent's intentional doing need not be caused to exist directly by the agent's volition to bring it into existence. It suffices that: (i) the agent's will be part of a psycho-physical causal context in which the agent's volition causes a primordial stage P which is in a direct causal chain to i; and (ii) the agent, although unaware of P and of how P is causally connected with i, can rely on his (unknown) causal context to bring about i by merely willing i to exist.

(D.3)   In the case of human beings the primordial stages of their doings are brain states; but *if* a disembodied self can act on the physical world, he could in principle perform doings whose primordial stages would be changes of different sorts in different objects.

(D.4)   In the case of human beings as we know them today the initial stages of their doings are bodily states resulting from their bodily movements; but it is conceivable that human beings could develop other powers, or that there may be agents with other kinds of bodies, so that the initial stages of their doings may be states of objects other than their bodies.

It is easy to imagine agents who could, for instance, move objects at a distance by simply willing the objects to move. This is not exactly the case with Ali Baba who could open the cave by saying "Open sesame". Ali's volition caused the initial stage of his vocal mechanism being in the appropriate state, and this is a bodily state resulting from bodily movement. We can picture the situation we envisage in (D.4) as one in which the agent can send, unconsciously perhaps, but automatically when he wills the distant object to move, some beams of special rays that cause the object to move. In such a case the process between the agent's primordial stage and the state of the objects just being moved by the beam of rays is like the unintended but relied-upon pocess linking Agens' brain state P and the initial state i of his fingers, which process underlies the truth of example (1) above. Another limiting law of doing is:

> (D.5)   If a disembodied self can both act on the world, and know what the primordial stages of his doings are, then his doings can have their primordial stages indentical with their initial stages.

Laws (D.3) and (D.5) do not imply that contemplative disembodied selves are viable – let alone disembodied selves capable of acting on the physical world. These are matters for the "larger" philosophical theory in which our discussion of actions and doings is to be embedded.

For Agens to act intentionally it is necessary that he have some intentions and that his volitions to realize such intentions be involved in the causation of the primordial stages of his doings. An agent can intend to bring about each of a long chain of states. Thus, in every intentional doing there is a terminal stage intended by the agent and perhaps a sequence of intermediary ones. In the example of Agens we have been discussing, *intermediary* stages are the state α of his gun after he fired it and presumably the states of the fired bullet right after it was fired and right before it penetrated Smith's body. These states were presumably envisioned by Agens. In any case,

> (D.6)   The intentional doing of an agent may have certain state both as its initial and as its terminal stage.

As we have said, the flow of energy goes beyond the terminal stage of an intentional doing. These are the unintended consequences of an intentional doing.

An *intentional doing* is, *inter alia*, by (D.1)–(D.6), a finite segment of a causal tree that starts with a volition, goes through a primordial stage to an initial stage, and proceeds to other envisioned stages.

> *Def.* 1. The fundamental element in an agent's intentional doing is his volition.

Def. 2. A causal chain V-P-*i*-α ... β is *more intentional* the more stages between *i* and α and between α and β the agent X envisions at the time of V.

2. ACTIONS, EVENTS AND PROCESSES

We have described the basic structure of intentional doing in terms of states of the agent's body and of the states of objects affected by the agent's doings. We have deliberately refrained from speaking of events. But we must bring events into our discussion. *Events* are the individual changes of states or properties that objects undergo. For example, Agens' gun acquiring state α is an event, and so is Smith's acquiring state β; events are also Agens' body entering into states P and *i*. Now, we cannot take the line segments in the diagram in § 1 that link the different states P, *i*, α, and β as representing events. Those segments merely represent the causal patterns that the realizations of events will adopt. In Figure 1 we must conceive of (real) events as the flow of existence or realization, so to speak, reaching given states. We conceive of a possible world as a complex system of causal patterns; *the real world is then simply that possible world in whose causal patterns existence or reality flows.* An event is realized when existence "reaches" a certain state at a certain position in the space-time scheme. A (real) *process* is then a continuous or uninterrupted total sequence of realized events between two given states separated by an interval of time.[2]

In our example of Agens' carrying out his intention of killing Smith by shooting him with his gun, we have already assumed that Agens' volition is an event, and represented it in the above diagram by a wiggle. But there are those events filling up the causal channels between each of the two listed states. Agens' doings are connected with the infinite strings of such events. Actions and doings, whether core doings or not, are in a sense events and sequences of events. The crucial thing to remember is that successful intentional doing requires that there be a steady flow of reality (or realization) from the volition, or its physical counterpart V_φ, all the way up to the terminal stage of the total doing.

We specify types of doings as follows, where V is not assumed to be different from V_φ, and if different it may be that V_φ, not V, causes P, and in such a case we are to understand 'V' to be a mere abbreviation of 'V_φ':

Def. 3. A *total intentional doing* is the full process V-P-*i*-α-β.

Def. 4. A *primordial intentional doing* is the process V-P.

Def. 5. An *initial intentional doing* is the process V-P-*i*.

Def. 6. An *intentional doing* is any process V-P-*x*, where *x* is either an initially or an intermediary, or a terminal stage.

Def. 7. An *initial* or *basic intentional act* is an event consisting of the realization of the initial stage of an intentional doing.

Def. 8. An *intentional act* is either an initial intentional act *i* or a process *i-x*, where *x* is either an intermediary or a terminal stage of an intentional doing V-P-*i-x*.

Def. 9. An *intentional deed* is any initial, intermediate or terminal stage of a total intentional doing.

In short, *doings* in our terminology start with a volition, and intentional *deeds* begin with an initial stage, both lasting through periods with highlighted stage times. Acts exist at times.

In the preceding definitions we have kept the adjective 'intentional' in order to indicate that the concepts introduced can be generalized to nonintentional ones. There are two natural generalizations. *First*, we can speak of a non-intentional doing or deed or action in connection with a process of the form V-P-*i*-β-*x* or the form V-P-*i*-*x*-β when we are interested in a state *x* that was not envisioned or intended by the agent in question. *Second*, and more radically, given a process starting with the agent's body and ending in some state *x* in which we are interested, we may say that the process or a segment of it is a doing, or a basic action, or a deed, whether the process starts from a volition or not. There are other ways of generalizing the concepts of doing and deed, but we will not consider them. Our primary concern is the connection between doing and thinking, i.e., with the structure of intentional doing, act, and deed. It may not be amiss to point out that the four words 'doing', 'act', 'deed', and 'action' are full of ambiguities and are often used interchangeably. Our definitions *Def.* 1–*Def.* 9 are *not*, therefore, analyses of all ordinary meanings of those words. They furnish technical meanings which coincide with some ordinary usages and can serve as tools in putting some conceptual order in our talk about action.

The word 'action' is very seriously ambiguous. In particular:

(W)   The word 'action' is used in at least four different types of related senses; to refer to: (i) certain properties or relations of agents; (ii) doings; (iii) acts, and (iv) deeds – as characterized above in *Def. 1–Def. 9*.

We use the word 'action' in sense (i) in Chapters 4–11, especially in Chapter 4, §9, when we discuss action-predicates. One of our main theses (defended in Chapters 5, 6, and 7) is that the elucidation of the nature of practical thinking requires that we distinguish between actions considered as circumstances and actions considered practically (i.e., prescriptively or intentionally). In all those discussions we speak of actions in sense (i). Actions in this sense are *universals* and can be instantiated by, or attributed to, different subjects *qua* agents. In that sense we speak of the action of killing, which many people can perform. Actions as universals are very peculiar; that is why we speak of actions being performed or being performable rather than of being instantiated. That peculiarity of action universals is precisely their connection with deeds and doings, which are the other meanings of 'action'.

Events as we explained above are not universals, but *particulars*. They are a sub-category of particulars beside the sub-category of individuals, i.e., persons, minds, and physical objects. Among the main differences between individuals and events are:

(a) Individuals do, while events do not, endure through time;

(b) Individuals undergo changes, but events are changes;

(c) Individuals have, as a consequence of (a) and (b), at least short contemporaneous histories; events can have posthumous histories, namely, the history consisting of the events later than the one we are interested in that lie in the same causal path; individuals and events both have pre-histories;

(d) the causal laws governing a world, whether possible or real, are laws for the regular succession of events.

Hence, to use 'action' to refer to events or processes does introduce a most serious risk of confusion.

Yet the word 'action' is sometimes used to refer to doings, whether intentional or not. A natural generic concept of action in sense (ii) is this:

> *Def.* 10. An *action$_{ii}$* of agent x is either an intentional doing of x or a process starting with a bodily movement of x that x could have performed intentionally in his circumstances.[4]

Something like *Def*. 10 seems to be relevant to normative systems that for some reason or other stipulate that a person is responsible for certain actions of his, whether he performed them intentionally or not, and sometimes even if he performed them unconsciously. In particular, laws enacted with the purpose of making sure that people refrain from certain undesired forms of behavior often make a person responsible for negligence or for acts which the person did not perform intentionally, but *could* in his circumstances, presumed normal, have avoided. This is the legal fiction of what a reasonable man is expected to do in standard circumstances.

The analysis of the sense of the 'could' in *Def*. 10 is a very tricky task which we shall, however, not undertake here. Such analysis belongs in the special theory of the legal institution as characterized in Chapter 1, §1.

When used in sense (ii) the word 'action' is also employed in more specific says. Some times it is used to refer to core intentional doings, and sometimes to refer to the segments of core intentional doings that go, inclusively, from the primordial to the initial stages of the doings in question.

Very often philosophers treating topics in the theory of action are not interested in the basic volitions or in the primordial stages of an intentional action. They tend to use the word 'action' in sense (iii) of (W), *i.e.*, to refer to what we have called acts. Then it becomes natural for them to use the following as the most general conception of action:

> *Def*. 11. X performs an *action*$_{iii}$ A just in cast there is a movement *m*
> of X's body and there is a process linking *m* to the realiza-
> tion of the state α characteristic of action A.

Def. 11 provides a sense of 'action' that is of interest from the point of view of practical thinking and rational action only on strong assumptions about the mind-body relationship. It of course allows the attribution to human beings not only of non-intentional actions but also of wholly unconscious actions. A generalization of *Def*. 11 is undoubtedly the one in use when somebody speaks of the actions of inanimate objects.

The word 'action' is probably less commonly used in sense (iv). But one can hear conversations like this: White: "Smith died yesterday"; Black: "*That* is Agens' action (doing)".

We are not interested in proscribing any usage of the word 'action'.

Our concern is merely the Aristotelian one of noting the multiple ambiguities of that word in the hope that attention to them will facilitate a
better understanding of standing disputes in the theory of action. We
shall, in §4 and §5, discuss two such disputes which at first sight look
almost insoluble, so that our characterization of the structure of doing
shows its worth.

3. THE CONFLUENCE OF AGENCY

In the preceding sections we have discussed the doings, the actions, and
the deeds of one agent. As we noted, the chief phenomenon is that of a
flow of existence or realization through a volition into the physical world,
part of the flow corresponding to what the agent envisions, but part
of it going beyond the agent's awareness and capabilities of knowledge.
But the flow is continuous or uninterrupted. Naturally, in a region of the
universe where there are several agents the flows of existence passing
through their volitions may branch out and have some converging
streams. Then the question that comes up is: Whose action is the one
that brought about a certain state we are interested in? Suppose, for
instance, that after Agens shot Smith, while Smith is bleeding, Jones
comes and shoots Smith destroying a different vital organ. When Smith
dies, who killed him? Suppose that Jones manages to aim at Smith and
sends off a bullet that passes exactly where Agens' bullet passed. Or
suppose that instead of shooting Smith, Jones stops the hemorrhage, but
then Smith dies of an infection caused by the bandage placed on his chest
by Jones. Suppose that Agens and Jones shoot at Smith from different
sides each destroying a vital function. Or suppose that Agens is determined
to poison Smith and prepares a lethal drink for Smith; then changes his
mind and sets the glass with the poison aside; then Jones fetches the glass
and gives it to Smith, who immediately dies. Who killed Smith? Perhaps
Jones did not kill Smith intentionally, but did he kill him unintentionally?

The above are only some relatively simple cases. The reader can imagine
how complicated ones can be concocted. The important truth that they all
reveal is that the flow of existence is steady and spreads about in all
directions in space. In such cases there is a confluence of streams of
existence. In some cases as in the double shooting of Smith by both Agens
and Jones perhaps each one of the shootings can cause Smith's death, and
it is natural to say that each shooter killed him, committing his own

manslaughter. But in the case of Smith's death partially caused by the infection resulting from Jones' bandaging Smith, Jones contributed, unwittingly perhaps, to Smith's death. The same is true in the poisoning case. But in general there is *no* natural way of cutting the flow of existence and trace it back to just one agent. Yet in practical life we often divide agency and blame and punish each agent involved in a confluence of existence, or punish only some of the agents. Such divisions of agency are often arbitrary, but justifiable. When we want to prevent obnoxious behavior we tend to be more inclusive in our distribution of punishments for small participation in confluent causations. Here we have again the legal fiction of the sensible person mentioned before. When, on the other hand, we want to encourage certain types of behavior and distribute prizes for those who succeed, we create more stimulation and competition by rewarding the involvement in confluent causations less generously.

There are, then, *arbitrary normative considerations* that enter in the allocation of actions, whether doings or deeds, to agents, not only in the case of isolated agents, but particularly in the case of confluent flows of event-realization. The study of the criteria for those allocations are connected with the purposes of the normative systems and, hence, the institutions involved. Therefore, such problems belong in the specific theories of institutions, as we characterized them in Chapter 1, §1. Here is then a further ambiguity of the word 'action'.

4. The Times of Actions

In our analysis of the structure of doing in §1 we have found that a total intentional doing includes several times: (1) the time of the volition; (2) the time of primordial stage; (3) the time of the initial stage; (4) the time of the terminal stage, and (5) the times of the intermediate stages. Of course, a doing has all the periods determined by those times. The other types of doings (primordial, initial, etc.) have only some of these times. A basic action has only (3), and an intentional act (by *Def.* 8) has (3) or (3) and other times from (4) and (5).

What is the time of an action? Given our analysis of actions in §2, this question is unclear. We must specify what sense of 'action' of the several ones examined in §2 is intended. Clearly, sense (i) of 'action' is not relevant, since we are dealing with the processes filling up the causal channels between a volition or an initial stage and some later stages, including in some normative cases effects not intended or envisioned by the agent.

Consider again the case of Agens who at 3 p.m. pulls the trigger of his gun aiming at Smith with the intent to kill him. The gun is a museum piece and fires at 3:01 immediately piercing Smith's heart, who dies at 10 p.m. the same day. At what time did Agens kill Smith? We are considering acts (in our technical senses), and they all involve different times and periods. There is, to start with, the initial act at 3 p.m., the intermediary act lasting from 3 to 3:01, and the terminal intentional act going on from 3 to 10 p.m., and there are also the times of the deeds. The question out of context is not definite enough. And given the different purposes we may pursue in different circumstances we may speak of different types of action on different occasions.[5]

Recently there has been a very lively controversy about the times at which actions are performed. In our example, some philosophers hold that Agens killed Smith at 3 p.m., thus identifying Agens' killing of Smith with Agens' basic act (in the sense of *Def.* 7).[6] Others [7]make this identification but then go on to point out, correctly, that Agens' basic act becomes a killing by the posthumous happening of Smith's dying seven hours later. Others[8] hold that Agens committed his killing from 3 to 10 p.m., thus identifying the killing with the terminal intentional act of Agens', (the normally visible part of Agens' total intentional doing), which spans the period between just a few second before 3 p.m. and 10 p.m. Clearly, these views are all correct in what they claim, given what they take as actions; their actual disagreement is perhaps a combination of their different uses of the word 'action' with their implicit claims that they are dealing with the ordinary meaning or the most ordinary meaning of the word 'action'.

5. THE IDENTIFICATION AND THE PLURALITY OF ACTIONS AND EVENTS

A more profound ontological issue about actions than the one about time, has been recently debated under the heading of the individuation of actions. I do not like the word 'individuation' here, not only because, as we explained in §2, we want to contrast individuals with events, but also because some philosophers engaged in the dispute defend a view of "individuation" of actions according to which actions are apparently in the category of propositions.[9] The issue is one about the identification or non-identification of actions and events. To introduce the topic consider Agens' homicide once more:

(1)   (At 3 p.m.) Agens moved his left index finger;
(2)   (At 3 p.m.) Agens pulled the trigger of his gun;
(3)   Agens fired his gun;
(4)   Agens shot Smith;
(5)   Agens killed Smith.

How many actions did Agens perform? Some philosophers, namely those who identify actions with initial acts in the sense of *Def.* 7, claim that Agens performed just one action. And they are absolutely correct: there *is* only one initial act (and only one initial doing). That initial act is the movement of Agens' left index finger in accordance with (1). This event has a posthumous history running from i to α to β in Figure 2.

So i becomes posthumously what causes α at 3:01 p.m. ... and γ at 10 p.m., etc. We can correctly interpret sentences (2)–(5) as describing episodes in the (necessarily posthumous) history of m and M.

The philosophers who take actions to be *processes* starting with the initial state i and ending at some later state α–γ refuse to identify Agens' triggerpulling with his gun-firing with his shooting Smith and with his killing Smith. And this is correct; for there *are* such acts (in the termino-

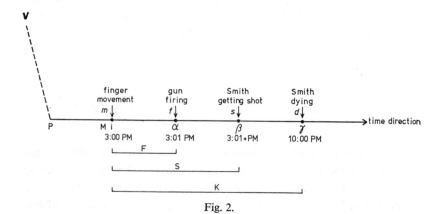

Fig. 2.

logy of *Def.* 7 and *Def.* 8) or processes as $m, i - \alpha, i - \beta, i - \gamma$, which are in the vocabulary of these philosophers Agens' actions are represented in the diagram by the vectors named M, F, S, and K. We can certainly interpret sentences (2)–(5) as attributing to Agens these acts.

Patently, there is no factual disagreement between the two views. The single basic act *m* is part and parcel of the multiple acts that have as other parts fragments of *m*'s (necessarily posthumous) history. The two views are correct about the non-linguistic facts; and their linguistic theses about the interpretation of sentences (2)–(5) are equivalent. They are the two sides of the one and the same coin, so to speak.

There are, however, other views on the identification of actions. On the first view just discussed, sentences (2)–(5) are taken to *describe* posthumous episodes of the initial act *m*. The propositions expressed with (2)–(5) attribute to *m* different logically independent properties. Obviously, the different properties are of different degree of importance in different contexts of discussion. E.g., for prosecuting Agens for homicide the truth of (5) is more crucial, than the truth of (2) or (4). Again the causal explanation of (5) is different from that of (1) and (2). These and similar considerations suggest to some philosophers that Agens' actions of killing Smith, shooting him, triggering his gun, etc. are different.[10] Here we move to deeper issues. Clearly, for the considerations just adduced it makes no difference whether Agens' killing of Smith occurs at 3 p.m. or lasts from 3 p.m. to 10 p.m.

The issue is now the more general one whether or not entities that have different true descriptions are different. At first glance it may seem both that the answer to that question is a rotund "yes" and that my way of putting the issue is, because of the temptation to such rotund answer, unfair to the philosophers who claim a plurality of actions on the grounds just given and the like. These appearances are symptoms of the depth of the issues which belong in general metaphysics and ontology. All I can do here is offer a glimpse of the issue and of my preferred solution.

The first thing to note is that we are now dealing with an entirely *different* issue from the one we discussed earlier in this section. It is an issue that in no way disturbs the claim made above that sentences (2)–(5) tell fragments of the posthumous history of the *same* action. Thus, we find once more a debate in which the two parties are not joining the issue. Let us explain this contention.

Consider, in order to develop the proper perspective, the well-known case of Oedipus in Sophocles' *Oedipus King*:

(11)   Before the pestilence Oedipus believed that the previous King of Thebes was dead;

(12)   The previous King of Thebes was the same as Oedipus' father.

(13)   It is not the case that before the pestilence Oedipus believed that Oedipus' father was dead.

These three propositions are all true. Yet if we take the *sameness* of (12) as identity we are led to the well-known puzzle that Frege emphasized so forcefully in recent times. For

(14)   If a is identical with b, everything true of a is true of b.

Then we should have that what is true of Oedipus' father according to (11) is true of the previous King of Thebes, namely:

(15)   Before the pestilence Oedipus believed that Oedipus' father was dead.

Thus we would contradict the truth of (13).

This is a serious puzzle that has to do with the nature of the mind and of the world outside. This issue has too much to do with the principle of the finitude of the mind, briefly discussed in Chapters 10 and 11. Naturally, different views can be developed depending in part on one's own general metaphysical presuppositions. One type of view attempts to reject principle (14), which is a fundamental law of identity. Other type of view is built upon the thesis that expressions like 'Oedipus believed that _____ was dead' do not (always) formulate properties, or something that can be true or false of anything. Other views recognize that the sameness spoken of in (12) is not (genuine) identity. One view of this type I have propounded elsewhere.[11]

I call the entity expressed at face value by each uniquely referring expression, like 'Oedipus' father' and 'the previous King of Thebes', *ontological guises*. These are atomic individuals, so to speak, composing by means of a certain relationship called *consubstantiation*, the ordinary complex individuals. To give a rough illustration, in the case of (11)–(13) we and Oedipus are dealing with the two ontological guises *Oedipus' father* and *the previous King of Thebes*, which belong together by consubstantiation into one ordinary object. Consubstantiation is the co-existence of guises into one ordinary object. Possible but inexisting individuals are unconsubstantiated with anything: they can be thought, but they lie in an isolation. For instance, the present King of France is isolated; it is consubstantiated neither with the young present King of France nor with the not-young present King of France: it has no properties, as is often said.

The consubstantiation theory has many complexities and consequences. (For the connoiseur, for instance, it rejects Russell's celebrated analysis of definite descriptions.) But it has many applications in different fields of philosophy.[12]

Now, let us show the relevance of all this to the identification of actions. Consider the initial act to which sentences (2)–(5) refer in any case. That act is describable as follows:

(21)   The initial act of Agens that caused his gun to be triggered;
(22)   The initial act of Agens that caused his gun to be fired;
(23)   The initial act of Agens that caused Smith's heart to become pierced;
(24)   The initial act of Agens that caused the death of Smith.

As we pointed out, these characterizations are hidden in (2)–(5). Hence, *no* argument can show that in some obvious sense one and the *same* act is being alluded or referred to in (2)–(5). That causal explanations and the propriety of certain punishments seem to force a distinction between any two of Agens' acts of gun-triggering, shooting, and killing is, then, not germane to the sameness that the philosophers of the initial action defend. The issue is of a different sort; namely, the one appertaining to Oedipus and his different ways of conceiving of the ordinary object that he conceived as the present King of Thebes. This can be readily appreciated by reflecting on the fact that causal explanations deal with determinate truths we are *interested* in; punishments are *deliberately* attached to pieces of behavior that have certain properties we want not to be exemplified; and so on. In all such cases we are dealing with psychological attitudes, both propositional and practitional (as discussed in Chapter 10, §1). Therefore, giving the principle of the finitude of the mind that we have taken pains to emphasize, in those cases we are dealing with aspects, with presentations, with ways of conceiving events. In short, we are dealing with *ontological guises of ordinary events*. What we need, then, is a theory of *co-eventuation* parallel to the theory of consubstantiation. But such theory belongs into the general metaphysics and ontology of events. The "local" problems within practical philosophy have been dealt with by reducing acts and doings to events and processes.

But, as we have insisted, the problem about *co-eventuation* is only a special case of a more general problem, the one illustrated by Frege's puzzle. To tie this down firmly, consider a standard move in discussions of identity. It is often said that the solution to Frege's puzzle above lies in noting that:

(26)   Laius under the description *the previous King of Thebes* [at the time of Oedipus] is believed by Oedipus to be dead;

while:

(27)   Laius under the description *Oedipus' father* is not believed by Oedipus to be dead.

Similarly, it is said:

(28)   Agens' moving his finger under the description *Agens' act of killing Smith* is unlawful and punishable;

on the other hand,

(29)   Agens' moving his finger under the description *Agens' pressing the trigger of his gun* is neither unlawful nor punishable.

This parallelism is fine. But by itself it does not solve any problem. The expressions of the form '*x* under description D' are terribly obscure. Curiously enough most people who speak that way do not trouble to explain what can be meant by such expressions. Most philosophers who favor that form of speech deny that there are any entities over and above the individuals, like Laius, and the events, like Agens' moving of his finger, with which the problem began. Yet obviously we have to proceed to the development of a theory.

In the case of Laius and Oedipus we are dealing with individuals for which we often have names. It is easy to think that: the name 'Laius' (somehow) refers to the individual *per se* directly while the descriptive locutions 'The previous King of Thebes' and 'Oedipus' father' refer to him indirectly through the attribution of certain properties. We can call certain uses of the name 'Laius' logically proper names, rigid designators, or whatnot. Of course, this terminology does not produce by itself any illumination, or even a view. The fact is that there is a distinction between names and descriptive phrases, which, however the theory of their distinction may be, provides a linguistic, if not an ontological, anchor for contrasting an individual with its descriptions. Since ordinary individuals are re-encounterable we can use the name again in connection with the same individual. Events (with the typical exception of Atlantic hurricanes) usually go unnamed. But this is really a weak reason for distinguishing the cases of individuals from those of events. The two cases are clearly parallel.

We should not dwell upon a certain trivial objection to contrasting a particular *per se* with particulars under descriptions. It is this. The word 'description' is often used by philosophers, since Russell in 1905, to refer to descriptive phrases of the form 'the ...'. Thus, the objection proceeds, the contrasts in (26)–(27) and in (28)–(29) make the truth of these propositions a linguistic matter: surely, there is nothing linguistic about what Oedipus believes or about the punishability of killing. Some philosophers hold that there is something linguistic about beliefs, and still others may want to claim that even punishability is a matter linguistic at bottom. Some of us, however, can interpret the word 'description' as referring to a set of properties, as when teachers of literature discuss descriptive compositions and consider whether X's description of hell is more frightening that Y's.

The crucial perplexity created by (26)–(29) is the contrast between Laius *per se* and Laius under the description *Oedipus' father*, or Laius *qua*, or as, Oedipus' father. What sort of entity is the latter? and what sort of entity is the former? Since Laius as *the previous King of Thebes* has a property which Laius as *Oedipus' father* lacks, they must be different. Furthermore, neither is identical with Laius *per se*. But how are they related?[13]

One view is to identify the *qua*- or as-components of entities under descriptions with the ontological guises introduced above. In our case, the as-components of Laius are the guises *The previous King of Thebes* and *Oedipus' father* briefly discussed above. Then we have the problem of Laius *per se*. On the Ontological-Guise view, Laius *per se* is the whole consubstantiation structure of all the ontological guises consubstantiated with (the guise) *Oedipus' father*. This view requires a certain view of proper names and descriptive phrases, and, more importantly, certain type of view of reference (which is the essence of conceptual activity) and of the mind. But these are all problems that lie much beyond our present plan. Yet they must be tackled with all the theorizing vigor and patience for data-collecting that the current philosophical climate permits, if we are to contemplate (and construct) the total pattern of practical thinking – and provide the ultimate philosophical foundations of our institutions, whether real or only possible. Those problems and the other problems in general metaphysics to the verge of which our investigation has brought us many times will have to be dealt with in another treatise.

NOTES TO CHAPTER 12

[1] The asterisks in this sentence indicate that the pronouns they attach to are quasi-indicators, i.e., are used to attribute to Agens demonstrative reference to time, place, and himself. See the materials mentioned in Chapter 6, note 5 and the text in Chapter 6 pertaining to note 5.

[2] In developing this conception of events as particulars I have been influenced by Donald Davidson's 'The Logical Form of Action Sentences', in Nicholas Rescher, ed., *The Logic of Decision and Action* (Pittsburgh: University of Pittsburgh Press, 1967); 81–95. See also his 'Events as Particulars', *Nous* 4 (1974): 25–32, and 'Eternal *vs.* Ephemeral Events', *Nous* 5 (1971): 333–349.

[3] A related notion of basic action has been proposed by Arthur Danto in 'Basic Actions', *American Philosophical Quarterly* 2 (1965): 141–148. For useful critical examinations of Danto's views see Myles Brand, 'Danto on Basic Actions', *Nous* 2 (1968): 187–190, and Frederick Stoutland, 'Basic Actions and Causality', *The Journal of Philosophy* 65 (1968): 467–475. For valuable wide-ranging discussions on problems concerning the criteria for identifying basic actions and the types of abilities that on some views are said to be basic actions, see Annette Baier, 'The Search for Basic Actions', *American Philosophical Quarterly* 8 (1971): 161–170, and Jane R. Martin, 'Basic Actions and Simple Actions', *American Philosophical Quarterly* 9 (1972): 59–68.

[4] In an interesting normative characterization of action David Rayfield has generalized this condition of possible intendingness to other persons than the agent: "(ii) someone, not necessarily [the agent], could on some occasion decide to run [which is his para-digm example at the juncture]". See his 'Action', *Nous* 2 (1968): 131–145.

[5] See John Vollrath, 'When Actions Are Causes', *Philosophical Studies* 27 (1975): 329–339, for a nice discussion of examples showing how a person's interest in timing an action can vary with context.

[6] This view is held by Donald Davidson. See his essays mentioned in note 2. It is held by Charles Daniels, from whom I learned much in our conversations on the nature of action in 1969–70. In his *The Evaluation of Ethical Theories* (Dalhousie: University of Dalhousie Press, in the Philosophy in Canada Monography Series, 1975), he develops very nicely the reversed contrast between action and perception: both have a time lag (the former toward the future, the latter toward the past) between doing [or perceiving] and what is done [or perceived].

[7] See Jonathan Bennett, 'Shooting, Killing, and Dying', *Canadian Journal of Philosophy* **2** (1973): 315–323. Vollrath, *op. cit.*, also emphasizes the posthumous histories of initial acts.

[8] For this view see Judith Jarvis Thomson, 'The Time of a Killing', *The Journal of Philosophy* **68** (1971): 115–132, and Lawrence Davis, 'Individuation of Actions', *The Journal of Philosophy* **67** (1970): 520–530. See also John Woods, 'The Formal Ontology of Death', forthcoming in Douglas Walton and John Woods, eds., *Understanding Death*. These are illuminating papers, and so is Vivian M. Weil and Irving Thalberg, 'The Elements of Basic Action', *Philosophia* **4** (1974): 111–138 in which they develop an account intermediary between Davidson's and Goldman's.

[9] See H-N. Castañeda, 'Individuation and Non-identity', *American Philosophical Quarterly* **12** (1975): 131–130, for distillation of the meta-physical issue of genuine individuation.

[10] For a sustained and charming attack on Davidson's view that Agens' shooting Smith is the same action as Agens' killing Smith, see Alvin Goldman, *A Theory of Human Action* (Englewood Cliffs, New Jersey: Prentice-Hall, 1970), Chapter 1. Goldman's views that those two acts are connected by level generation, which is a very intimate relationship, requiring co-temporality, is very much the same as the claim that they are the same act. The fact that an event can have different properties that are relevant in different contexts has given rise to views that equate actions in different ways with propositions or properties or abstract sets of entities. Some valuable papers propounding such views are: (1) Jaegwon Kim, 'Events and their Descriptions: Some Considerations', in Nicholas Rescher, ed., *Essays in Honor of Carl G. Hempel* (Dordrecht: D. Reidel Publishing Company, 1970), (2) Roderick Chisholm, 'Events and Propositions', *Nous* **4** (1970): 15–24; (3) R. Chisholm, 'States of Affairs Again', *Nous* **5** (1971): 179–189; (4) Wilfrid Sellars, 'Actions and Events', *Nous* **7** (1973): 179–202; (5) Neil Wilson, 'Facts, Events and Their Identity Conditions', *Philosophical Studies* **25** (1974): 303–321. See also Georg Henrik Von Wright, *Norm and Action* (New York: The Humanities Press, 1963, Chapter 2); and Charles Landesman, 'Actions as Universals: An Inquiry into the Metaphysics of Action', *American Philosophical Quarterly* **6** (1969): 247–252.

[11] See H-N. Castañeda, 'Identity and Sameness', *Philosophia* **5** (1975): 121–150, and 'Thinking and the Structure of The World', *Philosophia* **4** (1974): 3–40.

[12] See previous note.

[13] I agree with Davidson again: "The mention of 'descriptions' is obviously a gesture in the direction of ontology; but there can be no serious theory until we are told what descriptions are, and how attributions of attitude refer to them", in *Eternal vs. Ephemeral Events*, p. 341.

[14] See note 11 above. "Thinking and the Structure of the World" contains an appropriate theory of proper names, predication, existence, and propositional attitudes.

CHAPTER 13

THE AUTONOMY OF PRACTICAL THINKING AND THE NON-NATURAL CHARACTER OF PRACTICAL NOEMATA

In this chapter we explain how the system of views developed so far includes a very strong thesis about the autonomy of practical thinking in general and about moral thinking in particular. We also elicit the account, included in that system of views, of the non-natural character of the contents of practical thinking. Although practical noemata are not reducible to propositions, nevertheless there is a very important metaphysical sense in which purely practical noemata do not belong to the ultimate furniture of reality. (Of course, general metaphysics may in its turn establish that propositions or facts do not themselves belong to the ultimate furniture of reality.)

1. THE AUTONOMY OF PRACTICAL THINKING

Many philosophers have known that moral judgments are not reducible to non-practical propositions. But some of them have supported their insight with poor reasons. Many have thought that such irreducibility originates in the moral character of moral judgments. That this is a confusion is evident from our brief discussion of institutions in Chapter 1, §1 and from our discussion of normative systems in the early sections of Chapter 7. The *first fundamental truth about morality* is this:

(M∗) The irreducibility of moral judgments to non-deontic propositions derives exclusively from their deontic character.

The roots of the confusion about the source of the autonomy of morality are of different sorts, but one of the most important ones is the deep-seated desire to provide a justification of morality that would make it unavoidably valid for every agent. As we saw in Chapter 11, every agent has a motivational hierarchy governed by his concept of an overriding *ought*. This is a necessary structure of rational agency. Clearly, then, if morality can be identified with such a structure, every agent would automatically be bound by the principles of morality. But we must by all means avoid identifying morality with the structure of the overriding *ought*.[1]

We hold, then, the more profound thesis:

(P–Th*) Practical thinking is irreducible to contemplative thinking, and purely practical noemata are irreducible to propositions.

We have argued for this thesis piecemeal. In Chapter 6 we established that intentions are not propositions, and in Chapter 7 we argued that deontic judgments are built upon practitions. As a consequence, as we noted in Chapter 10, §1, practical thinking having both practitions and deontic judgments as contents is *not* contemplative thinking.

The fact that deontic judgments are built upon practitions suffices to establish their irreducibility to ordinary propositions. But we also hold the additional thesis:

(P–Th.D) Deontic operators are not reducible to non-deontic operators. Patently, (P–Th.D) is a minor thesis. It supports (P–Th*), but the absolutely crucial foundation of (P–Th*) is:

(P–Th**) The irreducibility of practitions to propositions, or to any other type of noema, lies on the irreducibility of the practitional copula-operator, which forms the practitional copula by operating on the propositional copula (as we explained in Chapter 10, §3).

The autonomy thesis (P–Th*) is grounded on (P–Th**) more deeply than it could be grounded by principles like:

Poincaré's thesis. Imperatives cannot be derived from a set of premises none of which is an imperative.[2]
Hume's guillotine. Ought-judgments are not implied by premises among which there are no ought-judgments.[3]

These theses allow that practitical thinking be a special kind of purely propositional thinking. They would, therefore, deliver in such a case only a minimal autonomy of practical thinking. But we have seen throughout the preceding investigations over and again that the cleavage between pure contemplative thinking and practical thinking is much more profound, and that, in reverse, contemplative thinking is a special case of practical thinking. (See Chapter 1, §2; Chapter 2, §1; Chapter 4, §5;

Chapter 5, §1; Chapter 6, §2–§5; Chapter 7, §10–§12 and §16; Chapter 10, §3; Chapter 12, §1–§3.)

Yet the main error of those two theses lies in that they present a seriously distorted view of the nature of practical thinking. As we have said before, the role of reason in the world as a survival mechanism for the agent (and his species) requires that it functions as a unitary mechanism capable of focussing fully on the fundamental unity of the world both as the subject matter of contemplative thinking and as the object of change by practical thinking. The unity of the world demands the unity of an effective reason, and this demands the unity of the contents of thinking, all thinking, in one master Representational Image. There *must*, therefore, be bridging implications connecting propositions and practical noemata. We have seen this theme developed in great detail throughout Chapters 1–12. Consequently, segregating principles like the above two theses are wholly out of order, by running against the "grain" of reason.[4]

This need for bridging principles of implication for the unity of the world is so profound and crucial that it pervades all the spheres of thinking. In general, we have

(TH*) All families of concepts, or properties, or entities are, by virtue of belonging to one and the same world, connected by general structural or implication principles which establish that unity of the world. More specifically: (1) the more intimately related two families of concepts or entities are, the more specific and less formal their connections are; (2) the more different two families of concepts are, the more need they have of standing in supporting hybrid implication relationships.

To illustrate the force of (Th*) let us consider some simple but general cases, which have already appeared in Chapter 3.

At the very first level of our study of implication in Chapter 3 we encountered several dyadic connections between propositions, and some monadic connections. In the case of the latter family we dwelled upon negation, and in the case of the former we concentrated on conjunction. And there are bridging principles relating the monadic to the dyadic family of connections. Among them is:

(P.1) A proposition of the form *not(p)* implies any corresponding proposition of the form *not(p & q)*.

We have in (P.1) a magnificent case of an implicate containing something not contained in the implicans – because it is a bridging implication principle.

In Chapter 3, §18 we studied briefly some of the most basic principles of the logic of quantification. Obviously, we had to have principles relating propositions to propositional functions. And we found not only structural principles that make connective compounds of propositions and propositional functions, but also principles of implication that link the two externally. For instance, a propositional function $*F(x)*$ implies a mixed propositional function $*F(x) \vee p*$.

Patently, the implication principles relating practitions to propositions that we studied in Chapters 4 and 6, as well as those relating ordinary propositions to deontic judgments in Chapter 7 and Chapter 11 are all grounded on the solid metaphysical foundation provided by (Th*). And these bridging principles are wholly incapable of blurring the profound autonomy of practical thinking. Furthermore, the genuine autonomy or irreducibility of practical thinking is compatible with the reduction of the Legitimacy-values of practitions (realized in Chapter 5 and Chapter 6, §8) and with the reduction of the truth or Legitimacy, if you wish, of deontic judgments (executed in Chapter 8), to both the truth-values of and the implication relationships between ordinary propositions. This reduction is, of course, part and parcel of the general network of bridging implications.

In short, then, implicational autonomisms are very deeply flawed. They are ill-conceived attempts at by-passing the labor (not very hard labor as our journey from Chapter 3 through Chapter 9 makes evident) required for the formulation of the logical structure of deontic judgments.

2. MORAL CLASSICAL INTUITIONISM AND MORAL NATURALISM RECONCILED

The system of views we have developed in the preceding chapters may be correctly said to recognize the merits of both the moral naturalists and the classical moral intuitionists. With the *intuitionists* we agree on several important theses, among which appear: (i) deontic judgments are propositions and have, therefore, implications governed by the general logic of propositions studied in Chapter 3; (ii) deontic judgments are not reducible to non-deontic judgments; (iii) deontic concepts or "properties" are very peculiar. With the *naturalists* we agree that the truth conditions of deontic judgments are all natural: (a) empirical facts about the motivational nature of the agent, his circumstances, and the causal connections governing his corner of the universe; and (b) logical truths. Roughly put, the intuitionists should be happy with our developments in Chapters 3, 4, 6, §1–§7, part of 8, and 9, and the naturalists should rejoice at Chapters 5, 6, §8, part of 8, 10 and 11. It seems, then, from our vantage position reached after the preceding investigation of the problems themselves, that the classical intuitionists and the naturalists had their eyes fixed on entirely different problems, where they were able to apprehend valuable insights; but because of certain prejudicial assumptions, they jumped to unnecessary denials of what they were not paying attention to. In particular, they did not distinguish well between the *meaning* of practical sentences and the *truth-conditions* of the noemata expressed by such sentences. In other words, their errors were created essentially by their not looking at the total system of problems. This is precisely the error we have been taking pains to avoid in these investigations. We have attempted to look at larger networks of problems and we have tried to connect the problems within the whole field of practical thinking both to one another and to the "larger" problems in general logic, ontology and metaphysics. That we can shed light on the dispute between intuitionists and naturalists is a piece of favourable evidence for the validity of our system of theories.

3. THE NON-NATURAL CHARACTER OF DEONTIC "PROPERTIES"

In a devious way the classical intuitionists and the naturalists agreed on a very central aspect of deontic judgments, namely, that the universe at its core, so to speak, does *not* have deontic judgments, that so-called deontic properties do not "really" belong *in rerum natura*, and that nature is uniform and unitary. This perception of the unitariness of nature led the intuitionists to claim that oughtness, wrongness, and the other so-called deontic properties are *non*-natural. And the same insight led the naturalists to attempt to reduce deontic "properties" to natural properties. This unitariness of nature is of a piece with what in Chapter 1, §3 we spoke of as the metaphysical or ontological primacy of pure contemplative reason. And we must end our study with a discussion of how deontic "properties" are *non*-natural (something which the intuitionists did not attempt to do in full). This account provides further light on the classical disputes between naturalists and intuitionists. And we can, if not close this historical issue entirely, at least transfer it to another level of discussion.

Moral intuitionists conceived of deontic words as expressive or predicative of properties. This conception is insightful in that it provides them with a solid basis for the application of ordinary propositional logic to deontic judgments. But it was wrong in that it prevented them from seeing the interesting peculiar logical structure of what deontic words express. They did not see that deontic words are not used to express predication, but *operations* that yield propositions from proposition-like complexes. They also lacked the appropriate conception of practition. Yet classical intuitionists saw quite clearly that so-called deontic properties are not ordinary properties. For one thing they are neither perceptible nor introspectible, nor is their exemplification generally implied by non-deontic facts. Of course, they did not have a proof of the latter, but they were prone to endorse Hume's guillotine. Deontic properties are, intuitionists said, non-natural properties.

From the perspective we have reached after our investigation into the ontological and logical structures of deontic judgments, we can explain the deep but murky insights of the moral intuitionists. They were very much justified in speaking of the non-natural character of deontic properties. To begin with, it is a verbal quible whether we use the word 'property' to refer to both operations and (natural) properties or only to refer to the latter. There need be no error at all in simply using the words 'property' and 'characteristic' in a wider sense than the one in which many of us are now inclined to use them.

And there is a point in saying that rightness, wrongness, and obligatoriness are characteristics. It is not merely that the words 'right', 'wrong', and 'obligatory' are adjectives. To say that an action A is right or that A is the right object to do an action to (with, for, ...) is to say something about A which holds for all people; it is to claim that any normal person in similar circumstances could in principle agree that A is right. The account of deontic truth given in Chapter 8, built on Chapter 5 and Chapter 6, and related to the view of Chapter 11 that oughts are ideal wants, provides deontic truth with objectivity, hence with intersubjectivity. (Please see those references.) As explained in Chapter 11, §3 an ought is an objectified ideal want. To say that an action is right is to say something about which we can argue and have contradictory beliefs. It is to utter a sentence that expresses something that can function as a premise or a conclusion in deductive inferences, governed (though not exclusively) by the rules of ordinary logic – regardless of whatever emotive or contextual implications it may have. It is also to classify action A. To be sure, this classifying is done through complex criteria. But legions of descriptive classificatory predicates involve complex criteria. The crucial thing, however, is that, as discussed above in Chapters 8 and 11, the ascription of oughtness, rightness, or wrongness to an object or an action is as objective and intersubjective as anything can be, even if it is a complex affair that relates to ends, decisions, conventions, and a large amount of facts, and one that presupposes the existence of a form of thinking oriented toward intentions and prescriptions.

(1)   Oughtness applies to proposition-like structures, namely, practitions, not to particulars or universals; i.e., it is an operation.

Furthermore:

(2)   Oughtness is a special kind of operation, not one that applies to propositions, but one that applies to practitions.

(3)   Oughtness is also special in another sense: it is not a pure operator that applies to practitions and yields practitions, and to propositions and yields propositions (like negation and conjunction): it applies to practitions and practitional functions only, and it yields just propositions and propositional functions: *it represents practitional structures as propositional.*

These features do make of oughtness a most peculiar property. They already explain part of its *dependence* on other characteristics or properties. When we say that X ought to go home we are somehow saying that a doing of X *qua* going home is *obligatory*. This is the sort of statement that, correctly, perplexed intuitionists.[5] How can the event of X's going home when it does not exist have the attribute of obligatoriness? Clearly, X's going home, if obligatory, is so regardless of whether X goes home or not. Yet obligatoriness does not seem to be an attribute of the agent X, but of his *going* home? These and related worries are the right philosophical worries about the ontological structure of ought-judgments. The worries were philosophically insightful.

In Chapter 7, §§1–10 we have developed an account of the ontological structure of deontic judgments that accommodates those insights. In Chapter 12 we have distinguished the crucial ambiguities of the word 'action'.

There is another non-natural feature of deontic properties. In accordance with Chapter 8, §1:

(4)   *X ought$_i$ to do A* is equivalent to *The practition *X to do A* is necessarily Legitimate$_i$*.

This property of oughtness, together with the properties discussed in Chapter 11, explains not only the connection of ought-judgments with reasons for action, but it also further explains the *dependence* of oughtnesses. Clearly, the oughtness of X's doing A depends on all the facts that enter into the context C that, in accordance with our discussion in Chapter 5, makes the practition *X to do A* Legitimate$_i$. Furthermore, the overriding oughtness of a conflict-solving ought-judgment is *toti-resultant* in that it depends on all the relevant facts that belong into the relevant absolute context. (See Chapter 5, §3). Moreover, as pointed out in Chapter 5, §1 and §3, the Legitimacy of a practition may very well depend on some false propositions. Hence, in general it is not the case that a set of true propositions implies that a practition is Legitimate (overridingly) or Legitimate$_i$ or that an ought-judgment is true.

Equivalence (4) is extremely important. It makes oughtness$_i$ (or *obligatoriness$_i$*) equivalent to necessary Legitimacy$_i$. Recall from Chapter 5 that Legitimacy$_i$ is an ontological property of practitions analogous to truth. It is an abstract, formal property, which may very properly be called non-natural. Indeed, even if truth may be considered a "natural" property of propositions, Legitimacy$_i$ is still non-natural in the sense that while propositions belong to the world in a primary sense, practitions do not: practitions are created by the conceptual machinery of a being who has practical reason, i.e., the power to think practically. (See Chapter 10, §3.)

There is more yet. Even if Legitimacy$_i$ is a natural property of practitions, *necessary*-Legitimacy$_i$ is not quite natural in the same sense. In Chapter 8, §2 we analyzed the *necessity* involved in equivalence (4) as implication. Thus, oughtness is equivalent to an implication. This definitely puts oughtness outside nature in the sense of the realm of just brute facts and their natural laws.

There is still *another* respect in which deontic properties are not natural properties. This is the metaphysical sense in which deontic properties do not belong to the basic schema of the world, even of a world with agents that possess and exercise the capacity of thinking practically, because in a certain sense deontic properties are dispensable for practical agents. Let us explain this in some detail.

4. THE DISPENSABILITY OF DEONTIC "PROPERTIES" OR OPERATIONS

Within our ordinary way of thinking about actions we cannot fail to encounter those indefinable, dependent, non-natural characteristics: rightness, wrongness, and obligatoriness. They seem ever present especially when we use attributive normative words rather than auxiliary verbs, and say things like "Action A is right (wrong, obligatory)". But this necessity of talking and thinking about such characteristics would be absolute if and only if the normative form of practical thinking and language were unavoidable for a practical being. On reflection, however, such unavoidability is found to be lacking. The whole category of normative noemata may be discarded without our life suffering a bit for it, except for some conceptual and linguistic complications.

As we have argued in Chapters 4, 6, and 7, prescriptions (or mandates) and intentions are not reducible to each other, and deontic judgments are reducible to neither. We argued that deontic judgments are propositions, and have defended the thesis that they are not reducible to non-deontic propositions. Thus, the totality of noemata that belong to practical thinking falls naturally into the following master structure:

I. *First-order noemata:* noemata about agents, their circumstances, their characteristics, and their actions, or about the world in general (including mathematics):
   A. Non-deontic propositions:
      1. "Natural" propositions

2. Other non-deontic propositions.
   B. Practitions:
   1. Prescriptions (and mandates)
   2. Intentions.
   C. Deontic propositions

II. *Second-order noemata:* noemata about first-order noemata, (i) in which properties like truth, Legitimacy$_i$, necessary falsity, being implied by, being equivalent to, and the like are predicated of first-order noemata, or (ii) which have constituents of type (i):
   A. Pure second-order noemata:
   1. Pure meta-propositions:
      a. Uniform pure meta-propositions: meta-propositions about noemata in just one of the three categories I.A, I.B and I.C.
      b. Non-uniform pure meta-propositions: meta-propositions that just relate two or all of the categories I.A, I.B and I.C.
   2. Pure meta-practitions, which can be uniform as well as non-uniform.
   B. Mixed second-order noemata: complex noemata that have both first-order and second-order noemata as constituents:
   1. Uniform mixed second-order noemata: meta-noemata involving a category I.A, or I.B, or I.C and its uniform pure meta-noemata.
   2. Non-uniform mixed second-order noemata: meta-noemata that connects noemata of first-order with a category I.A. I.B, or I.C, or with meta-noemata about another of those categories.

III. *Third-order noemata*
Etc.

We call *meta-normatives:* meta-propositions about deontic judgments, whether they are pure or not, whether mixed or not, and whether they are themselves deontic or not.

Now, our metaphysical thesis is this:
Deontic properties, i.e., deontic operations, do not belong to the

furniture of the universe, even of the universe of practical agents: deontic operations are created by normative thinking: the role of deontic operations is not really to guide conduct, but to facilitate practical thinking by providing a picture of properties that aid the imagination in the process of determining what to do ourselves or what others are to do. If rational agents were to dispense with their normative and meta-normative thinking, they would in principle be able to carry on, making plans, formulating purposes, reaching decisions, giving advice and orders, and the like.

The basis for this thesis lies in the results of Chapter 8 and in the practical primacy of practitions, especially intentions as we explained in Chapter 10.

As we noted in Chapter 11, the primacy functions of practical thinking consist of bringing about rational action through one's own decisions and of helping others to bring about rational action. Those fundamental practical functions are discharged fully by the imperative and the intentional segments of the total system of practical noemata, particularly if they are supplemented to the hilt by meta-propositions about practitions. By the results of Chapter 8 the complex meta-propositions about intentions and prescriptions formulated in Chapter 3, §1 and §3 and in Chapter 6, §5 can replace their corresponding normatives. In the case of motivational normatives we could also use imperatives or resolutives which would furnish their causal intention. Our deliberations could move from the facts, ends, and conventions to the Legitimacy-value of an intention, or imperative, and from the meta-propositions about the intention, or imperative, to this. Or, alternatively, we could enrich our present imperative and intentional discourse by developing imperatives and resolutions that could also be used unassertively, so that they could be used in deliberation or in reasoned commanding, requesting, advising, etc., without a causal intnetion.

We saw that normatives are not reducible to practitions, but we also noted that normatives presuppose practitions. This is the result of our logical investigation, arrived at in Chapter 7, §7–§10 and Chapter 11. This result makes it impossible to eliminate the practitional segment of the structure of practical noemata in favor of the normative segment. In general, part of the view that emerges from our investigations in Chapters

4–8 is, then, that *normatives are supernumerary,* and that, although more cumbersomely, the structure of practical noemata can discharge all its practical roles with the intentional, the prescriptive, and the meta-practitional segments.

Now, if a rational and practical being can get on just as well in the world without the language of normatives, the deontic properties rightness, wrongness, etc., will not be part of his world. But their absence would leave no hole; their disappearance would leave behind logically equivalent remainders: the semantical properties, Legitimacy and Non-legitimacy of prescriptions and intentions. That being can plan and act as always, recognize his circumstances, make decisions, and guide other persons' actions.

On the contrary, by way of contrast, a being's world devoid of colors would be limited. We are not making a point about language. Perhaps the cognition of colors is dependent on a color terminology, so that he who has no color language at all may be unable to have colors in his world. Be this as it may. The point is that if cognition of colors depends on the possession of a color terminology, then the colors of one's world go away with the color terminology, and on losing the terminology, one would lose both the enjoyment of colors and the identification of objects by color. The color properties are not eliminable with logically equivalent remainders that can do duty for them.

The deontic properties (or operations) are eliminable with logically equivalent remainders. They are like the shadows or mirroring images of those remainders. This is the metaphysical thesis suggested by the preceding arguments and discussions, and it deserves a precise formulation. For those philosophers who do not want to speak of propositions, we suggest that they read 'sentence' for 'proposition', 'language' or 'sub-language' for 'noematic system', and 'predicate' for 'property'. The metaphysical points we are about to make have, of course, a manifestation in language.

DEFINITION 1. $N(S)$ is *noematic system* = S is a set of properties or operations, $N(S)$ is a set of noemata involving at least one member of S, each member of S is involved in some noema in $N(S)$, and $N(S)$ is closed under all the logical operations present in its members.

For example: if S is the set of colors, $N(S)$ may be the totality of all propositions ascribing a color to some object, and the negations, conjunctions, disjunctions, and conditionals formed with such propositions.

DEFINITION 2. A noematic system N(S) is *truth-functional* = The only logical operations involved in the members of N(S) are copulation, negation, conjunction, disjunction, and quantification, or their equivalents (that is, the operations customarily denoted by 'not', 'and', 'or', 'some', and their equivalents).

A truth-functional noematic system of the properties blueness and yellowness can contain *This is both blue and yellow* and *Either this is blue or it is yellow*, but no propositions of the form *X believes that Y is blue* or *X sees (hears, feels) that something is yellow*.

DEFINITION 3. A noematic system (S) *presupposes* noematic system N(S') = It is logically necessary that whoever has a full understanding of N(S) must have some understanding of N(S').

To understand a proposition involving an analyzable property like being a bachelor it is necessary to understand the corresponding propositions involving properties which enter into the analysis of the property in question, like being unmarried, being adult and being a male.

DEFINITION 4. Noematic system N(S) is *dispensable* for noematic system N(S') = Every member of N(S) is logically equivalent to some member of N(S'), and N(S) presupposes N(S').

A trivial example of a dispensable noematic system is one made up of noemata involving some analyzable properties.

DEFINITION 5. A set S of properties is *partially conceptually dependent* = Every truth-functional noematic system N(S) is dispensable for some noematic system N(S'), such that no property of S' is a member or an analysis of a member of S, but no N(S') is dispensable for N(S).

It follows from this definition that analyzable properties cannot be conceptually dependent, unless some analyzing property is.

DEFINITION 6. A set S of properties is *fully conceptually dependent* = Every truth-functional noematic system N(S) is dispensable for some noematic system N(S′), but no noematic system N(S′) is dispensable for N(S).

We have seen that normatives are not reducible to practitions, by themselves or further combined with something else. We saw that normatives are logically equivalent to some meta-propositions that ascribe to practitions the semantical properties *Legitimacy* and *Non-legitimacy*. We also saw that those meta-propositions are not identical with normatives. Furthermore, we saw that a full understanding of normatives involves some understanding of imperatives and intentions. Hence, any truth-functional system N(S), where S is the set of normative operations (or properties if you wish) is dispensable for a noematic system M of meta-propositions about practitions and statements of fact, in accordance with *Definition* 4 above. On the other hand, practitions do not presuppose any understanding of normatives; clearly, statements of facts do not presuppose normatives. Hence the noematic system M of meta-propositions does not presuppose normatives; hence, it does not presuppose N(S). Thus, the former is not dispensable for the latter. Therefore, the deontic properties form, by *Definition* 5, a partially conceptually dependent set and, by *Definition* 6, also a fully conceptually dependent set of operations (or properties). They can be dispensed with without impairing our place and role of the world, without losing any facts of the world that supports our actions and plans or the facts that result from our actions and plans, in short, with no loss of reality.

By contrast, the color properties are not conceptually dependent. No proposition to the effect that an object has a certain color is conceptually equivalent to a proposition to the effect that the object has some property other than color. *X is red*, for instance, is equivalent to **X is red* is true*; but the latter presupposes the former. Suppose that the color orange were logically identical with the color between red and yellow, or that there were a complete list of colors. Then *X is orange* would be logically equivalent to *X is between red and yellow* or to *X is neither red nor yellow ... nor purple*. But *Between yellow and red* and *neither red ... nor purple* are, then, the same property of being orange, so that they cannot be members of the set S′ mentioned in *Definitions 5 and 6*. To dispense with colors is to lose an important part of the world.

Deontic "properties" are a creation of the very conceptual machinery of oughts, rights, and wrongs. But they are not merely subjective properties. They are intersubjective. To speak in Kantian style, they belong to transcendental subjectivity, i.e., to the form of subjective consciousness correlated with the normative conceptual framework. Though reflections of properties of practitions, deontic properties are non-subjective reflections that lie *there* in the conceptual framework itself ready to appear to practical consciousness.

To conclude, as the intuitionists correctly emphasized, the normative segment of the total network of practical noemata is patterned on the segment of natural facts. The normative substructure brings down, so to speak, to a par with, i.e., to the same first-order level as, the framework of practitions, the meta-structure of the Legitimacy of practitions as the framework of the grounds or reasons for actions. The normative framework is a framework carved out as an imitation of the framework of particulars and their properties. The normative substructure provides a "picture" or "transcendental schema" (to use Kant's term) of the Legitimacy values of prescriptions and intentions. A schema is, Kant tells us, "a general procedure of the imagination to furnish a concept with images".[6] Normatives provide practical thinkers (or users of practical language, if you wish) with the model of empirical facts so that they can "imagine" the deontic operations as non-natural properties inhering in objects, actions, or agents. We may suppose that the quasi-empirical "picture" inherent in the conceptual framework of normatives is of practical use to the practical creature. Since abstract thinking is harder and requires more intense concentration of attention and effort, a hypostatic framework that produces first-order "reflections" of the second-order properties of practitions introduces a valuable smoothness in the functioning of practical thinking. Deontic thinking is *au fond* nothing but a pictorial thinking that creates a facsimile of concretion that deputizes for the abstract thinking about the formal (abstract) properties of practitions.

NOTES TO CHAPTER 13

1 See note 1 to Chapter 1.
2 See Henri Poincaré, *Dernières Pensées* (Paris, 1912), p. 225, and R. M. Hare, *The Lanauge of Morals*, p. 28. For an examination of this thesis see The *Structure of Morality*, Chapter 6.
3 David Hume, *Treatise on Human Nature*, III, I, *i*. See the materials mentioned in note 2 to Chapter 1.
4 Hare has a segregrating thesis that is a converse of Poincaré's according to which

imperatives are always irrelevant premises of propositional conclusions. See *The Langauge of Morals*, p. 28 and my discussion of it in *The Structure of Morality*, Chapter 6 and in the paper mentioned at the end of note 1 to Chapter 1.

[5] See, e.g., H. A. Prichard, 'Moral Obligation', in *Moral Obligation* (Oxford: Clarendon Press, 1949), pp. 92ff.

[6] I. Kant, *Critique of Pure Reason*, A139.

INDEX OF NAMES

INDEX OF TOPICS

of propositions, prescriptions, intentions, and norms 32, 37ff, 44, 68, 75,
80, 89, 102, 106–109, 117–120, 137,
139–141, 143, 145, 194f, 225ff, 277ff,
284, 286f, 294ff, 305
qualified 195
See Belief, Enactment, and Intending
Endorsing
rehearsals of intending 277f, 280–284
Ends 134–139, 141–145, 177, 184, 240f,
243f, 278, 296
hierarchy of ends 142ff
ideal harmonization of hierarchies of
143f
English
connectives analyzed 63–68, 78f, 81,
100, 103f, 109, 111ff, 124, 173, 223
deontic words 27, 46f, 180, 190, 223,
229
inferential expressions analyzed 60,
100
infinitive construction expressive of
intentions 149ff, 165
logical words and imperatives 99ff,
112ff
logical words and intentions 173
mandate operator 93
modal and psychological words 183f
'Ought', and its tenseless perspicuity
223
prima facie deontic sentences 47ff
rules of speech deletion 291
two theses about "individuation" of
actions 322f
Entreaties 37, 91, 133, 141
Equivalence
between implication and deducibility
78, 102
between propositions 72, 78, 81
between the prescriptional copulation
view and the prescriptional predicate
view 97f
of propositions and pointing 241f
of the three approaches to implication
78, 81, 89, 102
Ethics
of communication 64
See Communication
Events 315–319, 328

compared with individuals, within the
category of particulars 317
identification of 321–329
their co-eventuation 326
Existence 315
flow of 315, 319f
See Reality, Fact, Truth
Experience
unity of xvi
of freedom 312
patterns of xv. xvi
practical. See Practical experience
Expression
characteristic of noemata 44
See Quotations, conventions of, and
canonical notation of structures by
propositions 241
Extensionality
of deontic judgments 157, 228–232,
236, 267–270
See Definite descriptions

Facts 46, 51, 56, 121, 145, 241, 280, 292,
331
Finitude
See Mind, finitude of
First-person 29ff, 41ff, 150–153, 155,
172–174, 178, 257
conception as subject of intentions
150f, 158, 169f, 172
element in all absolute contexts of
overriding Legitimacy for imperatives 145
irreducible to the third-person 155,
158f
point of view 135
pronoun 150ff, 171
propositions 158, 178
reference 42, 150, 158, 170, 243, 276–
284
senses 178
Form
logical. See Logical form
of life 142
Framework
conceptual 115f
Future, See Future framework
Freedom
experience of 312

to demand 246
to choose is a fundamental presupposition of practical thinking 134f, 137,
190, 246, 249, 250, 257, 280, 312, but
not established by the reality of
practical thinking 250
See Future Zone of Indeterminacy
Frege's point 158
Functions
See subheading'function' in Propositional, Deontic, Prescriptive,
Practitional
Future 41, 135ff, 245, 247, 280, 293
Framework 135–139, 141, 155f, 161f,
165, 168, 249f
Presupposition of open 136, 190, 246,
249f, 257, 280
tense 41, 159–168, 175
Zone of Indeterminacy 135–139, 141,
155f, 161f, 165, 168, 249f, 280

Games 181, 187f
Generalization
existential 83f, 86, 89, 124f, 177, 229ff
of truth-tables 119, 177
universal 83f, 86, 89, 124f, 177, 229f
Goodness 236 n5
Grammar
surface 151ff, 290
Grammatical
persons, their irreducible differences
155
Guises
ontological 178, 324–329

Happening 162f, 165f
Harmonization
of hierarchies of ends 143ff
Hierarchies
motivational 294ff, 303, 331
of claims or prima facie oughts 303
of ends 143–145, 241ff; harmonized
143
of needs 294, 303
of propensities constituting a thinker
275ff
History
of the world in Absolute, Legitimacy
145

posthumous, of events and deeds 315,
322f, 329
Hume's guillotine 11, 21, 90, 232, 298,
332

Hypothetical, imperatives and normatives, see Imperatives, hypothetical
Ideal
agent 306ff
harmonizations of hierarchies of ends
143f
of morality 145
possible worlds 250
wants, see Wants, ideal
world approach to deontic logic rejected 250f
Identification
of actions, see action, identification
of agents, see Propositions, and Action,
considered as identifiers
Identifiers
See Actions as identifiers
Identity 103, 230–235, 236, 259, 267
axiom for 259, 263; rule of derivation
for 263
deontic operators are extensional with
respect to 231f, 267–270
genuine, contrasted with consubstantiation 324ff
'If' 66ff, 111–114, 175f, 232ff
differs in thematic meaning from 'only
if' 67
never synonymous with ' ⊃' even in the
sense of 'material implication' 66,
113
See Conditional, and Connectives
Image
phenomenological, see Representational image
Imperatives 7, 92ff, 99–103, 111ff, 129,
141f, 146, 199
and logic 99–103
and Ought 21
and reasoning 129
hypothetical 20ff, 298–303,
305ff
pushing aspect of 291f
See Mandates and Prescriptions
Imperative-resolutive 51, 261

Sh-propositions 183f

Speech
  or linguistic acts 13ff, 32–48, 56, 63f,
    92, 92ff, 101, 109ff, 126, 127f, 133,
    171, 291; different from their con-
    tents 33, 38, 240
  prescriptive acts distinguished from
    prescribed acts 133f
  See Mandates

Statement 6, 32, 36
  See Proposition, Noema

States
  mental 163, 171
  of affairs 51, 136, 292
  of objects as results of doings 310–315

Structure
  and so is that of the implication
    between intentions 172–176
  common to a family of mandates 39,
    171
  of imperative implication is two-valued
    103–119

Subordinate
  clauses 156, 165, 171
  conjunctions and adverbs 111
  infinitive clauses 149–154, 165
  See *Oratio obliqua*

Subscription
  to ends 137, 143
  to systems of norms or rules 140
  See Endorsement and Ends, Intending,
    and Wants

Suggestions 40
  See Mandates and Prescriptions

Survival
  value 145, 284, 286, 293f, 345

Syntactical
  evidence for the contrast between
    propositions and practitions 92–96,
    151ff, 155ff, 162–168, 201–206, 208–
    214, 256

Systemic
  dimension 81
  nature of deontic judgments 190,
    233f, 240, 246

Tautology 69, 72f, 78, 122f, 165, 263

Tell to 39, 145, See Mandates, Com-
    mands, Advice and Requests

Tense
  agreement 223
  deontic operators, lack it 220–223
  future 41, 159–168, 175

Thematic
  differences in conclusions 59f; of
    negation expressions 109; of 'but',
    'and', and 'although' 65, 109
  dimension 59f, 63, 65, 67, 81
  ordering 67
  roles of inferential expressions 60
  roles of ordinary English connectives
    63–66, 103f, 109, 113ff

Themes
  of apprehension 67
  See Thematic

Theories
  philosophical. See philosophical
    theories

Thinking
  about time identity 278
  and language, see Language
  contemplative or propositional 5f, 8,
    51, 273f, 278, 281; its ontological
    primacy 8, 138f; its external
    causality compared with the internal
    one of willing 282ff
  episodes of 149, 275
  normative 4f
  practical 1, 5–16, 25–30, 36, 95, 112f,
    131, 134, 136f, 145, 150ff, 154ff, 170,
    195, 250, 273–284; its autonomy
    331–334; its logical and psycho-
    logical primacy 8, 67, 112ff, 134;
    effective 30; presupposes freedom
    134f, 137; ego-centered 145; has an
    internal causality 5f, 10, 123, 149;
    the fundamental phenomenon of
    277; endorsing, see Intending re-
    hearsals, and Volition; its ultimacy
    lies in the practical copula 278
  unity of 155

Time
  of action 223, 320f
  of circumstances can be later than that
    of intentional actions 162; and
    later than that of obligatory actions
    215ff, 220ff
  differences in mixed-intentions 162f

PHILOSOPHICAL STUDIES SERIES
IN PHILOSOPHY

Editors:

WILFRID SELLARS, Univ. of Pittsburgh and KEITH LEHRER, Univ. of Arizona

Board of Consulting Editors:

Jonathan Bennett, Alan Gibbard, Robert Stalnaker, and Robert G. Turnbull

1. JAY F. ROSENBERG, *Linguistic Representation.* 1974, xii+159 pp.
2. WILFRID SELLARS, *Essays in Philosophy and Its History.* 1974, xiii+462 pp.
3. DICKINSON S. MILLER, *Philosophical Analysis and Human Welfare.* Selected Essays and Chapters from Six Decades. Edited with an Introduction by Loyd D. Easton. 1975, x+333 pp.
4. KEITH LEHRER (ed.), *Analysis and Metaphysics.* Essays in Honor of R. M. Chisholm. 1975, approx. 330 pp.
5. CARL GINET, *Knowledge, Perception, and Memory.* 1975, viii+212 pp.
6. PETER H. HARE and EDWARD H. MADDEN, *Causing, Perceiving and Believing.* An Examination of the Philosophy of C. J. Ducasse. 1975, vii+211 pp.